FOUNDATIONS

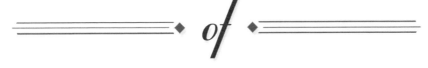

of

CHURCH
ADMINISTRATION

*P*ROFESSIONAL *T*OOLS FOR *C*HURCH *L*EADERSHIP

B*RUCE* L. P*ETERSEN*, E*DWARD* A. T*HOMAS*,
and B*OB* W*HITESEL*, EDITORS

BEACON HILL PRESS
OF KANSAS CITY

Copyright 2010 by Beacon Hill Press of Kansas City

ISBN 978-0-8341-2521-6

Printed in the
United States of America

Cover Design: Darlene Filley
Internal Design: Sharon Page

· **Library of Congress Cataloging-in-Publication Data**

Foundations of church administration : professional tools for church leadership / Bruce L. Petersen, Edward A. Thomas, and Bob Whitesel, editors.
        p. cm.
    Includes bibliographical references.
    ISBN 978-0-8341-2521-6 (hardcover)
  1. Church management. I. Petersen, Bruce L., 1942- II. Thomas, Edward A. III. Whitesel, Bob.
    BV652.F68 2010
    254—dc22

                                                                                                2010024493

10 9 8 7 6 5 4 3 2 1

CONTENTS

INTRODUCTION

David Wright
PhD, Dean and Professor, School of Theology,
Azusa Pacific University

Few other careers are as complex or as multifaceted.
>*You must be honest, but you must not offend.*
>*You must correct, but you must not discourage.*
>*You must hold accountable, but you must not dishearten.*
>*You must achieve greatly, but with little or no formal authority.*
>*You serve as example, foil, advocate, friend, counselor, and teacher.*
>*You are a prophet.*
>*You are a leader.*
Few other tasks offer either the demands or the rewards.
>*When you fail, you are as irrelevant as last year's outvoted politician.*
>*When you succeed, you become as dear as family.*
You work in a social context that no longer understands or respects your role.
But in those special moments when everything works, you bring hope where there is despair, love where the grim reality of broken life presses people down, and purpose to the lost and aimless.
You stand as God's ambassador to a world of desperate secularity, a reminder of the timeless, the sacred, the spiritual, the eternal.
No calling is nobler. No work is more fulfilling.
You are a church leader.

To succeed as a church leader, you need some uncommon characteristics—a divine calling, a thick skin, a sense of humor, and a stubborn streak, to name a few. A study by Robert Herman and Martin Butler looked at twelve qualities that characterize effective church leaders.[1] Their research employed three instruments: The Managerial Practices Survey (MPS), which is a well-known survey instrument

---

1. D. Martin Butler and Robert D. Herman, "Effective Ministerial Leadership," *The Journal of Nonprofit Management and Leadership* 9 (1999): 229-39.

with strong reliability and validity;[2] the Leader Behavior Questionnaire (LBQ), which is also broadly utilized and considered highly reliable;[3] and a lesser-known survey titled the Ministerial Effectiveness Inventory (MEI).[4]

Herman and Butler's research indicates that effective ministerial leaders are

- managers
- problem solvers
- planners
- delegators
- inspirers
- change agents
- shepherds
- communicators
- multitaskers
- students
- servants
- persons of integrity

Clearly, to succeed in that range of roles and responsibilities, a church leader will need a good set of professional tools. That's what this book is for—to offer professional tools for church leadership drawn from a set of management and leadership disciplines to which most ministers receive scant exposure during their preparation.

How We Created This Resource

We took a straightforward approach in creating this book.

1. We identified key disciplinary areas from the standard management curriculum taught in most masters of business administration programs.

2. We gathered faculty and business leaders we respect, those who exhibit strong expertise in each of these key areas. We asked them this question: *What four or five concepts from your area of management, administration, and leadership expertise would you like your church leaders to know?*

---

2. Gary Yukl, Stephen J. Wall, and Richard Lepsinger, "Preliminary Report on the Validation of the Managerial Practices Survey," in *Measures of Leadership,* ed. Kenneth E. Clark, Miriam B. Clark, and Robert R. Albright (West Orange, NJ: Leadership Library of America, 1990), 223-28.

3. M. Sashkin and W. Burke, "Understanding and Assessing Organizational Leadership," in *Measures of Leadership,* 297-326.

4. H. Newton Malony and Laura F. Majovsky, "The Role of Psychological Assessment in Predicting Ministerial Success," *The Review of Religious Research* 28 (1986): 29-39.

3. We distilled their responses into some of the key principles that informed portions of this book.
4. We surrounded these insights with supporting research and clarified them with examples from real-life situations.

THE NATURE OF MANAGEMENT, ADMINISTRATION, AND LEADERSHIP IN THE CHURCH

Before you dig into the heart of this book, permit us a few reflections.

All of us who have contributed to this book have been involved in ministry for many years. We've worked with church congregations, parachurch organizations, educational institutions, and business organizations. We are ministers, professors, administrators, and organizational managers. Perspective is one of the benefits of longevity, and as we've watched the church through the years, we've come to the conviction that churches and religious organizations, no less than business organizations, thrive when their leaders efficiently use a core set of managerial tools.

Unfortunately, most ministry preparation programs do little to provide these tools. One of our students recently told us that she has learned more valuable information about managing the church in her first few management classes than she learned in her entire ministerial preparation program.

Before you respond, let us assure you that we've heard and respect the arguments that the church is a divine organism. We believe, as do most church leaders, that God's kingdom grows and succeeds through God's blessing, not through human "management and administration." But the last time we checked, all of the churches and all of the religious organizations we know about are made up of human beings. Furthermore, in our experience, every one of these congregations and religious organizations exists in a social context. So, the church may be a divine organism. But it is also a human organization. Our point in this book is that successful ministerial leaders understand *both* elements of this identity and master a set of tools related to the leadership of *both* these elements.

LEADING THE CHURCH WELL

Leading well is also about capturing a vision, then putting in place what it takes for a group of people to achieve that vision. Most church leaders have some sort of vision. It may not be the right vision for the place and time, but at least on some level, that really doesn't matter. An organization actively pursuing a vision is healthier than one without any vision. The problem is that ministers often don't know the practical steps necessary to turn vision into reality. They don't have the organizational tools needed to accomplish what their vision calls them to do.

Talk about a recipe for frustration and disillusionment. Vision flounders on the rocks of unskilled leadership. What a tragedy! It doesn't have to be so. The missing link is the ability to develop and lead a healthy, dynamic, purposeful organization.

At this point we must also recognize that different church traditions place congregational leadership roles at different places within the church organization. For example, in some churches the senior or solo pastor is expected to lead the organization much as a CEO leads secular organizations. In other churches, the pastor is not expected to act as a CEO but is expected to be a counselor, a shepherd, a prophet, or a priest representing God to the people and the people to God.

Further, different church traditions empower congregational leadership differently. Whether a church has a board of elders, a board of administration, or a vestry, leadership in the church is often shared across groups of professional and volunteer leaders.

The point is that no matter with whom the task of organizational leadership lies, every church has its leaders. Those leaders need to know how to serve competently in that role. This resource is for them.

We offer one final insight, a simple plan for your professional development as leaders of successful organizations:

- You are *great* at something. Invest most of your personal development effort in this area.
- You can be *competent* at two or three more things. Keep learning in these areas.
- You must be *capable* at everything the job requires. Borrow all the brains it takes for your organization to succeed in these areas.

1

FOUNDATIONS OF ADMINISTRATION
THE BOOK OF ACTS AS CASE STUDY

Darius L. Salter

PhD, Educator, Pastor, Church of the Nazarene

The Book of Acts narrates function finding form, power directed into meaningful channels, and fire energizing and creating, rather than consuming and destroying. How can religion, the most privatized and internalized of human emotions and personal values, discover an institutional home and public form? How can organization simultaneously be human-directed and God-controlled? *Organism* and *organization* are derived from the same root word, but their common usage often connotes antithetical meanings. Both an organism and an organization necessitate interdependent parts, but the latter is often considered the death of the former.

Ironically, spirituality, the human experience that has been most mysterious and immaterial, has become a most visible and institutional cultural entity. Institutions require administration, the management of persons and machinery. Yet the demands of management often accumulate until the original intentions are lost in the evolving complexity of policies and offices. No one would argue that the infantile existence of Christianity, as narrated in Acts, is replicated in the twenty-first century church. Some very committed Christians would even argue that the explosion of miraculous spirituality, Christianity's supernatural mode of operation 2,000 years ago, has little to do with how the Church should function in contemporary society.

My personal observation is that primitive Christianity has provided, as it should, ethical, missional, and inspirational direction for the Church but seldom has it been considered a model for administration. Nowhere in the New Testament are we told how to organize a church. Nevertheless, though the Book of Acts cannot be translated into a manual on ecclesial management, this essay will argue for principles of church leadership and administration as relevant today as they were in the Church's earliest existence. In fact, a newly discovered trust in a theologically centered administration as narrated in Acts would solve many of the conflictual issues in today's church. I will also suggest that current administrative procedures are often far removed from New Testament thought and Christian intention.

Luke narrates God's formation of community, a story of communal life in the first thirty years after the resurrection and ascension of Christ. Community health presupposes rules of conduct and persons granted the authority to interpret and enforce those rules. The question is not whether administration is going to exist, but whether it is going to become an end in itself rather than a means for the stability and advancement of communal life. Salvific communities discover leaders who place the community's redemption beyond their own advancement. Early Christian leaders went about the daunting task of creating a government that renders more energy than it absorbs, an organizational structure sufficient for facilitating the community's mission rather than becoming the mission. The actors in Acts create organizational practices and procedures that add more than they subtract.

For this reason, the ongoing interest in the images and ideas of "church" in Acts should focus on emulating its missionary vocation and prophetic message, its resurrection practices, and the nature of its spiritual leadership—important claims on any congregation in any age—rather than on replicating outward forms of governance and worship or other time-conditioned practices.[1]

One may legitimately question whether any New Testament word represents a twenty-first century normative understanding of the word "administration." No Greek New Testament word can be translated "administration." The Authorized King James twice translates *diakonia* (service) as "administration" (1 Cor. 12:5 and 2 Cor. 9:12). The *New International Version* uses "administration" three times for the words *kubernēseis* (leading, guiding) (1 Cor. 12:28) and *oikonomia* (stewardship, management), from which we get the word "economy" (Eph. 3:2, 9). The *New King James* translates *kubernēseis* (1 Cor. 12:28) and *diakonia* (2 Cor. 9:12) as "administration." The *New American Standard* uses the word or a form of it five times: *kubernēseis* (1 Cor. 12:28), *diakonia* (2 Cor. 8:19-20), and *oikonomia* (Eph. 3:9 and 1 Tim. 1:4).

Though none of the above words accurately represents administration as executive oversight, they do enable us to definitively conclude that administration as a concept does exist in the New Testament and consequently in the Book of Acts, since the Epistles are addressed to the "Acts" churches. If we combine the ideas of the three Greek words above, we might define "administration" as guiding management through servanthood. We are tempted to infer from its

---

1. Robert Wall, "The Acts of the Apostles," *The New Interpreter's Bible,* ed. Leander Keck, et al. (Nashville: Abingdon, 2002), 10:28.

Latin twelfth-century origin that the word carries the Christian concept of ministry, to minister, but the English word "administration" refers more to carrying out duties of governance than it does acts of Christian service.

None of the above words appear in the Book of Acts. Yet Acts is the history of the Church finding its organizational legs. William Willimon refers to the Acts of the Apostles as "Christian Leadership 101."[2] The Book of Acts records life in community and the problems endemic to people with common purposes and differing perspectives about how those purposes should be carried out. Collective allegiance does not eliminate conflict inherent to communities living and working together, no matter how well intentioned they may be. Even the purest of motives are liable to misunderstandings generated by perceptions, temperaments, and ulterior motives, sometimes undetected by even the most sanctified individuals. Much of the New Testament was written as a historical response to crisis. The Book of Acts, as our earliest and most reliable history of the Church, documents the Christian community's action in the context of opportunities and problems. It is a plan of action in action, a series of situations comprehended by persons who claim to be followers of Jesus Christ.

God-Directed Guidance

The first administrative question the Church faced was how much to allow the Old Testament to dictate both its structure and its methodology. The first chapter of Acts (v. 26) narrates the choosing of a twelfth apostle by the casting of "lots." (The Greek word for lot is *klēros,* from which we derive the word "clergy.") This particular administrative procedure was rooted in the Old Testament. Most of Canaan was divided among the twelve tribes by the casting of lots. In other words, critical choices would be taken out of the hands of fallible persons and be placed in the hands of an all-knowing God. The Urim and Thummim, possibly two stones placed in the breastplate of the high priest, directed kings into war and other decisions of governance. We do not know how these stones gave direction. Possibly "yes" was written on one side and "no" on the other. Two yeses indicated that God was affirming rather than negating the action in question.

The methodology for choosing Matthias as the apostle to replace Judas sounds, if not irresponsible, at least archaic and primitive, today relegated to groups such as the Amish, who scorn modernity. But notice that the apostles selected two candidates through agreed upon criteria. "So one of the men who have accompanied us during all the time that the Lord Jesus went in and out among us, beginning from the baptism of John until the day when he was taken

---

2. William H. Willimon, *Pastor: The Theology and Practice of Ordained Ministry* (Nashville: Abingdon Press, 2002), 275.

up from us—one of these men must become with us a witness to his resurrection" (Acts 1:21-22 ESV). The person selected would have eyewitnessed both
Christ's earthly ministry and, at least, one post-resurrection appearance.

But even more importantly than prescribing rational and empirical param-
eters for making the above critical choice, the apostles prayed specifically for
God's guidance, for his will to be accomplished. The rolling of dice was saturated in prayer. Rather than writing this administrative decision off as obsoletism
cloaked in mysterious divining, we need to be reminded that church, unlike
McDonald's and Microsoft, is a supernatural business. While the Church need
not and should not circumvent sound business practices, these same practices
should not negate dependency upon God enabled by consistent and constant
prayer. Finding God's direction demands that we both carefully collect data and
examine it with spiritual eyes.

Church administration, if it is not going to be undermined by self-serving
interests, must be saturated with prayer. Prayer that takes place only in the face
of crisis simulates "water witching": "God, please don't let us make a mistake,
because if we do, it will be very costly." The magic of divining by looking at a
weather vane, or even depending on the Bible to fall open at a supernaturally
delivered reference, is much different than a constant attitude of prayer, which
is open to God's sovereign direction. Robert N. Bacher and Michael Cooper
sum up the divine-human synergy operative in God-controlled administration:
"In and through these processes, the community seeks a theological outcome
to determine God's intention in the situation. Is Yahweh a local deity or Lord of
all? Having found a communal answer to the question, they proceed to develop
corresponding strategies for preaching, fellowship, and exercise of authority."[3]
The casting of lots extended the Old Testament's radical monotheism, the exact
opposite of superstition and the shirking of responsibility.

Prayer does not eliminate good decisions based on all available criteria.
Rather, it grants God his due in the direction of his Church. Honest transparency releases control to God. For instance, Quakers historically have not voted
on the choice of leaders or business decisions. They have relied on a collective
consensus, directed by the Holy Spirit, referred to as the "sense of the meeting." The plus side of this methodology is maintaining unity within the body.
The downside is that the administrative process moves quite slowly for those
of us who immediately want to draw a line in the sand. "For it seemed good
to the Holy Spirit and to us" (Acts 15:28 NASB), while enhancing both spiritual
confidence and dependency, plus granting God authority in all matters great

---

3. Robert N. Bacher and Michael Cooper, *Church Administration* (Minneapolis: Fortress Press, 2007), 5.

and small, does not lend itself to immediacy—the urgent settling of all questions through a democratic process. The difference between Christian decision making in Acts and majority versus minority forging ahead by the contemporary church are often lost on us who have adopted an administrative mentality more akin to corporate America than Christian worship. Traditional Quakers never pronounce a benediction or dismissal prayer between a worship service and a business meeting. Business is a form of worship, a sacrament, a means of grace no less than singing or preaching.

Church administration is a sacred act done in the same way on both Sunday and Monday. Administration, which covets the wisdom of God, evidenced in prayer and Scripture reading, declares dependency upon God. Church administration, which is blessed by God, will eliminate self-sovereignty and self-sufficiency and at the same time demonstrate acquaintance with the most current management literature. All of us can benefit from reading Daniel Goleman and Peter Drucker and learning why Wal-Mart has become the largest retailer in the world.

A CHRISTIAN RESPONSE TO COMMUNAL CRISIS

The Acts of the Apostles should be more accurately titled "The Acts of God" or "The Acts of the Holy Spirit." Acts narrates observable manifestations of God's actions in the world: healings, ecstatic languages, supernatural interpretations, tongues of fire, visions, and God striking people dead. This supernatural activity camouflages the everyday details of communal life—details that become disruptive if not given immediate attention. The discernment of direction, systemic to any group enterprise, is part baseball strategy and part utopian experiment, the creating of a game plan for implementing mission and, sometimes, sheer survival. Luke Timothy Johnson precisely expresses this joint venture between God and human instrumentality in the Book of Acts: "With literary artistry and genuine theological sensitivity, Luke shows through the narrative itself how the diverse experiences of God's action by individuals are slowly raised to the level of a communal narrative, which in turn must be tested by the entire community in a difficult and delicate process of disagreement, debate, and the discernment of the Scripture."[4]

The "difficult and delicate process" is at no place better exemplified than in Acts 6, when disagreement arises between the Hellenistic Jews and the blue-blooded Hebrews over the distribution of food to the widows. What we don't know, since complaining is inherent to human nature, especially to church

---

4. Timothy Johnson, *The Acts of the Apostles* (Collegeville: The Liturgical Press, 1992), 16.

members, is whether the griping was motivated by actual inequity or by bickering between first cousins. Whatever the case may be, the apostles interpreted the accusations as sufficient to warrant action. The Jewish apostles, instead of siding with their national kin and alienating the Hellenists, authorized the church to select from themselves "seven men of good reputation, full of the Spirit and of wisdom, whom we may put in charge of this task" (Acts 6:3 NASB).

Organizational Structure or Charismata

The seven appointed to wait on tables are historically interpreted to be the first deacons in the Church. However, no one is referred to as a "deacon" in the Book of Acts. (Neither does the word bishop appear, unless the word *episkopēn* is translated bishop instead of leadership or office in 1:20.) Is there a distinct difference between Luke's understanding of church leadership and Paul's, the latter appointing elders in the various churches that he planted? Is administrative structure (bureaucracy) a necessary evil in the Christian Church? This question does not grant an either/or answer. It is clear that communities necessitate leadership. It is also clear in Acts that the Church deemed Holy Spirit-enabled gifts and graces far more important than trained and innate ability. The spontaneous and charismatic administration evidenced in Acts is largely absent from the normative practices of the twenty-first-century American church, which operates with a blend of both autocracy and democracy.

Is the government of the church going to look more like a micromanaged bureaucracy or a charismatic organism where lines of authority are unclear, programs are not neat, and ministries are unpredictable? This tension is genuine. Organization can overkill and stamp out life, or it can be so nonexistent that counterproduction and fragmentation undermine efficiency. Thus the Book of Acts narrates a tension between the structure of Judaism and the laissez-faire of Pentecost. Throughout Acts, hardly anyone asked permission to do anything. God directed Peter to go to Cornelius's house and Philip to wander out into the desert on an odyssey that was not even clear to him. Gradually, the church of Acts moved toward consensual sending, a communal blessing that does not so much grant permission but rather extends its blessing to what God has already ordered.

Administration in Acts increasingly distances itself from the traditions of Judaism, but structure and organization by the fourth century had developed to an extreme. Roman contamination afflicted church leadership to the point that they behaved much like heads of state. David Smith writes concerning ecclesiology "that the Church is within the confines and limitations of time and space. It cannot perform its mission without some kind of organizational features. It cannot minister effectively to the needs of mankind unless responsible officers perform acceptable offices."[5] How to prevent "organizational features" and "acceptable offices" from reifying and calcifying, becoming ends in themselves, has been a perennial problem for the church. Willimon prophetically declares, "An openness to the leading of the Holy Spirit requires a structure that is flexible, adaptable, lean and trusting in the surprising intrusions of the Spirit among us. The church is not meant for the mere maintenance of internal organizational machinery. The church is meant for proclamation and enactment of the gospel."[6]

Throughout the church's history the Holy Spirit has revived new forms of administration more reliant on New Testament images than on prevailing management models. The return to Scripture in a humble waiting on God produces egalitarian, sacrificial communities more in tune with the Holy Spirit than General Motors. Administration in the Book of Acts is nothing less than the reign of God. The church is a *sui generis* theocracy, a form of government that will not work in the world's institutions. This is not to say that New Testament models for governance cannot leaven worldly, administrative structures.

FLEXIBILITY IN STRUCTURE

Leadership in Acts was spontaneous, contextual, and often intuitive. The only way to lead others was to be a doer of the Word, equipped and energized by the Holy Spirit. Thus the leadership in the individual churches was neither monolithic nor unilateral. Henry Klopp argues that "a great deal of freedom was allowed in determining leadership structure and organization. Churches were not required to have the same structure. Contextualized needs helped shape church structure and organization. The church in Jerusalem, with its strong Jewish background and involvement of the first apostles, was organized and operated differently than the church in Antioch, with leaders such as Paul and Barnabas, than the churches planted by Paul in his missionary journeys."[7]

Administration in Acts is far less about earning a union card, paying one's dues, and longevity in the community, than it is about being called and equipped by God. New Testament administrators were servants. They were not people who told other people what to do. They did something. They were people in action, which characterized the highest-ranking apostles, Peter, John and later Paul. They led by example instead of giving orders to lesser subordinates. They gave themselves to the primary work of prayer and Scripture study so that they

---

5. David L. Smith, "Ecclesiology," *A Contemporary Wesleyan Theology,* ed. Charles Carter (Grand Rapids: Zondervan, 1983), 2:608.

6. Willimon, *Pastor: The Theology and Practice,* 282.

7. Henry Khopp, *The Leadership Playbook: A Game Plan for Becoming an Effective Christian Leader* (Grand Rapids: Baker Books, 2004), 62.

themselves might enter into the work of travel and proclamation. They created missional models for others to do the same.

The short attention span that Stephen focused on busing tables is surprising. Whether the apostles observed him as an effervescent personality spouting memorized Scripture as he served a heaping helping of mutton stew and discerned a promotion was in order, or Stephen simply took the initiative to do some street preaching, we do not know. What is even more critical to observe is that no job was too small for the most talented and that the apostles were not threatened when a waiter on tables invaded their territory. Stephen preached the longest recorded message in the New Testament, a sermon that demonstrated narrative proficiency in Old Testament history. Providence mandated that job descriptions were quite temporary, indexed by and open to the moment-by-moment nudging of the Holy Spirit. Both Stephen and Philip exemplified that there are no peripheral jobs in kingdom administration. Kingdom administrators are both humble and grateful for where God has placed them. And changes in office are not promotions but simply repositioning and redirecting in obedience to the Holy Spirit.

That the New Testament church as an organization was inchoate in regard to policy, structure, and practice does not mean it was careless about belief in procedure. It also does not mean that there was an egalitarian democracy that ensured everyone had an equal say in what defined the church's message and mission. Administration emerged and evolved in Acts as authority vested in persons, rather than a policy manual distributed to the various churches. Thomas Bandy notes that "the servant empowering organization does not need many policies; the fewer the better. . . . Even with a huge diversity of people in many different programs, the actual number of policies must remain relatively small. This means that policies must be made with extreme care."[8]

We know almost nothing of the job description given to the leaders appointed by Paul and Barnabas in newly planted churches (see Acts 14:23). Again, direction was gained through the spiritual disciplines of prayer and fasting. By reading the Pastoral Epistles we can conclude that character, love for God, self-control, and graciousness of temperament were at the top of the list. The ability to articulate the kerygma—the life, death, and resurrection of Christ supported by the Hebrew Scriptures—qualified the appointee for teaching. Most importantly, there existed a resonance between people and leaders who had been chosen by God. Darrell Guder contrasts the New Testament methodology of discerning leadership with the normative adversarial win-loose debates, parlia-

---

8. Thomas Bandy, *Spiritual Leadership: Empowering People to Do What Matters* (St. Louis: Chalice Press, 2007), 41.

mentary maneuvers, special interest lobbying, and majority rule that dominate the North American church. Guder writes that the ecclesial practice of discernment in missional communities is not simply to discover the will of the community but instead together to discern the will of God:

> It is the role of the Spirit to correct, convince, and lead those who profess faith in Jesus Christ into God's truth. Discernment requires this guidance because God acts, speaks in, and through the ambiguous circumstances of worldly life. . . . As the ecclesia of God, a people gathered and sent to be about God's business, the church is called to a way of making decisions that articulates and correlates with listening, hearing, testing, planning, and obeying together in the power of the Holy Spirit.[9]

CLARITY OF THE MISSION AND MESSAGE AS ADMINISTRATIVE TASK

The mission of the church in the Book of Acts is clear and unencumbered. Its purpose is to represent and spread the truth clearly articulated by Peter on the Day of Pentecost: "Repent, and be baptized every one of you in the name of Jesus Christ so that your sins may be forgiven; and you will receive the gift of the Holy Spirit. For the promise is for you, for your children, and for all who are far away, everyone whom the Lord our God calls to him" (Acts 2:38-39 NRSV). Peter had built his theological case from the Old Testament prophet Joel: "Everyone who calls on the name of the Lord shall be saved" (Acts 2:21 NRSV).

In Acts, one clear message defines and drives the mission. Christ is risen! He is alive! Do whatever it takes to let as many people know as soon as possible. The plan would not be accidental but proceed according to Acts 1:8. The "Jerusalem, and in all Judea and Samaria, and to the end of the earth" (NKJV) progression would at times be perceived through dreams and visions and at other times be directed by persecution—evil translated into good. The day Stephen was martyred, "a severe persecution began against the church in Jerusalem, and all except the apostles were scattered throughout the countryside of Judea and Samaria" (Acts 8:1 NRSV). Stephen's martyrdom was a tipping point, not ordained by God, but used by God to move the church out of its comfort zone. Stephen's sermon had ended with the most powerful conclusion of any message yet to be preached in the history of gospel proclamation: "I see the heavens opened and the Son of Man standing at the right hand of God!" (Acts 7:56 NRSV).

---

9. Darrell L. Guder, ed., *Missional Church: A Vision for the Sending of the Church in North America* (Grand Rapids: Eerdmans Publishing Co., 1998), 172-73.

Leaders in Acts are first and foremost stewards of the identity and integrity of the gospel. If these are lost, compromised, or contaminated, the organization has lost its reason to be. The Jerusalem council became the landmark case, an existential opportunity once and for all to state who makes up the church. "Council" may be an inadequate term for what is recorded in Acts 15, because one would hardly use the word "conciliar" in describing the meeting that took place in Jerusalem. Willimon states that "the Jerusalem conference serves as an example of biblical, adaptive, and transformative leadership, even though it served later as a proof text for fossilized conciliarism in the church."[10]

Paul and Barnabas had fallen into dispute with the Judaizers about whether "the Way," now called "Christianity," was going to require Gentile converts to be circumcised. Circumcision was the primary mark of identity for both Jewish nationalism and monotheism. Circumcision was the covenantal sign no less important than its covenantal creed, the Shema, Hebrew for "listen": "Hear, O Israel: The LORD is our God, the LORD alone" (Deut. 6:4 NRSV). Simply put, was the mark of Jewish identity going to be imposed on Gentile converts as essential to salvation? In fact, some would interpret Acts 15 as the historical event representing the entire theme of the Book of Acts. New Testament scholar Ernst Haenchen writes that in Acts "Luke the historian is wrestling, from the first page to the last, with the problem of the mission to the Gentiles without the law."[11] George Eldon Ladd may overstate the case but nevertheless accurately argues that "one of the central motives in Acts is the explanation of how a small fellowship of Jews in Jerusalem, for all intents and purposes, hardly distinguishable from their Jewish milieu became a Gentile fellowship in the capital city of the empire, completely free from all Jewish practices."[12]

This question was answered by appealing to the apostles and Pharisees who had converted to Christianity and were residing in Jerusalem, still interpreted as Christianity's headquarters in spite of Antioch's growing prominence. Peter presented the center of the argument, appealing to the event that had sealed the deal of God's promise of universal grace and the possibility of salvation for all peoples and all races. The command to eat unclean animals in his Joppa vision had liberated Peter, a very prejudiced Jew, to journey several days to the home of a Roman centurion named Cornelius living in Caesarea. Cornelius, having supernaturally received advance notice of Peter's visit, was more than ready to accept the message of salvation through Christ alone and lead his entire house-

---

10. Willimon, *Pastor: The Theology and Practice*, 280

11. Ernst Haenchen, *The Acts of the Apostles* (Philadelphia: Westminster Press, 1971), 100.

12. George Eldon Ladd, *A Theology of the New Testament* (Grand Rapids: W. B. Eerdmans, 1993), 391.

hold in a confession of faith. His extended family was baptized both with water and with the Holy Spirit.

Peter stated with no hesitancy to the Jerusalem leadership that the real distinction between Christians and non-Christians was not circumcision but the gift of the Holy Spirit. "And God, who knows the human heart, testified to them by giving them the Holy Spirit, just as he did to us; and in cleansing their hearts by faith he has made no distinction between them and us" (Acts 15:8-9 NRSV). Paul and Barnabas, at the same meeting, narrated similar accounts of inclusion that demonstrated God's acceptance and affirmation of persons who weren't particularly sensitive to and versed in the Jewish requirements for salvation. The only frame of reference that mattered for the new covenant was not circumcision, but faith in Jesus Christ.

James, the brother of Jesus, then quoted from Amos, who prophesied the offer of salvation for all people. James, who wasn't even a believer during Christ's earthly ministry, had unofficially evolved into the arch leader of Christianity. To believe in your brother as the Messiah requires greater faith than to believe in a miracle worker observed only at a distance. James declared in a somewhat arbitrary manner, "Therefore I have reached the decision that we should not trouble those Gentiles who are turning to God [with requiring circumcision]" (Acts 15:19 NRSV). James's statement, accepted by the majority (we have no evidence that the decision pleased everyone), was anything but a compromise. The decision was the clearly stated *sine qua non* of Christianity. Salvation is by faith alone, sealed by the transforming power of the Holy Spirit.

The additional requirements that would provide continuity between Judaism and Christianity were addendums, ethical requirements that were perceived to be important to Christian behavior rather than a preservation of Jewish nationalism. A person could be a Christian without being a Jew, but at the same time Jewish ethics helped inform Christian identity: abstention from sexual immorality, idol worship, and improperly prepared food (with the latter partially lost on those of us benefiting from the modern conveniences of refrigeration and chemical preservation). The watershed decision made within the context of a historical event would not only forever inform Christianity's message and mission but also demonstrate the dynamic nature of truth, an ongoing appeal to tradition and Scripture in the context of recurring situations. Thus quite possibly the most important administrative job in the Book of Acts was to historically and theologically interpret the faith and practice of the church.

There could be no doubt that the Holy Spirit enabled James to preserve the best of both worlds, to show respect for Jewish mores and at the same time, more importantly, to discern and disseminate the defining doctrine of Christianity, a creed that undermined the theological foundation of Judaism. Salvation would not be obtained through an adherence to the law but by belief in the sufficiency of the death and resurrection of Jesus Christ. Thus the central administrative task in Acts was to explore how to interpret, apply, and deliver this message.

THE CHARACTER OF LEADERSHIP

No narrative in the New Testament is more descriptive of the nature and character of New Testament administration than the farewell address by Paul to the Ephesian church. Acts 20, the narrative of Paul's longest pastorate, approximately two years, demonstrates Leonard Doohan's claim that "leadership is not what one does but rather who one has become through the opportunity of interaction with others in organizational life. It is a response to a vocation heard in the depths of one's heart."[13] Paul's leadership characterized communal life, empathy, endurance of persecution, hands-on help wherever possible, honest love, and house-to-house visitation, all the while supporting himself with a "tent-making" ministry. Paul conjures up Old Testament imagery from Ezekiel when he states, "Therefore I declare to you this day that I am not responsible for the blood of any of you, for I did not shrink from declaring to you the whole purpose of God" (Acts 20:26 NRSV). John McNeill writes in *A History of the Cure of Souls* that Paul, as the father of a great mission church, "was no iron hearted disciplinarian or bureaucratic official, but a brotherly Christian in need of the moral and spiritual support of the others."[14]

Church administration in the Book of Acts was anything but top-down management. Servant leadership expresses and exercises deep compassion for the needs and hurts that are constantly endemic to human existence. One of the primary purposes of communal life is to discover and minister to those communal hurts. Paul's authority was derived from a lifestyle that constantly stated that "I am one of you." His authority was earned, not imposed. Anthony Robinson and Robert Wall make the clear distinction between leadership arbitrarily imposed on a congregation because of credentials and titles, and authority that earns respect from servanthood. They state in *Called to Be the Church: The Book of Acts for a New Day*: "But there is a crucial difference between the expert and the leader. You make an appointment, have a consultation, get an estimate, obtain a service, and that's that. By contrast, a leader is part of a com-

13. Leonard Doohan, *Spiritual Leadership:The Quest for Integrity* (New York: Paulist Press, 2007), 17.
14. John McNeill, *A History of the Cure of Souls* (New York: Harper and Row, 1997), 83.

munity and belongs to that community. You go to see an expert, but a leader belongs to a community."[15]

Church administration needs to do everything in its power to circumvent the top-floor, corner office, "my time is more important than yours" demarcation between clergy and laity. Availability and communal life rather than a seminary degree or M.B.A. are the pillars that provide confidence in church leadership. This does not eliminate the problem of discerning a line between one's personal and professional life. It also does not disparage an acquaintance with management resources that is not dominated by them.

COMMUNAL AUTHORITY

Leadership in Acts is not trained but spiritually ripened and disciplined. This was the case in Antioch, Christianity's first developed community after Jerusalem. Persons came to the forefront through both spiritual gifts and disciplined commitment to the Christ who had saved them. Governance in Acts is defined by confidence in persons rather than a planned program or policy. We might assume that Simeon, Lucian, and Manaen, along with Saul, were mentored by Barnabas. They had comprehended the meaning of community, especially its corporate disciplines in the context of worshiping, and the spiritual disciplines of prayer and fasting. "While they were worshiping the Lord and fasting, the Holy Spirit said, 'Set apart for me Barnabas and Saul for the work to which I have called them'" (Acts 13:2 NRSV).

The response to the Holy Spirit's direction was not to vote, though there must have been discussions in the form of such questions as, "Are you perceiving what I am perceiving?" Prayer took the form of collective listening to both God and one another. Only after further fasting and praying did they enact the community ritual of laying hands on Barnabas and Paul, a rite of consecration and community blessing. Granting authority via symbolic rite was inherited from Old Testament practice. Kevin Giles explains that "the laying on of hands by those assembled therefore does not signify the bestowal of a ministry, or of the Spirit, but rather that from now on their ministry is no longer an individual one; they are from this point on representatives of their community. What they do, they do not undertake in their own name, but in the name of the community that has set them apart as its representatives."[16]

---

15. Anthony Robinson and Robert W. Wall, *Called to Be Church: The Book of Acts for a New Day* (Grand Rapids: W. B. Eerdmans, 2006), 237.

16. Kevin Giles, *What on Earth Is the Church? An Exploration in New Testament Theology* (Downers Grove: InterVarsity Press, 1995), 95.

Barnabas and Saul were so successful in their first mission that upon the healing of a crippled man the witnesses to the event attempted to confer on them the names of Greek gods. The two vehemently protested by tearing their clothes, a sign of abasement, assuring the crowd of their humanity. These first missionaries averted a primary temptation of charismatic leadership, the corruption of power, personality cultism that characterizes much of today's church leadership, especially in the contemporary megachurch. The incident also clarified the real mission of the church. More important than signs and wonders was the good news of salvation through Christ, a displacement of allegiance to false gods by the liberating grace of the living and true God.

Leadership as Godly Obedience

Leadership in the Book of Acts often depended on a direct line to God. Visions were often God's medium of choice in guiding the church and setting the agenda. It would have taken nothing less than a vision for Ananias to affirm and accept Saul, the Pharisee hit man who may have been headed to Damascus with Ananias as his target. A vision, which was divine instruction for Peter to trash most of the theology he had ever learned, sent the very prejudiced Peter to the house of Cornelius. A vision sent Paul to Athens, a city saturated with gods and pseudo intellectuals. Not the kind of place to peddle the "foolishness" of the cross.

Though visions may not be God's primary means of communication for the twenty-first-century church, the operational paradigm that God is in charge, or at least needs to be, is the same today as it was two thousand years ago. Though God doesn't always directly communicate in such dramatic fashion, he is no less concerned with the administrator doing his will. Every pastor's closing statement on life and ministry needs to be the same as was Paul's, who declared before King Agrippa, "I was not disobedient to the heavenly vision, but declared first to those in Damascus, then in Jerusalem and throughout the countryside of Judea, and also to the Gentiles, that they should repent and turn to God and do deeds consistent with repentance" (Acts 26:19 NRSV). God had told Paul where to go, where not to go, and even how long to stay (see Acts 18:9).

Conclusion

Administration in the Book of Acts is not a designated role, separating or positioning a person above others. Leaders evolve out of what they do: service, prophecy, evangelism, and the various gifts of the Spirit that are recognized as valuable to the edification of the community. These roles emerge as persons intimately relate to God, an intimacy evidenced by loving concern for those both inside and outside of the Body of Christ. The overarching theme for administration is that it seeks the guidance of the Holy Spirit for both the community's internal life and missional outreach. Administration is able to lead the flock without lording over the flock (see 1 Pet. 5:3). Its success is found in the sufficiency of God, diligently sought through prayer and often fasting. The three constants we have discovered are flexibility of form, attitude of servanthood, and supernatural empowerment. Administration in the Book of Acts is a spiritual authority, grounded in a relationship with God and a loving identity with those who are of the household of faith.

FOR FURTHER READING

Bacher, Robert N., and Michael Cooper. *Church Administration.* Minneapolis: Fortress Press, 2007.

Willimon, William H. *Pastor: The Theology and Practice of Ordained Ministry.* Nashville: Abingdon Press, 2002.

2
ORGANIZATIONAL LEADERSHIP
WHAT CHURCH LEADERS
NEED TO KNOW ABOUT . . .

Mark A. Smith

EdD, President, Ohio Christian University

"The servant-leader is servant first. . . .
It begins with a natural feeling that one wants to serve, to serve first.
The conscious choice brings one to aspire to lead."[1]

━━━━━━━━━━━━━━━━━━━ ◆ ━━━━━━━━━━━━━━━━━━━

WATCH OUT, JESUS, HERE I COME!

Pastor José had a vision. He wanted to see growth in several areas of the medium-sized church he pastored. Many of his parishioners supported his vision. José wrote down his ideas, created a plan, and developed some goals. He even included strategy on how to measure goal achievement in order to determine success. The plan was ready and he now could go change the world. His motto was, "Watch out, Jesus, here I come!"

But as the months passed, nothing happened. Each week Pastor José became more and more frustrated; depression and failure became his daily companions. As board members and business leaders watched from the sidelines, they saw what Pastor José was unable to see: he did not know how to lead forward with his vision. He always referred to the project as "his" project. When gathering a group to discuss new initiatives, he dominated the discussion, giving only token appreciation to others who shared viable ideas. At times he dismissed these ideas before the speaker had even finished talking. In Pastor José's mind, he alone knew how to make his vision a reality. After all, it was "God's vision." He worked even harder, putting in many extra hours to "grow the church." After two frustrating years, he resigned, certain that his parishioners "just weren't interested in change." He considered leaving the ministry altogether.

---

1. Robert K. Greenleaf, *The Servant As Leader* (Indianapolis: Robert K. Greenleaf Center, 1991), 7.

This all-too-familiar story is played out over and over again in the church. Why do visionaries sometimes fail? Why do church projects fail even when the top leaders support them? There are multiple answers, but one rises above the others—poor leadership strategies.

A BLUEPRINT FOR FAILURE

When talking about their pastors, many Christian business leaders express overwhelming support for "the man of God." However, these business leaders are quick to point out several traits that cause pastors to fail. Ironically, these same traits cause business leaders to fail:

1. The vision is the pastor's vision only.
2. The vision is not clearly communicated.
3. The vision does not include others.
4. The vision lacks careful planning.
5. The vision is poorly implemented.
6. The vision is never reviewed and updated.

Today, there is a critical need for men and women pastor/leaders to work with others to form a God-given vision and then lead the church forward in the implementation of that vision. These leaders must be principled and trustworthy. Six billion people are expressing a desperate need for compassionate, trustworthy leaders. Pastor, are you willing to be a world-changing leader? Are you open to changing *your* world? Our families, communities, churches, and organizations need a valiant response to this call if we are to make a world-changing difference in the next decade. This chapter offers you some strategies to use in changing your world.

DEFINING LEADERSHIP

Business leaders have a wide variety of leadership models or definitions from which to choose. To better understand the business leader's mind-set, pastors should review key principles from the world of business leadership.

Leadership is the act of modeling, serving, and communicating the values, vision, and goals of a community, team, or organization in response to a need. Many pastors fail to realize that they are leaders who lead organizations. In their overview of leadership strategies, leadership experts Warren Bennis and Burt Nanus describe these qualities as pivotal to effective leadership:

• Leadership is authority.
• Leadership is vision.
• Leadership is mobilization of forces.
• Leadership commits people to action.

- Leadership involves hard work.
- Leadership is associated with the strong.
- Leadership is both born and developed.[2]

The above list clearly shows that leadership not only involves numerous characteristics but also is difficult to define. Richard Chewning defines leadership in this way:

> Good leadership is an art. It provides direction and purpose for an organization. It elicits trust and helps employees focus on the big purposes of the organization. Leadership must be earned. It is voluntarily given by those who follow, not taken by those who lead. Followers perceive that leaders can work with them to provide opportunities to meet their personal goals while making a contribution to the goals of the business.[3]

Perhaps one of the most important aspects of leadership, Chewning adds, is understanding that "each of us can grow and develop leadership skills."[4] This should give hope to the ineffective pastor/leader. Knowing just how critical it is to be an effective leader, the pastor then should aspire to develop leadership skills in order to make a world-changing difference.

Daniel Goleman approaches leadership from a slightly different perspective but in a similar vein of thought. "Leaders set strategy, they motivate, they create mission, they build culture." Further, he says, the "singular job of the leader is to get results."[5] Pastors need to familiarize themselves with the business leader's perspective and focus on results. This is particularly true if the church board is comprised primarily of business leaders and if much of the discussion is framed by a business mind-set. Pastors often are frustrated by this "results focus," but much of their frustration can be reduced by establishing a clear agenda for the church—one that is capable of producing results. An agenda of results should include not only numerical and monetary growth but also spiritual growth, however difficult that might be to ascertain. Ironically, most pastors do not like the image or the pressure associated with a corporate inclination. Rather than see a dichotomy between the spiritual and the business mind-sets, it is more productive to view these two approaches as different means to the same

---

2. Warren Bennis and Burt Nanus, *Leaders: The Strategies for Taking Charge* (New York: Harper and Row, 1985).

3. Richard C. Chewning and others, *Business Through the Eyes of Faith* (New York: Harper-Collins, 1990), 133.

4. Ibid.

5. Daniel Goleman, "Leadership That Gets Results," *Harvard Business Review* (March/April 2000): 78.

end. Pastors need to understand that the church essentially is about results, and the primary result is to build the kingdom of Christ.

Leadership Styles

To avoid the pitfalls of ineffective pastoral leadership, pastors should understand the benefits and pitfalls of various leadership styles. Using a style that does not fit a particular project or group of people will only defeat the pastor's good intentions. Sometimes, elements of different styles can be combined for optimum results, allowing the pastor to connect style, characteristics, and strategies to facilitate world-changing leadership. Goleman reviews six leadership styles.[6]

1. Demands Immediate Compliance: Coercive Leadership

To coerce means to achieve something by force. A stylistic phrase would be "Do what I tell you." The underlying emotional intelligence competencies of the coercive leadership style are the drives to initiate, control, and achieve. For some odd reason, coercive leadership seems to be a preference with some pastors. Although a pastor must demonstrate strong leadership at times, coercive leadership is rarely helpful and more often than not causes congregational discomfort. Almost without fail the pastor who leads the church in this manner will end up weakening the church.

In extreme situations, such as a church split or a case of defiant sin in the church, coercive leadership may prove useful if it is employed with love and discretion. Business leaders exercise this style when turnaround is needed for a failing organization. In such cases, the coercive style can break unproductive business habits and shock people into new ways of working. It can be effective with problem employees when other methods have failed. It is also effective as a military model, necessitating immediate compliance. The coercive style is always appropriate during a genuine emergency, such as a natural disaster or terrorist attack. However, this is not suggested for any long-term plan.[7] While the coercive leadership style has merit in certain narrowly defined circumstances, it seldom should be used as an everyday model.

2. Mobilizing People Toward a Vision: Authoritative Leadership

An authoritative leader might be characterized by the phrase "Come with me." This leader is a self-confident, empathetic change catalyst. This style works

---

6. Ibid.
7. Ibid.

best when changes require a new vision or when clear direction is needed. Goleman describes authoritarian leadership as the ability to maximize "commitment to the organization's goals and strategy."[8]

The pastor who employs authoritative leadership is respected and goal focused. At times the authoritative pastoral leader will face discouragement if goals are not met. However, in being too goal focused, this leader may also overlook or forget people in the process of accomplishing goals.

3. Creating Harmony and Emotional Bonds: Affiliative Leadership

An affiliative leader often will use the phrase "People come first." This leader's strengths are empathy, relationship building, and communication. Affiliative leadership works best to heal rifts in a team or to motivate people during stressful situations. Goleman describes the affiliative leader as one who "leads by building strong emotional bonds and then reaping the benefits of such an approach, namely fierce loyalty. . . . They share ideas; they share inspiration."[9]

The pastor who is an affiliative leader works constantly at relationships. While this leader may frustrate some who are goal focused, over the long term the affiliative pastor will be respected for harmony of vision and purpose.

4. Forging Consensus through Participation: Democratic Leadership

The democratic leader's catchphrase is "What do you think?" This leader exemplifies collaboration, team leadership, and communication. The democratic style works best when building employee buy-in or consensus, or in order to receive input from valuable employees. Goleman explains: "By letting workers themselves have a say in decisions that affect their goals and how they do their work, the democratic leader drives up flexibility and responsibility."[10]

The strength of this leadership style for pastors is the fact that many people are involved in the decision-making processes. This style tends to broaden the church base and include many people; however, some will view this style with concern because decisions are not made quickly or efficiently.

5. Setting High Standards: Pacesetting Leadership

"Do as I do—now" characterizes the pacesetting leader. Setting high standards of performance, the pacesetter is noted for conscientiousness, initiative,

---

8. Ibid.
9. Ibid.
10. Ibid.

and the drive to achieve. Pacesetting leadership works best when the goal is to get quick results from a highly motivated and competent team. "The pacesetting style has its place in the leader's repertory, but it should be used sparingly," Goleman advises. "The leader sets extremely high performance standards and exemplifies them himself. He is obsessive about doing things better and faster, and he asks the same of everyone around him."[11]

The pastor who is a pacesetting leader tends to come into the church organization for specific purposes (such as leading a construction project or increasing growth dramatically within a short timeframe) and stay for short periods of time. Because of a get-it-done attitude, this pastor may be applauded by business leaders. The same attitude, however, may frustrate others in the congregation. In the follow-up years, a relational pastor may be needed to balance the growth associated with the pacesetting pastor.

6. Developing Future Leaders: Coaching Leadership

The coaching leader's underlying competencies are empathy, self-awareness, and the ability to develop others. The coaching leader's catchphrase is "Try this." This style works best as a way to help employees improve performance or develop long-term strengths. Goleman explains: "For instance, the coaching style works particularly well when employees are already aware of their weaknesses and would like to improve their performance."[12]

The pastor who employs this leadership strategy must build a trust relationship with a select few members. This trust relationship is built on admission of needed improvements and a willingness to resolve those issues. The pastor who commits to this style primarily uses it with staff in one-on-one sessions. While coaching leadership is not best applied in large groups, the overall approach may be conducive to guiding a large group.

WHICH STYLE IS BEST?

Goleman believes that the most effective leader will master four or more styles.[13] Pastors should study their individual leadership styles in light of these six, modifying and adapting various elements in order to improve interaction skills and be more effective in their leadership roles. A pastor must ask which style is best in a given situation. The following questions should initiate reflective thinking about which style is appropriate:

---

11. Ibid.
12. Ibid.
13. Ibid.

1. Does the problem identified need immediate action with strong leadership?
2. Does the situation require motivational leadership?
3. Does the situation need consensus?
4. Does the identified need area require high performance standards?

THE SERVANT LEADER

In approaching this book for pastors, the authors are biased toward a servant leadership approach to leadership. In recent years, the term "servant leader" has captured the attention of those seeking to implement Christian ideals in the workplace—even in the business world. A servant leader influences people to collaboratively work toward shared visions and goals in order to produce results for the common good. It is the act of modeling, serving, and communicating the values, visions, and goals of a community, team, or organization in response to a need.

In his Organizational Leadership Assessment, Jim Laub describes effective servant leaders as those who

- display authenticity,
- value people,
- develop people,
- build community,
- provide leadership,
- share leadership.[14]

Although they do not call it servant leadership, James Kouzes and Barry Posner support the underlying philosophy. Summarizing extensive research in *The Leadership Challenge*, they note five key leadership practices that promote change:

1. Challenging the process (status quo)
2. Inspiring a shared vision
3. Enabling others to act
4. Modeling the way
5. Encouraging the heart[15]

These five practices embody servant leadership. The spirit of this leadership style transmits a sense of trust and respect while influencing people to produce the intended results. This evokes in those being led a sense of appreciation, optimism, freedom to improve and advance, motivation, involvement, and owner-

---

14. Jim Laub, "Servant Leadership," OLAGroup.com, http://www.olagroup.com/Display .asp?Page=servant_leadership.

15. James M. Kouzes and Barry Z. Posner, *The Leadership Challenge: How to Keep Getting Extraordinary Things Done in Organizations*, from The Jossey-Bass Management Series (San Francisco: Jossey-Bass, 1995), 1-2.

ship. Effective and caring leaders can stifle or liberate the talents and skills of the team or organization. The effective pastor should strive to unleash the talents and creativity of those under his or her leadership.

World-Changing Servant Leadership

After reviewing leadership definitions, styles, and strategies, and after talking with numerous business leaders, we offer this definition of world-changing servant leadership for pastors:

Pastoral World-Changing Servant Leadership is the ability to identify compelling needs, to initiate the collaborative action required to envision solutions, and to influence people and resources to serve others for a better future. This leadership is an active, purposeful, skilled, service-led influencing of others to further facilitate change or growth, enabling the team or community to achieve both corporate and individual goals.

Qualifying leadership in this way, a pastor—embodying a servant mind-set—becomes an active participant in leading an organization forward. Rather than allow circumstances to control the church organization, the pastor leader adopts a proactive, not a reactive, focus. The effective leader does not sit by and allow the church to remain status quo but focuses instead on forward movement. Leading coordinated action often means the difference between a church's success and failure. It also marks the difference between an average leader and a world changer.

Check Your Leadership Inventory

Since the process of becoming a world-changing servant leader requires action, it is essential for leaders first to assess their inventory of a key characteristic—compassion, which is seeing a compelling need. I love and have been involved in the church for many years. In fact, I am a pastor. Yet I see so many pastors who fail to notice the compelling needs around them. Pastor-effective leadership is gleaned by studying your community and identifying the needs. Once you identify the needs, you must develop an action plan. It starts with compassion and seeing needs.

The pastor must be a compassionate public leader. As I spoke recently with a school superintendent about leadership, he shared his ideas about how dynamic leaders should lead in the public sector. His list was inspiring to his leadership team, the faculty, and the school/community. He noted that great leaders transmit a compassionate spirit and the behaviors of a servant leader. In so doing, they provide

1. love and devotion as they encourage and strengthen others;

2. wisdom and good judgment as they guide and counsel others;
3. authority (caring and helpful influence) as they protect and support others;
4. goodness as they supply and comfort others;
5. equality as they work with others in the spirit of love and unity.

Servant leaders are promoted to a position of authority over those under their care. Servant leaders must not use coercive and positional power to lord it over people, nor should they act tyrannically. Instead, servant leaders are called to love, care, serve, train, and empower those they lead. One should never choose to exploit and control others. Rather, the focal point of leadership should be meeting the needs of those being served.

Identify Key Leadership Factors

Too many leaders fail to understand and appropriately use three key leadership factors: authority, responsibility, and accountability. In a seminar in Dallas, Dr. George Selig, provost of Regent University, shared his definitions of these key factors:

1. **Authority** is the right to make decisions.
2. **Responsibility** is the obligation to make decisions.
3. **Accountability** is being evaluated on how authority and responsibility are applied.

Effective pastors empower others. They delegate authority, responsibility, and accountability to the trustworthy. And they find mutually compatible ways to monitor and assess progress.

Pastor, how do you evaluate yourself? Do you delegate authority? How and in what areas? How would you evaluate the leaders you have empowered? What changes can you make to master or improve in these areas?

Inspirational Servant Leaders

The following stories illustrate how servant leaders have changed the world. This section is designed to help you pick up leadership styles or strategies that will further facilitate your growth. Pay close attention to the circumstances that framed the worlds of these leaders and how their actions changed the world.

Listen Up, Men!
Esther: A Woman Pastor

Esther is a biblical figure who changed her world. When she first appears in the Bible, she is an orphan Jewess named Hadassah, "also known as Esther" (Esther 2:7). Within four years she is a queen, the wife of Xerxes, the king of Persia. Although this position gave her tremendous power, she managed it wisely.

From her humble beginnings, Esther became God's instrument to save the entire Jewish population.

Thinking of being a world changer? Esther is someone from whom you can learn important pastoral lessons. Many consider her to have been Israel's best pastoral leader overall. Author Edith Deen highlights several leadership strategies that Esther modeled as she led the Jews out of harm's way.[16]

1. She gained favor with the people.
2. She used sound judgment.
3. She always thought of others first.
4. She was willing to sacrifice her position and even her life to save others.
5. She was dedicated and loyal.
6. She exhibited character.
7. She was fearless.
8. She was prudent.

Esther is a pattern for each of us to follow. Could it be that the characteristics listed above would resolve the situation that you so desire to change? Perhaps one of the greatest problems in the church today is the lack of leadership strategies and involvement from the church organization's "common folks." Why is it that so few of the laity speak up when a church or church organization seeks to resolve problems? Among the reasons are these:

- Some are afraid to speak up.
- Some feel they have nothing valuable to offer.
- Some are not involved in the church, so feel voiceless.
- Some feel their ideas are not valued because of past rejection.
- Some simply do not care.

And, even more tragically, some pastors are too controlling and closed to new ideas. Esther changed her world. Who is the Esther in your church? Which of Esther's leadership strategies would work for you?

Mother Teresa: A Church Leader with a Servant's Heart

Mother Teresa of Calcutta is a contemporary leader who impacted the world through servant leadership. She was responsible for bringing the plight of Calcutta's street people to the world's attention. When she first walked onto Calcutta's streets, the poorest of the poor were living and dying there. Many were lepers. Many were children. No one seemed to be doing anything about their desperate situation or deplorable conditions. Her heart was so moved by

---

16. Edith Deen, *All of the Women of the Bible* (San Francisco: Harper Collins, 1988), 148-51.

their overwhelming need that she decided to take action. She began to work as a "missionary of charity," ministering to the lepers.

In his book *Something Beautiful for God,* Malcolm Muggeridge describes Mother Teresa as epitomizing servant leadership by choosing "to live in the slums of Calcutta, amidst all the dirt and disease and misery."[17] He describes her as having a "spirit so indomitable, a faith so intractable, and a love so abounding, that he felt abashed."[18]

Mother Teresa is known for having changed the plight of many lives. However, it is important to remember that she went about changing the world one heart at a time. Love was her modus operandi, the key to her tremendous influence. Will this same M.O. work for church leaders?

In modeling leadership characteristics, Mother Teresa exhibited these qualities:

1. An outstanding work ethic
2. Love for others
3. The ability to see the need
4. A vision to change the plight of the needy
5. A plan to implement her vision
6. The ability to organize resources
7. The ability to galvanize an effective vehicle for change (i.e., the Mothers of Charity)[19]

It is readily apparent that Mother Teresa saw a need and committed herself to changing the world. The characteristics of great leadership seem to converge in the key behaviors she modeled and taught throughout her life. She clearly saw the relationship between leadership and God's kind of love. Mother Teresa has many leadership qualities from which to learn.

President John F. Kennedy: A Shining Light

Although President Kennedy was not a pastor, he is an example of a person who saw a compelling need and was a servant leader for the cause of civil rights. In his all-too-brief time in office, President John F. Kennedy will be remembered for his inspirational leadership in the troubling days of the early Civil Rights struggle. His ability to articulate hope and forward thinking was a shining light to a country coming to grips with its conscience. Among his most powerful leadership skills were these:

17. Malcolm Muggeridge, *Something Beautiful for God: Mother Teresa of Calcutta* (Garden City, NY: Image, 1977), 17.
18. Ibid.
19. Ibid., 17.

1. The ability to create vision
2. The ability to effectively communicate the vision
3. A passion for excellence
4. The ability to motivate people toward a common cause
5. The ability to lead the cause

President Ronald Reagan: Visionary Leadership

President Reagan was not a pastor either, but his vision for the nation to end the Cold War and promote democracy was an example of visionary servant leadership. Ronald Reagan will be remembered not only as one of America's greatest presidents but also as one of the finest leaders of all time. He said that our goal as Americans was "to have the vision to dream of a better, safer world, and the courage, persistence and patience to turn the dream into a reality."[20] This statement underscores his strong belief that one man can change the world. History is already validating that belief, as information continues to emerge revealing President Reagan's part in the subsequent fall of Communism. Democracy prevailed through his visionary leadership. Author Dinesh D'Souza concludes that President Reagan was governed by three basic elements of leadership:

1. Vision—the ability to frame conviction and visualize destination
2. Action—the ability to get from here to there
3. Consent—the ability to articulate vision and rally the people[21]

From different political spectrums, Presidents Kennedy and Reagan inspired the nation and modeled servant leadership. In so doing, they advanced noble causes and changed the world. The pastor who is aligned with servant leadership becomes an active participant in making the world a better place. Rather than allowing circumstances to control people, the pastor influences positive action to control circumstances as led by the Holy Spirit. Leading coordinated action is the difference between letting life change you and taking measures to change life.

WORLD-CHANGING LEADERSHIP AS EXEMPLIFIED BY JESUS CHRIST

In looking briefly at some well-known servant leaders in this chapter, we have identified certain characteristics and practices pivotal to successful servant leadership. Additionally, to effect substantive change in the world—to be a world changer—key strategies are necessary. As we focus on these strategies,

---

20. Dinesh D'Souza, *Ronald Reagan: How an Ordinary Man Became an Extraordinary Leader* (New York: Free Press, 1997), 228.
21. Ibid.

we would do well to study the person that even secular writers on leadership acknowledge to be perhaps the most influential leader of all time: Jesus Christ.

World-Changing Leadership Involves Sharing Vision

One writer suggests that "Jesus knew his mission statement, and he did not deviate from it. He declared that his mission was, in essence, to teach people about a better way of living." Further, in describing his leadership style, she says that Jesus was "a leader who, like many of us, had to depend on others to accomplish a goal."[22]

Jesus Christ had a vision. That vision was to change the world with a message of love, one person at a time. A healthy, creative mind produces vision. Individuals and organizations are always in critical need of vision. Outstanding, world-changing leaders possess great vision. They change the seen and envision the unseen. Their creative vision convicts, inspires, and enables people to achieve peak performance and attain extraordinary goals. That is exactly what Christ did as a leader. This was Jesus' vision statement: "I have been given all authority in heaven and on earth! Go to the people of all nations and make them my disciples. Baptize them in the name of the Father, the Son, and the Holy Spirit, and teach them to do everything I have told you. I will be with you always, even until the end of the world" (Matt. 28:18-20 CEV).

With this simple vision statement the world was changed.

World-Changing Leadership Involves Developing Others

Jesus developed others by reproducing himself in them. Great pastors transmit excellence by loving, serving, and teaching their followers. As leaders develop those around them, they first must "manage themselves" by discipline. Followers will trust someone in a leadership role who is disciplined and consistent in behavior.

We must remember that world-changing pastors are also preparing world changers. Too many pastors have conformed to society's standards and have either been changed by those standards or have become indifferent to the problems around them. Great leaders reproduce the leadership strategies of Jesus Christ in those they manage, teach, and serve. The improvement, growth, and spread of world-changing endeavors will occur in direct proportion to the supply of world-changing pastors/leaders.

---

22. Laurie Beth Jones, *Jesus, CEO* (New York: Hyperion, 1995), xvii.

World-Changing Leadership Depends on Integrity

Stephen Covey became a best-selling author by espousing the idea of "principle-centered leadership." He suggests that "principle-centered leadership introduces a new paradigm—that we center our lives and our leadership of organizations and people on certain 'true north' principles."[23]

Pastors who commit themselves to world-changing endeavors will be faced with several critical issues:

- How do I use power?
- How do I use wealth?
- How do I use positions of influence?

Pastors must constantly safeguard against temptations to abuse these privileges. The best protection involves principled leadership and accountability. In my relatively short lifetime, I have seen many pastors fall because of their lack of accountability to God and to others. Even on individual projects, pastors/leaders must resist the tendency to promote themselves as the solution providers. This does not mesh with the character of Jesus Christ. His very character was the essence of "pure motives."

World-changing pastors are needed today, it's true, but these can only be men and women of character—those who will advance a cause for the benefit of others. An example of foundational pastoral leadership principles can be found in this passage: "Just as shepherds watch over their sheep, you must watch over everyone God has placed in your care. Do it willingly in order to please God, and not simply because you think you must. Let it be something you want to do, instead of something you do merely to make money. Don't be bossy to those people who are in your care, but set an example for them" (1 Pet. 5:2-3 CEV).

QUESTIONS FOR PASTORS

As you prepare to take leadership initiative for a project, ask yourself these key questions:

1. Do I really see a need before me?
2. Am I committed to hard work?
3. Am I committed to serving others?
4. Is there a church project that I passionately want to pursue?
5. Can I enthusiastically share the vision with others?
6. Am I willing to take a risk with this pursuit?
7. Am I open to listening to the criticisms of others?

---

23. Stephen R. Covey, *Principle-Centered Leadership* (New York: Free Press, 1991), 18.

8. Am I ready to give fearless leadership?
9. Will this project allow me to model integrity?

The Legacy of Servant Leadership

Why was Jesus Christ the greatest servant leader of all time? After being with his disciples only three years, he had so profoundly ingrained his principles in them that an entire world was changed—and continues to be changed. Thus as leaders in a world-changing effort, we must constantly instill in those around us the desire to complete the job even after we are gone.

Pastor, the challenge is before you to become a servant leader. Servant leaders are people of character and integrity who see needs around them, influence and build relations with others, commit wholeheartedly to change the world, communicate an action plan, and are accountable in accomplishing that plan. Every business leader in the world would love that kind of pastor. Are you up to the challenge?

Perhaps the greatest test of pastoral leadership is what happens after the leader is gone. Does the vision continue? Will the organization fail? Is the church developing other leaders to take the place of the pastor in the future? Just as Jesus Christ mentored and led twelve disciples to fill leadership roles, the pastor who is an inspirational servant leader must do the same. In the case of Jesus Christ and Christianity, the ripples continue to spread!

One man.
Twelve men.
And the world is changed.
Wow! What a leader!

3
STRATEGIC PLANNING
PLANNING TO MEET THE
MISSION OF THE CHURCH

Edward A. Thomas
PhD, Associate Professor of Management,
Mount Vernon Nazarene University

An inclination to plan beyond a year is sometimes foreign to most people. How true is this idea of the clergy? The closest most get is using the lexicon to preach sermons throughout the year or developing a mission and/or vision statement without ever implementing it. Yet there are many businesses that fail by not paying attention to the environment around them or the direction they wish to go over a period of time. This is true for the church.

Once a business class was asked what they considered to be the greatest book on strategy. Several members answered the Bible. They were correct. God initiated his plan in the Garden of Eden in Genesis 2, built a nation to receive the Messiah with numerous prophecies pointing the way, unfolded the plan of salvation in the New Testament, and revealed the final victory at the Holy Book's end. When humankind fell to sin, God had a plan to rescue the race of Adam. Even Jesus said a king will not invade another land without considering the consequences and the means to do so (see Luke 14:31-32). Thus such a planning process is biblical.

No pastor should substitute the planning process for the spiritual leadership of the Holy Spirit. Everything a pastor does should have the blessing of God's Spirit on his or her endeavors. There are four things a pastor must do when coming to a church for the first time as the pastor: (1) love and respect the people, (2) pray, (3) preach, and (4) lead and direct the church. This last issue is the principal concern of this chapter and book. Many ministers often see in their early pastoral ministry that this issue is especially important, and their education or lack of it in this topic is dependent on where they attended school. It has been found that one Christian denomination may lose up to 30 percent of its clergy within their first ten years, and the greatest consensus (90 percent in the survey) agreed that they had not received the training for leading such an organization.[1] A multidenominational study has also confirmed that leaders are not receiving enough training to be effective in their local churches.[2] The tools in this book are designed to assist pastors in attaining the effective, efficient managerial leadership qualities churches need. Gaining proficiency in these tools begins by grasping the big picture—strategic planning.

THE NEED

As stated earlier, God demonstrated how important strategic planning is. Churches have often relied on what they have been doing for years as their guide for the future even if it is not effective. It is like the average worker living from week to week on a paycheck. Churches often live from week to week on routines.

John Beckett, owner and president of R. K. Beckett Industries in Cleveland, stated that one reason many businesses fail is that they often neglect to keep up with the larger picture of what is going on around them.[3] Review technology as an example. In the early days of the home computer there were Commodore and Atari computers. Though they were not quite user friendly, they did the basic job. Apple had its Mac, and IBM came along with their PC. IBM had the 086, 286, 386, 486, and all the Pentium series. In business, it would be disastrous to fall behind. Whether one belonged to the computer industry or was just an end user, technology dictated the need to keep up.

Similar thinking applies to the church. What is happening in the political (regulations), economic, and demographic world that may affect you in the church? Or what is happening in your local church community or your denomination that has its influence on the church. What about the parishioners? What keeps them satisfied? All of these factors and more set a pastor apart from one who is practicing through a veil of ignorance or assumes that every dynamic factor and person is sailing on the status quo. If a pastor wants to be faithful to his or her calling, that pastor must display a quality of leadership that demonstrates he or she knows where he or she is going and how to manage the details to arrive there.

Strategic planning can help the pastor access the church's strengths and weaknesses, look for ministry opportunities, and avoid most threats facing any church. Now, what does a pastor do with threat information? He or she plans to

---

1. R. Wells, *Factors Associated with Burnout* (Miami: Barry University Adrian Dominican School of Education, 1996).

2. David A. Roozen, "Are Seminaries Failing the Test?" *Faith Communities Today* (2001).

3. John Beckett, personal communication, 2007.

be effective. And just a spiritual note here is needed. The pastor who relies on the guidance of the Holy Spirit will have the perfect partner in ministry. So as a worker approved by God, use the valuable tool of strategic planning to help build his kingdom.

The clergy has often heard the line "free the laity." This is how it starts. Don't be afraid to let them enhance the ministry of the church so that you may enhance your call to the ministry. Remember Jesus needed twelve disciples to win the world. We are no better than our Master (see John 13:16). So figure out where you want to go in the future, what the purpose is of your church's existence, and generally how you are going to get there, and then the details can be worked out with an organized plan.

STRATEGIC PLANNING PROCESS

According to Bryson, a church should adopt the following process when it begins to enter the strategic planning phase:

1. Initiate and agree upon a strategic planning process with the church's governing board or council.
2. Identify organizational mandates.[4]

This chapter contains some examples but is not an exhaustive list of mandates (also known as objectives) that will happen only when the strategic process is part of your church's ministry:

- Fulfilling the Great Commission of Matthew 28
- Seeking and saving the lost and sanctifying their hearts
- Caring for the poor, orphans, and widows
- Developing a community and fellowship of believers
- Meeting denominational budgets and missionary and Sunday School goals
- Developing a viable children's and youth ministry
- Developing a Christian school
- Developing a retirement center
- Engaging in community outreach and sponsorship of community events
- Fostering gender and age-specific ministries

Point No. 1 of the planning process stated above is simply to get your governing board and key leaders to spend time thinking about where they want to go and how they want to do it. If a couple was planning a honeymoon trip to Niagara Falls, they would want to map out the route to their destination or risk getting lost. People attend churches that have a purpose.

---

4. J. M. Bryson, *Strategic Planning for Public and Nonprofit Organizations* (San Francisco: Jossey-Bass Publishers, 1995).

Point No. 2 answers the question "What are we here to accomplish?" There are four sources of these mandates (or objectives). They could be God-inspired, biblical, denominational, or local community directives or needs. When this step is first introduced, a pastor may expect to receive very broad generalities or the "deer in the headlights" stare. The goal here is to get the group to be specific and validate their choice with one of the four sources of the mandates.

An annual review of the plan should be initiated once the entire plan is developed and implemented. Answer questions such as, "Did we hit the target?" or "Are there adjustments needed?" This step will keep the church moving in the established direction or reveal reasons why the leaders may want to shift the focus of their direction. This way the church stays current. Any good organization will do this. The early church shifted its focus from the Jewish to the Gentile element in the Book of Acts. Follow the direction of the Holy Spirit and audit the changes in your community. There will be more on this concept later.

Once the parishioners buy into this planning system (and keep it always surrounded in prayer), they will take this plan seriously. The mission of the church will take on an important priority especially as results start happening. What follows now is a description detailing the main part of the planning stages of successful strategic planning.

THE PLAN

The overview (first part) of a written plan report should be a brief summary of the entire report describing the strategic plan's highlights. This serves as a brief introduction and provides a wonderful outline for someone who may be new to the process after the plan is finished. Many executives use a summary when they are too short on time to read a new report. Don't overlook this. It may save a lot of time explaining the developed plan to someone who is curious about it. Also this part is the last section written. A summary needs to be completed for the sake of conciseness.

The first major section should define the mission of the church. It should explain the church's purpose to those you serve in the community. The mission statement should answer the "how, when, and where" of what the church is doing to accomplish it purpose and goals. Here is an example from the school where the author works: "Mount Vernon Nazarene University exists to shape lives through educating the whole person and cultivating Christ-likeness for lifelong learning and service."[5]

5. "Information About" page, http://mvnu.edu/information.asp.

The university's mission statement contains two important points. The first is the values clarification of the university ("exists . . . for lifelong learning and service") and the second supports its core competencies (to supply a stated purpose: "shape lives through educating the whole person and cultivating Christlikeness"). Both of these phrases support the "how" or describe the objectives of the organization. The mission statement is brief to allow people to remember the mission, but the organization can add in an additional supporting statement more details that "clarify" (called simply a Clarification Statement) what the organization does. This statement may include the history of the organization, current preferences of the organization's members, available resources, and distinctive competencies.[6] This can also supply the "when and where" if not included in the mission statement.

The vision statement is forward looking and describes the direction the church is going, plus this statement should answer the questions of "what and why."[7] "What" is the overall reason that the church exists as a denominational and community church. Keep it simple, as short as possible, and straightforward. Use uplifting and encouraging terms. This is your guiding expression of your local corporate faith, so keep it memorable. The vision sets the direction, energizes the people, and sets the boundaries for the goals that will be set. The following describes an effective vision: "*[a]* imaginable [visualization], *[b]* desirable [attractive or motivating], *[c]* feasible [practical], *[d]* focused [centered], *[f]* flexible [not set in stone], and *[g]* communicable [inspiring]."[8] Here is an example from the same school: "Mount Vernon Nazarene University: An Academic Community of Faith, Shaping Christ-like Leaders for Lifelong Service and Global Impact. Ephesians 4:11-13"[9]

The "what" ("An Academic Community of Faith") and the "why" ("Shaping Christ-like Leaders for Lifelong Service and Global Impact") are present here. Vision gives the people the purpose of the church and a point to start their service. Since most individuals love mental pictures of things or people they hold dear, a creative and imaginative vision statement will allow the members to know where the beginning point and future ending point are. The vision statement may also allow for the incorporation of other points along this road. A university's vision statement may include different types of educational levels

---

6. Garry Smith, Danny Arnold, and Bobby Bizzel, *Business Strategy and Policy* (Boston: Houghton Mifflin, 1991).

7. Arthur A. Thompson, A. J. Strickland III, and John E. Gamble, *Crafting and Executing Strategy* (Boston: McGraw-Hill, 2008).

8. J. P. Kotter, *Leading Change* (Boston: Harvard Business School Press, 1996), 72.

9. "MVNU Student Handbook." MVNU, 2007.

(traditional, graduate, or professional offerings if the organization so wishes) or services that may be offered in the future.

Never underestimate the power of vision to motivate a person. It clarifies direction, motivates people, and coordinates actions.[10] A vision will save time and resources on how and what to do, since the purposes of ministry are known and captured in the vision statement. Church members will put their time and energy in the goal set before them. No more wandering for forty years in the wilderness as the Hebrew children did in the Old Testament. Simply, everyone will be on the same page, with no one doing his or her own thing. This is a great force for leadership, to have unity in purpose.

Additionally, a church may want to include a value statement. This may be optional, since values may have been incorporated in the mission and vision statements. This can become a statement of faith that the church holds true as norms about its ministries (i.e., children's or senior adult ministries), which it considers its core competencies or what it does best.

The second major section of the plan report should be the scanning of the macro environment surrounding your institution. It is made up of the following traits:

1. Demographic—What statistics are reflected in your national, community, or church environment? What are the trends for the population? What are the income statistics, and educational or job opportunities (unemployment) that affect your church?
2. Economic—What is happening in the national, regional, and local economies?
3. Regulatory/legislative—What are the government trends in laws and regulation at all levels that have an effect on your church?
4. Social/cultural—What social trends are currently affecting your people? What are the latest activities, interests, and opinions that the culture is pursuing?
5. Technological—What are the latest gadgets and electronic devices that may have an impact on your church?
6. Environmental—What "green" factors concern the church?

Here is a little secret. A pastor may also find ideas for sermon generation or ideas for future ministries by monitoring these traits. Remember, the big picture is what many businesses fail to keep an eye on and a major reason why they fail. They fall asleep and miss opportunities and possible threats. Sounds a bit like the parable of the ten virgins in the New Testament. And this has been

---

10. Kotter, *Leading Change,* 69-70.

a criticism of the church from outsiders who say the general church ignores the welfare of society and has grown inward. What is happening in your big picture that is affecting the local church? Does anyone in that local congregation have any idea? This is why this section is a valuable tool for the pastor's administrative toolbox.

The third major part of the report should be a reflection of the religious community within which the church finds itself. This writer pastored a smaller church sandwiched between four large churches holding different doctrines of faith: one denominational Pentecostal church, two independent churches (one that was strongly promoting Bible studies and special topic seminars and the other emphasizing music and youth), and one large mainline Calvinistic church. People in the community had their choice of where to attend. Why would they choose a smaller church? Was it important to know how these other churches ministered in order to find our church's ministry? Our smaller church had as an advantage a day-care center that it hosted in its facilities as a contact for young families, and the church tried to specialize as a niche ministry to families. After our church discovered through the use of the U.S. census data that people would drive up to a twenty-mile radius to go to church, the church's ministry area expanded and this kept the church from feeling claustrophobic amid the larger churches in its community.

Pastors do not like to think of neighboring churches as competition, since the church is in a sanctified work, but the truth remains. Other churches do want your members even though it is never stated out loud. So it is advantageous to know what they are doing to attract new people (even people looking for a church home for the first time). Can that form of outreach and worship style or ministry work in your congregation or not? Or will there be a duplication of the other church's ministry, thus offering an unnecessary ministry that will be ineffective, as well as not allowing your church to have an advantage in reaching new people?

One final question that is needed to complete a community scan of the church's environment is to ask what changes may occur in the near future. The driving forces for change might stem from the macro forces described previously or be derived from changing needs in the community or changing ministries from area churches.[11] The pastor can pick up this data from listening to people around the church and from other pastors as they gather in fellowships and pastoral meetings. Where is your church positioned to make an impact in relation to what others are doing?

---

11. Smith, Arnold, and Bizzel, *Business Strategy and Policy,* 89.

The fourth major part of the report should be a look internally at the local church environment or missional capabilities. This will make your environmental review complete. Start with the basic church organizational makeup—its five internal environmental factors: (1) personnel—skills, leadership, gifts; (2) ministries—internal, external; (3) finances—pros and cons; (4) outreach—what is working or not; and (5) organizational structure—strengths or impediments.

A good tool is a SWOT (strengths, weaknesses, opportunities, and threats) analysis. For each of the five internal environmental factors, list the strengths, weaknesses, opportunities, and threats. Second, take each of the four sections of the SWOT analysis and consolidate them into a master SWOT review. Group the strengths of all five environmental factors together and contrast them with the consolidated groups of weaknesses, opportunities, and threats. Then you can determine which strengths can be built up for ministry, which strengths need to be shored up against weakness, which strengths can open doors of ministry, and which strengths can provide defense against external threats. This type of strength assessment is where the planning of strategy starts. The SWOT analysis allows a person to visualize where the church is currently in a description of skills and processes for completing their mission.

Let's look at the organization for missional capabilities based upon four basic organizational cultures: defenders, prospectors, analyzers, and reactors.[12] The defender can be characterized as a church that keeps an inward focus and maintains the status quo amid whatever happens around them. It is business as usual week after week for this type of church. Gains and losses are evened out. They do enough to attract people to replace any that may leave or die but have little impact outside their nominal ministries.

Prospectors will look for any opportunity to build and enlarge old ministries and develop new ones. They are aware of what their community needs and react accordingly. There may be a need for a senior citizen's fellowship or a Bible study in their community at the senior center, and the church meets that need. Or there may be a need for youth activities (Upward Bound Basketball, etc.) or a "young family with children" focus (a "parents' night out" social/Bible study). How about a Sunday School class for young mothers or just a fellowship/book study (the Bible or a religious book) as a ministry to this group? Prospectors are very change oriented and less traditional in style, worship, and ministry.

---

12. Raymond E. Miles and Charles C. Snow, "Organizatioal Strategy," *Marketing Management: A Strategic Decision-Making Approach* (Boston: McGraw-Hill/Irwin, 2008), 217-19.

They pursue any possibility that affords an opportunity to minister to others and build the kingdom for God.

Analyzers are a group that seeks to keep a strong core of its traditional programs but follows after change and opportunities that are presented to them. They are very aware, just as the prospectors, of the needs in their community. They will use their current (traditional) structure of organization and expand their current ministries to incorporate extended new ministries or develop new ones after careful evaluation of new waters. They will be flexible in designing an organization to fit their new culture but still retain a core structure of the status quo.

Reactors have no visible strategy. This type of church may have even developed a mission statement, but that is as far as they got. They keep to the status quo for organization/culture and may lack leadership to move them off center. They may feel that their best days are past. If this group is complacent, declination will set in.

Thus the leadership must look at itself and determine what form of organizational structure will lead them to carry out the Great Commission of Matthew 28. Whether the church is traditional or contemporary in style, the leaders' philosophy and strategy or, simply put, their attitude is what will determine and energize their vision and mission in reaching their objectives.

COMMUNITY POSITIONING

The fifth major section of the strategic planning report should answer the question, "What is the perception of your church in your community or its value as it is perceived by the community?" Develop a survey for both the church members and the outside community on the ministries, programs, and perception of the local church. Distribute it to the internal members and then to the outside community and compare results. The survey may be eye opening. The positioning of both groups' perceptions based on the values derived from the survey will serve as a guide for developing the forthcoming strategies.

STRATEGIES AND OBJECTIVES TO DEVELOP BIBLICAL ALTERNATIVES

There are different strategies for growth, stability, and declination. First let's look at growth, since this will be the most requested and approved strategy.

1. Increase frequency of contact with the target community. Find new ways to reach out through current ministries with increasing frequency.
2. Increase usage of current ministries. Use various events, promotional methods, public relations, and so on, to attract visitors in increasing frequency.

3. Develop new applications (for changing old wine from old wineskins to new wine in new wineskins as the Bible states) by finding new purposes or methods for current ministries.

Another way is simply to research your community's environment and find the community's needs and wants (internally and beyond the four walls of the church). Use surveys or focus groups, or simply walk around meetings and talk with people and community (and church) leaders. Then develop a group that shares a vision as a guiding coalition. Brainstorm ways to develop the means and financial objectives.

Next there are general strategies for stability. Sometimes this is all a pastor can do because there is little chance for growth. The church may simply not be ready for growth, or there are internal factors, such as complacency, or external factors, such as economic decline in which people are moving away to find work. This does not have to be a time of no growth. A church at some point still needs to replace members who are not attending, or it will face declination. Growth is just slower or less aggressive at this time. Using the same methods for growth just discussed, a church can slowly reach out to others. A pastor can use the methods on a smaller scale to match the resources and the enthusiasm level in the church. Then maybe someone will declare that growth is possible again and begin more active pursuits in outreach.[13]

The last strategy, the one pastors don't like to talk about, is a declining strategy. Sometimes after a loss of members (for whatever reason), it is time to retrench or downsize. Some churches have a limited lifespan.[14] They will someday die. But before yours does, try a turnaround strategy. Cut any ministries that are draining resources and will not fit into a future vision of the church. Downsize to fit the current need in ministry and resources. Don't carry deadwood. But once you do this and the situation stabilizes, then consider using the growth strategies, if this is the new vision, or just harvest what you have and keep the process at the new smaller efficiency level. It may not be the right time for the church community to grow for various reasons. The church may just need a time for healing and reflection for spiritual renewal.

Now let's move on to the implementation of the strategies.

IMPLEMENTATION

What is more important, the planning or implementation of a plan? If you said both, you are right. The late great coach Vince Lombardi stated that the

---

13. Smith, Arnold, and Bizzel, *Business Strategy and Policy*, 241.
14. Tom Nees, "Do Churches Have to Die?" *Holiness Today* (May/June 2008): 8-9.

"best made plans never blocked anyone."[15] Until the plans are set into motion, no one can predict the outcome. On the other side of the coin, if no one is responsible or accountable to carry out the plans, nothing is accomplished. In this case, a prime example would be for a pastor to get up in the pulpit one Sunday and declare out of the blue that the church will start a home visitation ministry this coming Tuesday night and everyone is to be at church at 6 P.M. Does a program need to be in place, were key leaders informed, and was the rest of the congregation given a heads up about this? If none of these matters were addressed, implementation in this situation starts with very poor planning on the part of the pastor. Then if no one shows up at the designated day and time, nothing will get done. On the other hand, if planning was done and the announcement was made weeks in advance, then a group may come. Thus both sides of a plan, planning and implementation, are necessary.

The following are basic steps (who, what, how, and when) to effective implementation:

1. Choose a leader or a guiding coalition depending on the complexity of the driving force or ministry. A coalition brings more expertise and leadership to a strategic project. One leader may be an alternate choice for expediency and urgency. This is the principle of accountability. This is their job to get done.[16]

2. Develop a list of critical tasks, roles, and key functions.[17] What are the forces or procedures necessary to accomplish goals that have been set? What skills or training are needed? If training is required, then do it. What relationships are significant? What type of person will work well and fit into the requirements of this missional service? What are the roles—leader, trainer, worker, encourager, prayer, and so on? How will these roles meet and blend to be effective?

3. Develop a budget (the second part of the implementation process in the end-of-chapter outline). Use the zero-based method of budgeting. After researching the tasks in step 2, assign a dollar amount to each task that requires an expenditure of money. This method allows the coalition to find out what the cost is and allows for budgetary review later.

4. Develop a timeline. Have a time set for the critical stages before the prelaunch of the items mentioned in the first three steps. Set a date to launch and set specific times to review the process.

---

15. Thompson, Strickland III, and Gamble, *Crafting and Executing Strategy,* 358.

16. J. Stewart Black and Hal B. Gregersen, *Leading Strategic Change: Breaking through the Brain Barrier* (Upper Saddle, NJ: FT Prentice Hall: Pearson Education, 2002).

17. Smith, Arnold, and Bizzel, *Business Strategy and Policy,* 333.

5. Monitor the plan (the third part of implementation in the end-of-chapter outline).[18]
   a. If it requires low involvement, low risk, and low cost to implement a plan, then review once a month.
   b. If it is a high involvement, high risk, and costly new program, meet every two weeks for the first two months and then at set milestones of either time or accomplishments to review the status of the project. Remember, the longer the term of the project, the greater the risk of success or failure will loom over the individual or committee in charge of the plan.
6. Anticipate the possible need for contingency plans (the final step in the end-of-chapter outline). Not everything goes according to the original plan. Sometimes the results surprise us and are better than expected. Sometimes they are worse.
   a. If the plan is doing better than expected, be ready ahead of time with a plan to expand to meet the demand of the increased task.
   b. If the plan hits all targets, stay with the current plan.
   c. If the objectives have fallen short of the goals, then
      (1) increase the inputs needed to achieve the goals,
      (2) stay at the current level if still satisfied with the current results with no additional inputs,
      (3) or reduce the inputs to meet realistic expectations and results, find an alternative strategy (see next line), or stop the project.
7. Alternative strategies include the following:
   a. Fortify—stay with what you have currently at this effective level of ministry. Be sure resources are enough to keep the level of effort sustained.
   b. Flanker strategy—add additional services to complement the main thrust or simply have additional resources available (i.e., access to a counselor in a teen ministry).
   c. Expansions—offer your current members extensions or improvement of current ministries if that is the primary target or offer current members an opportunity to partake of any new ministries. This will serve as an extension of the established program (the old may find new life).[19]

18. John W. Mullins, Harper Boyd, Jr., and Orville C. Walker, Jr., *Marketing Management: A Strategic Decision-Making Approach* (Boston: McGraw-Hill/Irwin, 2008).
19. Ibid.

d. Other strategies:
   (1) Leap—while in the process of developing a ministry or program, another opportunity that is more promising presents itself; switch resources to the opportunity.
   (2) Niche or focus—if one avenue or segment of the targeted group(s) has fulfilled the targeted objectives while the rest of the targeted groups have not, focus on that segment (i.e., a children's ministry blossoms while a senior adult ministry does not).
   (3) Withdraw and regroup.[20]

When the implementation begins, try for short-term wins in order to boost the confidence of the church. Short-term, smaller victories are better than a long-term, large victory.[21] People will grow bored, tired, or lose faith if accomplishments are long-term. Short-term gains build confidence, competence, faith, and a strong belief in the mission. It is like a professional baseball team trying to make it to the playoffs in the fall. They need to win a certain number of regular season games to qualify and prove first to themselves that they belong in the playoffs. They know they have the skills to do so.

Be sure to adopt any accomplishments into the culture of the church, especially if the program is new. Cement the accomplishments of the goals and objectives into the very nature of what the church is or into its values. This step will aid in solidifying the results and making them permanent in the lifestyle and faith of the church.

Conclusion

God gave us the greatest strategic plan of all time starting in the Book of Genesis and finding its fruition in Jesus Christ. And the plan is still unfolding today. The Bible tells me so. Why not follow this biblical model and give your church the blessed opportunity to be Spirit led (always by his guidance we dream and act) plus have a roadmap governed by a vision and a plan with the practical determination to fulfill the Great Commission in Matthew 28? Start with a dream, then plan.

Outline of a Church Strategic Plan

I. Overview—A Summation of the Plan Written Here
   A. Mission, Vision, Values
   B. Macro Environment

---

20. Ibid.
21. Kotter, *Leading Change.*

C. Community Environment
D. Local Church Environment
   1. SWOT
   2. Missional Capabilities
E. Strategies and Objectives for Biblical Alternatives of Action
F. Implementation
   1. Who, What, How, and When
   2. Budget
   3. Monitoring: Weekly or Monthly Reports
G. Contingency Plan

4

GOALS AND OBJECTIVES
STRATEGIZING FOR THE MISSIONAL CHURCH

Stephen W. Dillman
PhD, District Superintendent, Pittsburgh District,
Church of the Nazarene

◆

As one denomination, the Church of the Nazarene, approached its centennial, church leaders declared that the mission of this denomination is to "make Christ-like disciples in the nations."[1] For one hundred years, this mission appeared to be assumed. The Great Commission of Matthew 28:19-20 was a common basis for mission statements created by local church leaders and only amplified by adding identity and strategic statements. Identity statements answered the question, "Who are we?" and strategic statements answered the question, "How are we going to fulfill the Great Commission?"

GOAL-ORIENTED MISSION

In the latter half of the twentieth century, churches seemed quick to adopt—though rarely adapt—professional business practices. This may have been due to the accessibility of readable books by popular business authors, an increase in interest about the subject of leadership, and an emerging body of scientific evidence showing a cause-effect relationship between best business practices and a successful bottom line. With the decline of church attendance, Sunday School attendance, and church membership that followed the baby boomer increases of the post-World War II era, the church was looking for something or someone or both to turn things around. Business practices and the leaders of successful organizations seemed to offer some answers.

One of the early church voices to draw on the business and scientific worlds for help was Donald McGavran. He also drew from sociology, anthropology, psychology, and theology to understand the changing world and create an effective strategy for mission theory and practice.[2] While the church often

---

1. NCN News, "Overview of Mission 2007," February 23, 2007, Nazarene Communications Network, http://www.ncnnews.com/nphweb/html/ncn/article.jsp?id=2919.
2. Donald McGavran, *Understanding Church Growth* (Grand Rapids: William B. Eerdmans Publishing Company, 1970), 5.

characterized its mission as evangelism, McGavran reframed the issue as one of church growth. He introduced church leaders to concepts such as culture analysis, community needs, individual readiness to the gospel, evangelistic strategies, and more to bring the often-ethereal mission of evangelism down to a set of strategic and achievable goals.

With McGavran and others influencing how the church went about fulfilling its purpose, goal-oriented strategies were common. These tended to fall into the following categories: imposed, reactive, and traditional.

Imposed goals were established by the institution and were often accompanied by incentives to get people to bring more people into the church. Growth, more than evangelism, was the emphasis.

Reactive goals were also common but rarely articulated, since these goals appeared to be less noble. Evangelism was the stated goal, but the objective of evangelism was church-centric for the purpose of survival, award, recognition, or fund-raising. Reactive goals reflect a broad category of organizational leadership theory called transactional leadership where leaders try to "sell" the vision with compelling and persuasive arguments.

Traditional goals focused on the responsibility and duty of the church people to win the lost. Believers were admonished to witness to their faith.

Path-Goal Theory and Imposed Goals. According to Bernard Bass in his encyclopedic *Bass and Stogdill's Handbook of Leadership*, path-goal theory reinforces change in a follower by showing the follower the path (i.e., behaviors) through which rewards may be obtained.[3] The leader's responsibility is to clarify the goals as well as the paths to those goals. This body of research shows that this clarification enhances the follower's psychological state and arouses the follower to increase his or her efforts to perform well. Follower satisfaction is tied to achievement of the goal.

In the case of imposed goals, the path-goal theory suggests that a local church, district, or denomination will achieve certain goals and cause people to feel good about achieving them when those goals are clearly defined and communicated. Additionally, a positive outcome is predicted when there is a reward attached to the achievement. How does this work in a local church? A local church pastor and board might set a goal for a record attendance on Easter Sunday. This goal is communicated along with the promise of a reward such as a special Easter memento for all who attend. A strategy or path is suggested, which can be as simple as asking members to fill a pew or as elaborate as a

---

3. Bernard M. Bass, *Bass and Stogdill's Handbook of Leadership: Theory, Research, and Managerial Applications,* 3d ed. (New York: Free Press, 1974), 46.

Friends' Day celebration. Together, the goal and path provide a roadmap that enables the pastor and congregation to move toward their desired outcome of a record attendance.

The positive side of this type of goal-oriented strategy is a clearly defined outcome. There is no internal debate. The negative side is the "one-size fits all" nature of the goal setting. A congregation may learn to ignore these imposed goals as too expensive, too hard to implement, or requiring more people and commitment than is available. If the organization loses its personal touch, the goals start to appear mechanical or self-serving. Followers may find it difficult to customize or contextualize the goals as they are encouraged to work in lockstep with each other for the benefit of the organization.

Transactional Leadership and Reactive Goals. Transactional leadership is just what it sounds like. The leader "sells" a vision or goal to followers who "buy in" to it. The leader entices followers to support the vision by communicating a compelling reason to do so. Interestingly, this process is based on reciprocity. The leader tries to influence followers and is under their influence as well. Effective transactional leaders adjust to the expectations of followers and, in doing so, earn more influence. As a leader responds to followers, followers learn to trust the leader, giving that leader the power to call followers to the vision or goal.[4]

Reactive goal setting is a ripe environment for transactional leadership. In the church, the pastor looks for early "wins." These achievements earn the pastor credit with the congregation. Often, this effort is connected to the leader's ability to identify issues and demonstrate an expertise for dealing with them. The pastor becomes a Moses who is able to lead the people to the promised land (i.e., the goal).

A negative side-effect of transactional, reactive goal setting is the emphasis on success and the measure by which success is evaluated. One difficulty is the requirement of a problem that allows the leader to demonstrate expertise and earn the right to lead. But being transactional and setting reactive goals can be positive when pastors are able to communicate their motives as selfless, rising out of their love for God and the people they serve. This is also a good time to create and discuss a shared or empowered leadership.

Transformational Leadership and Traditional Goals. Transformational leadership calls followers to work for transcendent goals and for aroused higher-level needs for self-actualization rather than immediate self-interest.[5] In other

4. Gill Robinson Hickman, *Leading Organizations: Perspectives for a New Era* (Thousand Oaks, CA: Sage Publications, 1998), 345.
5. Bass, *Leadership and Performance*, 11.

words, pastors call congregations to think more about winning the lost than their personal spiritual development. The goal is numerical regard of the spatial condition of the church. Because the goal is couched in simplistic terms, it has the benefit of being easily communicated and quickly understood by the followers. It makes measuring the spirituality of the congregation a simple process, since any self-interest is viewed as carnal and, therefore, unacceptable. Numerical goals value conversions, baptisms, and enrollment in Sunday School classes where new believers are discipled. If local efforts to evangelize the community are ineffective, the congregation can transfer their evangelistic interest to missionary work, sending money and supplies as tangible expressions of their desire to see people saved. A problem with this approach is its simplicity. This approach becomes somewhat anachronistic. As the church becomes more complex, the needs of the people become more varied, and the culture changes the expectations of those people the church is trying to reach. The simple structure cannot sustain the weight of change.

BEING MISSIONAL AND MISSION-ORIENTED: GOALS AND STRATEGIES

What does it mean to be missional? Darrell Guder gives a clear and succinct response to this question:

> We have come to see that mission is not merely an activity of the church. Rather, mission is the result of God's initiative, rooted in God's purposes to restore and heal creation. "Mission" means "sending," and it is the central biblical theme describing the purpose of God's action in human history. God's mission began with the call of Israel to receive God's blessings in order to be a blessing to the nations. God's mission unfolded in the history of God's people across the centuries recorded in Scripture, and it reached its revelatory climax in the incarnation of God's work of salvation in Jesus ministering, crucified, and resurrected. God's mission continued then in the sending of the Spirit to call forth and empower the church as the witness to God's good news in Jesus Christ. It continues today in the worldwide witness of churches in every culture to the gospel of Jesus Christ, and it moves toward the promised consummation of God's salvation in the *eschaton* ("last" or "final day").[6]

---

6. Darrell L. Guder, "Missional Church: From Sending to Being Sent," in *Missional Church: A Vision for the Sending of the Church in North America*, ed. Darrell L. Guder (Grand Rapids: William B. Eerdmans Publishing Company, 1998).

Who are called to be missional? The simple response is "everyone"—leaders and followers, clergy and laity. Alan Roxburgh notes that the usual leader-follower concepts derived from business models are not sufficiently grounded in a missional theology to be much help here. These are more functional than fundamental. He says, "In the missional community all are ordained to ministry in their baptism; all receive the same vocation to mission; and all are gifted in various ways for that mission as they participate in the twofold journey of the reign of God that is both inward and outward."[7]

At this point, we have arrived at the heart of this chapter. The following sections identify six missional goals that are grounded in Scripture and derived from what Guder calls a "theocentric reconceptualization of the Christian mission."[8] With each, examples of goals and strategies will be suggested as starting points for implementation. The author is indebted to Dr. Charles Zink for most of the following outline.[9]

The Great Commandment

Jesus replied: "'Love the Lord your God with all your heart and with all your soul and with all your mind.' This is the first and greatest commandment. And the second is like it: 'Love your neighbor as yourself.' All the Law and the Prophets hang on these two commandments." (Matt. 22:37-40)

If Jesus said that loving God and one's neighbor as oneself are the foundational commandments, then we need to start here and note the key words.

The Greek word for "love" is a form of the word *agapē*, a word that Christians often associate with a godly love. However, it has a broader meaning in 2 Timothy 4:10, where Paul says that "Demas, because he *agapes* this world, has deserted me." *Agapē* love, then, is an all-consuming desire for someone or something to the point that one is willing to sacrifice everything for the object of that love.

---

7. Alan Roxburgh, "Missional Leadership: Equipping God's People for Mission," in Guder, *Missional Church*, 200.

8. Guder, "Missional Church," 4.

9. On January 13, 2005, this author lost a colleague and friend to pancreatic cancer. Dr. Chuck Zink served as district superintendent on the New England District and, for the last few months of his life, as the denominational director of Clergy Development for the Church of the Nazarene. His titles and position did not define his life; his commitment to growing the kingdom of God did. His passion was to see the Church reach out to lost people with the transforming love of God. The methodologies were not critical concerns. The bureaucracies were loved but irrelevant. Success was defined by the simple question: Are you doing the mission of Jesus Christ? For Chuck it was framed in the words of Jesus Christ himself: "The Son of Man came to seek and to save what was lost" (Luke 19:10) and "Go and make disciples" (Matt. 28:19). Many of the missional priorities in this section come from his heart and mind. They are a tribute to his life and commitment to being missional.

When Jesus added the words "love your neighbor as yourself," he was referring to a passage in Leviticus 19:18. Of the list that God told Moses to say to the people, Jesus chose this one admonition to call the second greatest commandment. It is the only admonition that speaks of love and parallels the first commandment to love God. This is also part of the *missio Dei* (the mission of God) that calls for his chosen people to evangelize the nations. It is not about living peacefully with one another or being nice to one another. This is part of the salvation story that God has been telling since creation.

The degree of love is expressed in the absolute sense of the word "all," as in all your heart, soul, mind. This is the foundation for all the other missional goals. It is where we must start before moving on to structure, programming, and plans that we believe will fulfill the mission of the church. It is worth spending as much time as necessary to ground one's followers in this fundamental commandment. Here are just a few suggestions:

- Use the privilege of the pulpit and podium to speak about the Great Commandment and speak of it often.
- Before any program or plan is discussed, spend time talking about how this program or plan fulfills the Great Commandment.
- Incorporate the Great Commandment into the articulated mission statement of the church.
- Tell stories of how the Great Commandment is changing lives or let those who have been transformed as a result of people living out the Great Commandment tell the story themselves.
- Follow the admonition of the Shema (Deut. 6:4-7) and start embedding the Great Commandment into the minds and hearts of the children.
- Develop some avenues for people to express the Great Commandment that are not tied to institutional goals or personal satisfaction but give them an opportunity to rise to the level of sacrificial and altruistic love.

Great Commission

Then the eleven disciples went to Galilee, to the mountain where Jesus had told them to go. When they saw him, they worshiped him; but some doubted. Then Jesus came to them and said, "All authority in heaven and on earth has been given to me. Therefore go and make disciples of all nations, baptizing them in the name of the Father and of the Son and of the Holy Spirit, and teaching them to obey everything I have commanded you. And surely I am with you always, to the very end of the age." (Matt. 28:16-20)

Having established the only proper motivation, we can now address the most important instruction to the missional church—the Great Commission. It is a mistake to start here or to assume that this is a singularly outward focused commission. Missional theologians see this as a command to focus inwardly and to move outward into the world. As congregations see themselves as reflections of the *imago dei* (image of God), they embrace the priority of God to bring the nations under his Lordship. As Milfred Minatrea says, "In his image, the Body of Christ will seek to accomplish his purpose. Those who bear his image are sent to serve his mission, *mission dei*, in the same way that Christ was sent to accomplish the Father's purpose."[10]

The inward focus is as important as the outward focus. In his commission to his disciples, Jesus makes two inward references. First, he clearly implies that the authority given to him to accomplish the mission of God has also been given to them. His authority in them enables them to go and make disciples. Second, if there was any doubt that his authority is theirs, Jesus reminds them of his continual presence that would become a reality on the Day of Pentecost. Authority and presence on the Day of Pentecost—this was expressed as power for witnessing that comes with the infilling of the Holy Spirit.

The outward focus is condensed into the words "go and make disciples," though it encompasses more than that. There is the evangelistic element, to be sure. There is also incorporation into the body through baptism, and there is discipleship to teach believers to know and obey the words of Jesus. This outward focus is legitimate only as it reflects the inward focus of people who embrace their transformation into the image of God and live as God's missionaries in the world. The missionary activity of the Great Commission flows out of having a heart for God and having the heart of God. Minatrea expresses this as the four dimensions of mission: love God, live his mission, love people, lead them to follow. Each, in turn, creates the self-perpetuating cycle of missional churches.[11]

How can a local congregation and congregational leaders incorporate this inward/outward focus?

- Spend time developing a permanent plan for spiritual formation. It might start with a personal plan and move on to training leaders and then inviting the entire congregation to intentionally develop their spirituality and intimacy with God.
- Take advantage of key holidays to develop the congregation's understanding of God's mission. Christmas, Easter, and Pentecost are just three

---

10. Milfred Minatrea, *Shaped by God's Heart: The Passion and Practices of Missional Churches* (San Francisco: Jossey-Bass, 2004), 8.

11. Ibid., 17-20.

times when one can deal with the inward/outward focus of mission. Don't overlook the Christian calendar for other times when sermons, lessons, and events can highlight the mission and keep it constantly before the people.

• Create multiple ways for people to participate in the Great Commission based on the spiritual gifts of individuals within the congregation. For example, someone with the gift of hospitality might be willing to host a small group in their home, while someone with the gift of teaching might be willing to lead the group.

• Tell the stories. Some are going; some are responding. Personalize the Great Commission so that the congregation sees it in concrete and not just abstract ways.

The Great Commitment

On one occasion, while [Jesus] was eating with them, he gave them this command: "Do not leave Jerusalem, but wait for the gift my Father promised, which you have heard me speak about. For John baptized with water, but in a few days you will be baptized with the Holy Spirit. . . . But you will receive power when the Holy Spirit comes on you; and you will be my witnesses in Jerusalem, and in all Judea and Samaria, and to the ends of the earth." (Acts 1:4-8)

When the day of Pentecost came, they were all together in one place. Suddenly a sound like the blowing of a violent wind came from heaven and filled the whole house where they were sitting. They saw what seemed to be tongues of fire that separated and came to rest on each of them. All of them were filled with the Holy Spirit and began to speak in other tongues as the Spirit enabled them. (Acts 2:1-4)

The ultimate commitment to an inward focus that cleanses an individual from self-interest and empowers that person for outward service comes with the infilling of the Holy Spirit. The essence of carnal sin is the self-sovereignty that breaks the first commandment given to Moses for the people of God: "You shall have no other gods before me" (Exod. 20:3). This rebellious belief that mere humans can be gods is demonstrated as egotism, self-idolatry, self-centeredness, narcissism, and self-absorption. For many, this type of human behavior is unacceptable regardless of one's faith position.

Strategically, this is a critical factor in the people of God becoming a missional people. Since being missional includes the intentional act of putting oneself and one's resources at the disposal of God for the purpose of advancing his kingdom throughout his creation, church leaders will not likely be successful in transforming the church into a missional people until there is a movement away from self-sovereignty to a total surrender to the will of God and his purposes. How can this happen?

- Preach intentionally, consistently, and specifically about holiness and entire sanctification.
- Highlight examples of surrendered lives and celebrate these people within the body of Christ.
- Integrate the preaching and teaching on holiness into as many opportunities and age-groups as possible.

The Great Community

They devoted themselves to the apostles' teaching and to the fellowship, to the breaking of bread and to prayer. Everyone was filled with awe, and many wonders and miraculous signs were done by the apostles. All the believers were together and had everything in common. Selling their possessions and goods, they gave to anyone as he had need. Every day they continued to meet together in the temple courts. They broke bread in their homes and ate together with glad and sincere hearts, praising God and enjoying the favor of all the people. And the Lord added to their number daily those who were being saved. (Acts 2:42-47)

A growing theme within writings about the church is the theme of community. Whether you are reading about the emergent church or the church championing social justice or the missional church, community is the context for meaningful Christian practice and behavior. It is more than a sense of belonging. It is the understanding that in Christ, we contribute to the meaning of others—Christian and non-Christian alike. Minatrea says, "Missional communities seek to live authentic lives as disciples of Jesus Christ and, in doing so, validate the transformational promise that God does change lives. As missional communities reflect the grace of Jesus Christ in their lives, they also share the availability of grace with others, creatively and clearly."[12] This is done in small groups where believers eat and witness to friends and family. Also, the community gathers corporately to teach, preach, lead prayer, administer the sacraments, and organize systems of benevolence. Inagrace Dietterich writes the following about this kind of community:

This communal reality of holy living, mutual support, and sacrificial service the New Testament calls *koinonia*. Challenging the old competitive order

---

12. Ibid., 23.

of independence, self-interest, and private privilege (*idios*), Christian community indicates a new collaborative order of interdependence, shared responsibility, mutual instruction, and commonality (*koinos*). Within this new company of believers studying, sharing, eating, and praying together, the promised fulfillment of creation is visible, tangible, and experienced, even though not yet perfected.[13]

The missional community is characterized by unity and generosity. This is more than just what a missional community does; this is about who a missional community is. It is about the character of the community as much as it is about its activity. Unity goes beyond agreement and is more akin to marital oneness. Individual preferences and personal rights are willingly and intentionally surrendered so that we have a common identity in Christ and adopt his mission as our own. This internal commitment is externalized as generosity where individuals say, "What's mine is yours," and collectively says, "What's ours is theirs."

Strategically, missional leaders might consider the following:

- Spend time teaching the theological roots of being a missional community: identity, character, motivation, and vocation.
- Encourage development of small groups and create regular opportunities for communal worship, education, fellowship, and benevolence.
- Encourage radical obedience to the Holy Spirit and celebrate the stories of transformation resulting from the Spirit's intensity and focus as he works in and through people.

The Great Compassion

Then the righteous will answer him, "Lord, when did we see you hungry and feed you, or thirsty and give you something to drink? When did we see you a stranger and invite you in, or needing clothes and clothe you? When did we see you sick or in prison and go to visit you?" The King will reply, "I tell you the truth, whatever you did for one of the least of these brothers of mine, you did for me." (Matt. 25:37-40)

Earlier, generosity defined the missional community. Believers sold possessions and gave to others as they had need. Compassionate ministry does not come cheaply. There is a cost. This section addresses the recipient, the motivation, and the acts of compassion.

Who are we, as a missional church, supposed to care enough about that we will spend our time, money, and energy on them? Jesus says that we are to

---

13. Inagrace T. Dietterich, "Missional Community: Cultivating Communities of the Holy Spirit," in Guder, *Missional Church*, 143.

care about everyone whom he cares about—those whom he loves like family ("these brothers of mine") and those whose needs limit them from full participation in the kingdom of God ("the least of these"). This is more than just having a benevolence fund and distributing food or gas vouchers to everyone who asks. Compassion calls the missional church to engage the person who is in need, to enter this needy world, to learn more about a person than a name and address, to discover the roots and address the cause of the need, and to personally care about the individual. It would be easier to give out vouchers. However, being compassionate at this level means that we are ministering to Jesus—being Jesus to people he loves—and receiving the ministry of Jesus.

The acts of compassion are many but can be summarized as follows: Acts of compassion are those actions that meet a need for someone who cannot meet that need himself or herself. These needs are holistic in nature, since they can be physical (assisting someone with a disability), emotional (comforting someone experiencing grief), political (advocating for change in a national policy that discriminates against someone), legal (assisting someone to find a qualified attorney), educational (helping someone find vocational training), and more. When we help someone who cannot help himself or herself, we are loving that person and, in turn, loving Jesus.

To help a congregation participate in the Great Compassion, the following strategies may be considered:

- Help establish teams of volunteers to work at a local food bank, after-school tutoring program, or some other community program that targets people in need.
- Develop support-group leaders for grief, addiction, divorce, and parenting groups, especially among those who can empathize.
- Build relationships with local nursing homes and correctional facilities that provide opportunities for regular ministry.

The Great Cost

I have been crucified with Christ and I no longer live, but Christ lives in me. The life I live in the body, I live by faith in the Son of God, who loved me and gave himself for me. (Gal. 2:20)

Leading a missional church is not easy. It is more than a call to commitment. It is more than a call to loyalty or duty. Inviting people to become part of a missional church is inviting them to sacrifice themselves for the cause of Christ without any reciprocal promise that there is something in it for them. Self-will and self-ego are willingly "crucified" for the sake of the mission. However, there is a promise. The promise is that there is a resurrection after the crucifixion. In this scriptural analogy, Paul is saying that the resurrected self is one that embodies the spirit of Christ who came to redeem the world from sin and call the redeemed to join him in that mission. When the spirit of Christ fully lives in us, we will give ourselves to the mission in the same measure that he gave himself for us. In other words, we are called to be totally devoted to the mission with all that we are and all that we have.

Minatrea notes that this will change the membership requirements of a local church.[14] Membership will not be more restrictive—all may join. However, the requirements of Christlikeness, devotion to the mission, and one's willingness to give sacrificially of self, time, and resources may result in fewer, but stronger members.

The cost of being missional will not be an imposed cost. The church will not decide what the cost is. The Holy Spirit will. That will require the missional leader to teach followers how to be spiritually disciplined and sensitive so that they can discern the leading of the Spirit. Spiritual formation will be an important part of the missional church agenda.

This suggests that the strategic leader will consider the following:

- Preaching and teaching on becoming a missional people will include specific opportunities for people to respond, such as altar calls, invitations to be discipled, and chances to see models of sacrificial love in action.

- Membership classes are required in a missional church. Besides the usual material on church history, structure, and standards, the class will include ways to discover followers' spiritual gifts and strengths, discuss expectations upon church members to serve, insist on the importance of tithing and giving offerings as investment in the mission, and offer specific choices for missional involvement with the expectation that a potential member will choose one.

- Spiritual formation will become part of the DNA of a missional church. It won't be an annual event or a periodic topic of discussion. Specific and consistent efforts will be made to help missional members develop a spiritual life that helps them discern the leading of the Holy Spirit. The Spirit who knows us and knows what we have to offer will not hesitate to call us to obedience and participation in the mission of Christ.

---

14. Minatrea, *Shaped by God's Heart*, 29ff.

STRATEGIC PLANNING

There is nothing wrong with strategic planning or any other business practice or model when applied to a missional objective as long as we understand that the mission initiates the strategy and not the other way around.

Two basic planning techniques can be easily adapted to the missional church. SMAART goals can be established. SMAART (or SMART) goals are goals that are specific, measurable, achievable, action-oriented (omitted in some uses), results-oriented, and timely (or time-based). This explanation will utilize the longer acronym. SMAART goals (with two A's) have been attributed to Peter Drucker in 1954 and made popular by many others.[15]

Specific goals are just that—specific. The goal answers the questions of who, what, when, where, and how. Specific goals have been shown to have a much greater probability of being accomplished than general goals.

Measurable goals are easily evaluated on some identifiable criteria. For instance, a food bank might count the number of clients served each month. Keeping track of this number will help to evaluate the effectiveness of the ministry. The food bank might also track the number and type of cereals that its clients request so that it has enough of the popular kinds and does not take up inventory space with unwanted kinds.

Achievable goals are attainable but not trivial. Set the goal high enough to be challenging but not so high that people are discouraged from trying. Do not be afraid to adjust goals upward or downward along the way. Goals can be dynamic.

Action-oriented helps frame the goal in the active voice. It is one thing to say, "People shall be received into our fellowship with love and acceptance," and another to say, "We will receive people into our fellowship with love and acceptance." It is the same thing but said in the active voice. It becomes a determination and commitment when the goal is action-oriented.

Realistic goals are goals that fit the situation, circumstances, resources, personnel, skills, and strengths of the organization. A pastor of a church with 30 people attending told his denominational supervisor that the church would run 1,000 on its hundredth anniversary, just five years away. In a community that numbered less than 800, this was probably not a realistic goal. If this pastor had suggested that the church would have 100 in regular attendance by its hundredth anniversary, the goal would have been more realistic and achievable.

---

15. Peter Drucker, *The Practice of Management* (New York: Harper and Row, 1954). However, there is no direct reference to this acronym in his book. Still, the basis for this type of goal setting is derived from Drucker.

Timely or time-based goals stay in perspective and have a timeframe for being accomplished. The pastor mentioned above had a time-based goal and knew that the goal had not been achieved when the church celebrated its anniversary. While it would have been more fun to have met the goal, the deadline served to end the attention on a goal that was too discouraging. Timely goals help the organization by structuring the steps for achieving the goal around the calendar and creating a celebration date for the goal's (hopeful) achievement.

There is another planning strategy that can help once goals are established. A SWOT analysis assists leaders and their followers to assess what might help or hinder the organization in accomplishing its goals. SWOT stands for Strengths, Weaknesses, Opportunities, and Threats. It is best done in a group environment among a leadership or ministry team. It is often done as an early step in the planning process so that valuable time and resources are not wasted on less effective ideas. A missional goal can benefit from this analysis, even if that goal seems to be the leading of the Holy Spirit. SWOT analysis does not set the goal. It helps the team understand what it will take to accomplish the goal and develop implementation and intervention strategies to that end. SWOT simply asks, "What resources do we have or can we get to accomplish the goal?" "What are we lacking that could hinder the accomplishment of the goal?" "What are the potential benefits to all our constituency if this goal is accomplished?" and "What or who might be a negative factor in the accomplishing of this goal?" This process can be a spiritual process as the participants learn to discern the leading of the Holy Spirit who is part of the omniscient Godhead. It can be a faith-building exercise as participants recognize the positive and negative factors within a Spirit-led goal.

In summary, while current planning models can be effective, many do not begin with a scriptural understanding of mission. It is not just a matter of doing the right thing. It is doing the right thing for the right reasons.

5
DEVELOPING A BUDGET
USING THE BUDGET AS A RESOURCE TOOL

D. Martin Butler
DMin, PhD, Dean for Administration,
Nazarene Theological Seminary

In the minds of some ministry leaders a budget is something that constrains ministry. That is, they see a budget as a straightjacket that keeps missional entrepreneurs from doing real ministry. These kinds of leaders have heard far too many board members say, "We can't do that; it's not in the budget."

Conversely, some ministry leaders see a budget as an entitlement. They reason that if it is in the budget, they are entitled to that much money and they will do everything within their power to spend all of "their money" for fear of having their allocation reduced next year.

Obviously, both of these views of a budget are incorrect. A well-drafted budget does not constrain real ministry. Rather it directs resources into ministry. And a well-drafted budget is not an entitlement to be spent. Rather it is a guide to help the church prioritize and monitor its revenue and expenses.

Technically, when you think about developing a budget, you should look beyond dollars to human and physical resources, as well. Members, friends, and constituents enable the ministries of the church with human resources (staff and volunteers), physical resources (church facilities), and fiscal resources (revenue). Having acknowledged that, however, this chapter will focus exclusively on financial budgeting.

One more caveat: this chapter emphasizes the development of the day-by-day operating budget of the church, which includes salaries, programs, mortgage payments, denominational commitments, and so on. Budgeting for a building program lies outside the scope of this chapter and is a science unto itself. Not all of you will be involved in constructing a building or remodeling a facility during your career. But if that opportunity confronts you, understand that a capital budget is different than an operating budget. Work closely with denominational leaders, architects, contractors, and lenders when developing a construction budget.

THE ADVANTAGES OF A
WELL-PLANNED OPERATING BUDGET

It forces the church to plan ahead. Planning, in general, is something most of us acknowledge is important, but few of us practice as much as we should. One decided advantage of taking the church through a budget planning exercise is that it forces the church to plan ahead and think ahead.

It encourages the church to evaluate programs. Budget planning causes the church to ask tough questions about programs and personnel. During the budget process you need to assess the extent to which the church is realizing its ministry objectives. For instance, a church may be in the habit of spending several thousand dollars each year on an outreach event that was very effective twenty years ago, but which has had a declining attendance in recent years. This calls for asking the tough question, "Are we seeing missional results from this program, or do we need to discover other places to invest our resources?"

It helps to establish priorities. It would be a mistake to say that the area of ministry in which we invest the most funds automatically identifies our highest priority. That is much too simplistic of a response to a complicated matter. However, it is true that where we spend our money tells us something about our priorities. A budget planning process helps the church to ask if it is spending money in the right places. So although the amount of money we spend on a ministry doesn't tell the church everything about its priority, it is one indicator.

It gives the church clear direction. A well-drafted budget has clearly stated revenue and expense goals that help the church focus its energies. Many churches (particularly small- to medium-sized churches) struggle with trying to do too many things. As the church determines its direction and gets the funding of those matters down on paper, it provides a roadmap into the future.

It authorizes spending in advance and saves time. If the church adopts a budget and if the revenue is coming in commensurate with that budget, ministry leaders already have the authorization they need to spend. You do not have to spend thirty minutes in every board meeting voting on whether or not to buy paper plates for the kitchen. There seems to be an inverse relationship between the size of a church and the length of board meetings. Large churches often have a board meeting that lasts sixty to ninety minutes each month. Some small churches have board meetings that start at 6 P.M. and members struggle to get home in time to watch the late-night news. Part of the reason for this is that if there is not a spending plan (a budget), then time is taken to vote on nearly every expense.

It allows more people to be involved. Later in this chapter I will suggest a budget planning process that involves a budget committee and all ministry leaders. When you get several people engaged in the writing of a budget, you develop ownership of the ministries of the church. Many laypersons have no idea how much money it takes for utilities, office supplies, Sunday School literature, and so on. As you involve people in helping to determine dollars to be spent on these matters, you help them see that the church is "us" and not "them."

It leads toward accurate and clear reporting. The most important question a treasurer should answer in a board meeting or to a congregation is not, "How much money did we raise and spend last month?" Instead, he or she needs to answer the question, "How much money did we *plan* to raise and spend last month?" One could falsely be led to believe everything was fine if the only thing the treasurer said was, "We raised $7,236 last month and spent $7,225. We have $11 in the bank." Without more information, one does not know if this is good news or bad news. What if the church needed to raise $10,000 last month in order to meet annual commitments? A properly designed budget and a proper, periodic reporting system on that budget gives ministry leaders the information they need to make critical decisions about the direction of the church.

It promotes better stewardship. As you involve the congregation in understanding more about the finances of the church and as you report to them more accurately what you need to raise in order to keep pace with expenses, people will be more likely to give. There should be no secrets in the church about finances. What the pastor is paid, how much was spent on travel, what is spent on missionary endeavors, and so on, should be public record, and as that information is made available through a budget, the congregation is more likely to be generous.

It makes life easier when filing for a loan or completing reports. In my first church we were faced immediately with the need to go to the bank to borrow money to meet an obligation that had been overlooked. The money was clearly due and payable, and the church had no resources. The district superintendent (the denomination's leader for the region) advised me to go to the bank to borrow the funds. When I talked to the banker, he told me that we would need to provide documentation about how much the church raised and spent during the last three years and what our plans were for the next few years. Needless to say, I had to scramble because the church had never operated with a budget. I had to dig through past checkbooks and ask lots of questions of members to develop a sense of how the money had been spent in the past in order to put together some kind of a plan for how the money would be spent in the future. It took me several weeks to compile documentation that would have been easily available had the church been practicing a budgeting and reporting system.

It cuts down on impulse buying. We have all heard that we should never shop for groceries when hungry because we will buy things on impulse. Impulse buying can leave a family with more month left than money, and it can certainly ruin a church's resources. I held a revival in the church of a former student a few years ago, and he told me this true story: His church had no spending plan and no money. A group of men were working on the roof of the parsonage trying to fix a leak when someone began complaining about the church lawnmower. Everyone chimed in with agreement that it was really a hassle to come over to the church as a volunteer to mow the grass and to find that the mower did not work most of the time. Suddenly one of the men said, "Hey, I notice we have a quorum of the board right here. I move we buy a new lawnmower." And before this young, green pastor could say a word, on the roof of the parsonage they voted to buy a lawnmower. Although it may be true that a lawnmower was needed, without a spending plan one does not know what other commitments were waiting for those same dollars. A well-drafted budget provides a plan for meeting ministry needs and cuts down on impulse spending.

What Kind of Budgeting Should a Church Pursue?

Several methods of budgeting exist. You will find persons on your board who follow certain procedures where they work. They may want to impose those processes upon your church. That may be appropriate, but it may also be damaging. Some budget processes (particularly for governmental agencies and large corporations) are very complex. It takes knowledge of the financial field and sophisticated insights to read and understand such reports. The main thing to consider when selecting a method for the church is whether it is simple enough for persons unfamiliar with financial jargon to understand.

For instance, some organizations utilize *program budgeting*. In this method all costs are associated with a particular program, function, or "cost center." One divides all salaries, utilities, building payments, office supplies, and so on, among ministry functions such as worship, evangelism, fellowship, and discipleship. Although this sounds appealing at the outset because it will let you know how much it costs to operate a certain segment of the church's ministry, it is also very cumbersome. To divide the monthly utilities, the building payment, a portion of the pastor's salary, and so on, among the various programs or outcomes is not an easy chore. Besides, who is to say what percent of the pastor's time should be allocated to discipleship, fellowship, community service, or worship?

Other organizations with which your board may be familiar follow the practice of *zero-based* budgeting. In this budgeting process, all programs, personnel, and so on, must be rejustified each budget cycle. That is, you must go back to ground zero each year and prove the necessity of each program or employee. Such a process is very time-consuming. Should we evaluate the past to see if what we have been doing is effective? Absolutely! Should we ask the VBS director, the Sunday School superintendent, or the missionary president to go back to "ground zero" every year and justify why the church needs their program? Probably not. My experience has been that true zero-based budgeting is usually not necessary in most church settings.

Other organizations follow the practice of *line item budgeting*. This method is sometimes critiqued as incrementalism (simply taking last year's figures and adding a percentage increase). Under this practice the well-funded ministries get more and more money while the more sparsely funded ministries seem to never catch up. A 5 percent increase for a department that already has a $20,000 budget provides a lot more revenue for that ministry than a 5 percent increase for a department that has a $2,000 budget. The reason line item budgeting is conducted so frequently is because it is much less time-consuming than zero-based or program budgeting.

I advocate a combination of line item and zero-based budgeting. I call it *strategic budgeting*. In this method attention is given to whether or not a program should be continued (zero-based), but builds upon the past costs (line item). For most churches, the past is a good indicator of the future. The fact that you spent $1,000 on casualty insurance last year is a good indicator of what you might spend this year. There is no sense in justifying whether or not to have casualty insurance. This method of taking last year as a good starting point and adding or subtracting costs as needed while prioritizing programs for the future is a very effective and "doable" process for even the smallest church.

BUDGET CATEGORIES (CHART OF ACCOUNTS)

A budget document should not only help you see what the church has spent on certain items but also be designed to provide information needed for reports to the local church board and to the denomination. In the denomination in which I serve, the pastor completes a document titled "The Annual Report of the Pastor to the District Assembly." It asks for lots of statistics about attendance, church programs, and so on. One of the major sections of the report is the finance page where expenses are to be reported according to certain categories. In my opinion it is extra work for the treasurer and pastor to design a budget and financial reporting system for the local church that fails to answer the questions that will inevitably be asked. That is, a budget should be designed with the "end in mind." It needs to be designed to provide reports that answer questions that are being asked on both the local and denominational level.

Some denominations want to know how much money is raised through tithe and also how much is raised through the Sunday School, missions program, and so on. If your denomination is looking for this kind of information, then I suggest your revenue budget be broken down into these same categories. Some denominations want to know how much money is spent on local programming versus regional, educational, or foreign mission expenses. If that is the case for you, I suggest you design your budget categories around these same major categories.

Regardless of denominational expectations, however, I think it is essential that a local church understand how much it is spending on its local programming versus the amount of money it is providing for ministries beyond the local church, such as denominationally supported colleges and missionary programs. I served on a church board once where all of the budget categories were established around the major committees of the church. That looks like and sounds like a good idea. But monies being sent outside the local church to fund denominational programs were mixed in with local costs. The amount of money spent on local outreach efforts were commingled with the amount of money being sent to the denomination for world evangelism because both amounts were reported as expenses of the outreach committee. Similarly, the discipleship committee mingled expenses for the local Sunday School with amounts sent to denominational educational institutions. This method fails to help a church understand what it actually costs to operate the local church. Keep track of local operating expenses separately from expenses for other ministries outside the local setting.

Budgets and budget reports should be easy to understand. When I became treasurer of a large church, I followed a treasurer who was a CPA. Thank God for professional accountants. I am not bashing them here. But he kept the records in a sophisticated accounting system that he used in his office for other business clients. He gave the board a seventeen-page report each month. In the first board meeting after my election, I gave them a three-page report patterned after the denominational reporting system. A board member (who, by the way, was highly educated and had been in the denomination most of his life) commented, "For the last year I have had no idea where we stood financially. I was afraid to admit that the seventeen-page report from the former treasurer meant nothing to me. I did not know what it said or how to interpret the facts. This report tonight is clear and understandable. Thank you." Financial reporting isn't brain surgery. It can be simple and precise. And the report should be built around the budget.

INDIVIDUAL BUDGET LINES

Above I suggested a budget be broken down into at least two main categories—local church expenses and expenses for programs outside the local church. Your budget may have these two main categories or ten main categories. Regardless of the number of main headings, however, you need to plan carefully for the various budget lines within each category. Stop and think for a moment about all of the items that need to be funded. The list below is simply representative of some local church expenses:

Salaries
Benefits
Professional Business Expenses
Mortgage Payments
Parsonage Expenses
Utilities
Repairs
Equipment Upgrades
Small Groups
Worship
Advertising
Office Supplies
Photocopies
Social Activities
Flowers and Gifts
Maintenance Supplies
Evangelism
Insurance
Youth
Children
Sunday School
Missions

The number of budget lines is almost endless and will vary from church to church. Some churches want to know how much was spent on each separate utility (gas, water, electric, etc.). Others simply want to know how much was spent on utilities, in general. If you prefer the former, you will need a budget line for each one. If you prefer the latter, you will need only one utility budget line. However, I think it is critical to keep a budget report for the board brief and to the point. So although you may have fifty or more subcategories, when reporting to the board, summarize them into a shorter list of major categories and then make detailed information available to those who are interested in more specifics.

I am frequently asked what percentage a church should spend on salaries, mortgage payments, and so on. The answer is, "It depends." Let me explain. Besides teaching church finance, I also teach personal finance. In family budgeting, persons often ask what percentage of their income they should spend on groceries, house payment, car payment, and so on. I answer, "It depends." If you have five children, you will spend a greater percentage of your money on food than I will at my house where we have an empty nest. If your home is new, large, and located in certain portions of the country, you will pay out a larger percentage of your income for housing than the person who lives in an older, smaller, and less competitive housing market.

These same principles hold true for the church. There simply is no magical formula for how much you ought to spend on certain things. Each church must establish its own set of values and priorities. The obvious fact is this: the more you spend on one item, the less you will have to spend on others. There is no such thing as an independent financial decision. They are all interdependent.

There are some benchmarks, however. In most churches at least 10 percent of revenue is given to "others" outside of the local church. That is, in support of denominational programs and other commitments beyond the local church, at least 10 percent of the operating budget is spent. In some denominations that amount can be as much as 20 percent.

It is quite common for salaries and benefits to consume 35 percent to 50 percent of the operating budget, depending upon the size of church. In small churches I have seen that figure go above 50 percent (if you count in the cost of maintaining the parsonage for the pastor), while in larger churches it may be closer to 35 percent. At the medium-sized church where I serve on the board, our goal is to keep personnel costs for all employees (lay and clergy) to 40 percent of the budget. But there is no magic number above or below which a church must stay in this regard.

This raises the question of how much a minister should be paid. His or her pay should be based upon education, years of experience, and pay scales in the area for ministers and other professionals. It should not be based upon whether or not he or she is married and has a family. The reality is that many small churches cannot provide enough compensation for a full-time minister. In some denominations roughly half of their clergy workforce is bivocational. Even in churches where a full-time salary is intended, salaries are often less than ideal. However, it is time for ministers to stop making offhanded comments about how little they are paid. If a church is spending upwards of 50 percent of the budget on the minister's compensation, there is little more we can expect of these faithful laypersons who are, in some cases, giving sacrificially to keep the church doors open.

If salaries make up the largest segment of the operating budget, coming in a close second would be costs of maintaining the facilities. It is not unusual for a church to spend between 25 percent and 35 percent of its budget on mortgage payments (or rent), utilities, multiperil insurance, and repairs/improvements to the church building.

So considering the percentages listed above, you can see if you spend 20 percent on ministries outside the local setting, 50 percent on salaries and benefits, and 30 percent on maintaining the facilities, you have nothing left for office supplies and flowers for the bereaved, let alone for programs for the youth, children, and adults. Churches need to control the costs of personnel and facilities so money is available to operate the VBS, buy Sunday School literature, pay for music for the worship team, and so on.

THE BUDGET PLANNING PROCESS

The process of drafting a budget takes approximately four months. I recommend that you begin immediately after the eighth month of the current year. If, for instance, your year starts in July, you would begin the budget process in March. Don't make the mistake of waiting until the new year begins and new officers take office before you start your budget planning. Many churches wait because they want the new Sunday School superintendent to establish her own budget or the new building and property chair to assess the physical plant needs. The problem with this approach is that you could be sixty days into the new year without a budget plan in place and that puts you behind from the very start. Instead, allow current ministry leaders to establish the budget for the new year with the understanding that the budget will be reviewed part way through the year. If major changes are needed by the new leader, those matters can be considered when the budget is reviewed.

For the purposes of this chapter, I am assuming a July 1 to June 30 year and suggest the following steps:

1. Review values and mission. The board should spend time in the March meeting reviewing mission and priorities for the new year. These should be clearly communicated to all department heads.

2. Decide in the March meeting what type of budgeting you will do (program, zero-based, strategic, etc.).

3. Appoint a budget committee in the March board meeting to direct the process and to review the requests submitted by ministry leaders. This committee should be of manageable size. Keep the group small enough to be able to

act quickly and collectively. In small churches I recommend that the key leaders of the church (Sunday School superintendent, missions leader, youth leader, treasurer, and pastor) serve as the budget committee. In larger churches it makes the most sense that the same committee you have been using all year as the finance committee serve as the core of the budget development group. This group can be supplemented with a few additional members during the budget development process.

4. During March conduct a data search of what has been spent so far in the current year. This task is usually completed by the treasurer. I recommend that the treasurer develop a budget worksheet for each ministry department. In the "item" column the treasurer lists the budget lines for each ministry department and then fills in the amounts for the first two columns of numbers, leaving the ministry head to put numbers in columns three and four. The last column is completed by the budget committee later if reductions are needed to bring the budget into line with revenue projections.

Sample Building and Grounds Budget Worksheet

Item	This Year Budget	This Year to Date	This Year Projected	New Year Request	Revised Budget
Repairs	$2,000.00	$900.00			
Utilities	$7,500.00	$5,235.00			
Mortgage	$30,000.00	$20,100.00			
Supplies	$3,000.00	$1,115.00			

5. When the treasurer has completed the first two columns of numbers, he or she should distribute the worksheets to ministry or department heads. The ministry head makes projections about the total that will be spent this year and then enters the budget request for the new year. If a new venture is being added that has not previously been funded, a new line can simply be added to the worksheet. The final column is reserved for the budget committee to use in making any revisions to the budget based upon revenue projections. The document is delivered by the department head back to the budget committee no later than May 1.

6. The budget committee reviews requests according to income projections (see Determining Revenue below). If changes are needed, consult with ministry heads about reductions and enter the revised figures in the last column. This give and take between the budget committee and ministry leader is vital. No one wants to have his or her budget cut without dialogue. A budget commit-

tee should not presume to cut items out of a budget or to reduce budget requests on its own. That would place far too much power in the hands of a few who may not know all of the reasons behind a budget request. Instead, reductions should be solicited from the ministry leader.

7. Present the balanced budget to the board in the June meeting for its approval. As indicated above, budget planning documents and monthly budget reporting documents should be succinct. Every budget presentation should have three things:

a. A line-by-line list of expenditures and how those compare to the previous year. If possible, this should be one page in length and should have the same columns as the budget worksheet.

b. Separate pages supporting the summary numbers listed on the one-page budget. That is, if the one-page document lists $3,000 for supplies, the supporting pages could give the breakdown of how much of that is for stationery, toner cartridges, and so on. These pages are informational only and should not be an occasion for people to begin nit-picking over trivial details.

c. A revenue forecast (see below).

8. Depending upon church polity, you may want to distribute the budget to the congregation for its approval. In the denomination in which I serve, congregational approval is not necessary, but I still like to announce that budget documents are available on a table in the foyer for anyone who would like to have a copy. Once again, openness and candor is essential to stewardship development.

DETERMINING REVENUE

It is no mistake that I have placed the decision about how much revenue a church can generate after the process of determining ministry priorities and soliciting budgets. Far too often we get this backward. We ask the treasurer how much he or she thinks we can raise next year and then we allow that figure to limit our dreams and the vision God may be giving us. It is critical to go through the exercise of looking at all programs of the church and setting dollar values on those programs before comparing them to revenue. Sure, it may mean that some items will need to be reduced or eliminated, but everyone in the budget development process needs to see what we would like to do compared to what we ultimately determine to be reasonable based upon revenue projections.

Determining revenue for the new church year is not a difficult matter. Although you could estimate the income of the congregation and multiply that amount by 10 percent, you probably would not have a clear picture of projected revenue. Unfortunately, many of our parishioners do not tithe. Instead, I recommend that you analyze giving trends and forecast growth/decline for the new year.

Ask the person who tracks giving for income tax reporting purposes to prepare a report listing how many persons give to the church, but do not list names on the report. Break the report down by giving category—those giving less than $500 last year, those giving between $500 and $1,000, those giving between $1,000 and $2,500, those giving between $2,500 and $5,000, those giving between $5,000 and $10,000, and those giving more than $10,000. Note on the report any giving units at each level who left the church since the calendar year ended and how many new giving units have come. If it is known that a key family is transferring out of the city in the near future because of a job change, ask that this donor be flagged as well. Armed with this information you can estimate within a few hundred dollars what the current pool of givers might give in the new year. When you know this information, you can then add new sources of revenue that you anticipate receiving throughout the new year. This process results in a relatively accurate revenue projection.

Clearly, in the middle of all of this financial analysis, the pastor and budget committee must be in earnest prayer seeking God's direction on the matter. God sometimes desires to stretch our faith.

Monitoring the Budget

A budget does no good unless someone is willing to blow the whistle and stop expenditures that are running out of control. It is the responsibility of the finance committee, treasurer, ministry leaders, and ultimately the board to be sure the budget is followed.

However, this is not to say that the board should be involved in month-by-month decisions about what bills to pay and what not to pay. I recommend that you pass a series of resolutions at the beginning of each church year that define the ground rules for what the treasurer can pay without further authorization. Here are some suggested resolutions:

1. Approval of the operating budget by the board shall constitute permission to spend funds within that spending plan. The treasurer needs no further authorization to disburse funds requested within budget lines by appropriate ministry leaders.

2. No entity may request more than a sixty-day advance on their budget without the approval of the finance committee.

3. The building and grounds committee may spend up to $1,000 on projects without the approval of the finance committee or the board if the

project comes from their budget. The finance committee and the board must approve expenditures of larger magnitude.

One aspect of monitoring the budget is tracking cash flow. It is not enough to need to raise $100,000 a year, but you must raise a certain amount each month in order to pay salaries, utilities, and so on. I recommend that the treasurer develop a spreadsheet that shows the income and expenses by month for the past several years. In this way, you will know when to panic and when not to panic! If you are running behind on your revenue projections, but know that historically you always have a very large offering in December, you can relax a bit. If, however, your revenue the last three months is running behind the same months in recent years, you have reason to put on the spending brakes.

Finally, the best way to monitor the budget is to insist on a written report from the treasurer each month. Oral reports cannot give enough detail to allow the decision makers to know if the income and expenses are progressing according to projections.

REVISING THE BUDGET

A budget is not the law of the Medes and the Persians. It is a spending plan that can be adjusted if revenue and expenditures warrant it. However, it is very confusing if you change the budget every month. Instead of revising the budget every time someone thinks of a new project to fund, build a contingency fund into the original budget that can be used for such purposes. Revise the budget, if necessary, but I recommend it be done only once at the six-month interval. The exception to this general principal would be if a church is experiencing rapid growth or decline. In such cases immediate attention should be given to budget adjustments.

FOR FURTHER READING

Berkley, James D. *The Dynamics of Church Finance.* Grand Rapids: Baker Books, 2000.
Henry, Jack A. *Basic Budgeting for Churches.* Nashville: Broadman, 1995.
Hotchkiss, Dan. *Ministry and Money.* Herndon, VA: Alban Institute, 2002.
Malphurs, Aubrey, and Steve Stroope. *Money Matters in the Church.* Grand Rapids: Baker Books, 2007.

6

ORGANIZATIONAL BEHAVIOR
GRASPING THE BEHAVIOR AND PERSONALITY OF A CHURCH

Bob Whitesel

**DMin, PhD, Professor of Missional Leadership,
Wesley Seminary at Indiana Wesleyan University**

"Even if you are on the right track, you'll get run over if you just sit there."
—*Will Rogers, American humorist*[1]

═══════════════════ ◆ ═══════════════════

GROWTH INHIBITORS

"Our consultant told me I was part of the problem," Pastor Bill declared. "And he is right." Bill pastored First Baptist, a church that averaged over 200 in weekly Sunday attendance. Although the church had been growing for three of the past five years, it had plateaued during the two most recent years. Still, the community surrounding the church continued to add new residents. Sensing underlying growth inhibitors, church leaders hired me to help them conduct a SWOT analysis and develop a strategic plan. My analysis concluded that four key factors were thwarting the church's growth.

First, the church had an inadequate network of small groups. Small groups—whether they are Sunday School classes, task groups, committees, or home Bible study groups—are the interpersonal foundation of a growing church. First Baptist had only seven such groups in a congregation of almost 350 members.

Second, the congregation did not have a clear idea of what kind of church it wanted to be. Some wanted the church to become more like the charismatic/Pentecostal church down the road. Others wanted to maintain their Baptist distinctiveness, including an altar call after every service. Still others wanted to focus on their thriving music program, which attracted people from across the region. These concurrent and numerous directions in which the church was headed were laudable, but too diverse for most attendees to ascertain where

---

1. Quoted by Fred R. David in *Strategic Planning: Concepts and Cases,* 9th ed. (Upper Saddle River, NJ: Prenctice-Hall, 2002), 157.

exactly the church fit. Thus many people kept from fully committing to First Baptist, fearful that the church might become something they would not enjoy.

A third factor inhibiting First Baptist's growth was the changing median age of the community. Twenty years earlier, the community had primarily consisted of retired blue-collar workers, whose neatly trimmed houses dotted shady, peaceful streets. However, in the last seven years the community had started to experience an influx of Generation Xers looking for reasonably priced housing and safe streets for their families. The church also was experiencing the entry of baby boomers and their families. Pastor Bill had welcomed these families, even as the new attendees began to outnumber the mostly retirement-age members of the congregation. Feeling that they were losing control, the aging members began to subtly resist change. Bill felt caught in the middle and even had considered leaving.

A fourth key inhibitor was the new size of the congregation. When the number of attendees passed the 200 mark, the church's internal structure began to change. However, the leadership structure did not change with it. Prior to the beginning of growth five years earlier, the church had fewer than 100 in attendance. But now, after three years of growth, followed by two more years of moderate and then low growth, the church had entered a new size structure. Bill and the church leaders continued to administer the church as if it were still a church of 100 attendees, relying on a small staff who tried to do most of the labor-intensive tasks themselves. Staff burnout loomed.

From the pulpit, Bill shared with the congregation the growth inhibitors I had identified, as well as the action steps the strategy groups had decided to undertake. There was one more area to address—and this was the hardest for Bill, for it dealt with a needed change in his leadership style. "Our consultant told me I was part of the problem," Bill declared. Silence spread across the auditorium. "And he is right," Bill continued. "I've been leading this church like it is a church of a hundred, because that's the only size of church I've ever led . . . till now. However, I'm ready to move forward. But it's going to require some changes in First Baptist—and in Bill."

It didn't take long for First Baptist to regain its strong growth curve. Another church two blocks down the street and of similar polity did not fare so well. Comprised of aging members, that church closed two years later. But First Baptist, due to growth plans and Bill's humble leadership, turned a corner and became a vibrant, growing congregation of multiple generations. Soon even a name change reflected its vibrant and affable personality, as First Baptist Church became known by the more informal appellation: First Church.

The Tools of Organizational Behavior

Defining Organizational Behavior

The transition from an aging and/or declining church to a healthy, well-managed congregation did not come easily. But it came deliberately, as the leaders incorporated many of the tools listed in this chapter. Before we list these tools, let's define organizational behavior.

In their seminal text on organizational behavior, Professors Debra Nelson and James Quick describe organizational behavior as "the study of individual behavior and growth dynamics in organizational settings. It focuses on timeless topics like motivation, leadership, teamwork, . . . exceptional performance, re-structuring organizations, . . . [and] what happens when organizations . . . face the pressure to become current, competitive, and agile."[2]

While it is not possible in this chapter to examine in depth every aspect of organizational behavior, I will focus on four primary principles:

1. *Leadership.* First, we will look at the important role of leadership and the difference between simply good leaders and great ones. We will see that great leaders customarily are not autocrats but facilitators and mentors, training others to succeed.

2. *Motivation.* Next, we will look at how to motivate volunteers and staff to achieve outstanding performance. By grasping the future direction and personality of a church, those involved will work together for progress.

3. *Teamwork.* We will see how small groups help build cohesiveness and unity as a congregation grows beyond the "fellowship" atmosphere of a small church. And we will see how these small groups can effectively meet the social as well as the ministry needs of a growing congregation.

4. *Adapting Organizational Structure and Management Styles.* As a congregation grows, its organizational structure and management styles must also evolve, just as it does in secular businesses. If they do not evolve, the church will cease to progress and may even die due to an outdated organizational leadership.

Leadership

Effective leadership is one of the most crucial factors in creating and sustaining organizational growth and health. Resources on this important topic are

---

2. Debra L. Nelson and James Campbell Quick, *Organizational Behavior: Foundations, Realities, and Challenges,* 3rd ed. (Cincinnati: South-Western College Publishing, 2000), xxi.

abundant, readily available, and embrace a surprising number of good ideas. However, for our purposes in this book—which examines what business school instructors wish church leaders knew about management—I will tackle some of the more overlooked yet critical aspects of effective church leadership.

Effective Leaders Learn Fast and Keep on Learning

"Seminary was a great experience. But most of what I learned about managing a church came from the first three churches I almost killed." Thus Bill summed up what he had learned about strategic church management. "Seminary is great for theology, history, and the like," Bill continued. "But there ought to be courses that teach pastors how to manage the church. Because without them, like me, through trial and error, you might kill a congregation first."

Bill has sounded a clarion call that echoes continually among church leaders I have encountered. While the classic disciplines of theology, history, and spiritual formation are adequately addressed in seminary, very few schools offer courses that deal with the management and organizational behavior of congregations. Yet it is this latter topic, and not the former, that leads most often to pastoral dissatisfaction and turnover.

James Belasco, professor of management at San Diego State University, and Ralph Stayer, CEO of Johnsonville Sausage, put it this way: "Success is a valuable teacher, provided it does not lull us into complacency. Whatever puts us where we are will not take us where we need to go. Circumstances change; leaders must change also, or be left behind. The skills learned to be a good supervisor will not help anyone be a good president. Continued learning is crucial to continued success."[3]

Consequently, great church leaders will be quick, tenacious, continual learners. To achieve this, church leaders must avail themselves of opportunities to attend continuing education classes, as well as business courses at local colleges, universities, and/or online. The proliferation of MBA programs attests to the business sector's belief that graduate study is crucial for effective twenty-first-century leadership. In addition, congregations must allow and encourage their leaders to participate in continuing education.

Effective Leaders Are Driven by a Clear Purpose

Rick Warren pastors one of the few churches in America that has not plateaued but continues to grow. He stresses the importance of the pastor being

---

3. James A. Belasco and Ralph C. Stayer, "Why Empowerment Doesn't Empower: The Bankruptcy of Current Paradigms," *Business Horizons* 37, no. 2 (March-April 1994): 29-41.

driven by a spiritual and noble purpose.[4] Warren believes (as well as the authors of this book) that Jesus' Great Commission in Matthew 28:19-20 is the heart of that purpose—the force that should drive pastors and churches. Jesus uses four verbs in this passage (in italic in the following quote): "Therefore *go* and *make disciples* of all nations, *baptizing* them in the name of the Father and of the Son and of the Holy Spirit, and *teaching* them to obey everything I have commanded you. And surely I am with you always, to the very end of the age."

The sentence construction of the original Greek makes it clear that three of these verbs are modifying another, more central verb, and that this central verb is what Jesus identifies as the focus or goal of this Great Commission. The Greek sentence construction identifies the imperative verb "make disciples" as the goal of this commission. The participles "going," "baptizing," and "teaching" are part of that disciple-making process. Peter Wagner points out that the *going, baptizing,* and *teaching* are "never ends in themselves. They all should be used as a part of the process of making disciples."[5]

However, the goal of *making disciples* has to start first with the pastor. It is nearly impossible to generate a purpose from the ground up. Thus selecting an appropriate pastor is critical to the success of discipleship. A church that calls a pastor, or a denomination that appoints a shepherd, must carefully screen each candidate to ascertain the purpose that drives the candidate and to ensure that this purpose coincides with God's purpose. Failure to address this stage circumspectly will lead to frequent detours from God's intended course.

Effective Leaders Are Driven by Ethics

The leader of an organization sets the moral and ethical tone for that organization. The Bible warns, "Whoever can be trusted with very little can also be trusted with much, and whoever is dishonest with very little will also be dishonest with much" (Luke 16:10). The Bible also sets challenging expectations for various leaders in both 1 Timothy 3 and Titus 1, calling them, among other things, to "be above reproach" (1 Tim. 3:2), "not [be] a lover of money" (v. 3), "have a good reputation with outsiders" (v. 7), "not [pursue] dishonest gain" (v. 8 and Titus 1:7), and "[love] what is good" (Titus 1:8).

An ethical culture is imperative for the well-run and Christlike organization. An example of ethical solidarity with suffering employees is evidenced in Carl Reichardt's leadership of Wells Fargo Bank during the bank deregulation

---

4. Rick Warren, *The Purpose-Driven Church* (Grand Rapids: Zondervan, 1995), and *The Purpose-Driven Life* (Grand Rapids: Zondervan, 2002).

5. C. Peter Wagner, *Frontiers in Missionary Strategy* (Chicago: Moody Press, 1971), 22.

crisis. Reichardt stated, "There's too much waste in banking, getting rid of it takes tenacity, not brilliance."[6] Reichardt let his employees know that everyone, even those at the top, would suffer as the bank weathered the deregulation crisis. This included asking his executive leaders to suffer with the rank and file. He froze executive salaries, closed the executive dining room, and sold the corporate jets. He even rejected reports from surprised subordinates who submitted their reports in fancy binders. "Would you spend your *own* money this way?" he asked. "What does a binder add to anything?"[7] From Reichardt's example of shouldering the pain with his employees, his company emerged from the crisis to become one of the primary banking providers in the twenty-first century. For more examples, see P. E. Murphy and G. Enderle's article, "Managerial Ethical Leadership: Examples Do Matter," in *Business Ethics Quarterly.*[8]

Effective Leaders Are Driven by Five Behaviors

The following five behaviors of effective leaders were first codified by Professors Debra Nelson of Oklahoma State University and James Quick of the University of Texas at Arlington.[9]

1. *Effective leaders accept the uniqueness of each organization.* No two organizations are alike. The leader who says, "I've done that before" or "I've led a church just like this one before" may not be innovative and creative enough to adapt to each church's unique situation. Thus pastors who acknowledge the changing nature of management and leadership, as well as the uniqueness of each organization, are far more likely to lead with innovation rather than to fall back upon outdated strategies.

2. *Effective leaders must be willing to bring about change without creating destruction.* Today there is a widespread notion that to create something new, you have to do away with or abolish what worked in the past. "I thought you had to start with a clean slate," Bill said, describing his first two pastorates. "And so, I got a lot of our older people off key committees and replaced them with young people. . . . I thought the church was going to die without radical surgery, and so I decided to get rid of the old way of doing things for the sake of the church's health."

---

6. Carl E. Reichardt, "Managing: Carl E. Reichardt, Chairman, Wells Fargo and Co.," *Fortune* (February 27, 1989), 42.

7. Research interview conducted by Jim Collins in *Good to Great: Why Some Companies Make the Leap . . . and Others Don't* (New York: HarperCollins, 2001), 128.

8. Patrick E. Murphy and Georges Enderle, "Managerial Ethical Leadership: Examples Do Matter," *Business Ethics Quarterly* 5 (1995): 117-28.

9. Nelson and Quick, *Organizational Behavior*, 404.

Unfortunately, the "status-quo old slate" at the church was more successful at getting rid of Bill.

The idea of destroying the past to create something new is a major tenet of postmodern philosophy, exemplified by philosopher Richard Rorty. Rorty declares, "Great edifying philosophers destroy for the sake of their own generation." Called "deconstruction," this concept of destroying the old in order to replace it with something new is a key ingredient in many popular leadership paradigms.[10] However, management professors such as Nelson and Quick point out that this is a poor leadership strategy.[11]

Staying Power: Why People Leave the Church Over Change and What You Can Do About It proposed that change is accompanied by a six-stage process with five triggers. By adjusting just two of these triggers, organizations can bring about change in a unifying manner without alienating either their status-quo members or their change proponents. Thus the good news is that you can have change and keep your aging status-quo members too. Deconstruction is not necessary.[12]

3. *Effective leaders must have a genuine concern for people.* A genuine concern for people is especially important today when pressures to physically grow a church seem to take precedence. Since organizations are made up of people, leaders that succeed are those who seek to understand, empower, and improve the quality of their workers' lives. Martin Luther said, "To love is not to wish good for another person; it is to bear another's burden, that is, to bear what is painful to you and which you do not bear willingly."[13] Management researcher Jim Collins concluded, "Compared to the high-profile leaders with big personalities who make headlines and become celebrities, good-to-great leaders seem to have come from Mars. Self-effacing, quiet, reserved, even shy—these leaders are a paradoxical blend of personal humility and professional will. They are more like Lincoln and Socrates than Patton or Caesar."[14]

---

10. Ed. L. Miller, *Questions that Matter: An Invitation to Philosophy*, 4th ed. (New York: McGraw-Hill, 1996), 203-8.

11. Nelson and Quick, *Organizational Behavior*, 404.

12. Bob Whitesel, *Staying Power: Why People Leave the Church Over Change and What You Can Do About It* (Nashville: Abingdon Press, 2003).

13. Quoted in Donald Bloesch, *Freedom for Obedience: Evangelical Ethics in Contemporary Times* (San Francisco: Harper and Row, 1987), 33.

14. Jim Collins, *Good to Great: Why Some Companies Make the Leap . . . and Others Don't* (New York: HarperCollins, 2001), 12-13.

4. *The effective leader must be willing to let the right individual lead at the right time.* Great leaders recognize that as organizations change, leadership changes too. As Bill recognized, the management skills he used in small churches would not succeed with his latest church's new size (around 200 regular attendees in a membership of 350). Effective leaders recognize that the changing nature of organizational behavior will require them either to change their leadership style or to hand the reins to a different leader.

5. *Finally, an effective leader also will be a good follower.* Effective leaders do not know it all. Instead, they rapidly absorb information from varied sources. They read, they listen, and they seek advice. They do not trust in their own intuition only but seek the advice, counsel, and correction of God, friends, and colleagues.

MOTIVATION FOR OUTSTANDING MINISTRY

At the heart of organizational behavior is an organization-wide motivation that produces outstanding results. By outstanding results I mean ministries, programs, and events that in anointing, quality, and excellence grab the attention of unchurched and dechurched individuals. These results are "outstanding" because they stand out among the distractions and attractions of secular culture.

Motivation for outstanding ministry must pervade the entire organization. It begins when an organization discovers its core competencies and builds mission and vision statements upon those core competencies. A resulting understanding of strengths and weaknesses, combined with a resolute faith in a church's mission and vision, drives the organization forward in unity. In his look at "good-to-great" companies, Jim Collins found that "every good-to-great company embraced what we came to call the Stockdale Paradox: You must maintain unwavering faith that you can and will prevail in the end, regardless of individuals. *And, at the same time*, have the discipline to confront the most brutal facts of your current reality, whatever they might be" (italics Collins').[15]

At Every Level

In order for this motivation to pervade the entire organization, it must be exemplified most clearly and robustly at the top. Elmer Towns, dean of the School of Religion at Liberty University, often quoted C. T. Studd's words about foreign missions: "The light that shines the farthest shines the brightest at home." In other words, the motivation for effective and robust foreign missionary action

---

15. Ibid., 13.

begins with an even more robust mission program in the home church and its surrounding environs. Leadership, for Towns, must be exemplified and modeled from the source outward.

In addition, an effective leader must transfer the ownership for this outstanding performance from the senior management to every person involved in the organization. Belasco and Stayer tender an especially probing illustration in their article, "Why Empowerment Doesn't Empower: The Bankruptcy of Current Paradigms."[16] Let's look at the true story they cite. The original story described a "company" and its "employees," but I've modified it by changing the business terms into church administration terms:

> Early in our leadership careers we became grounded in [lay] involvement. We read a lot about it, and it sounded good. . . . We began by holding [church-wide] meetings to solicit [congregational] participation. . . . It rapidly deteriorated, however, into a [gripe] session. [Congregants] kept bringing up situations that needed fixing. We made long lists of things to fix and worked hard to fix everything before the next meeting. But this turned out to be a full-time job. We told ourselves, "You have to demonstrate good faith. It will take time. Eventually they'll run out of things to fix and you can get on with solving the [church's] real problems." Fixing their problems, after all, was part of our leadership responsibility. Eighteen months later, we were still receiving long lists to fix at every meeting. We ran out of patience before they ran out of lists. In retrospect, the problem is clear to us. We were owning all the responsibility for fixing the problems.[17]

Eventually, Belasco and Stayer discovered that the missing ingredient was a transfer of ownership for fixing the problems from the leadership to the workers. Leaders must help workers understand that *everyone* should identify *and* fix the problems. In the church scenario, this has been labeled "layperson's liberation." It liberates the church volunteer to participate in all aspects of identifying and eliminating problems, while demonstrating outstanding performance.

Diffusion Theory

As Belasco and Stayer found out, the process of transferring ownership is challenging and, thus, must be carefully undertaken. To graph this process, let's outline a seven-step process for "trickling down" goals from the leader to the

16. Belasco and Stayer, "Why Empowerment Doesn't Empower," 29-41.
17. Ibid., 29-41.

average participant. This outline is an abbreviated form of what is called "diffusion theory" in the management field.[18]

1. *Start by envisioning yourself.* Through prayer, Scripture, research, and input, gain an understanding of where your organization is and where God intends it to go.

2. *Envision your circle of accountability.* These are trusted friends and colleagues that can provide accountability and perspective. Allow them to further refine the vision/mission.

(Note: in some church structures, Steps 3 and 4 may be reversed due to the leadership structure.)

3. *Envision the staff.* The staff often will bear the brunt of change and its ramifications. Thus, early in the process, staff members should be informed and asked to tender advice regarding the mission/vision.

4. *Envision the leadership core.* By leadership core, I mean the primary administrative and decision-making council, board, or vestry of the church. Support from this group is vital for successfully trickling-down ownership. This step, along with step 3, must be undertaken deliberately but judiciously.

5. *Envision the informal leaders.* Every church has "gatekeepers" and opinion makers who need to understand and embrace the mission/vision. Do not forget these individuals, treating them with the same respect and regard you gave official leaders in steps 3 and 4.

6. *Envision your congregation.* Only now is it time to approach the congregation. Too many leaders fail to transfer ownership because they *start* with step 6. From the pulpit or lectern, they will announce some new idea or plan. "It's just a way to gauge response," Bill said about one such public proclamation. However, leaders, both formal and informal, are usually caught off guard by such experimentation. As a result, leaders often will form poor initial opinions—not due to content, but to congregational discomfort with the surprise.

7. *Envision your community.* Now you can go public. Once the organization has fully accepted ownership for the new idea, change, or mission/vision, only then should the outside community be given a chance to peruse it. This not only preserves unity in the organization but also promotes a unified manifestation to an observant world all too familiar with our disagreements.

---

18. Bob Whitesel and Kent R. Hunter, *A House Divided: Bridging the Generation Gaps in Your Church* (Nashville: Abingdon Press, 2000), 111-20.

TEAMWORK:
HARNESSING THE POWER OF SMALL GROUPS

Defining Small Groups and Teams

Small groups by definition are "any group of three to twelve people formally or informally meeting approximately one or more times a month within the church fellowship network. Though they may on occasion be comprised of more than twelve individuals, the cell group's cohesiveness is rarely found in meetings of more than twenty individuals."[19]

Some small groups function as teams. The term "team" connotes a small group with a task orientation. Teamwork is the product of these interdependent teams as they engage in a project, mission, or task. In the business sector, they may be called quality circles, maintenance teams, task groups, strategy teams, or management teams.

However, in the church context, small groups may also be convened to provide fellowship, accountability, and/or acceptance. When this occurs, we simply call them small groups.

The Benefits of Small Groups and Teams

Productivity

The reason we include the term "teams" is because companies have learned that teams are especially helpful in accomplishing work that is complicated, complex, or interrelated or that involves more work than one person can handle. When knowledge, skills, talents, and/or abilities are dispersed across many organizational members, teams can help put together a comprehensive strategy to address a need.

This is especially true in volunteer organizations such as the church. In these organizations, no one person may have the time (even if this individual has

---

19. Bob Whitesel, *Growth by Accident, Death by Planning: How NOT to Kill a Growing Congregation* (Nashville: Abingdon Press, 2004). The designation of these small groups as "cell groups" is somewhat unique to the church environment. Page 140 states, "The 'cell' designation was initially designed to stress this group's ability to divide and multiply as it grows, in much the same manner that a human 'cell' divides and multiplies. I have kept this designation because this diversifying aspect of the small group is important if the group is not to become a closed circle. Small groups should be seen as growing, living organisms that may shed dead elements and add new ones as they thrive. As the larger organism (the church) grows, the division and multiplication of cells into parallel units is important if church growth is to take place logically and coherently."

the talents) to accomplish all aspects of a task without burnout coming into play. Thus teams become the backbone of volunteer organizations, helping to forge a network of people to accomplish a complex task.

Small groups are also capable of providing an accepting and supportive environment in which spiritual growth and breakthrough can occur. For many people struggling with emotional, spiritual, or behavioral issues, the small-group environment becomes the most productive venue for progress toward wholeness.

Integrated Involvement

Teams and small groups provide a place where people can belong. They have also been called "kinship groups," for they foster family-like kinships.[20] Through their involvement in a group, people recognize where they fit into the bigger picture. Often when I ask clients to tell me where they fit in their congregation, they describe the small group or team in which they participate.

If newcomers do not find or become a part of a team or small group, they may feel that their talents remain untapped or unrecognized. If suitable small groups or teams are not available, newcomers may conclude that the church is too big and impersonal (or too small and clannish) to offer such opportunities. In either case, newcomers may seek involvement in a different congregation.

Psychological Intimacy

Psychological "inter-reliance" is a very important by-product of the team and small-group environment. It is here that participants can open up without fear of being ostracized or isolated for their feelings and/or beliefs. And it is here that the Holy Spirit seems especially adroit at breaking down barriers, opening up individuals to new ideas, and coalescing participants into a surrogate family. Corporate America has long recognized the social-psychological benefits of groups and has sought by way of teams to re-create some of this cohesiveness and solidarity. But the church must not abdicate this responsibility to the business realm. The church should be the primary venue for people to develop a psychological intimacy established on an understanding of their Creator and his creation.

Types of *Teams* in the Church

In New Testament times, task-oriented teams were organized when necessary. Acts 6:1-4 shows how the early disciples organized a team of servers:

---

20. C. Peter Wagner, *Your Church Can Grow* (Glendale, CA: G/L Publications, 1984), 107-8.

In those days when the number of disciples was increasing, the Grecian Jews among them complained against the Hebraic Jews because their widows were being overlooked in the daily distribution of food. So the Twelve gathered all the disciples together and said, "It would not be right for us to neglect the ministry of the word of God in order to wait on tables. Brothers, choose seven men from among you who are known to be full of the Spirit and wisdom. We will turn this responsibility over to them and will give our attention to prayer and the ministry of the word."

Since that pattern was first set with the early believers, the church has actively embraced task-oriented teams.

Types of *Small Groups* in the Church

Fellowship-oriented small groups have emerged over the last 500 years, when Protestant churches began to use "gender" as a primary way of dividing churches into two subgroups. It is continued today in the Amish/German Baptist traditions: "Men on one side . . . women on the other." In 1872, B. F. Jacobs, a Chicago produce broker, persuaded the Sunday School Union to adopt classes graded for differing "ages." Thus the Sunday School was born. Out of these Sunday Schools came a system of age-specific small groups.

From 1935 to 1965, "marital status" was added to "gender" and "age" as a designation for organizing new small groups. This was an era when nearly all adults were married. As a result, "singles groups" now met apart from "married groups."

In the early 1970s, a new subgroup emerged. A culture of never-married or formerly married individuals gave rise to distinctive subgroups under the "singles" umbrella. Some groups that fell under this heading were parents without partners, single mothers, divorce recovery groups, and widows and widowers.

Then, in the mid-1970s, perhaps as a response to the Church Growth Movement's emphasis on discipleship as a "process," new groups were organized along "stages of faith development." Groups were now available for new converts, seekers, and/or mature Christians. The current popularity of the Alpha Course, a user-friendly introduction to Christianity created at Holy Trinity Brompton, an Anglican congregation in London, is an example.

With that in mind, many churches might look like figure 6.1, composed of a multitude of formal groups/teams (solid lines) and informal groups/teams (dotted lines).

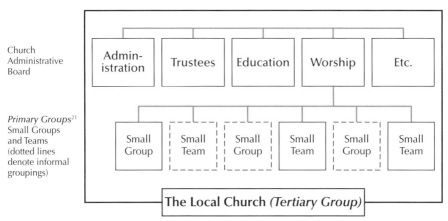

**Fig. 6.1. Small groups and teams in a
typical worship department of a congregation**

How Many Small Groups Are Needed?

Figure 6.2 offers general guidelines for the minimum number of small groups or teams needed to produce a healthy congregation. When a congregation successfully integrates the number of small groups in each category listed below, that congregation will exceed the minimum threshold required to develop healthy interpersonal environments.

Target Goals for Small Groups or Teams	
Type of Small Group or Team	*Percentage of Average Weekly Worship Attendance*
Adult Sunday School Classes	4% (minimum)
Prayer Groups and Teams	4% (minimum)
Outreach Teams—teams that present the Good News to unchurched and dechurched people; the evangelistic mandate	4% (minimum)

---

21. The secondary groups, not shown here, will be explained under the "Functional Structure" section and illustrated in figure 6.5.

Outreach Teams—teams that meet the physical needs of unchurched and de-churched people; the cultural mandate	4% (minimum)
Worship & Celebration Teams—teams involved in leading worship and the execution of celebration duties	5% (minimum)
Fellowship, Self-Help, Bible Study, and/or Home Groups—non-Sunday morning	6% (minimum)
Administrative Leadership Team—non-Sunday morning	8% (minimum)
TOTALS	35% (minimum)

Fig. 6.2. Target goals for small groups or teams in a congregation

Growth by Accident, Death by Planning: How NOT to Kill a Growing Congregation describes four steps to creating a sufficient number of small groups or teams for churches of any size.[22] Use these steps to ensure that your church has a sufficient number of small groups and teams.

1. Use figure 6.2 to determine the number of small groups and teams in your church, and the number you need.
2. Create organic groups and teams, using demographic, skill, social, and interest data to create groupings. It is important to create teams around natural and not artificial interests and skills. Many churches simply assign people to a group, often by geographic proximity. At other times, nominating committees assign people to teams (committees) based on their availability or their lack of a good excuse. However, effectively functioning teams will be based around shared goals, gifts, or needs. *Growth by Accident, Death by Planning* further outlines four substeps for creating "organic" groupings based on demographic, skill, social, and interest data.[23]
3. Consider using a staff-level human resource director. Churches are discovering the benefit of designating a "human resource director" to

---

22. To investigate these steps in more detail, see chapter 10 of Whitesel, *Growth by Accident.*
23. Ibid, 142-48.

oversee volunteerism, skill development, continuing education, and assigning individuals to an appropriate group or team.

4. Make small groups and teams a key part of your church personality,
along with prayer, worship, outreach, and the Word.[24]

ADAPTING ORGANIZATIONAL STRUCTURE AND MANAGEMENT STYLES

Another important tool for understanding the strategic future of a congregation is to project how the organizational structure and management styles will
evolve as the organization grows. Let's first look at a simple diagram (fig. 6.3)
that demonstrates how businesses grow.

Simple — Functional — Multidivisional Business Structures

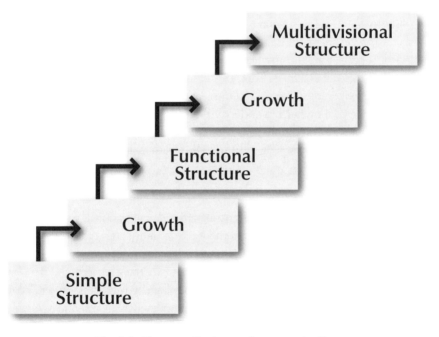

Fig. 6.3. The growth stages of an organization

---

24. To better understand how the axiom "Word – Prayer – Outreach – Worship– Small
Groups" provides a necessary foundation for a flourishing church, see Whitesel, *Growth by
Accident,* chapter 10.

In the organizational behavior of the business world, firms grow through these three stages: the simple structure, the functional structure, and the multidivisional structure. Let's look at these stages and how they are paralleled by similar stages of growth in churches.

Simple Structure

The simple structure is the basic structure of a small business or a small church. In the business context, an owner/manager makes all major decisions and monitors all activities. In the church scenario (100 or less attendees), the pastor makes all major decisions and monitors all progress toward goals.

Earlier in this chapter, we illustrated a situation that fits the simple structure scenario. Belasco and Stayer recounted the problem with the "long lists of things to fix" and how the leaders were unable to get past the lists in order to accomplish their vision for the organization. "Eighteen months later, we were still receiving long lists to fix at every meeting. We ran out of patience before they ran out of lists."[25] The organization Belasco and Stayer described had functioned to that point as a simple structure: the leader(s) were expected to make all major decisions and oversee all activities. Thus, even though the organization had grown to the next level, workers still expected the leaders to fix the problems themselves, rather than take goal ownership and join the leaders in solving the problems.

Many churches encounter this situation when a pastor, familiar with leading a simple structure church, is thrust into the leadership of a congregation that has grown to the next size, the functional structure.

Functional Structure

Functional structure means organizing around an organization's "functions." This customarily results in the establishment of "departments." A functional structure allows for some autonomy, along with a higher degree of specialization. In the business context, an accounting department may emerge, research and development may become a separate area, and sales may have its own department. While each department may have its own director, the organization essentially remains one entity, with departments carrying on specific duties.

In the church context, a congregation may develop departments of music, Christian education, youth, missions, building maintenance, outreach, and so on. Often, each department has a departmental head that reports to the senior leader. Churches can grow to 500+ within the functional structure. However, if they want

---

25. Belasco and Stayer, "Why Empowerment Doesn't Empower," 29-41.

to grow beyond a predominately single-generational church and reach multiple generations, they must adopt the next structure, the multidivisional structure.

Multidivisional Structure

In business, the multidivisional structure means the organization literally becomes two or more companies under the same umbrella. An example is General Motors, which includes divisions such as Chevrolet, Pontiac, Saturn, and Cadillac. Each division provides the same commodity: a vehicle for transportation. But each division provides this commodity with its own style, image, and corporate culture.

In the same way, churches grow into multidivisional structures when they reach out to multiple generations. Because different generations worship, fellowship, learn, and reach out to their friends using different styles and structures, trying to blend generations can cause undue friction.

Thus, in the church context, this divisional structure might be represented by a congregation with separate boomer, Gen Xer, and builder/senior sub-congregations. Each of these internal wings or divisions within the church might have its own worship service, Sunday School format, and outreach programs. Still, all three generations would remain part of the overall organization. Leaders of each generational wing could exploit synergies between generational sub-congregations. As such, each generation could contribute to the health of the overall organization. This becomes especially important when one division is weak. The popularity of the Pontiac and Chevrolet divisions of General Motors helped Cadillac stay afloat during the nebulous '90s.

Many churches try to thwart this inevitable and healthy multidivisional structure by blending ministry among several generations. Blending church ministries is analogous to the failed missionary strategies of the nineteenth-century Europeans who tried to force Africans to adopt European culture and language in order to convert them to Christianity. These failed efforts are a testimony to the danger of confusing culture with theology. While theological consistency is important, the European strategy was not successful because it failed to inculcate its message into the "heart language" and cultural customs of the people.

In contrast, two centuries earlier, Saint Patrick was successful in winning the Celts to Christianity. He did this by rejecting the strategy Peter Wagner calls "the creator complex, where we try to make over people in our image."[26] Rather, Professor George Hunter points out that Saint Patrick was successful because he translated the Good News into the symbols, language, stories, customs, and

---

26. Wagner, *Frontiers in Missionary Strategy*, 97.

culture of the Celts.[27] Hunter demonstrates that for older generations to reach younger generations today, older generations must allow indigenous strategies modeled after Patrick's success with the Celts. Hunter concludes, "The supreme key to reaching the West again is the key that Patrick discovered. . . . The gulf between church people and unchurched people is vast, but if we pay the price to understand them, we will usually know what to say and what to do; if they know and feel we understand them, by the tens of millions they will risk opening their heart to God who understands them."[28]

Regardless of changing generational demographics in the community, any church of 100 or more members can grow steadily with multiple sub-congregations if it allows each generation within the church to develop its own style of ministry while maintaining theological consistency.

Now let's look at figure 6.4 to see how churches grow through simple-functional-multidivisional structures.

Simple—Functional—Multidivisional Structures in the Church Context[29]

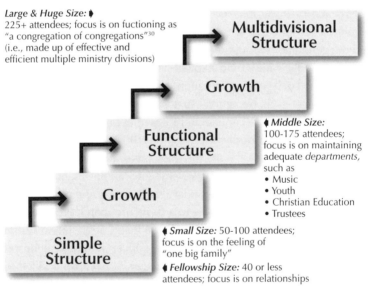

Large & Huge Size: ◗
225+ attendees; focus is on fuctioning as "a congregation of congregations"[30] (i.e., made up of effective and efficient multiple ministry divisions)

Multidivisional Structure

Growth

Functional Structure

◖ *Middle Size:*
100-175 attendees; focus is on maintaining adequate *departments,* such as
• Music
• Youth
• Christian Education
• Trustees

Growth

◖ *Small Size:* 50-100 attendees; focus is on the feeling of "one big family"

Simple Structure

◖ *Fellowship Size:* 40 or less attendees; focus is on relationships

Fig. 6.4. The growth stages of a church

---

27. George G. Hunter III, *The Celtic Way of Evangelism: How Christianity Can Reach the West . . . Again* (Nashville: Abingdon Press, 2000), 47-55.

28. Ibid., 121.

29. Size designation from Lyle E. Schaller, *The Multiple Staff and the Larger Church* (Nashville: Abingdon Press, 1980), 27-31.

30. George G. Hunter III, *The Contagious Congregation: Frontiers in Evangelism and Church Growth* (Nashville: Abingdon Press, 1979), 63.

In both the business context and the church context, as the organization grows through each stage, a different management structure and a different style of leadership will be necessary. If these adjustments do not occur, the organization's growth will stall. The church world often refers to the factors that stunt growth as "growth barriers." Business people call these same factors "growth stages" because organizational behavior changes as growth occurs.

Remember, churches tend naturally and frequently to divide into sub-congregations based on generational preferences. In figure 6.1 we described small groups/teams in congregations. Let's update that in figure 6.5, showing how generational sub-congregations emerge once a congregation grows beyond 100 attendees in weekend worship.

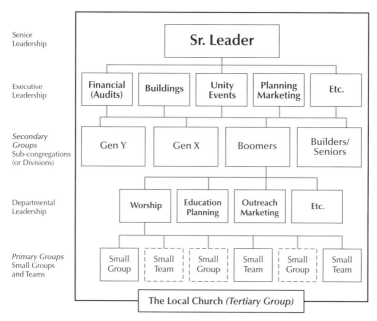

Fig. 6.5. Church structure with generational sub-congregations in a boomer worship department of a congregation

Sub-congregations: The Overlooked Key to Managing the Growing Church

Generational sub-congregations (designated Gen Y, Gen X, Boomers, and Builders/Seniors in fig. 6.5) naturally develop as the church passes 100 attendees. These sub-congregations can be the key to strategically managing the growing church. Much like business divisions in the multidivisional structure (see fig. 6.3), which are given some degree of autonomy and self-rule, these sub-congregations must be granted space and autonomy in order to thwart conflict. First, however, they must be recognized. When leaders do not recognize the existence of generational sub-congregations, they can expect five results:

1. *Conflict.* People in the church want to be "one happy family," but they cannot reconcile this altruistic vision with the generational propensity to worship, learn, and reach out through different procedures and programs. The result is generational conflict, tension, and self-justification.

2. *Control Issues.* One generation will seek to control decision-making power. Thus the controlling generation will create what it considers to be appropriate programming for other generations, only to frustrate and irritate other generations who view these programs as inappropriate to their needs.

3. *Polarization.* Generations will polarize over approaches to ministry, viewing the church with an "either our way, or the highway" approach. This division over change usually progresses through six stages. *Staying Power: Why People Leave the Church Over Change, and What You Can Do About It* scrutinizes these six polarizing steps and shows that by adjusting just two of the triggers, unity can be preserved.[31]

4. *Bias.* Sub-congregations that feel stonewalled or overlooked eventually will leave the church and start a church of their own (or affiliate with a congregation of similar generational preferences). The downside to such a church split is that those who leave usually will polarize around age preferences as well. Thus those who leave will soon become part of a generationally biased church like the one they left. So, regrettably, the cycle starts again.

5. *Frustration.* Pastors and leaders will become frustrated because they do not understand that they must lead two or more distinct generational sub-congregations. Frustrated with generational differences and the inability of sub-congregations to get along, leaders often will leave the church. However, the answer is very simple, one that is employed consistently in the business world: Allow the church to become separate generational sub-congregations or divisions, each with its own style of ministry, education, and worship. While values and doctrine should remain consistent, generational predilections are accommodated in much the same way that a family accommodates certain style preferences of its teenage children.

---

31. Whitesel, *Staying Power,* 53-168. Because of the intricacy of this topic, I encourage the reader to read this earlier volume. It describes the polarization process, suggests corrective steps, and includes questions for team discussions.

A church comprised of several mutually accepting and mutually beneficial sub-congregations can be called a "multigenerational church." *A House Divided: Bridging the Generation Gaps in Your Church* defines "multigeneration" or "Multi-Gen" in this way: "The multigenerational church is a holistic congregation with three or more distinct generational sub-congregations peacefully coexisting under one roof, one name, and one leadership core."[32]

Figure 6.6 briefly describes each of these generations and the preferences that can readily polarize sub-congregations.

Name	Birth Years	Cultural Preferences	Church Preferences
Seniors *Rationale of name:* They are the senior group, the oldest living generation in the church.	Born before 1926	Cultural preferences mirror the Builders (see below).	Church preferences mirror the Builders (see below).
Builders *Rationale of name:* They *built* the Western world into a worldwide military and economic power. Their heritage means they appreciate fine craftsmanship, seeing it as a reflection of their God-given skills and a vital part of their worship.	Born between 1927 and 1945	*Perspective on change:* Stability. They want constancy and few changes in a world already beset by the insecurities of old age. *Learning:* Builders prefer the lecture format. *Legacy:* They built the Western world into a safe and secure environment.	*Church size:* 75-300 *Affiliation:* Mainline *Church emphasis:* Need to be heard. *Worship style:* Traditional hymns, customary liturgy. *Best worship times:* Sunday morning and evening, Wednesday evening.
Boomers *Rationale of name:* The term "boomer" was appropriated by media pundits to describe an increase in births after World War II in much the same way that a "boom town" in Old West parlance was a town that sprouted up overnight due to the discovery of gold or silver.	Born between 1946 and 1964	*Perspective on change:* Experimentation. Boomers like to experiment to find new and more efficient ways of doing things. *Learning:* They prefer the participation format, where questions are encouraged. *Legacy:* Through innovation and creativity, they made the world a better place (however, in the process they did not necessarily make the world a safer place).	*Church size:* 300+ *Affiliation:* Independent *Church emphasis:* Needs of the congregation. *Worship style:* Modern (soft rock), with use of choruses. Some, but limited, media usage. *Best worship times:* Sunday morning, and Saturday or Friday evening. Not weeknights.

32. Whitesel and Hunter, *A House Divided*, 83.

Generation X		*Perspective on change:*	*Church size:* 200-300
Rationale of name: Originally, the X was intended to portray a nihilistic bent. However, Gen X tends to be a very religious generation.[33]	Born between 1965 and 1983	Radical experimentation. Gen X likes to experiment even more than Boomers, often combining seemingly incompatible concepts. *Learning:* They prefer the Socratic format, where questions and dissent are encouraged. *Legacy:* They saved the world from itself (pollution, terrorism, overpopulation, etc.).	*Affiliation:* Mainline, due to the perceived security that mainline affiliation affords. *Church emphasis:* Needs of the community. *Worship style:* Interactive postmodern (edgy rock) with extensive use of media, videos, etc. *Best worship times:* Sunday morning and Friday evening. Not weeknights.
Generation Y		Cultural preferences are still developing.	Church preferences are still developing.
Rationale of name: While some have tried to call them the "millennials" because they were raised in a period spanning two millennia, the Y designation (simply meaning they followed the X generation) seems to have stuck.	Born between 1984 and 2002	*Perspective on change:* Gen Y embraces electronic community, living, and communication for better living. *Learning:* They prefer a hyper-Socratic format; active confrontation and discord lead to insight. Also prefer electronic communication in all areas. *Legacy:* Gen Y wants to be the generation that is plugged into all areas of life.	*Church size:* 75-300 *Affiliation:* Unknown *Church emphasis:* Gen Y needs to be closely connected to one another, even if not in physical proximity. *Worship style:* Postmodern (edgy rock), with even more use of interactive media, videos, etc. *Best worship times:* Sunday morning and Friday evening. Not weeknights.

Fig. 6.6. Generational differences

Managing Sub-Congregations

Managing in the Functional Structure Stage

Approaching church management from an understanding of generational congregations can thwart a myriad of problems. As departments emerge and the church passes the 100 mark in attendance, the church leadership must adapt to the changing circumstances. It can evolve in much the same way as the sole proprietor's leadership in the "simple structure" business evolves into a team leadership approach. Just as the sole proprietor establishes department heads of directors to oversee each department, so too must the senior pastor ("president" in the business context) delegate responsibility and authority to "department heads" in the "func-

---

33. Ibid., 62-63.

tional stage." The failure to fully and sufficiently empower and delegate authority to departmental leaders is one of the greatest oversights of church leadership.

Managing in the Multidivisional (Sub-Congregation) Stage

When the church reaches the next level (225+ in worship attendance), the church needs to undergo a transformation into the M-form or multidivisional structure. In this structure, each sub-congregation (or division) is more autonomous: "associate pastors" or divisional leaders oversee budgets, outreach, ministry development, worship, discipleship, and so on, within their generational age-grouping.

Figure 6.7, which is configured the same as figure 6.5, demonstrates how a church can grow into a healthy and balanced "Multi-Gen" congregation of four divisions.

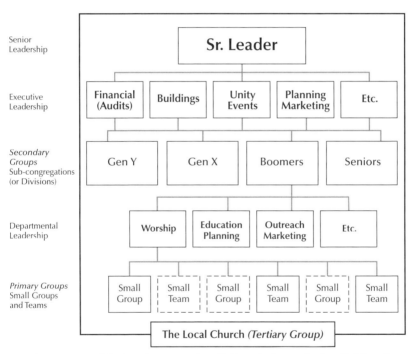

Fig. 6.7. A Multi-Gen Congregation.[34] (For clarity, only the divisional leadership and small groups/teams of one sub-congregation are shown.)

---

34. The business student will be familiar with figure 6.7 as the "cost-leadership" structure. In this structure, certain management functions are retained at the executive level to prevent replicating them in each sub-congregation. The financial accountability department, building maintenance department, unity-building event planning, and strategic planning are retained at an executive level. Utilizing this process helps to cut costs. Yet, even in this scenario, control over disbursement of funds, program creation, and ministry style are retained in each sub-congregation or division.

Managing the New Small-Group Environment

Generations born in and after 1946 appear to prefer the small-group environment for developing social, spiritual, and task networks. However, management styles must change to effectively manage this new organizational building block. In figure 6.8, Professor Larry Hirschhorn points out some key differences in management style that must be employed in the new small-group environment preferred by younger generations.[35]

Old Team Environment (Preferred by Builders and Seniors)	New Team Environment (Preferred by Boomers, Gen X, and Gen Y)
Members follow orders.	Members exploit team synergies to generate innovation.
Team depends on a supervisor to chart its course.	Teams have considerable authority to chart their own steps.
Members are a team because people conform to direction set by the manager. No one rocks the boat.	Members form a team to collaborate in the face of their emerging right to think for themselves. People both rock the boat and work together.
People cooperate by suppressing their thoughts and feelings. They want to get along.	People cooperate by using their thoughts and feelings. They link up through honest and direct talk.

Fig. 6.8. Old and New Team Environments

Figure 6.8 implies that managing in the new small-group environment requires a much less autocratic style than it did previously. Thus those born before 1946 often will feel uncomfortable participating in or managing groups in the new small-group environment. As such, leaders born before 1946 must learn to delegate a great degree of authority, as well as grant a lot of leeway for groups to struggle along as they chart their own course.

Just as granting such autonomy to sub-congregations will feel alien to older generations, this autonomy will seem natural to younger generations. Thus leaders must be careful to avoid a "disconnect" between older members of the organization and younger members due to different expectations and predilections. The authors of this book believe that diversity is a reflection of God's variety in his creation.

---

35. Larry Hirschhorn, *Managing in the New Team Environment*: *Skills, Tools and Methods* (Reading, MA: Addison-Wesley Publishing, 1991), 13-14.

APPRECIATING THE NEXUS OF CHURCH BEHAVIOR AND HEALTH

Just as the skilled pastor should have a basic understanding of counseling and psychology, a rudimentary understanding of organizational behavior should also be seen as indispensable. Those shepherds who are bereft of such skills may need to surround themselves with staff and/or laypeople qualified in these vital disciplines. A foundational understanding of the behaviors and personalities of organizations must be integrated into leadership strategies to ensure their appropriateness and viability.

7
GOVERNANCE
THE ORGANIZATIONAL STRUCTURE OF THE CHURCH
David Wilson
DMin, General Secretary, Church of the Nazarene

For the past thirty-one years, it has been my privilege to work with a variety of church governing boards: as pastor, district superintendent, seminary and university trustee, and general secretary for the Church of the Nazarene. Most of these experiences have been very positive because of the relationships among the members and the organizational energy provided by board leadership.

These experiences have not been accidental. Two factors have contributed to these boards' effectiveness. One is, at all levels, in the local church, with university trustees, and general church administration, there was a strong level of trust between the governing board and the staff that managed the day-to-day operation. One person, or even a small group, regardless of giftedness, will not have all the answers needed to keep an organization moving in a positive direction. Discontent emerges when a board and staff try to dominate or control each other, allowing seeds of mistrust to develop.

This is especially true in the relationship between the pastor and the church governing board. The board is comprised of members of the congregation who have invested time and financial resources over many years. Pastors come and go with fresh plans and new ideas. They expect buy-in from their boards, while board members, because of their tenure, desire consideration. Problems arise when either one tries to restrain or manipulate the other.

Second, trust between staff and boards is typically found in places where each party respects the other and the roles they play in helping the organization to be successful. Boards and staff have distinct responsibilities, and difficulties often arise when these roles are not recognized or allowed freedom to function.

What are those roles and how are they defined?

GOVERNANCE VS. MANAGEMENT

There are two key concepts that define the roles played by governing boards and staff: governance and management.

Governance addresses direction, resources, and structure. Specifically, governance deals with strategies that set direction, assures that there are sufficient financial resources and accountability for their use, and facilitates the development of leadership.[1]

Management produces programs and activities that help to accomplish what the church wants to do. The pastor and/or staff are usually responsible for this function. They develop, implement, and manage the details behind the programs.[2]

In many churches, the lines of responsibility are blurred because there is not sufficient staff to develop and manage programs. Key lay leaders share this accountability with their pastor. Pastors of small congregations may depend on their boards to not only work with the programs but also suggest ideas that will move the church closer to accomplishing its goals.

The critical role of the board is governance. What are the elements of good governance and how is it carried out in relation to congregations?

ELEMENTS OF GOOD GOVERNANCE

Setting Direction

The first element of good church board governance is establishing direction for the congregation. Two critical questions must be considered: What do we want our church to be? and What is our strategy for getting there? There are three components in establishing direction: articulating mission, vision, and values.

The pastor plays an important role in helping the board and congregation in this process. Frequently in Scripture, God raised up a leader and communicated a vision for his people. In a similar way, the pastor prayerfully gains a sense of vision and will cast that vision to help the board and congregation see the germ of an idea of what the church can be.

Admittedly, casting a new vision is often easier than reshaping the vision of an established church. In established churches, it is often assumed that people

---

1. Marc Smiley, "Governance vs. Management," Marc Smiley Organizational Development, http://www.marcsmiley.com/marcsmiley/tools/html_files/staff_management/governance_management.html (accessed May 12, 2008).
2. Ibid.

know the answers to such questions as who the church is, what its purpose is, and how it's going to get there. Grappling with those concerns is considered by some to be a waste of time—especially if other pastors have tried and failed, or if there was no follow-up to the earlier work. In a new congregation it is natural to take time to study identity questions and efforts are often quite productive, especially if the pastor is skilled in involving others in a group process.

Effective pastors are able to grasp a basic idea and have the ability to help board and congregation share this perspective. Wise pastors do not develop this idea in a vacuum; rather, it begins to grow as they pray and as they ask questions and listen to members of the congregation as they testify to their personal stories and share their memories of church life. This dialogue gives members a sense of connectedness with pastoral leadership and with the first step in the direction-setting process. The capacity for communicating vision helps to build excitement and brings people together to articulate mission and then work toward the mission's fulfillment.

As the seed of the idea is planted and begins to take shape, the board can begin to work with the pastor in developing clarity of mission. Everything the board does centers around mission, and for that reason, time spent on developing and communicating the mission is crucial. A succinct, carefully worded statement of mission provides clarity of a church's direction in ministry.

Simply stated, the mission statement describes the church's overall purpose.[3] A mission statement is not best formulated by one person alone, but is strengthened when there is a variety of contributing voices. Pastoral leadership in the process is not only necessary but also expected.

The starting point for establishing a mission statement is with Scripture. The teachings of Christ express his expectations for his followers, what they are to be, individually and corporately. He tells his disciples how they are to relate with God and with fellow believers and what their attitudes and actions should be to those who do not share their faith. In Matthew 28:19-20, he succinctly summarizes the mission of the church as going to all nations and making disciples. A thorough study of Scripture is a vital starting point for pastors and boards who want to gain a clear understanding of what the church is to be.

Because the teachings of Christ provide the basic framework for mission, the mission statements of all congregations will have common elements. Distinctive components will emerge as two other dimensions are considered. One is denominational objectives. This is not an issue for groups that choose not to

---

3. Carter McNamara, "Basics of Developing Mission, Vision and Values Statements," http://www.managementhelp.org/plan_dec/str_plan/stmnts.htm (accessed September 5, 2008).

affiliate themselves with a denomination; but for those that do, it is a matter of integrity to stay aligned with the theology and practices of the parent organization. Key questions to consider are, What are the distinguishing characteristics of who we are in our denomination? Together with other churches that share the denomination's name, what beliefs are we trying to promote? What do we want to accomplish?

Another distinctive component for consideration in establishing a church mission statement is the church's environment, its culture. There are times when the location of a church will help define its mission. What are the needs of the neighborhood and the community at large? What is the age demographic? The main employers? The socioeconomic levels in the community? What is the target for ministry? The interests, talents, and abilities of the congregation are other aspects to consider.

When all of these factors have been evaluated, the board can begin to formulate the mission statement. The key to this work is "the simpler the better." Wordy mission statements are hard to remember and to communicate. If they are too complex, the focus can be lost.

Once established, the mission of the congregation cannot be overcommunicated. The congregation needs to hear it stated and explained often from the pulpit by the pastor, in small groups by board members, in church membership classes, and even in casual conversation. The statement should be in print and memorized by everyone in the congregation. A visitor who asks about the mission of the congregation should receive an answer from every member. Understanding the mission of the church helps promote a spirit of unity and focus.

The author has taken time to describe one way of arriving at the articulation of mission because as the board develops strategies and plans, makes financial decisions, and selects leaders, the question of mission will always be the primary consideration. "How does this decision impact our mission?" should be the most frequently asked question during church board deliberations.

There is a tension between "staying the course" and making sure the mission remains relevant. A congregation cannot change its mission quickly or often without a compelling reason. Once the mission of the congregation has been established, it should not be easily changed unless a significant shift occurs that impacts the "picture" of the church's future (i.e., changing demographics, a shift in financial resources in the community, etc.).

During a time of pastoral change, a congregation that knows its mission has a clearer picture of the kind of pastoral leadership it needs and, thus, is able to ask questions that reveal a candidate's "fit." A congregation that does not have a firm idea of "who we are" is particularly vulnerable during pastoral transitions.

Pastors often have an agenda that fits their style of ministry and may seek to steer mission in a compatible direction.

A church board will follow its work on articulating its mission by developing a vision statement. While a pastor's vision may be stated generally and serve as the catalyst for setting direction, establishing a vision statement is specific and becomes the inspiration and framework for strategic planning.[4]

A vision statement describes an ideal outcome—inspiring, energizing, and helping to create a mental picture of what the church will be like by a specified future time. The vision should be stated powerfully and emotionally in a phrase or paragraph. Brevity is not crucial in a vision statement. Whatever space it takes to paint the picture should be used. The vision should be stated optimistically and should contain a "wow" factor. It should tap the imagination and open eyes to possibilities.

The third component in setting direction is expressing a statement of values. Values are beliefs and norms, developed from traditions and social and family sources, that navigate through our decisions in life. The congregation's values provide boundaries and will define the limits to which they will go in achieving their vision. Values express the priorities of the congregation and how members act within the organization.[5] The values of a Christian group like the church will reflect the spirit and attitude of Christ himself and will emanate from the Great Commandment, loving God with all one's heart, soul, and mind, and one's neighbor as oneself (see Matt. 22:37-39).

These three components in establishing a church's direction—mission, vision, and values—provide the basis for board governance. Together they form a starting point for determining priorities and a measuring stick for evaluation.

Strategic actions can begin being developed only when mission, vision, and values are clarified; but these are only starting points. One of the greatest failings of pastors and church boards is spending a great amount of time on statements but not following through by implementing plans and identifying who should be accountable for getting this done. Mission and vision statements by themselves change nothing. They serve only to focus a pastor and board; they do not say "how" the mission will be achieved. Many churches reach the "now what?" stage and go no further. Programs and activities must be developed to answer the "how" questions. Discipline is needed to not let the direction-setting process stop with articulating mission. Both pastor and board share responsibility for follow-through.

---

4. Susan Ward, "Vision Statement," http://sbinfocanada.about.com/od.
5. McNamara, "Basics of Developing Mission."

The responsibility for the development of programs and activities designed to help the congregation accomplish its mission is a philosophical question with two parts. The typical board in a new or small church operates as a committee of the whole, and it has a high degree of participation in deciding what kinds of activities the church will use. As a church grows and matures, there is a shift to a committee structure, and the pastor/pastoral staff plans, develops, implements, and administrates the programs and activities.

The author contends that a congregation does not have to wait until it is "large enough" to move to a committee structure and for the pastoral team to assume programmatic responsibilities. The greater question is the willingness of the board and pastor to make the shift. The burden on the pastor is training laity for board leadership. The burden on laity is being available to be trained and to accept time-consuming leadership of board committees. If these responsibilities are not accepted, confusion will result and changes will be made with more difficulty.

The shift also involves focusing more intently on the work of one committee rather than having general knowledge of all the business of the board. Great trust is required to believe that another committee has discussed an issue completely and that their recommendation to the whole board is acceptable. Trust is built when committees take their responsibilities seriously, and thorough treatment is given to issues that arise. Committee leaders will be prepared to answer the questions of board members who have not been part of the research and development of a recommendation.

A congregation takes a giant step forward when the pastoral team assumes leadership in planning and implementing programs. Even in small or new churches, the pastor can develop a lay staff that can help dream and plan ministries that move the church toward accomplishing its mission. At that point the board's responsibility shifts to evaluating and dialoguing about plans presented by the pastoral team and, of great importance, assuring that the activity helps to fulfill the church's mission. Making this shift has its challenges, but when it happens, both pastor and laity are released for more satisfying ministry.

When the pastoral team is allowed to take responsibility for programs and activities, the board is able to focus in greater measure on the fiduciary aspects of their assignment.

Financing the Program

The second element of good governance is the responsibility for raising and managing the finances of the church. There is a business side to congregation life that must be carefully observed so that the main thing—spreading the gospel and making disciples—is not hindered by an overemphasis on money or a poor reputation in the community.

A challenge that faces every board is to not let financial issues control the destiny of the congregation. Not everything can be figured with the point of a pencil. There has to be room for God's people to be stretched in their faith and for God to have the opportunity to show that the church is not a standard business. The church is a community of faith—faith in God's reconciling work and his desire to advance his kingdom through the church. Ultimately, he supplies what is needed to accomplish this task.

The full financial picture is seen and pressure for paying the congregation's obligations is felt most strongly by the board treasurer. It is natural, then, for the treasurer to be a "voice of reason" in board meetings and, at times, even become possessive of the checkbook. A delicate balance must be maintained between operating with sound financial principles and being willing to take steps of faith when God opens doors and when he leads in directions that do not seem reasonable. Treasurers who hold too tightly to the checkbook may stymie the faith process of the board. It is prudent to have standard operating procedures that can be interrupted by unusual opportunities that are in keeping with God's plans.

Every church board is wise to have a finance committee, charged with the responsibility to create and monitor the budget. This committee may be comprised in a number of ways. One way is to have board committee chairs compose the finance committee. This gives each committee a voice in budgeting and financial management.

Another way is to have a separate finance committee with no other board committee responsibilities. The positive side of this method is that the finance committee has fewer distractions and more time to devote to financial management. The downside is the perception, among the finance committee members themselves and within the board, that this is an elite committee that wields great power.

The pastor may be involved in the budgeting process and may even give strong voice; but pastors cannot be the final voice. The pastor and others who work with the finances of the church are protected by a checks and balances system that involves others and limits their access to the checkbook.

For example, neither a minister nor immediate family member should ever be authorized to sign checks. This practice opens the door to questioning the pastor's integrity. Good business principles call for a valid check-writing policy to be designed by the finance committee and approved by the board as their first order of business. This policy includes the names or positions of those authorized to sign checks. Financial irregularities stemming from the pastor's involvement in the check-writing process usually leads to termination and, if the charges are serious enough, the end of vocational ministry.

The second order of business for the finance committee is the development of the annual budget (see chapter 5 for complete details). Every church needs a working budget. A budget is a spending plan that reflects the church's priorities, enables the church to be proactive rather than reactive in response to immediate needs, and guides the church when there is a shortfall or surplus.[6]

When a church establishes spending priorities, it says not only how it *will* spend money but also how it will *not* spend money. A church cannot say yes to every request, regardless of legitimacy. This is where understanding the mission of the church is vitally important. The budget will reflect mission. If a potential budget item does not contribute to accomplishing the mission, regardless of merit, it will not be included in the budget.

A board will begin the budgeting process by looking at the last three to five years of giving and expenditures. By studying these numbers and even charting them, it is possible to see trends emerge. Growth and/or decline is noted. In addition, internal factors to be considered are changes in major givers, the number of givers, and patterns in giving. "Patterns" refers to monthly income over the course of the year. External factors to be considered are utility increases, the health of major employers in the community, and economic indicators such as the price of gasoline and food. These factors will help the board to determine the projected income for the year.

The next step will be to look at fixed expenses. This refers to the cost of "keeping the doors open." No matter what happens in the church, these expenses continue as long as the church is in existence. These expenses must be paid before anything else. They include the mortgage, utilities, insurance, and pastoral compensation.

The author's experience has been that about 40 percent of a church's income will be spent on pastoral support. In a large church the 40 percent is spread among members of the pastoral staff and includes both salary and benefits such as housing and insurance. In some smaller churches the 40 percent rule will not be sufficient to provide pastoral compensation, and the church will be forced to allow the pastor to supplement the salary given by the church. Churches that have just completed building programs may have excessively high mortgage payments, and a reduction in staff will be necessary, reducing the amount spent on pastoral compensation.

---

6. Ibid.

An element for budget consideration that is often overlooked is an amount for deferred maintenance. As buildings age, repairs are needed. Furnaces and air-conditioning units need to be replaced. Whenever possible, a church should begin to set money aside for major repair work.

When fixed expenses have been deducted, the balance of the projected income is available for ministry projects. There are two ways this income can be divided. One is for the pastor and finance committee to evaluate the ministries and give each a share. The ministries then develop a budget for what they want to accomplish during the year. This is known as "top-down budgeting."

"Bottom-up budgeting" is when ministries project the dollars they will need to reach their goals during the coming year. When a finance committee is comprised of board committee chairs, each brings an "asking budget" to help the committee put the ministry budget together.

In either case, the major question for budget inclusion is, "Will this project, program, or activity contribute to the fulfillment of our mission?" A board might start by looking at major programs and ministries that specifically address a mission need and direct those funds to the ministry that will carry out the plans.

Quite often available dollars will not be sufficient to meet all the needs and dreams. The board will be forced to indicate which ministries and programs will have the highest priority for the year. A second level of priorities may be established for those times when there is a surplus in the bank account. It does happen, especially when a church aggressively addresses the needs of reaching its community.

The final budget will be communicated to the congregation, in writing and with a verbal explanation. Wise boards will take great care in keeping the financial needs before the congregation by placing in worship folders, newsletters, and electronic communications a breakdown of how the church is doing in meeting its budget. Usually there are four columns in the report: the monthly need, the amount received on a given Sunday, the projected annual budget, and an indication of where the finances are to date for the year. At midyear, the board will evaluate and address the issue publicly.

Two or possibly three times a year, attention will be given to helping the membership stay current with their commitments to financial giving: at the beginning of the fiscal year, at the end of the calendar year (many members are conscious of how charitable contributions impact their taxes), and in the last part of the fiscal year as the church works to reach its annual financial goals.

Because people may easily lose the sense of urgency, it is good to celebrate short-term victories. This produces excitement and enhances further interest.

Financial Accountability

The third aspect of good governance is financial accountability. There are three major areas: weekly counting policies, monthly financial reports, and yearly audits.

When offerings are being counted, a minimum of two persons, unrelated to each other, and never the pastor or a pastor's immediate family member, will be on the counting team. In addition, the same two people should not count the offerings every week. An envelope numbering system should be used to assure privacy. Deposits are placed in a locked bag and taken to the bank's night deposit.

The church treasurer is responsible for presenting monthly reports to the church board. These reports will tell not only the monthly activity in the operating account—income and expenditures—but also how money is being managed for future projects, the balance in various ministry accounts, savings and investments, and if the congregation is reaching anticipated income levels. The treasurer must take great care in providing accurate information and be realistic when an exciting idea is presented that does not have adequate financial support. At the same time, the treasurer is wise to guard against possessiveness and control.

One area of financial accountability that is often overlooked by church boards is the annual audit. Two typical reasons given are that it suggests a lack of trust in the treasurer and that the church cannot afford the cost. In reality, the audit protects the treasurer, and the church cannot afford not to have the audit.

The church financial records should be audited every year. This can be done through an internal audit, where qualified members of the congregation access the authorized expenditures by the church board by comparing the board minutes with account records. There are different levels of audits done by a certified public accountant, some more affordable than others. The key is to make sure an audit is completed and the report made public. The need for audits cannot be overemphasized.

One other area of financial accountability by the board is selecting a financial secretary who is charged with the responsibility of keeping the giving records of members and other contributors. This person must be above reproach in matters of trust and confidentiality. Some pastors choose to know the record of giving of church members, but outside of the pastor, no one else, not even the spouse of the financial secretary, should know the level of contribution. This officer of the church will be the one who provides giving statements that are signed and given to the church members at the end of each year. There are members who understand giving more in terms of charitable deductions on their taxes rather than stewardship, and they will give great attention to the accuracy of reports.

Leadership Development

The fourth aspect of good governance is leadership development. Careful attention needs to be given to the kinds of people who will serve best in board leadership roles.

When board selections are made, several characteristics should be considered.

First, board members should be representative of the congregation. That means the board will be as diverse as the group of people they represent. They also speak for members of the congregation who depend on the board to represent them in the decision-making process. The author has often said to board members, "A significant number of people in this congregation thought you could serve the church well and voted for you to be on this board. Represent them well."

Second, board members will be models for other members of the congregation. Any time a person is elected to a leadership role in the church, the standard for his or her life and conduct is raised. More is expected, not just within the church but also in the community in which they live. Board members will want to protect the integrity of the congregation by the way they conduct themselves in their business dealings, in their neighborhoods, and in all other aspects of their society.

Within the church board itself, members will be model churchpersons. They will participate in the life of the congregation in their attendance, involvement in various programs and ministries, and especially in their financial support. Most churches elect only those who have a record of faithful giving. This is right and proper.

Finally, board members function best when they stay informed. This will require them to speak up in board meetings, asking questions that provide insight and clarification. A board member who is willing to address difficult issues with the church's best interest in mind is often greatly appreciated by congregation members.

One dimension of development is preparing members of the congregation for board leadership. Electing board members who are not ready to assume leadership roles can be devastating for a board and congregation.

Paul warns against putting young believers in positions of authority (see 1 Tim. 3:6). One reason is that they may become disillusioned by seeing the "business side" of the church and by fellow members with strong personalities.

Another reason is the opportunity for arrogance, seeing leadership as a superior position rather than a place for humble service.

Young Christians can be given opportunities to serve on ad hoc committees and in positions with lesser responsibility that allow them to grow into major leadership roles. Pastors and boards may also identify potential future board members and offer training options that will introduce those with leadership gifts to board processes. Knowing what is expected and how to conduct oneself as a board member will help new members transition more easily.

Newly elected board members will get off to a better start if they are provided an opportunity for orientation to board functions and responsibilities. The orientation gives the new member a chance to learn about how business comes to the board, church finances, committee job descriptions, and the expectations of those who serve as board leaders. Each church has its own culture, and even those who have been in leadership roles in other congregations need to be oriented to how the board in their present location functions.

A wise pastor will take time in every board meeting to give attention to board development issues. There are many responsibilities that are taken for granted, and gaps in understanding are revealed in times of crisis. Important areas such as the church's insurance policies, screening those who work with children and teens, financial protocols, operation policies, and even the spiritual leadership of board members in the church—these and many other aspects of board responsibility can be addressed in a fifteen-minute presentation in each meeting. In addition, a weekend board retreat or leadership day offers the board a chance to develop teamwork and to address leadership issues in an unhurried setting.

The board will also want to give attention to helping its pastor develop his or her leadership skills. Making it possible for the pastor to attend workshops and seminars is one way. Another is for laypersons skilled in various aspects on the business side to offer their services to pastors who may be in a learning phase of ministry or who do not have strength in a given area. Laypersons can help "make" their pastor as he or she provides leadership for their church.

When a church board understands its role and embraces the opportunity to lead, the members will experience a sense of fulfillment and the belief that they are contributing to the advancement of the gospel. Many board members experience personal growth as they give themselves to the joy of helping to lead the church.

8
STAFFING
SELECTING AND DEVELOPING HUMAN RESOURCES FOR THE CHURCH

Alan Nelson
DMin, Executive Editor, *Rev! Magazine*

◆

The most important, single key for effective ministry, other than the touch of God, is staffing. As a pastor for more than twenty years and now in a role serving thousands of pastors in various denominations, church sizes, and styles, I'm convinced that the single biggest difference between effective and ineffective ministries is how they engage people in roles of serving.

When our first church plant was growing, I remember thinking, "If only I had more money, we could really take off." I was so naïve. I thought that money was the key, but it's not; it's good people. Throwing money at staff is not the solution either. That's good news for many of us who will lead churches that can't spend much money on personnel. Approximately 85 percent of churches in America are under 200 in average worship attendance. As economics tighten, most churches will lack sufficient budgets to hire additional staff, but you still need good people.

BIBLICAL STAFFING MODELS

In Exodus 18, we read a story similar to the typical local church pastor. Moses was trying to do too much himself. From sun up to sun down, he was fixing people's problems while they waited in line. Obviously, Moses wasn't doing everything on his own. Others organized food and water, managed housing, tended the ill, and so on. But Moses was doing far more hands-on work than he should have. Jethro observed the problem and then suggested a solution. Equip leaders to supervise groups of 10, 50, 100, and 1,000. Moses needed to move from me to we.[1]

---

1. Alan Nelson, *Me to We* (Loveland, Colo.: Group Publishing, 2007).

In the New Testament, we see a similar method when Jesus recruited his staff of twelve. We have no indication he ever paid them. Perhaps they bartered time for room and board. He looked in their eyes and said, "Follow me." The power of personal invitation still works today. Jesus invested most of his messianic ministry in the dozen who'd eventually "do even greater things" than him (John 14:12). The power of teamwork was evident in how Jesus pastored. His ministry to the masses could be seen primarily as opportunities to provide his staff with on-the-job training.

If Moses and Jesus are insufficient models of staff development, then a quick look at Paul should round out God's design. In Ephesians 4:11-12, Paul provides the job description for pastors: "It was [Jesus] who gave . . . some to be pastors and teachers, to prepare God's people for works of service, so that the body of Christ may be built up." The work of the pastor is to equip others to serve. That is his or her primary service.

As pastors prepare others to serve and as these people use their gifts, then we find what we're striving for among our people—unity and maturity. "Until we all reach unity in the faith and in the knowledge of the Son of God and become mature, attaining to the whole measure of the fullness of Christ. Then we will no longer be infants, tossed back and forth by the waves, and blown here and there by every wind of teaching and by the cunning and craftiness of men in their deceitful scheming" (Eph. 4:13-14).

Based on this passage, one of the primary reasons for the lack of spiritual maturity we see in our churches, in spite of decades of attending services and programs, is that pastors are doing too much of the ministry themselves and not enough equipping of others to use their gifts in serving each other. Staffing begins with equipping those currently in our congregation more than with hiring professionals from the outside to minister to the people.

PASTORAL PARADIGM SHIFT

The pastor-centric ministry paradigm in most American churches is neither biblical nor effective. The typical Western pastor has assumed the role of doing ministry instead of equipping the ministers. These are significantly different tasks and skill sets. Unfortunately, we tend to replicate what we've seen done, perpetuating a model of ministry that has little theological support. Most of us will need to make a major shift in our ministry paradigms in order to embrace a more biblical approach to pastoring.

While we are responsible that people receive ministry, we are not responsible to do it ourselves. In Acts 6, the apostles heard complaints about the unfed widows. They excused themselves to preach and delegated others to care for the widows. In Mark 1:35-39, Jesus got up early to pray. While he was in prayer, he was found by "parishioners" needing help. He immediately left for another village. No single person, no matter how gifted, can fulfill the needs of a congregation. No staff, no matter how large, can do it either—nor should they.

The result of pastors and pastoral staff preparing people to use their gifts to serve each other are threefold:

1. *People mature by receiving ministry from others who are using their gifts.* Only God grows people, but his grace flows through spiritual gifts. When a pastor or staff member strives to serve outside of his or her gifting, the result is frustration due to a lack of growth in the receivers and pending burnout of the givers.

2. *People gain ownership in ministry.* The more people are involved in serving others with their gifts, the more they feel the ministry is theirs. Psychologists refer to this as ego-involvement. Ego in this sense refers to a sense of identity, "I am." When people feel that they own ministry, they are more apt to give time and money to it. One of the primary reasons many churches struggle with tithing of time and finances is because they've allowed the few to serve the many.

3. *People mature by serving others through their gifts.* As the Spirit moves through us, we reap the benefit of discovering our purpose. We begin to give up self-centeredness, the engine driving the sin nature, manifesting unholy fruits (lust, stealing, lying, etc.). The result is maturity, not an up-and-down neurosis (see Eph. 4).

The temptation of professional ministry is assuming that if we're good enough to get paid, we should be doing it ourselves. John Wesley multiplied ministry by engaging lay leaders to pastor local parishes, while the circuit-riding preachers dropped in to preach and teach. It was Acts 6 on steroids.

Consider how you can elevate key people to the level of staff, with all the benefits and responsibilities thereof, but without pay. One equipping pastor I know has volunteers who supervise various paid church staff members. He realizes that some of the best people will never want to be paid and that the church could never pay enough people to accomplish God's mission for it. Another church sets up office space for volunteers that is better equipped than the paid staff's. A pastor who made the decision to become an equipping church said to his staff, "If we catch you doing ministry yourself, a year from now, you'll be fired. From this point on, you're to develop and train teams of people to do the ministry." He began holding staff accountable to work through others. Some didn't make it. Most did. The change transformed the congregation.

CHALLENGING ASSUMPTIONS

Three staffing assumptions deserve challenging when it comes to making this paradigm shift.

1. *The pastor is the ministry expert.* Just because you've been trained professionally does not make you "the" expert. God has given various gifts to a variety of people in every congregation so that they can be more effective in using their gifts than a nongifted person who's been trained. The goal of the pastor is to come from seminary and create a practical seminary in the local church, training ministers for service in the church and community. When a church depends on one trained pro, or even a handful of them, there will always be a bottleneck in ministry. Multiply; don't add.

2. *Hire for talent.* This is the proverbial mantra in staffing. Old school says go after the best musician, children's minister, youth pastor, and small-group leader. But being a good player is usually different from being a good coach. Hire coaches, not players. The latter tend to be self-running ministry leaders, often with egos requiring feeding. Look for people who have proven track records in developing teams, work through people, and know how to motivate. Teams will always outperform individuals in the long run.

3. *You can't hold volunteers accountable.* The reason so many of us believe this is because we've set the bar low and have failed to cast the vision that inspires people to do the incredible for God. Today, corporate employers are realizing they have to think of paid staff more as volunteers, if they want to retain them. The inverse is true in volunteer organizations. Giving people the freedom to make choices, establishing accountability systems, and providing feedback loops are not only possible but also often attract the strongest players. When we raise the bar of kingdom work, we get higher rewards. You reap what you sow.

ESTABLISHING EXPECTATIONS

When you get a group of pastors together, it's only a matter of time before staff discussions arise. There's something about working together that brings out the best and worst in us. The horror stories of staff conflict, an inability of finding quality people, needing to fire bad people, and all that goes into functioning as a ministry team can keep us awake at night.

I heard a counselor claim that nearly all anger is a result of unmet expectations. If you receive lousy service at a restaurant, you get upset if you were expecting good service. You don't get upset if you expected to be treated poorly.

A lot of church conflict could be significantly reduced if parties communicated and clarified expectations.

Here is a practical way to reduce the collision of expectations.

Focus on the Three Cs: Character, Competency, and Chemistry

Character has to do with who a person is and the values he or she brings to life and work. Is the person a hard worker? Does he cut corners? Will she deceive you? Can he be trusted with guarded information? Is she spiritual? All of these are heart issues, relating to our ethics, morality, and judgment. Compromising in this area, especially in the ministry, will nearly always lead to regrets. The best way to judge future behavior is to investigate past behavior. This does not mean a person cannot be forgiven and change, but look for patterns and trends. Talk to people who've known the person. Listen for words describing the person such as "honest," "high integrity," and "very spiritual." These are character matters.

Competency has three aspects that make up the acrostic SET: skills, experience, talent. Skills are trained behaviors, whether it's a software program, developing messages, playing an instrument, or running a sound system. Training improves skills. Experience refers to how much know-how a person has from actually doing the task. Classroom education often does not translate into the real world. What's the person's track record? Longevity is a sign of experience. It's possible to do the same thing for a number of years and only have experience in that one area. Talent has to do with natural aptitude and capacity to gain a skill, whether it is leadership, music, communication, prayer, evangelism, or counseling.

Chemistry is the third ingredient. While being far more subjective in nature, this element is important because we all have a sense of whether or not we relate to and get along with someone. Being on the same page is vital to team play. Philosophy of ministry is more significant than theology and doctrine when it comes to working well together. Temperament and emotional intelligence are also keys, especially in leaders. If you have a gift of discernment, use it. If you don't, find a couple people who do and intentionally have them interact with this person. Don't rely solely on feedback from two or three. Expand the interaction to those who'll likely minister with this candidate. Ask them to confidentially debrief their thoughts and impressions.

I know of one congregation that had good long-term pastoral staff. So when they began searching for a senior pastor, they went after one who got along with the existing staff. The search committee wanted to be sure the new pastor fit the others. The process worked. The pastor has now been there several years, following a well-loved former pastor. Most of the same staff continued. This is chemistry, how we get along and feel when we're around a person. All it takes is one individual to disrupt the harmony of a team, board, or staff.

Here are some indicators to look for when testing chemistry.

- Does the person seem comfortable around others on the staff/team?
- Is there natural rapport and friendly conversation that emerges?
- After you leave this person's presence, do you have an overall positive, happy feeling, or is there a tinge of relief or melancholy?
- What do references say about how this person gets along with others, handles conflict, and relates as a ministry team member?

While it sounds as if you're looking for perfection, you're not. All strengths have shadow sides and every person brings a certain amount of baggage, blind spots, and weaknesses. The information you need to try and gather for these three are how heavy, how large, and how many. The better you are, the more effective you'll be in finding a person who'll thrive in the role for which he or she is being considered.

The best staff members have all three Cs. If you're missing character, the person is apt to self-destruct and/or lose valuable trust that is needed in spiritual leadership. If competence is light, you'll have a really nice person who just doesn't perform. This is a stewardship issue. If you're weak on chemistry, you may have a person who performs, but who is not well liked by teammates and is forever butting heads with colleagues or the organization as a whole. People ask, "If you're going to compromise on one of the three, which would it be?" The answer is, "None." If you do, there's a high price to be paid.

PROCESS ISSUES

There are a battery of assessments and instruments available to help reveal a person's wiring. Ask around to see what other churches, consultants, or human resource people you know use. The power of the right assessment is that it can reveal how a person processes information, interacts with people, and views life in general. This will naturally be revealed over time, but you want to know this in advance and reduce the risk of a poor fit. That's the benefit of hiring from within the church, where the person is already known and tested. The weakness is usually in the area of competency and training and in the political collateral if the person does not work out. It's easier to train someone in a skill than it is to change character or hope for different chemistry.

I've made some hiring and recruitment errors in the past, going against my "gut" feeling, thinking that we'd make it work. When I did this, I usually regretted my decisions. I've talked to scores of pastors who, in spite of their best selection processes, have experienced horror stories, good hires gone bad. There is no perfect system, but that's all the more reason to be intentional and thorough. The breakdown is usually in failing to validate the three Cs, check references, and get multiple inputs from people around you and in trying to fill a spot too fast. It's very tempting, when a key position has been empty for a time, to fill it and move on. But you'll spend a lot more time afterward, mopping up after problems and tossing in bed, because you rushed the process.

We see processes like these in the Bible: Moses recruited people for various roles in Exodus 18, David was preselected as the future king, Jesus picked the Twelve, and the apostles replaced Judas and then discerned that Stephen should be the one to oversee the feeding of the widows (Acts 6). Discernment, being in tune with the Holy Spirit, and seeking wise counsel are all important components. Never hire or recruit alone. Even the best of us have blind spots and can miss things. The beauty of this is that when someone doesn't fit, it's a shared responsibility as well.

Three types of people are important to include as part of your "wise counsel." Get feedback from those who are going to interact with this person on a somewhat regular basis. Let them know that an opinion is not the same as a vote, but seek their input. Include someone who has the spiritual gift of discernment, who can give you a "read" on a person's spirituality and detect something that might be amiss in God's will. Finally, make sure you have someone with HR (human resource) experience, as this training and experience are invaluable in ministry settings. Most of us hire so few that it takes us quite a while to get really good at it. It's not only your life you're complicating in a bad hire but also the life of the person being invited into a wrong role.

Fit is key. Don't say, "She's the wrong person." Rather, "It's the wrong role for her." God gives everyone gifts and abilities. Our job is to help find roles for people in our church. That is called equipping. When hiring a person, we want to make sure there's a good fit. Unless we have a very clear set of expectations for the role and have thought through what type of skills and abilities are needed to succeed, we won't be able to make a good match, or at least with confidence. "Hoping it will work out" is usually more wishful thinking than it is faith.

One of the biggest failures I've seen in church work is that we let our good hearts get in the way of wise judgment. Mercy gifts can negatively bias a hiring process. You want the very best that you can afford and usually even better. We should not lower our standards or let compassion skew our vetting process.

The general rule is that the more important the role is, paid or unpaid, the more thorough you need to investigate, requiring greater time and money investment. Asking a person to hand out a worship folder or flip a flapjack for a men's breakfast is one thing. Considering a youth pastor or board member is quite another.

BEST PRACTICE IDEAS

A single chapter in a book is insufficient to address all staff issues, so here is a list of points that raise issues I hear about with pastors across the country.

- Know the dos and don'ts of HR (human resource) issues. You're vulnerable to lawsuits if you're not savvy about what you can and can't ask in an interview and how you record issues leading up to a dismissal.

- Always check references but realize that legally, a former employer can only share certain information, so be shrewd in what and how you ask questions.

- Immerse yourself in the growing number of books that deal with equipping, lay mobilization, and doing ministry by team.

- Be a ministry coach. Don't think you have to have all the answers. This does not empower others. Ask questions. Learn coaching skills so you can better develop staff without acting as though you know it all.

- Think externally focused. While you need to cover the bases in the nursery and worship team, many of your people will jump at the opportunity to demonstrate grace by building a Habitat home, visiting a homeless mission, and teaching English as a second language. The new apologetics is serving. Think outward, not inward, and you'll engage twice as many people in serving.

- Pay as well as possible. Few of us work in a church for the money, but it sure helps attract and keep quality staff members, especially when other offers come their way.

- When you have an underperforming staff member, meet with him or her so that expectations are clear. Document this in writing and even ask the person to sign a form, denoting that he or she understands the content of the meeting. If performance does not change, do this again and establish a deadline for "sustained improvement," as underperformers often improve for a short period and then lapse. This allows you to avoid serial confrontations.

- Establish written protocol to clearly communicate what is and is not acceptable, especially in terms of male-female meetings and communication.

- Have a clearly written job description for every ministry role, paid or unpaid, including a length of term. This is a great tool for engaging people who want clarity before committing. This is primarily a communication document, but it also provides guidelines for accountability.

DEVELOPING STAFF

Our research with *Rev! Magazine* shows that leadership development is consistently one of the highest needs among pastors. We get so busy "doing" ministry that we take little time developing those who supervise ministry and others. We're so busy chopping wood that we don't sharpen the axe. Even if we think of developing people, we're sometimes unsure what to do. Here are some practical ideas.

Write a Plan

I taught a seminary class called "Developing People." As I prepared for the course, I realized that no church I know has a written strategy for how they develop people, yet that's what we're in, the people growing business. What should people expect in our ministry or church? How do we help them grow or at least develop their own soul growth plan? What kind of people are we trying to produce? How are we helping leaders grow in skills? How are we developing them spiritually? How can we equip them to be more effective in their ministry roles? Take time to write a plan, being exact in your thinking and getting everyone on the same page. When I consult with a church about leadership development, we get the people engaged in the task and then plan a schedule of developmental readings, workshops, and growth opportunities.

Team Building

The goal in ministry is to accomplish tasks through the community. If you don't facilitate community as a ministry team, you probably won't see it happen in your congregation as a whole. Push back on the taskmasters for time to laugh, pray, teach a leader lesson, and go on an occasional retreat, experiential trip, or social outing. Let your more driven people understand that this is vital for effective teams as well as modeling what they should be doing with their ministry teams.

Training

Do we have the competency we need? What do we need to improve on? How can we get better? Whether it's visiting a thriving church, attending a workshop together, or discussing a ministry book, take your training seriously. One pastor I know has made it the largest line item in his budget, because he understands the importance of training his staff, both paid and unpaid.

Vision Casting

Thousands of pleas for your people's attention distract them from what your church is striving to accomplish in ministry and its purpose for doing it.

Your role as the team leader is to keep the vision strong by using multiple means and creative ways to get their attention. Every four to six weeks, you need to do a mini vision cast or you'll drift and lose passion. Jesus had the opportunity to live 24/7 with his disciples for three years. We don't, so we're all apt to weaken in our commitment and clarity.

Accountability

How are we holding each other accountable to the tasks, moral standards, and accomplishments? I've found that very few churches have a formal means of measuring progress other than attendance and offerings. The difference between control and accountability is that the former tends to de-motivate by micromanaging. The underlying message is, "We don't trust you, and you're not competent." Healthy accountability says, "We believe you can deliver, and we want to help you succeed in what you do." Moral lapses happen in ministry often for lack of proper accountability.

Feedback

Why is it we fear feedback in ministry? Is it because we don't want to be held accountable, or do our egos get in the way? "We are God's appointed." In our book, *The Five Star Church,* Stan Toler and I introduce a variety of ways for gaining feedback in order to improve the quality of our ministry.[2] When we do not seek it proactively, it often bubbles up negatively through critique and criticism. You'll need to figure out how you can gather feedback from your staff about how you're doing, but in a way that is constructive and allows people to be as anonymous as possible. You will also want to see how people are feeling about the programs and ministries in your church, not to be judgmental, but to see how and where you need to improve both programs and staffing. Never assume you know what needs to be done. Intentionally gain input, whether it's about nursery care, sermons, music, or any number of related matters.

Managing Conflict

The two biggest ministry discouragers are critique and conflict. You will never be able to fully avoid these nagging elements. Even though you're in ministry for noble reasons, to serve God and help people, others will judge your actions, question your motives, and cast their opinions. The good news is that people tend to complain when they care. Developing a thick skin while retaining a sensitive heart may be the greatest personal challenge you'll face emotion-

---

2. Stan Toler and Alan Nelson, *The Five Star Church* (Ventura, CA: Regal Books, 1999).

ally. But even if you do a good job receiving criticism and managing expectations, you will still have conflict. The apostle Paul had it. The disciples had it among themselves, and Jesus had it with the Twelve. Because Christians wrestle with how to appropriately handle anger, we often sweep it under the rug or try to put patches on it. The right kind of conflict is good, because it enhances communication, improves outcomes, and engages people. The wrong kind can shake us to pieces and result in hard feelings and people leaving the church. Equip yourself in conflict management skills so that you can model this for others, because it is a part of staffing.

THE "L" FACTOR

In most congregations, the single most overlooked area of stewardship is tapping those with leadership capacity. These are the 100 and 1,000 group leaders mentioned in Exodus 18. When you have people who are successful entrepreneurs, who manage others in their business, and who are community catalysts casting vision and innovating, you'll want to find a unique role for them. Many pastors are intimidated by these people and either avoid them or give them token roles ushering or directing traffic in the parking lot. These individuals will almost never volunteer in response to a bulletin announcement or pulpit plea. You have to go after them one by one. After you get one or two, you'll be able to get more, because leaders are aware of their peers. They are far less apt to invest in something that is overly managed, small thinking, and lacking in vision.

What is needed is what I call "3-D Leading: Discern, Disciple, Deploy."

Discern

Because most pastors do not have the gift of leadership, they struggle trying to discern other leaders. The adage "It takes one to know one" holds true in this area. To determine who has natural leadership gifts in your church, consider who others look to in conversations, who supervises ten or more people at work, and who has the ability to get things done through others. Sometimes, people with a lot of opinions are leaders, meaning you may be able to transform your critics into allies with some savvy engagement. Listen for stories in their past where they led. Ask your congregation, "If I disappeared tomorrow, who would you look to in this church to lead it during a transition?" Intentionally build rapport with these individuals over coffee and meals; spend time with them in their homes and work environments.

Disciple

If you want to add ministry, disciple anyone interested. But if you want to multiply ministry, disciple influencers. The pastor should only and always be discipling those who will either become leaders in the church or community or who will become disciplers of others. Turning over church authority to spiritual neophytes is not wise, as mentioned in 1 Timothy 3:6. While the text suggests a recent convert, a better understanding is someone spiritually immature. There are a lot of people who are not new believers, but who should not be in roles of leadership, because they lack emotional intelligence and spiritual maturity. Once you've discerned who is gifted in leading, personally invite these people into a six- to eighteen-month Bible study that you personally lead. This allows the influencers to know and trust you, and you them.

Deploy

Once leaders have been developed spiritually, then you need to unleash them. Staying in touch over coffee and in informal settings is vital, but don't try to micromanage these people. They need room to run. Let them cast vision. Allow them to run their ministries or projects as they please. Within reason, your role is merely to empower and coach, not to oversee or control. Accept advice from them, because most pastors can significantly benefit from those who are gifted and experienced in leading. This is how God has wired them. They can discern things in organizations, strategy, and structure that inhibit progress. Our research with stuck churches shows that those individuals with catalyzing gifts have either left or become marginalized by ministry managers who see these people as troublemakers and boat-rockers.

High-capacity people need to be given a unique role, not because they are better, but because they are different. Savvy pastors who discover a ten-talent individual will do their best to create an opportunity for that person, not force the person into an existing position that may not fit him or her well. These pastors understand that given the right opportunity, a high-capacity person will make things happen.

WHERE TO BEGIN

The best place to begin healthy staff development is in the mirror. You will tend to attract healthy people if you're healthy and unhealthy people if you're unhealthy. Every seminarian and ministerial candidate should go through a process of in-depth counseling to look for potential gaps or family or origin issues that often deter us from efficacy, often without our knowing. It was not until middle age that I found myself in a place where I sought this help, and it has made a significant difference. I'm confident that the first half of my ministry would have been significantly improved if I'd had that help earlier in my path. Don't wait for ordination processes to require this. Be proactive and seek assistance in this area. Because we tend to reproduce who we are, staff development begins in our mirror. As one of my friends says, "The greatest gift we give to others is the energy we invest with God and in personal growth."

SUMMARY

Staffing is the single most important aspect of ministry, next to the anointing of God. It's about people. The primary responsibility of the pastor and ministry leaders is to prepare others for works of service. You do this by getting the right people into the right roles and modeling ministry by team. Think *we*, not *me*. You will undoubtedly run into snags, but the better you are at assessing people's personalities, talents, passions, and character, the more effective you'll be at unleashing the potential of your church.

9
PEOPLE DEVELOPMENT
MENTORING CHRISTIANS TO MAXIMIZE THEIR EFFECTIVENESS

W. C. Dishon
DMin, Professor of Religion and Chaplain,
Mount Vernon Nazarene University

The theme of this chapter goes to the heart of the purpose and mission of the church. When Jesus said, "Therefore go and make disciples of all nations, baptizing them in the name of the Father and of the Son and of the Holy Spirit, and teaching them to obey everything I have commanded you" (Matt. 28:19-20), he had far more in mind than gathering a crowd or making converts. While conversion is basic, it is only part of a much larger process of developing people, helping them to become all that God has had in mind for them to be, all that God has saved them for and wants them to be. Those of us involved in ministry have the awesome privilege of being part of that process!

Recently, a megachurch that has been widely recognized as a model for relevance and effectiveness in our postmodern society has concluded that while effective in gathering a crowd and even in leading people to faith in Christ, they have not been nearly as effective in helping those people to develop and grow toward maturity as disciples of Jesus Christ. That conclusion has resulted in extensive study and reflection as they seek ways to become more effective in the full challenge of the Great Commission.[1]

The task of Christian ministry is so much greater than building an organization or developing a great following. Our challenge, and privilege, is to be workers together with the Spirit in the process of developing mature disciples of Jesus Christ. *The Living Bible* paraphrase of Romans 5:2 says, "For because of our faith, he has brought us into this place of highest privilege where we now stand,

---

1. Greg Hawkins and Cally Parkinson, *Revealed: Where Are You?* (South Barrington, IL: Willow Creek Association, 2007).

and we confidently and joyfully look forward to actually becoming all that God has had in mind for us to be." What does he have in mind for us to be? He wants to work by his Spirit to help each believer develop into a Christlike person. The apostle Paul gives a succinct statement of this process and its goal: "It was he who gave some to be apostles, some to be prophets, some to be evangelists, and some to be pastors and teachers, to prepare God's people for works of service, so that the body of Christ may be built up until we all reach unity in the faith and in the knowledge of the Son of God and become mature, attaining to the whole measure of the fullness of Christ" (Eph. 4:11-13).

The Living Bible paraphrases verse 13 this way: "until finally we all believe alike about our salvation and about our Savior, God's Son, and all become full-grown in the Lord—yes, to the point of being filled full with Christ." It is that grand process that we are privileged to participate in as co-laborers with the Spirit!

When one keeps this larger, complete challenge of the Great Commission in view, one's understanding of and approach to ministry is shaped by it. For instance, is the pastor a manager or mentor? Is he or she a supervisor or shepherd? Is he or she a CEO or servant? Each of these terms, or labels, evokes a particular perception of the pastoral leader's approach to his or her role and/or function in it. Obviously, the pastor often functions as a manager of ministry. But is he or she merely a manager? Is that his or her primary function? Or should the managerial function be seen as part of a larger, even more important task of mentoring people, always seeking to move them toward maturity in Christ? A pastor who sees himself or herself as primarily a manager will approach both work and relationships much differently from a pastor who sees his or her primary task as mentoring those to whom and with whom he or she ministers. A pastor who merely manages tends to focus on tasks more than people. A manager-mentor considers the people involved in those tasks and is more concerned about their growth and development.

Interestingly, in recent years much has been written in management and leadership literature about the importance of mentoring in the business and corporate setting. One such book is titled *The Manager as Mentor* by Michael J. Marquardt and Peter Loan. In it, they state that "mentoring is sweeping through corporate America and is attracting attention in government and nonprofit sectors as well."[2] While acknowledging that "a culture of greed and individualism" has characterized some in the corporate world in the past few decades, they

---

2. Michael J. Marquardt and Peter Loan, *The Manager as Mentor* (Westport, CT: Praeger Publishers, 2006), 4.

also point to a growing number of businesses, including a number of the top 100 best companies to work for, who are seeking to nurture a culture of servant leadership. In fact, they conclude the following:

> Success in the twenty-first century will require a very strong form of transformational leadership reminiscent of Maslow's higher needs of employees: security for self and family, love and respect, opportunities to grow, and sense of purpose in life. As we shall see, the qualities that the new organization will seek in a manager are the same ones that characterize the mentor.[3]

If that is true in the corporate environment, how much more is it true in the church! Those in pastoral ministry should allow the concept of mentoring to inform their understanding of the pastoral role and to shape their approach to and function in that role. God wants to work in and through those whom he has called and commissioned to encourage and enable his people to learn, grow, and develop until they become all that he has in mind for them to be. This is the ultimate concern of the Great Commission and is the ultimate purpose of the gifts and graces of the Spirit!

Dictionaries remind us that the term "mentor" comes out of Greek mythology where Odysseus entrusted his friend Mentor to guide the development of his son, Telemachus. The term usually refers to a trusted counselor or guide. Mentoring, then, is the relationship between persons in which the mentor provides guidance, advice, support, and feedback to the mentee(s).

The pastor's role as mentor is rooted in the biblical picture of Christ as the Good Shepherd. In John 10:14, Jesus reminds us that the shepherd knows and is known by his sheep: "I am the good shepherd; I know my sheep and my sheep know me." That spells relationship! And that relationship is essential to effectiveness in helping people to become all that God wants them to be. Further, Jesus indicates that as the Good Shepherd, he will even lay down his life for his sheep, doing so out of love for them: "Greater love has no one than this, that one lay down his life for his friends" (John 15:13 NASB). The familiar words of Psalm 23 are a strong picture of that care and provision. The good shepherd always cares for the sheep and has their ultimate best interest at heart.

In his recent book *Church Is a Team Sport*, author and pastor Jim Putman calls for a return to the concept of the pastor as shepherd. He asserts that "shepherding earns you the right to lead."[4] Citing examples from his experience in a

---

3. Ibid., 19.
4. Jim Putman, *Church Is a Team Sport: A Championship Strategy for Doing Ministry Together* (Grand Rapids: Baker Books, 2008), 101.

rapidly growing and now large church, he explains what that caring looks like and involves. Putman concludes that "strategy is not what people follow. They follow a shepherd who has earned the right to be followed."[5] As the old adage says, "People don't care how much you know until they know how much you care." Then knowing how much you care, they are more likely to trust you.

That trust is essential to the mentor relationship and process. Referring to the mentoring relationship, Marquardt and Loan state that "trust is the most important part of the relationship and is especially crucial at the beginning."[6] Another recent book calls trust "the one thing that changes *everything*."[7] The author advocates the necessity of trust in all relationships, whether personal or business.

Basic to that trust is integrity. In John 10, Jesus contrasts the good shepherd with one whom he calls a thief. Church history is littered with examples of those who were involved in ministry for personal motives rather than for spiritual purposes. They could not, should not, have been trusted. Often they inflicted much pain and did great damage to people and to the church. Unfortunately, the possibility for such still exists today. Too many stories could be cited of situations where pastoral leaders have asserted strong pastoral leadership (too often a euphemism for heavy-handed, authoritative control) with little apparent regard for the impact on the people who were the church. Instead of establishing a strong, caring relationship that might have earned the trust of their congregations and thus the right to lead, these pastoral leaders doggedly insisted on their way. And the results were devastating to many of those involved.

A 2006 Forced Termination survey conducted by the Church Minister Relations' Directors network in cooperation with LifeWay Christian Resources reported that one of the major reasons for such termination was that "the pastor's leadership style is too strong."[8] It indicated that "church leaders and members can have the perception that the pastor has a leadership style that seeks to have everything his way. In some instances, this is a reality more than a perception."[9]

Whenever a pastor's leadership style is too strong or his or her personal desires/interests take precedence over the welfare of those to whom he or she ministers, it is likely that sheep (people) will be used and abused. Whenever a pastoral leader allows his or her own strong desire to "grow the church" to su-

---

5. Ibid., 216.
6. Marquardt and Loan, *The Manager as Mentor*, 65.
7. Stephen M. R. Covey, *The Speed of Trust: The One Thing That Changes Everything* (New York: Free Press, 2006), 1.
8. Bob Sheffield, "Avoid the Top 5 Reasons for Pastoral Terminations, Part 2, Leadership Style," LifeWay Christian Resources, http://www.lifeway.com/article/167645/.
9. Ibid.

persede his or her concern for the welfare of those who are the church, people are likely to be hurt. If we permit, the enemy of our souls and of the church will utilize even otherwise legitimate desires, dreams, and goals to sabotage the development of the people of God and the solid building of the church of Jesus Christ. Therefore, we must allow the Spirit to help us discern more clearly what motivates us in ministry. Is it genuine love for God and God's people? Or have we allowed other lesser, possibly personal, motivations to cloud our vision of God's purpose for his people, his church? For Christlike shepherds, there should be no conflict between our understanding of that vision and our motivations.

Such is certainly a far cry from the kind of relationship taught and modeled by Christ, the Good Shepherd. Scripture teaches that love for God and for one another should always condition and guide our expressions and actions. Both our inner motivations and our methods and actions should be consistent with the standard of love.

Just as the good shepherd is concerned about the welfare of the sheep and cares for them, so those involved in pastoral ministry are to care, genuinely care, for their flocks. Such terminology may sound archaic in our day of technological development and sophistication. Often it seems that those in pastoral leadership prefer the CEO model of the corporate world to the biblical model of the shepherd. But to the word picture of shepherd, Christ adds another that is equally challenging. In Matthew 20:25-28, he said, "You know that the rulers of the Gentiles lord it over them, and their high officials exercise authority over them. Not so with you. Instead, whoever wants to become great among you must be your servant, and whoever wants to be first must be your slave—just as the Son of Man did not come to be served, but to serve, and to give his life as a ransom for many."

Interestingly, the concept of servant leadership enunciated and personified by Christ has gained wide recognition in recent business leadership literature. Robert Greenleaf's book *Servant Leadership: A Journey into the Nature of Legitimate Power and Greatness*, first published in 1977, led to numerous others related to this topic.[10] As the term "servant" suggests, the leader "serves" those whom he or she leads. This turns upside down our usual pyramidal picture of leadership. Instead of the leader at the pinnacle of the pyramid and everyone else below, the leader is on the bottom, serving and supporting the followers. As recorded in John 13, Christ demonstrated this in the familiar incident in the upper room just before his betrayal. Though the disciples were so "position-

---

10. Robert K. Greenleaf, *Servant Leadership: A Journey into the Nature of Legitimate Power and Greatness* (New York: Paulist Press, 1977).

conscious" that they refused to serve one another, Christ stooped to serve them all by washing their feet. Then he indicated that they, and we, should likewise serve one another.

How often, though, do we in the church mimic the world, in this case, the corporate world? How often do we as pastors see ourselves as CEOs giving visionary leadership to our churches as we attempt to grow or build a great organization—all to the glory of God, of course? In a recent article titled "Church Leadership that Kills Community," Gilbert Bilezikian wrote,

> Church leaders must return to the basic teachings of the New Testament to redefine their own ministries of leadership. Far too often, the prevailing models of church leadership are uncritically imported into the church as constructs borrowed from the corporate business world or from secular systems of administration.
>
> As a result, multitudes of congregations are saddled with structures of leadership that violate the New Testament prescriptions for community life and stifle or distort its biblical expression.[11]

He then notes that Jesus specifically prohibited such imitation of the world's models when he said, "It shall not be so among you" (Mark 10:43 ESV). Jesus continues by stressing the principle of servant leadership as normative for his church (see Mark 10:40-45).

While the pastor can learn from many sources, what he or she learns elsewhere must be filtered by the teaching of God's Word. He needs to allow the shepherd-servant concept to challenge his or her presuppositions and approach to pastoral leadership and ministry. The pastor needs to remember that, like Christ, he or she is here to serve rather than to be served. The good shepherd discussed above is a servant to his sheep. Combining these two terms, the servant-shepherd becomes the biblical model for those who would enable their people to grow and develop toward the goal of becoming all that God has in mind for them to be.

The pastor's understanding of his or her role and approach to pastoral leadership are critical to the fulfillment of the challenge of the Great Commission to make disciples, to help people to develop into mature, Christlike persons who live out their faith in their daily lives as gifted, enabled, and led by the Spirit. Those who would be effective in developing mature, Christlike disciples must remember that they are called and commissioned by the Great Shepherd as under-shepherds who are to serve in his stead.

---

11. Gilbert Bilezikian, "Church Leadership that Kills Community," *WILLOW Magazine* (Summer, 2008), http://www.willowcreek.com/WCAnews/story.asp?id=WN10I32008.

The apostle Peter never forgot the risen Christ's challenge and commission, "Feed my sheep" (John 21:15-17). Probably toward the end of his life, Peter reminded those to whom he wrote,

> Be shepherds of God's flock that is under your care, serving as overseers—not because you must, but because you are willing, as God wants you to be; not greedy for money, but eager to serve; not lording it over those entrusted to you, but being examples to the flock. And when the Chief Shepherd appears, you will receive the crown of glory that will never fade away. (1 Pet. 5:2-4)

When those in pastoral ministry approach their task as servant-shepherds, mentoring in its broadest sense will be a natural result. Their work, whether preaching and teaching, planning and programming, personal counseling, or performing some other function or task, will be colored by the desire to encourage and enable the growth and development of those to whom and with whom they minister. And the caring relationships established by the servant-shepherd attitude and approach to pastoral leadership will open the way for such mentoring. When the people realize that you genuinely care, they will trust you and will be much more likely to hear what you say, whether from the pulpit or one-on-one. They will be more likely to respond positively by internalizing and acting upon what you have to say. This is true on both the individual and organizational levels. In part, this reflects the fact that they will feel secure in the knowledge that you really do have their best interests at heart; thus they can safely accept and respond to your ministry and leadership.

Assuming that a pastor's understanding of and approach to pastoral ministry is consistent with the servant-shepherd model of Christ, what does he or she do to encourage and facilitate the development of those to whom and with whom he or she ministers? Let's consider several possibilities.

First, the power of the pulpit is primary. The preaching and teaching of the Word is still central to most Protestant worship. This is especially so among those who are considered to be evangelicals. This provides the pastor with an excellent opportunity to communicate the truth of God's Word and to relate it to life in today's world. Just as Christ frequently taught the people, as in the Sermon on the Mount, so the pastor should teach the Word. When people are bombarded by so many other voices throughout the week, how critical it is that they hear the clear preaching and teaching of God's Word at every possible opportunity! In addition to personal reading and study of the Word, all benefit from the instruction and inspiration that comes through Spirit-anointed preaching. Consistent exposure to biblical truth is imperative if a person is to grow in the Lord. Not only do people hear the call of God to salvation through the clear,

Spirit-anointed preaching of the gospel, but they may also hear the Spirit speaking about issues in their lives that need to be dealt with or areas in which they need to change and grow.

If the pastor would mentor his or her congregation through preaching and teaching, the pastor must model his or her message. When the pastor's message is demonstrated in his or her life, both the pastor and the message have credibility. When people know that the pastor practices what he or she preaches, they are more likely to accept and act upon the message. Further, the servant-shepherd pastor will know the felt needs of the congregation and will relate the truth of the Word to them. Thus he or she seeks not only to comfort and encourage but also to instruct and nurture. While there will always be people who seemingly forget what they have heard as soon as they leave the service, many will know that the Spirit has spoken to them in their need and will respond in faith and with gratitude.

The goal of moving people toward Christ and Christlikeness should guide the pastor's preaching plan and preparation. As a servant-shepherd who actively cares for his or her people, the pastor will have a good sense of where the people are and the variety of needs among them. Also knowing where they need to be biblically, the pastor will prayerfully seek the guidance of the Spirit while planning his or her preaching ministry. In this process, the goal of developing Christlike disciples should be kept clearly in mind.

While there is real value in preaching series, topical or textual, there will be those times when the Spirit prompts a pastor to lay the series aside and address something that is of concern at that moment. As a parent can turn a mistake or accident into a "teaching moment," the pastor who is sensitive to the Spirit and to the needs of the congregation can turn "happenings" into valuable instructional moments. Often people are more open to the truth and the work of the Spirit in such moments and are more ready to respond.

Creativity and variety can enhance effectiveness in the preaching, teaching, learning process. Sometimes, simple "tools" can become instrumental in communicating truth and/or retaining it. For instance, in one sermon series, lighthouse refrigerator magnets were distributed to each family to be used during the series as visual reminders that we are the light of the world. A variety of props can also be used effectively for visual demonstrations or object lessons. Mundane things such as small electric appliances can demonstrate the necessity for Christians to be "plugged in and turned on" to the power of the Spirit. Today, video clips are readily available to illustrate a truth or to set up its presentation. Anything that helps to secure attention and/or to clarify the message could be used as long as it is consistent with the message and the larger biblical context.

However, anything that might distract from the message because it is too involved or requires too much time should be avoided.

Seminars and/or workshops may also contribute to this teaching-learning process. Whether conducted by the pastor or by others from within or outside the congregation, relevant, well-planned, well-timed seminars and/or workshops can be effective in helping people to move toward maturity in Christ and in his service. These settings provide extended time to consider topics that are pertinent to the people's growth and development. In today's busy culture, whole-day workshops or weekend seminars cannot be conducted frequently, but occasional ones can be highly beneficial.

Another beneficial possibility is the use of small groups. During the past three to four decades, much has been written about the role of small groups in the church. Church history solidly supports the idea that small groups can be instrumental in promoting spiritual growth as well as surrounding people with a network of caring believers. John Wesley and early Methodism are prime examples. New believers were expected to participate in small groups for the purpose of instruction, accountability, and support. And such involvement in small groups can still contribute to the spiritual growth and development of the participants.

Some believe that growth takes place best in such small groups and do their best to encourage all in the congregation to participate in one. Accordingly, church calendars may be adjusted to accommodate meeting times for such small groups. While small groups can be highly effective in nurturing a sense of caring and of community, my experience also suggests that for small groups to effectively nurture their participants toward growth, they need at least minimal structure and direction. Guidance in some progressive Bible study is helpful if the group is to do more than "share and care." While even that has obvious value, value that in its own way contributes to nurture and growth, greater growth can be achieved through the group study of the Word as well. As small groups share the truth of the Word and its relationship to their lives, as well as sharing their needs, concerns, and weaknesses, they can encourage and nurture one another toward greater growth spiritually.

In addition to small groups, one-on-one mentoring may also play a positive role in this whole process. This may be accomplished through formal structures that pair a mentee with a mentor or they may be informal and spontaneous. For instance, in one congregation that I pastored, an older lady who was an experienced Sunday School teacher was asked to take a younger lady who was a new Christian as her assistant. The goal of that arrangement was twofold: the older lady would mentor the younger one, both in her new faith and in teaching

Sunday School. The arrangement was a positive one for both. Both grew person-ally and the class grew as well. Such arrangements could be made in many areas of the church's ministry and would be beneficial to all involved.

Implied in the mentoring arrangement just mentioned is the idea of ap-prenticeship. The younger lady was an "apprentice" to the older, more experi-enced teacher. Such "on the job" training and experience could be highly valu-able in developing ministry skills. Years ago, I appealed to a lady who was a talented educator but who had never been actively involved in the ministry of the local church to assist in the direction of Vacation Bible School. She agreed to serve as assistant director for one year with the understanding that the follow-ing year she would direct and I would assist. For several subsequent years, she continued to direct VBS and to train others in the process. Such apprenticeship is an effective means of training people in ministry. And it is equally valuable in the spiritual growth and development of both persons involved. Often the men-tor expresses that he or she has learned and grown as much as a result of the relationship as the mentee.

For years while pastoring, I met with men, either one-on-one or in small groups, for breakfast for the purpose of encouraging and nurturing them in their faith. Often we used a simple Bible study as the basis for our sharing. We dis-cussed their concerns in the light of Scripture and prayed together for God's guidance and strength in applying its truth to our lives. The goal was to help these men to grow in their understanding of the Word and their application of it to their lives whether at home, in the workplace, or at the church. To borrow George Barna's phrase, the goal was to help them to "think like Jesus,"[12] to de-velop a biblical worldview, and to make decisions in the light of it. Books, such as the classic *In His Steps*, by Charles Sheldon,[13] and other more recent books that focus on living out one's faith, can be used to both stimulate discussion and to challenge people to "think like Jesus" as they live out their faith 24/7 whether in the home, neighborhood, school, or workplace.

This brings us to another tool that can be effective in helping people to be-come all that God wants them to be—books. In spite of the visual nature of to-day's society, well-selected books can be a valuable asset in this process. Across the years, I have frequently recommended books both to individuals and to the whole congregation and have often made them available either on loan or for

---

12. George Barna, *Think Like Jesus: Make the Right Decision Every Time* (Nashville: Integrity Publishers, 2003).

13. Charles Monroe Sheldon, *In His Steps: What Would Jesus Do?* (New York: Grosset & Dunlap, 1935).

purchase. A well-stocked, proactively managed church library and/or bookstore can contribute significantly to the growth of the people.

Some churches have established a series of courses that build on one another as they walk participants through scriptural teachings that are essential to understanding the Christian faith, developing a biblical worldview, discovering their spiritual gifts, and becoming active in service to others. Such courses are repeated periodically to provide opportunity for those new to the church to participate and for others to do so at the appropriate levels. This is a commendable way to intentionally encourage people to move toward maturity as disciples of Jesus Christ.

At times, such courses or similar seminars/workshops can be viewed as a means of encouraging and/or equipping people for participation in ministry in the local church. Certainly this is a worthy goal. However, it should not be our only goal. Rather, we should remember that we are called to be disciples 24/7. For most of our people that will involve life in the home, the neighborhood, and the workplace. We should remember, too, that ministry is much broader than what takes place in the church or its programs. Wherever our people are they should live lives of love and let their light shine. They should demonstrate their faith in and love for Jesus Christ as they serve those around them wherever they are, however opportunity presents itself.

This was impressed upon me by an incident that occurred during my childhood. A man who was active in the church and served in several official capacities was also a well-known businessman in the community. One day as my father, who was pastor of that church, visited with this man at his business, the businessman made the remark, "I can't operate my business on Christian principles. If I did, I'd go broke." At best, this statement revealed a woeful lack of understanding of the biblical nature of discipleship. At worst, it could have revealed a deliberate disregard for those teachings of Scripture that were "inconvenient" for this man. Unfortunately, one of the unforgettable experiences of my childhood is the sight of this man later walking down the center aisle of that church accompanied by a police escort required by a restraining order issued because of attempted bodily harm toward another person, my father. That's an extreme example, but, for me, a vivid one of the failure to consistently live out one's faith.

Another man, a printer working for a commercial printing company, came to me concerned about a large printing job that had just come to his press. The material to be printed was inconsistent with his morals and values as a Christian. He was conflicted about involvement in the printing and distribution of such material. Yet he feared losing his job if he questioned the company's involvement with this type of material or especially if he refused to have any role in printing it. After talking and praying about it with his wife and his pastor, he went in to the owner of the printing company the next day and told him that he would not be involved in the printing of such material in the future. He expected to be fired on the spot. To his surprise, the owner said, "Let me think about this tonight and we'll talk tomorrow." The next day, the owner thanked the man for standing by his principles and indicated that he had decided that he did not want his company to be involved in or associated with that kind of material and that he was cancelling the contract to print it.

The stark contrast of these stories reminds us that those of us in pastoral ministry have a tremendous challenge and awesome opportunity to help our people to understand the implications of their faith for the choices they make, even in the workplace. In an age of extreme relativism when selfishness and greed can justify almost any action, when corporate scandals leading to massive failures are increasingly common, how desperately our society needs the leavening influence of men and women of faith and conviction, men and women who have the courage and/or boldness of the Spirit to stand up for what is right, regardless of the consequences. In a time when the enemy seeks to silence the voice of faith, to exclude it from public discourse, how much more are those needed who will stand up, step forward, speak out, and do so in Christlike love and wisdom as the Spirit empowers them.

Another man was involved in corporate management when the Spirit began to nudge him about being light and salt in that setting. As he began to make some discreet inquiries, he discovered a small group of believers who were meeting for a brief Bible study and prayer during their lunch hour. He joined them. A few months later, as the national day of prayer approached, he and this small group decided to sponsor a prayer time at the flag pole in front of their corporate headquarters in the heart of one of our major cities. They posted some simple announcements around their building and hoped for 20 to 30 people to participate. On that day, more than 125 gathered at the flag pole for prayer. Seeing what was happening, people from other nearby office towers also joined them. This response encouraged other believers who worked for that company to identify themselves and other small groups were formed. Later, a "Celebrate Jesus in the Workplace" banquet attracted more than 200, with some employees coming from other cities to participate. Only God knows what could be accomplished if believers around the world would allow the Spirit to guide and empower them for ministry in the workplace.

Like the apostle Paul, who said, "I have become all things to all men so that by all possible means I might save some" (1 Cor. 9:22), our goal should be to use every means available to us that would help us to be more effective in fulfilling our purpose to make Christlike disciples, people who think like Jesus and live out their faith wherever they are. While conversion may be instantaneous, developing mature Christlike disciples is a long-term process, one that will challenge our Spirit-inspired vision, insight, and creativity, one that will require Spirit-empowered discipline and determination to implement effectively. But just as he did in the Book of Acts, the Spirit can and will do so today wherever he finds ready, willing servants. After all, ultimately this is his work, not ours. We have the awesome privilege of sharing in the work he is doing in the hearts and lives of people. And we can do so with the confidence expressed by the apostle Paul: "For because of our faith, he has brought us into this place of highest privilege where we now stand, and we confidently and joyfully look forward to actually becoming all that God has had in mind for us to be" (Rom. 5:2 TLB).

FOR FURTHER READING

Mallory, Sue. *The Equipping Church: Serving Together to Transform Lives* (Grand Rapids: Zondervan Publishing, 2001).

Ogden, Greg. *The New Reformation: Returning the Ministry to the People of God* (Grand Rapids: Zondervan Publishing, 1990).

Stevens, R. Paul. *The Other Six Days: Vocation, Work, and Ministry in Biblical Perspective* (Grand Rapids: William B. Eerdmans Publishing Company, 1999).

Trueblood, Elton. *The Incendiary Fellowship* (New York: Harper and Row, 1967).

Warren, Rick. *The Purpose-Driven Church: Growth Without Compromising Your Message and Mission* (Grand Rapids: Zondervan Publishing, 1995).

10
TEAM BUILDING
WORKING TOGETHER AS
GROUPS WITHIN THE CHURCH

Rick Ryding
EdD, Pastor, Centralia, Washington, Church of the Nazarene

❖

Chaucer begins the Prologue to Canterbury Tales with these lines: "When April comes, and with her gentle showers has banished the dreary month of March, when in every copse, and valley the young trees bud and flowers show their heads, when birds make melody in the fresh morning time, then men's hearts long for the wide air and joys of the open roads. It is the time for pilgrims."[1] In the twenty-first century, however, spring brings thoughts, not of pilgrimage, but of baseball.

I can remember those blustery days of early spring, when notices went up on the high school bulletin boards announcing an upcoming informational meeting about tryouts for the baseball and softball teams. When the day for the meeting arrived, hundreds of wannabes gathered in the school gymnasium. Tryouts were slated for the following Monday, Tuesday, and Wednesday. First cuts would be announced on Thursday.

If you were fortunate enough to make the cut, you were invited to participate in two weeks of conditioning, bonding, and rehearsing the fundamentals of the sport you thought you knew inside and out. Infielders scooped up grounders, outfielders shagged flies, and pitchers snapped off curve balls. Everyone took their turn at the plate, making contact. When the team had honed their essential skills, the coach began to develop offensive and defensive strategies and drilled the squad until everyone's response became second nature. There was no such thing as a "routine fly ball" if there was a runner on base.

Being a part of a team is not an easy experience. It's fraught with struggle and pain. You have to submit yourself to the coach and your teammates, letting

---

1. M. Sturt and E. C. Oakden, *The Canterbury Pilgrims: Being Chaucer's Canterbury Tales Retold for Children* (The Project Gutenberg, 2003), http://www.fullbooks.com/The-Canterbury-Pilgrims1.html.

go of your own dreams, wishes, and need to be the hero. It means being confident to play your best when your gifts and skills are needed and humble enough to cheer for your comrades when their gifts and skills are called upon. Baseball is not a one-man show, but a team sport that requires getting to know one another well, learning how each player thinks and responds, trusting each other to give their best, communicating openly, affirming one another when things go awry, and becoming a team that plays as one.

I learned a lot about teams from playing baseball and other sports in my younger years. But it was in my early years of ministry that I met a coach who taught me how to build ministry teams. I met him at a Serendipity workshop in Dallas, where he introduced me to a baseball diamond model of team building. His name was Lyman Coleman. In this chapter, I will share with you what I have learned about teamwork in order to create a model of effective team building.

1. BIBLICAL PERSPECTIVES ON TEAMWORK

Most of Western culture is built on the strength of the individual. Our heroes have rugged personalities and fight against overwhelming odds. Sometimes they battle all alone for truth and justice. The characters that John Wayne, Sylvester Stallone, and Jean-Claude Van Damme portrayed were solitary, tenacious, resourceful people who dealt a death blow to evil. Many cartoon and comic book champions are portrayed in the same way. Yet this is a mythic ideal. Other heroes worked in pairs in the company of trusted companions. The Lone Ranger partnered with Tonto. The Cisco Kid rode with Pancho. And Don Quixote, in search of the impossible dream, traveled with Sancho Panza.

The Bible is full of heroes who singlehandedly fought for righteousness. Yet they were not alone. God was with them, empowering them, guiding them. Noah, Abraham, Joseph, Moses, Joshua, Gideon, David, Elijah, and Paul are all solitary figures who found themselves linked up with others at certain points along their journeys. Noah had his family, Moses had Aaron, Joshua had Caleb, Gideon had 300 faithful warriors, Elijah had Elisha, and Paul had Barnabas, Silas, Timothy, and a host of other compatriots who worked with him. In reality, the kingdom of God is not about being solitary but about being in company with others for the common task of doing God's will. We need each other for encouragement, strength, perseverance, and effectiveness in our calling. The old adage from Ecclesiastes says, "A cord of three strands in not quickly broken" (3:12).

Partnerships in ministry are evident throughout Scripture. Yet how those partnerships were forged into effective teams is not always evident. One strategy was presented to Moses when he was overwhelmed with the responsibility of settling the disputes of the Israelites in the desert. Jethro, Moses' father-in-law, suggested Moses could work more effectively if he were to divide the work by appointing God-fearing and trustworthy men who would administer justice over groups of thousands, hundreds, fifties and tens. They would solve the easier cases and send the more difficult cases to Moses for his verdict. Administrative teams made Moses' work more effective and less taxing. The account is found in Exodus 18.

Perhaps the greatest example of team building comes from Jesus himself. In the calling of his disciples, Jesus is very intentional. He prays, discerns, decides, visits, and invites each of the men to leave what he is doing in order to follow him. Jesus' goal for his disciples encompasses spiritual formation, team building, and on-the-job training. He plans, from the outset, to turn over his ministry to them when he has completed his Father's will. The disciples would not only be doing what he had been doing but also be empowered to do even greater things because Jesus would send his Spirit to remind them of all he had taught them, to guide them into all truth, and to help them with the responsibility of ushering in the kingdom. Such delegation would be the catalyst for the great influx of many people who would be "called out" to become the church. They, too, would experience the same fellowship, the same formation, and the same training to carry on the ministry of Jesus.

The church would discover, early in its existence, the need for teamwork. In Acts 6, a dispute arose over an inequity in the allocation of resources. It seems the Gentile widows and orphans were not getting their fair share in the daily distribution of food. The problem was easily dealt with. Seven men, full of the Holy Spirit and faith, were appointed to organize the benevolence work of the church. This allowed the apostles to continue their work of preaching, teaching, evangelizing, and expanding the influence of the church.

The distribution of labor within the ranks of the church prompted Paul to describe the church as the "body of Christ," the dwelling place of God's Spirit and the corporeal reality among humanity. In 1 Corinthians 12, Paul articulates that Christ's body is made up of many parts, each having a specific function, yet all interdependent on all other parts. The unique gifting of each part determines its function. As cells form tissues, tissues make up organs, organs function in systems, and systems interface together to be a living organism, so the church is a living organism comprised of people with unique gifts and graces who each do their part to function together as an integrated whole. Qualities such as healthiness, togetherness, community, cohesion, intimacy, and oneness are to mark believers' lives in Christ and with each other. Yet the deep qualities of life together do not simply appear when people come to faith in Christ, become part of a local church, or begin to serve others. Just as Jesus was intentional about forming his disciples into an effective team, so we too are responsible for doing the same thing. There are methods for facilitating a healthy, functioning ministry team.

2. THE VALUE OF TEAMS

The human experience really has not changed much over the last 3,000 years. Leadership is still a difficult responsibility, particularly if you try to do it all alone. Many rely on their educations, their internships, the examples of mentors, and their reading and prayers to do their jobs effectively. Yet if pastors do not mobilize the laity to partner with them in the work of ministry, they find it to be a lonely, taxing, and stressful job. Burnout is a common malady among caregiving professionals, including ministers. Through team building, we can tap into the spiritual gifts and graces of believers, train and equip the laity, empower people for ministry, involve more folks in service, and become more effective as a church. In so doing, we are faithful to the teaching of Paul in Ephesians 4.

A team is a group of people, bearing unique gifts and skills, called together for a common purpose, and developed into a cohesive unit to reach a clear objective for a certain period of time. These can be care groups who form to listen and minister to each other. They can be learning groups who grapple with new concepts from Scripture or other spiritual resources for the purpose of growing in grace. Other people come together to complete projects using their unique knowledge and skill. Still others are missional, reaching out in creative ways to the needs of the people in their world. The goal is to be the healthy, functioning body of Christ, whose members demonstrate love for one another and for the people in their world.

To be a part of a healthy ministry team is to understand the church experientially. It is one thing to be able to talk conceptually about the characteristics and qualities of life together in Christ, and quite another to experience those qualities at work in your relationships in the body of Christ. Team building is not an optional new program to create "warm fuzzies" for your parishioners; it is an essential strategy for enabling the church to be the church.

3. IMPORTANT CONSIDERATIONS BEFORE BUILDING MINISTRY TEAMS

a. Begin Slowly and Intentionally

An important caution with any ministry idea or method is to "take it slow." This is especially true at the beginning of your work in a new parish. It is vital that you build relationships over the first few months, get a feel for who's who and how things function, and discern where, when, and how you will introduce team building into the life the church.

A major mistake made by many leaders is to see themselves as entrepreneurs whose ideas are just what their new congregation needs. To many parishioners, it must feel as if the new minister assumes the congregation is ill and needs a new magic potion. What they are anticipating is a minister who will spend time getting to know them, learning their history and listening to their ideas before launching a new campaign. New strategies for major change should not be introduced within the first six months or even within the first year if the minister wishes to have a long-term relationship with the church.

b. Investigate the Culture and Climate

Beyond getting acquainted with the individuals and families of the church, the pastor or associate must learn to assess the culture and climate of the congregation. Every organization has both a culture and a climate. In the simplest terms, an organization's culture is "the way we do things around here" and the climate is "the way we feel about how we do things around here."

Each congregation has a unique history that has been shaped by the following:

- Its demographics—urban, suburban, or rural location; the age distribution of its members; social-economic strata and trends; educational achievements of the people
- Its core values—mission and vision, theological beliefs, language, architecture, political structure, and governance
- Its history—stories of its dreams, visions, plans; the victories and defeats; the heroes and villains
- Its spiritual depth and tone—discipline, commitment, service, outreach and evangelism

Culture assessment begins by careful observation and conversation to learn the history of the church—its ups and downs, victories and failures, joys and sorrows, and so on. These are captured in the congregation's stories. Spend time listening to the tales told as you visit with congregants over meals or coffee. Values, beliefs, and convictions will reveal themselves in conversations, policies tucked away in church minutes and other records, and patterns of behavior observed when people gather for worship, fellowship, and meetings. Measures of past strategic effectiveness are revealed in statistics, master plans, and even the layout and condition of the church building.

The church's climate will be most visible in the attitudes and relational patterns of the parishioners in response to the cultural topographic of its values, structures, and patterns. Sharp, harsh terrain may be evidenced by rigid ideas, legalism, and judgmental relationships. Gentler landscapes may elicit optimistic, grace-filled relational patterns.

Team building is a prescription, not a panacea, for a healthy church. Some people or groups within the church will be ready for a "spiritual and relational fitness" program to enhance their lives and ministries. Other folks will need the healing ministry of spiritual formation in a small-group context in order for them to return to personal spiritual and relational health before they can contribute to the well-being and effectiveness of the congregation. A prayerful assessment of your local church's culture and climate will help you discern how, when, and with whom to begin team building.

c. Facilitate Team Building

As a Christian leader, you are called "to prepare God's people for works of service, so that the body of Christ may be built up until we all reach unity in the faith and in the knowledge of the Son of God and become mature, attaining to the whole measure of the fullness of Christ" (Eph. 4:12-13). This means you must see people with fresh eyes, envision their potential, nurture their hearts, and cultivate their gifts and graces so that they might love God and their neighbor with all that is within them. You are to mine the gold that lies within individuals and the church. This might be the most difficult challenge you face as a leader. There are marvelous books and courses on the art of facilitation and the craft of collaboration that will open the church to a new way of being, a new way of seeing, and a new way of being together.

d. Develop a Strategy for Team Building

While participating in a Serendipity workshop in Dallas, I experienced a small-group strategy that transformed over 200 strangers into ministering communities within eight hours. I had never experienced a method by which openness, trust, caring, and prayerful support could be so easily and safely developed among new acquaintances. In that one day, my approach to ministry was transformed. So what did Lyman Coleman, the director of Serendipity House and the leader of the workshop, do that marked me for life? He presented a philosophy and four-stage method that integrated task achievement and relationship development into a team-building model. The model he used was a baseball diamond.

Understanding the four stages of team building provides a clear picture of what it takes to build and work together as a team. For instance, a baseball team has to advance runners from first base to second base, from second to third, and then from third base on to home plate, if they are to score a run. So it is in building teams for ministry. The process must follow the same base path, from first to second to third and then home. Trying to shortcut the strategy does not work in baseball or team building. You've never seen a baseball player hit the ball to right field and then take off running to third. He would be automatically called "out." Many leaders believe they can take their church directly to third base without doing the work that must be done at first and second base. This is not a workable option. So how does the baseball diamond model work?

TEAM BUILDING: NURTURING RELATIONSHIPS AND EFFECTIVE MINISTRY[2]

Second Base: Affirming to Stabilize Community in the Midst of Storms and Chaos

Problem Solving

Communication

Decision Making

Trust

Third Base: Creating New Community Norms of Effectiveness Through Self-emptying

First Base: Storytelling to Form Community

Goal Setting

Accountability

Celebrating Our Transformation into True Community or Koinonia

First Base: Storytelling

Lyman Coleman called first base the history-giving base. Others have labeled it the "forming" stage. Reaching first base is the beginning of a process that establishes trust and develops open communication, which are both essential to a healthy team environment.

Many people are not comfortable telling their story. They are not sure what to reveal, or if it is safe to do so. Others do not see the value of wasting time on the "touchy-feely" stuff. So for many folks the norm for self-revelation is to give their "name, rank, and serial number" and then get down to business. Not so when building an effective ministry team. People need to gain insights into

---

2. The baseball diamond motif in this section is an adaption, modification, and expansion of a model developed by Lyman Coleman and included on pages 25-27 of his *Encyclopedia of Serendipity* (Littleton, CO: Serendipity House, 1980).

the other members of the team that go beyond the obvious facts. The methods used at first base are very simple. They follow five principles. They must first of all be *safe*. Early in a team-building relationship it is neither wise nor sane to invite people to share things that could be used against them. People must have a safe environment in which to tell their story from the simplest facts to the more tender experiences of their lives. Team members have to earn the right to receive the deeper, sacred thoughts and feelings of their colleagues. This should happen as trust is developed over time.

The second guideline is *confidentiality*. Simply said, what is spoken within the group stays within the group. Break confidentiality and the currency in the group's trust account will be spent!

The third principle is the experience must be *fun*. There are hundreds of categories from which to draw questions that probe safe, interesting areas of a person's experience. Personal preferences in food, music, literature, film, and vacation destinations are a few sources that gently reveal more about each participant.

The fourth principle is *incremental risk*. Over time people move from stating their preferences to addressing their perspectives on life issues with openness and honesty because their knowledge of each other has established basic trust within the group. Interpersonal knowledge is an ingredient essential to trust.

The fifth principle is *challenge by choice*. Challenge by choice means that when given an opportunity to say or do anything in the group setting, a person has the right to pass without prompting, goading, prying, critique, or judgment. Each individual has the right to say, "No, thanks. I'd rather not respond to that question just now. I'm not feeling comfortable enough to share." As relationships blossom and grow, and trust is enhanced, people do rise to ever greater challenges because they know they retain the right to respond without fear of discrimination or pain. When there is enough currency in the group's "trust account," team members will become more vulnerable with each other and will reveal more about themselves.

The best source for first base questions is the *Serendipity Encyclopedia*.[3] Used copies can still be purchased from Web-based book sellers.

Second Base: Affirmation

Second base has been pegged as the "storming" base. Why? Every group will experience conflict at some point in its life. It doesn't take long. Whenever people work together, the seeds of conflict are sown when purposes are unclear,

3. Lyman Coleman, *Serendipity Encyclopedia* (Littleton, CO: Serendipity House, 1997).

processes are rigid, perspectives and preferences differ, and resources are limited. It does not matter whether the group is a standing committee of the church board or a well-oiled team, conflict will arise. What does matter is the work done by the team at first base! If the leader has taken the time and used the methods that enabled the members of the team to get to know one another beyond the cursory interpersonal information, then the team has already deposited currency in their trust account and experienced open, honest communication. Why does this matter? It gives each team member a more thorough awareness and understanding of the other players on their team and more confidence in them as people. When the conflict and the chaos arise, each person has a clearer picture of every other person on the team and can affirm each person for who he or she is—the person's character, the person's passions, the person's ideas—not as the individual who is acting out his or her frustration over an issue.

The deep personal knowledge you have of a Christian brother or sister is a catalyst for seeing him or her through God's eyes, loving him or her unconditionally, and affirming his or her character in even the most chaotic episodes of teamwork. When circumstances change, problems become conflictual, and emotions bubble over, it is possible to become affirming and redemptive and then take the time to deal with the festering issue. Declare a hiatus and move into a problem-solving mode. How does this work?

Creative Problem Solving

Many people see conflict as chaos that leads to dissolution of a team or congregation. Other folks recognize group turbulence as an opportunity for creativity; a means of capitalizing on the diversity of the group and its ideas.

- Begin by acknowledging the team is in conflict and that this is normal.
- Affirm your faith in each of the persons on the team and your confidence in them to work through the crisis.
- Identify and define the problem that is stirring up the emotions, stalling effective work, and threatening the team.
- Agree on the method you will use to address the problem, and the rules that will guide the process and protect team members and the integrity of the team. This means you stay focused on the main issue and not individuals on the team or in the church.
- Open several ways in which to communicate during the problem-solving process. Open dialogue can be supported with discussion in pairs and trios. If issues are particularly dicey, then comments can be jotted down on sheets of paper and read anonymously to the group. Avoid generalities. Always be specific.

- Acknowledge all side issues and agree to deal with them at another time.
- Suspend all judgment on persons, their character, and their motives. Intentionally listen to each person in order to hear what he or she is saying and feeling. Each person needs to be able to say in response to the listener's restatement, "Yes, that is what I am thinking, saying, and feeling."
- Seek a "win-win" outcome by focusing on concerns and not endorsing positions.

Conflict is inevitable, but it does not have to be detrimental or destructive. Storms can be weathered. Chaos can be transformed into order. Differences can be used to advantage to solve problems creatively and make decisions collaboratively.

A team that is comfortable with its uniqueness and the differing perspectives of its members can experience freshness and a vitality that breaks down the wall of conventional thinking and moves them "outside the box." From this vantage point, the team members can see new possibilities that never crossed their radar. Methods like brainstorming invite participants to see the sky as the limit, offer far-out ideas, and then piggyback more creative options on top of these wild ideas. This is where the "creative zone" begins to produce the solutions that did not exist before. Now the team is experiencing new ways of being together as a group. This is a collaborative approach to problem solving that sets the stage for making team-based decisions where all the members are of "one mind." This can only happen when the team leader or coach has worked the process to establish mutual appreciation and respect between team members.

Collaborative Decision Making

There are many ways to come to a decision in a group. As a leader you can simply make the decision, take a straw poll of your members, solicit insights through interviews and discussions, cast a ballot, or seek consensus. With a well-functioning team, the foundation has been laid to move toward an integrated decision that is owned by the team. Ownership is the critical issue. If a group of people has invested in the problem-solving and decision-making processes, then the final outcome and its implementation will be more effective. Why? There are more advocates for the decision, more people who believe in the required course of action, and cheerleaders who will encourage and motivate the congregation to support the decision and the new direction on the team or congregation!

A collaborative style of decision making invites rich discussion, creative problem solving, openness to a variety of ideas that lie outside the box, and a tendency to refine the final solution to make it truly fit the local situation. Though some would disagree, this process of problem solving, decision making, and community building is modeled on an old story known as "Stone Soup," attributed by some to the Brothers Grimm and popularized by Marcia Brown.[4] The story describes how three soldiers returning home from a war stop by a small town to request a meal and a place to sleep. Finding the townspeople suspicious and reticent to give them food and lodging, the soldiers alter their request to include only a fire, a large pot, some water, and three large smooth stones with which they can make stone soup. Intrigued by the possibility of soup from stones, the villagers provide the essential elements and finally all the ingredients for a community feast and festival! What did the soldiers do to elicit such support? They used curiosity to invite participation and ownership in the meal as each person brought what they had to the soup pot. A simple meal of hearty soup became a village celebration. As the villagers later declared, "Imagine! Soup from stones!"

Collaborative decision making is simply inviting people to participate in a creative project in which they help design, develop, and implement creative new ministries. In the process, they discover the new heights to which they can go as they work together as teams under the direction of the Holy Spirit.

Third Base: Effectiveness

Having reached third base, the team has come to the place where they have achieved a new way of being, a new way of seeing, and a new way of being and working together as a group. They have a new love and respect for one another, new confidence in their ability to work together, and greater effectiveness in doing what they have been called together to do. All this became possible because they followed the "base path" from first to second and on to third. Being transformational, this process brings about a change within each team member. Each person has to let go of his or her own ambitions and perspectives in order to be guided by the same vision, be bound together by the same Spirit and purpose, and be sustained by the same selfless love and concern for one another. This is inherently a spiritual process that must be embraced if effectiveness is to be realized.

At this stage of the team-building experience, the old has gone and the new has come. The group has established a new set of norms for their life together as a ministry team. They have become more than a group of people gathered to complete a task; they are a compassionate community who love and care for one another. This hospitality—the ability to create a safe haven where you are always welcome to be yourself—is the foundation for ministry to others. In this new rela-

---

4. Marcia Brown, *Stone Soup* (New York: Simon and Schuster, 1947).

tionship, each member has the opportunity to be open with and accountable to the other players on the squad about their own concerns, issues, and goals. These may be personal, relational, professional, or spiritual in nature. As the members are vulnerable with their partners in ministry, they create an environment of love and submission, confession and forgiveness, prayer and encouragement, discernment and guidance, wisdom and confidence. In this safe and healing place, a person can be transformed and make course corrections on his or her journey. The team is an incubator for spiritual development and formation.

As each person experiences this renovation of love, the team becomes a mature body of believers whose life together is expressed in deeper dimensions of humility, love, and ministry toward one another, as well as evolving goals for their service to the church, community, and the world.

Home Base: Christian Community

In baseball, you must reach home to score a run. In team building, to reach home means to rejoice in the Christian community we have experienced as we have reached the goals we have set for ourselves, our ministry team, and our congregation. At other times, when we have not realized our goals, we still celebrate what God has done within each person and the life of the group. That is, we are rejoicing in loving others, being loved in return, and what we have experienced and achieved together. This is expressed in our worship, celebrations, and ongoing service as together we go deeper into the love of God by rounding the diamond again and again.

The essential requirement of the New Testament is that we love one another. Christian spirituality is all about becoming like Christ as individuals and as a body of believers. The process begins with confession, repentance, and redemption, and it continues with an awareness of sin's deep roots within our nature and a desire for cleansing and emptying and the infilling of the Holy Spirit. We believe these experiences are wrought by grace through faith in a moment of time, yet continue as growth in grace over time, while we encounter life together in Christian community. As Paul said to the Corinthians, "And we, who with unveiled faces all reflect the Lord's glory, are being transformed into his likeness with ever-increasing glory, which comes from the Lord, who is the Spirit" (2 Cor. 3:18).

How and When Do You Begin Team Building?

Team building is more a way of life than it is a program to be implemented. It is an experience that embraces the heart and mind and penetrates the practice of ministry. People cease to be a problem to be solved but become a mystery to be entered into. You see your people with fresh eyes as you listen to their stories— their histories, their joys and sorrows, their victories and struggles, their passions and weaknesses. You find yourself asking simple "get-acquainted" questions that are both safe and fun while you chat in the foyer, meet for coffee, or while driving to an event. Small-group life is restructured to make room for storytelling as an essential element to growing together with trust, openness, and love. Committees and boards can find moments in their business agendas to share nuggets of information with each other. A word of caution! There can be a steep learning curve for people who expect the working groups of the church to be "all business." Carefully planned history-giving experiences slowly change the culture and climate of a group's life to be more compassionate, creative, and effective.

When you are ready to build the first ministry team, it is vital that you begin with a weekend retreat! A place apart is the perfect environment in which to facilitate the following:

- Protracted history-giving experiences
- Trust-building initiatives
- Communication exercises
- Tension and conflict resolution
- Brainstorming creative new ministry ideas
- Becoming familiar with the personal spiritual formation process
- Dreaming
- Setting goals
- Forming strategies for the year ahead

If the retreat facility has either a ropes course or set of initiative elements, the retreat center staff becomes an additional resource for you. Reconnoiter the retreat facility in advance of the retreat, explain your goals to the program staff, and explore the possibilities they have for using these tools to facilitate building your team.

Final Thoughts

While building an effective team, you will also be nurturing Christlike disciples who are equipped to trust, to communicate openly and with vulnerability, to affirm one another during turbulent times, and to see diversity as a source of creativity. Christian community is comprised of people who have emptied themselves of all but love in order to be hospitable and redemptive to one another and to all who enter their lives. The goal of team building is to create effective ministry that flows from the heart of each individual and the team!

11
Managing Outreach
Orienting the Church Toward Achieving Its Mission

Bob Whitesel

DMin, PhD, Professor of Missional Leadership,
Wesley Seminary at Indiana Wesleyan University

"You can give people responsibility and authority; but without information
they are helpless. Knowledge is the ultimate power tool."
—Bill Gates[1]

══════════════════════ ◆ ══════════════════════

Growth of a Little Country Church

Corinth United Methodist Church sits on a peaceful country road only a few miles from a bustling university town. Less than a mile from the church, new homes are being built to accommodate Gen X and boomer families moving into the area. However, for most of these new residents, Corinth UMC is invisible.

For many years, Corinth UMC had been situated in the ideal location. It was across from a small schoolhouse that had been the center of this farming community until 1955. After the school closed and relocated, a four-lane bypass had cut a swath across the adjacent farmland, cutting off Corinth from the nearby town. Although the road on which Corinth sat intersected the bypass, few community residents traveled the country road because it was a dead-end lane.

However, Corinth had an energetic new pastor and a dedicated team of lay leaders. They were of one accord in realizing their future was hampered by their nearly invisible location. Subsequently, a team was launched to map out appropriate programs and a marketing strategy to inform the community of the new ideas emanating from the church down this "dead-end" country road.

---

1. Bill Gates, *Business @ the Speed of Thought* (New York: Warner Books, 1999), 408.

They met with me to discuss their choice of a leader for their marketing team. "We've chosen June Mason (a pseudonym)," began Jack. "She's got the best understanding of what needs to be done." June's farm abutted the church property, and she was the matriarch of one of the oldest families in the church. Definitely of the builder generation, and somewhat refined and retiring, she was not the candidate I envisioned. It seemed to me she might be out of touch with the marketing strategies and outreach ideas this church needed. I was soon convinced otherwise.

"We built the church here in 1937 because we wanted to be across from the school, to minister to families," June said quietly. "We've got to keep that tradition alive. And the steeple was our advertisement for years," she continued. "We built the prettiest steeple and lit it too. Some people complained about putting a light on it. But it was to remind the people that there was a church here. But now people can't see it from the bypass. It's too far away. So we're going to start ministries that will be what our steeple used to be: a light to tell the community that Christ is here."

Over the next several months, June's team created an amazingly sophisticated strategy consisting of family-oriented programming, advertisements, radio ads, an eye-catching logo, a billboard, directional signage to the church, and even advertisements on placemats in nearby restaurants. The exhaustive nature and creativity of this plan was nothing short of amazing, especially considering that it had been created under the auspices of someone who did not fit my image of the ideal "marketer." I soon learned that June's appearance belied her outgoing and likeable personality. Her deep concern for the church reflected an intuitive understanding of its problems. In addition, she had run a farm for many years. Whether dealing with grain, cattle, or churches, she understood the importance of marketing.

Before long, Corinth was enjoying a surprising influx of newcomers—more in one three-month span than in the entire previous year. With a newcomer assimilation process in place, Corinth began to add new Sunday School classes and fill its daycare center. This little country church in the wrong location was buzzing with an excitement that amazed visitors. June had led the charge into the world of marketing, a realm many churches hesitate to go.

MARKETING: AN IGNOBLE TASK?

Many churches hesitate because they consider marketing strategy to be an ignoble task for the church. There is no such timidity in the business world. According to research conducted by executive recruiting firm Korn/Ferry International, most CEOs and executives start out in the company's marketing division.[2] Professors Louis Boone of the University of Alabama and David Kurtz of the University of Arkansas point out that approximately fifty percent of the cost of all products is due to marketing costs the company feels are necessary to reach people.[3]

Why does the business world feel so compelled to invest in marketing, while the church eschews such endeavors? The reason may be marketing's reputation for abuse. Bait-and-switch advertising, false advertising, price fixing, and deceptive pricing are just a few of the maladies that have tarnished marketing's image. However, in every human realm, including marketing, there is the temptation for manipulation and exploitation. In our discussion of managerial ethics, chapter 18 of this book underscores this reality. Although marketing can be abused, it must not be shunned simply because of its potential for misuse. Marketing is a valuable tool for getting across a message. As such, it becomes another resource the Christian can use to communicate the Good News.

Let's begin our investigation into marketing with a definition: Marketing is basically about meeting needs. Viewing marketing through this lens, we can identify four components.

The Four Stages of Marketing

Stage One: Identify the needs of people.

Stage Two: Design something, such as a ministry or program, to meet those needs.

Stage Three: Communicate information about those ministries and services to the people who need them.

Stage Four: Evaluate the satisfaction levels of those who receive the ministry and/or service.

From this four-stage definition, many church leaders immediately will recognize that they are already involved in some marketing. Most churches are engaged in stages one and two. However, because many people regard stage three as suspect, it is the stage the church often ignores.

In chapters 3 and 4 of this book, which focus on strategic planning, we examined stages two and four.[4] So in this chapter we shall address stages one and three.

---

2. Louis E. Boone and David L. Kurtz, *Contemporary Marketing,* 11th ed. (Mason, OH: South-Western Publishing, 2004), xxxix.

3. Ibid.

4. Often, the four stages of marketing are addressed by several disciplines concurrently. In the business world, the marketing department may work with executive management to establish strategic goals. Thus stages are often a combined effort of several disciplines. This is why we address stages two and four in the earlier chapters on strategic planning.

"Outreach" Instead of "Marketing"

Before going further, let's look at an alternative designation for marketing. Because the term "marketing" has a somewhat callous resonance in church circles, I shall use the more amenable (and theologically defensible) term "outreach."[5] By outreach, I will mean a strategy that addresses the same four areas or tasks explained above and diagrammed in figure 11.1.

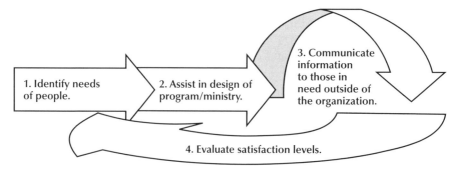

Fig. 11.1. The tasks of outreach

STAGE ONE: IDENTIFY THE NEEDS OF PEOPLE

To Whom Are We Reaching Out?

To identify the needs of those to whom we are reaching out, we first must ask the question, "Which people?" In the business realm, this group is often referred to as an organization's target. But "target" has an unpleasant ring in the ears of many Christians. However, the term "mission field" historically has been an acceptable synonym, one that identifies the people a church feels it has a mission to reach.

Avoid Outreach Myopia

As a church begins stage one, it should first conduct an honest self-appraisal to ensure that it is not suffering from outreach myopia. Labeled "marketing myopia" in the business world, this is the malady that occurs when an organization is too shortsighted to see beyond what it is doing now. AT&T for years saw itself strictly as a telephone company. After deregulation, it had to escape this

---

5. The business world also has begun to embrace "outreach" as an alternative term for marketing. In many universities, such as The Pennsylvania State University, the marketing department is now called Penn State Outreach Marketing and Communications (http://www.outreach.psu.edu).

myopic view and transform itself into a multifaceted communication network. This expanded understanding thwarted myopic tendencies and allowed AT&T to successfully branch out into new and profitable areas, including the Internet, cable TV, international satellites, and wireless communication.

Outreach myopia arises when a church becomes so consumed with the day-to-day running of the organization that it fails to address or identify the needs of those outside their fellowship. Jesus appears to address this myopia when he urged his disciples to "open your eyes and look at the fields! They are ripe for harvest. Even now the reaper draws his wages, even now he harvests the crop for eternal life" (John 4:35-36). Jesus' analogy that his disciples must be harvesters harvesting a "crop for eternal life" reminded them to see their mission field and its magnitude.

Find Your Mission Field

Finding your mission field requires hard-nosed investigation into two areas: (1) the things that you do well and (2) the needs of your mission field.

What an organization does well can be defined in its core competencies. However, identifying the needs of your mission field involves a five-step process. Let's look at this graphically in figure 11.2 before we investigate each section individually.

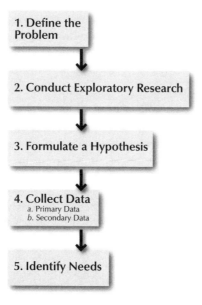

Fig. 11.2. The outreach research process

1. Define the Problem

Defining the problem begins with conducting a strategic analysis of the organization. This includes a SWOT analysis, which investigates the strengths, weaknesses, opportunities, and threats to the organization.

In the church management field, identifiable church illnesses are often referred to as "pathologies."[6] These terms are employed because problem conditions are more readily embraced by congregants when described in terms of maladies that affect the "body" of Christ (the church). Common church illnesses include the following:

- **Geriatrophy**. This term comes from combining the word "geriatric," the branch of medicine that deals with the diseases of old age, with "atrophy," indicating a wasting away or failure to grow. Geriatrophy is the wasting away of an aging church because it does not have an influx of younger generations. This is the primary killer of churches in America. Younger generations often feel the aging congregation neither sufficiently understands nor reaches out to them. Thus younger generations go elsewhere. This further weakens the aging congregation, leading to an eventual and painful demise. *A House Divided: Bridging the Generation Gaps in Your Church* describes a seven-step growth process to facilitate the peaceful coexistence of three generations.[7]
- **Ethnikitis**. This church illness is caused by a change in the ethnicity of a neighborhood. It is the second biggest killer of churches in America.[8]
- **People Blindness**. This malady prevents a church from seeing the important cultural differences that exist between groups of people who live in geographical proximity. These differences tend to create barriers to the acceptance of the church's message.[9]
- **Hyper-cooperativism**. Hyper-cooperativism describes a local church's loss of identity when all or most of its outreach efforts are conjoined with those of other congregations. Studies have shown that in interdenominational outreach efforts, fewer people respond to the outreach.[10]
- **Koinonitis**. Sometimes called "fellowship inflammation," this term is derived from the Greek word for fellowship, *koinonia*. This describes a

---

6. C. Peter Wagner, *Your Church Can Be Healthy* (Nashville: Abingdon Press, 1979).

7. Whitesel and Hunter, *A House Divided*.

8. C. Peter Wagner, "Principles and Procedures of Church Growth: American Church Growth" (lecture, Fuller Theological Seminary, Pasadena, California, January 31-February 11, 1983).

9. Ibid.

10. Wagner, *Frontiers in Missionary Strategy*, 139-60.

church in which spirituality and unity are so high that newcomers and/ or unchurched people are hindered in their efforts to be assimilated. If growth does occur, it is usually "transfer" growth of Christians from other churches.

- **St. John's Syndrome**. This illness is congregational "lukewarmness" about which Christ warned in Revelation 3:16. It is characterized by an apathetic attitude toward spiritual disciplines and formation. It is often the disease of second-generation churches.
- **Sociological Strangulation**. This malady occurs when the facilities/staff are unable to keep up with the influx of people. The famous "80 percent Rule" is that if in any regular service your worship facility is 80 percent full, you are entering into sociological strangulation. "The shoe must never tell the foot how big it is," stated Robert Schuller.[11]
- **Cardiac Arrest**. As the name implies, this is a serious and all-too-common church illness. Sometimes, the "heart" of the congregation has been so hurt by some traumatic event that the congregation would rather die than continue on as before. *Staying Power: Why People Leave the Church Over Change and What You Can Do About It* examines this serious problem and explains how unity can be preserved.[12]

When Are You Not Ready for Marketing?

Several of the above maladies are internal illnesses that must be dealt with before a church can initiate an external outreach strategy. Koinonitis, St. John's Syndrome, and Cardiac Arrest in particular must be addressed before a church reaches beyond its walls. In such circumstances, it is more important to make progress toward internal unity and wholeness than it is to initiate an aggressive outreach strategy.

Don't Market Beyond Your Reach

Defining your problem also means defining the scope of that problem. If your problem is Geriatrophy and you need to reach younger generations, first determine how far you should expect those generations to travel to your church. Marketing or reaching out across a geographic zone that is too large may limit your success.

In looking at outreach, we can identify two limiting factors regarding scope: geographic reach and social reach.

11. As quoted in Wagner, "Principles and Procedures of Church Growth."
12. Whitesel, *Staying Power*.

Geographic reach means finding the geographic size of your mission field. For most congregations, this will be the size of the area from which they attract existing and potential constituents. To discover your geographic reach, take these five steps:

1. Place pins representing existing attendees on a physical (or computer) map. Draw a boundary around the area where most of these pins lie. This is your rough geographic boundary (RGB).

2. Look at major transportation arteries that connect your church location with potential constituents. Compute how far along these arteries a person could travel in 12½ minutes. (However, if you live in a metropolitan suburb or a rural area, increase this to 22½ minutes.) In a different color ink, draw a boundary around this area. This is your potential geographic boundary (PGB).

3. Now draw a third boundary (using a third color ink) that roughly falls between the two boundaries. This is your combined geographic boundary (CGB). Most of your outreach should be confined to avenues that target your mission field in your CGB.

4. Recalculate your RGB, PGB, and CGB yearly.

Social reach means that a congregation should not attempt to reach out to those who are too far removed from its categories of age and/or ethnicity, unless it is willing and prepared to make sweeping cultural changes. For example, a congregation comprised of Hispanic builders/seniors (born in and before 1945) may successfully reach out to Hispanic boomers. The only social barrier will be age. However, if that same Hispanic builder/senior congregation sought to reach out to Asian-American boomers, the combination of two social barriers (age and ethnicity) might thwart the process.

Another more common scenario would be if a predominately builder/senior Caucasian church tried to reach out to boomer Hispanics moving into the neighborhood. The combination of two social barriers (age and ethnicity) means that success would be more tenuous. However, if a congregation's survival was at stake, such chasms might need to be bridged. In such circumstances, the reaching organization will have to radically subdue its own preferences and even adopt the culture of those they seek to reach. This is similar to missionaries in a foreign mission field, who are expected to respect and even embrace the cultural preferences of those they seek to reach. The lesson here is to cross as few social barriers as necessary for survival when calculating your church's mission field.

2. Conduct Exploratory Research

The next step in locating your mission field requires researching the problem, both theoretically and practically. This is often the second most overlooked step (next to step three). In step two, leaders should undertake the following:

1. **Read** books, articles, research, Internet pages, and so on (both Christian and secular), on the perceived problem. Do not limit yourself to one source. Delve into a variety of information sources.

2. **Look for successful examples** of organizations that have overcome the problem you are facing. More often than not, problems besetting your church will be common to the other churches in the area. Overcome any inclination toward competition or envy, and enthusiastically investigate churches that have been successful in overcoming the problem you are encountering. But be careful that you do not simply accept their explanations. Pastors often attribute growth to the wrong sources.[13] Thus, conduct an independent investigation of the churches you think might be overcoming the problem you face. Look closely, and use impartial judgment.

3. **Get outside help**. During this stage, an outside consultant is invaluable. Denominational departments often offer such help, but these can be influenced by denominational preferences or politics. As is also true in the business world, an independent and outside consultant may be the best utilization of your money. The Great Commission Research Network serves as a clearinghouse for consultants trained in the mechanisms, procedures, and strategies of church management, growth, and health.[14]

3. Formulate a Hypothesis

Step three is the most overlooked area in the process of identifying your church's mission field. Frequently, initial insights gained in steps one and two can be so euphoric that leaders will forget to sit down and codify the problem. Before researching the mission field, it is imperative to know what you are looking for.

For example, many churches will discover that they are suffering from unbalanced generational ratios. In the case of Corinth Church, June's marketing strategy team discovered that 70 percent of the congregants were aging builders/seniors (those generations born in and before 1945). However, an investigation of county records revealed that boomer and Generation X families (those fami-

---

13. Whitesel, *Growth by Accident, Death by Planning*.
14. The Great Commission Research Network, http://www.ascg.org/home.

lies born after 1945) made up 72 percent of community residents and were the area's fastest growing segment. So the team discovered that Corinth Church's generational ratios were opposite the community's ratios. Thus the church was suffering from geriatrophy.

Corinth then formulated a hypothesis: "Corinth is dying because we do not have programs and ministries attractive to community residents born after 1945." To test this hypothesis, they advanced to the next step.

4. Collect Data

To confirm its hypothesis, an organization must look at primary and secondary data.

Secondary Data

Secondary data is data that is already published. The marketing strategy team at Corinth Church investigated governmental, denominational, and business data to better understand the new people moving into the area. It soon became clear that these new people were boomers and Gen Xers with young children. The large home sites and quiet country life were attractive to families who were moving to the outskirts of the bustling university town.

Secondary data resources available from county offices, planning commissions, libraries, and the Internet include (but are not limited to) the following:

1. *Monthly Catalog of the United States Government Publications*, published annually
2. *Statistical Abstract of the United States,* published annually[15]
3. *Survey of Current Business*, updated monthly
4. *County and City Data Book*, published every three years on counties and cities with over 25,000 residents

Primary Data

Primary data is information collected specifically for the task at hand. Usually this is conducted through a process called "sampling." Sampling requires taking a representative "sample" of an overall population and deducing certain area-wide conclusions. While those unfamiliar with sampling may question its accuracy, research confirms sampling to be a very reliable barometer of community needs.

A House Divided: Bridging the Generation Gaps in Your Church explains how a church can conduct a simple sampling of community needs. These sug-

---

15. U.S. Census Bureau, "Statistical Abstracts," http://www.census.gov/prod/www/abs/statab.html.

gestions appear below in abbreviated form. For a fuller explanation (along with sample phone and interview scripts), see especially chapter 7 of *A House Divided,* "Step 3: Identify the Needs of the Unchurched."[16]

Methods to Identify the Needs of the Unchurched

Focus Groups

As small gatherings of six to twelve individuals, focus groups are designed to bring to the surface feelings that often remain buried in one-on-one interviews. Focus groups help organizations "focus" on information or advice from the group. Four guidelines should direct a focus group.

1. *Group makeup.* Groups should be made up of those in your mission field. For example, convene a group of nonattendees if you wish to solicit advice on what nonattendees are looking for in a church. Regrettably, churches often poll existing members to discover what should be done to minister to outsiders. This will yield an inaccurate perspective—one conceived by those already on the inside. You will get more of the same and, thus, more of what has not worked in the past.

2. *Group location.* Choose a neutral location in which to convene a group. Many unchurched or dechurched people will feel awkward in an ecclesial setting. Put them at ease by meeting them on their own turf, such as in a library, school, city building, or other public facility.

3. *Meeting setup.* It is important to have a comfortable and private meeting venue. Make sure the chairs are comfortable. Have writing utensils, paper, and refreshments available. In addition, ensure that the location is not open to public scrutiny. People will share more freely if they feel they are in a comfortable, private, and accommodating environment.

4. *Use a moderator.* A moderator will help to facilitate, but not dictate the direction of the conversation.
   a. The moderator's job is to
      (1) put the focus group participants at ease;
      (2) implement the focus group agenda;
      (3) steer the group away from controversial topics and injurious remarks;
      (4) tactfully elicit comments from less verbal members;
      (5) keep the discussion on track.
   b. The moderator's agenda should pattern itself along these lines:

Introductions

Moderator: "Let's introduce ourselves . . ." *(Moderator introduces himself or herself. Participants introduce themselves.)*

---

16. Whitesel and Hunter, *A House Divided,* 144-60.

MODERATOR: "The purpose of our focus group is to discover *(put your hypothesis here)*. Your advice will be very helpful to us. In addition, the meeting will conclude promptly at *(give the time)*." (In the case of a church suffering from *geriatrophy*, the hypothesis might be: "*The purpose of our focus group is to discover what people your age are looking for in a church . . .* ")

Data Gathering (Sample)

MODERATOR: "Why do you think some people of your age choose not to attend church services?"

PARTICIPANTS: *(Response)*

MODERATOR: "What do you perceive to be the needs of people your age?

PARTICIPANTS: *(Response)*

MODERATOR: "What needs of people your age can the church best address?

PARTICIPANTS: *(Response)*

MODERATOR: "If you could tell the pastor of *(your organizational name)* one thing, what would it be?

PARTICIPANTS: *(Response)*

(Close the meeting with acknowledgment and gratitude.)

One-on-One Interviews

These types of interviews are the best avenues for obtaining detailed information. However, they also can be intimidating for the interviewee. Thus it is best for a church to approach this judiciously, undertaking the following guidelines:

1. **Door-to-door or street interviews**. These types of interviews are not as well received today as they were in the 1950s and 60s. Some groups, such as Campus Crusade for Christ, successfully used these methods to speak personally with millions about their relationship with Christ. However, because overly zealous marketers have utilized these approaches, today it is best to proceed with caution. If you decide to conduct a door-to-door or street interview, follow the sample guidelines in figure 11.3 to ensure that you conduct your research effectively and appropriately.

2. **Phone Interviews**. Because of the caveats of door-to-door and street interviews, the telephone interview has become increasingly popular. Again, interviewees may be reticent because of the overuse and questionable practices of a few. Proceed cautiously, using a variation of the sample survey in figure 11.3.

3. **The number of interviews required**. Demographers have discovered that a random sample of 1,500 people can provide surprisingly accurate information about the larger population as a whole.[17] However, many congregations will find this beyond their "person power" to conduct. Nonetheless, a reasonably

---

17. David G. Myers, *Exploring Psychology* (New York: Worth Publishers, 1990), 13.

effective alternative is to sample 1 percent of your mission field. For instance, if you discovered from the U.S. Census abstract that there are 30,000 Gen Xers in your mission field, then a sample of 300 (1 percent of 30,000) would give a reasonably accurate picture of their needs.

The questions in figure 11.3 can serve as a guide to testing your outreach hypothesis in any of the above types of one-on-one interviews.[18] (In this example, the goal will be to uncover the needs of a younger generation.)

"Hello. My name is *(name)* and I am conducting a short survey for *(name of congregation)* in *(city/town)*. Would you mind if I asked you a few anonymous and brief questions?"

- *If* "YES," *continue.*
- *If* "NO," *conclude by saying,* "Thank you for your consideration. Good-bye" *(if through the phone), or* "Have a good day" *(if through personal interview).*

Survey Parameters

"We wish to interview individuals who were born in the years *(year)* to *(year)*.[19] Were you born in or during these years?"

- *If* "YES," *continue.*
- *If* "NO," *conclude by saying,* "Thank you for your time. Good-bye/Have a good day."

Open-ended Questions

QUESTION NO. 1: "What do you think a church could do to help people age _____ to _____?"

QUESTION NO. 2: "Why do you think people age _____ to _____ do not attend church services?"

QUESTION NO. 3: "What are people your age looking for in a church?"

QUESTION NO. 4: "What advice would you give me so that a church could help people age _____ to _____ more effectively?"

QUESTION NO. 5: "Are you actively involved in a church, synagogue, mosque, or other religious house of worship at this time?"

Conclusion

"Thank you for your time. Your advice will help *(name of congregation)* of *(city/town)* better address the needs of people in our community(ies). Thank you. Good-bye" *(if through the phone), or* "Have a good day" *(if through personal interview).*

Fig. 11.3. Sample survey questions

---

18. Whitesel and Hunter, *A House Divided*, 156-58.

19. For Generation X, birth years are 1965 to 1983; for boomers, 1946 to 1964; and for builders, 1945 and before. Birth years are easier to use than specific ages, since the latter will keep changing. However, it is helpful to use the exact ages in the remainder of this survey.

5. Identify Needs

Finally, your task is to identify the specific needs of your mission field so that you can select strategies based upon these needs. Several processes can be helpful in this area. One of the most productive and easiest to implement is called the debriefing and correlation procedure. This process is threefold:

1. Immediately upon completion of the interview, meeting of the focus group, or other sampling method, the leader(s)/moderator(s) should rank the needs they perceived. At that same time, they should write down creative ideas and suggestions generated during the interview process.
2. After all interviews have been conducted, the leaders/moderators should meet on their own and combine all rankings into a master list, ranking them from most to least prevalent.
3. Gather all leaders/moderators and correlate responses and suggestions gleaned from the interview process. Then proceed to stage 2.

STAGE TWO: SELECT STRATEGIES TO MEET THE NEEDS OF YOUR MISSION FIELD

We investigated the tools for selecting strategies on strategic planning in chapters 3 and 4. With that in mind, let's look at figure 11.4 to see how strategies that might meet the needs of those in Corinth's mission field could be graphed.

A List of Needs This list of needs was culled from the data-gathering process.	Potential Strategies Brainstorm to create a list of potential strategies.[20]
Child care for working mothers of pre-school children.	Day care provided by the church. Carpooling service for preschoolers in the area. Have the youth group organize child care on Saturday morning so mothers can grocery shop or spend time with other mothers. Serve a breakfast for mothers with pre-school children once a week from 6 to 8 a.m. Staff it with stay-at-home mothers or Builder/Seniors.

---

20. Whitesel, *Growth by Accident.*

After-school care for school-age children.	Kids' club provided by church after school day ends.
	Join with other community churches to provide after-school recreational activities.
	Start an after-school choir called "Praise Kids."

Fig. 11.4.[21] **Mission needs and strategies**

Use figure 11.4 as a basis for the marketing team and the strategic planning team to rate each strategy based upon how well it builds upon your SWOT analysis. Then implement each strategy (the most highly rated first), as resources and time allow.

STAGE THREE: COMMUNICATE INFORMATION ABOUT APPROPRIATE MINISTRIES AND SERVICES TO NEEDY PEOPLE

Outreach Caveats

Employing football terminology, author Herb Miller once urged churches to "throw your message to wider receivers."[22] By this, Miller meant that a church must share its message effectively and widely to those outside its walls. Many churches attempt this but often fail to witness any response from the community because of one or more of the following caveats:

1. **Results are expected too quickly.** Many times a budget committee will allocate money to advertising and then attempt to judge success or failure within a short span of time. In the marketing realm, years may be required to establish customer loyalty. Thus marketing is a long and slow endeavor. While evaluation is important, evaluating results of strategies that have been implemented for less than eighteen months to two years can be hasty. Visiting a church (much less joining one) is an important cultural, spiritual, and personal decision. Often a great deal of time will elapse before results are identifiable.

2. **Christians advertise in the wrong places, typically to other Christians**. Every Easter I am amazed by the sheer number of churches that advertise on the religious page of local newspapers. Nestled among

---

21. Whitesel and Hunter, *A House Divided*, 160.
22. Herb Miller, *How to Build a Magnetic Church* (Nashville: Abingdon Press, 1987), 15.

dozens, if not hundreds, of similar ads, a small church such as Corinth has little chance of increasing visitor flow. Unfortunately, ads on the church page are predominantly read by other Christians, not by the unchurched people most churches are attempting to reach. Unchurched people most likely decide what they will do this weekend by reading the entertainment page or the sports page. Thus, for the church, these pages (that often cost more) can yield the biggest return on investment, since they reach more unchurched people with their message.

3. **Christian advertisements often promote the same things as other churches**. Churches have many differences, but they also have many things in common. Thus, when churches promote their commonality with similar sayings, they can overwhelm and confuse the reader. For example, one church page at Easter was filled with churches offering "a place for your family to grow," "contemporary ministry for today's families," and "family friendly and Christ centered." These descriptors were all variations of a fundamental desire to welcome people into fellowship and discipleship. Now, there is nothing wrong with this objective, for we have seen that discipleship is the goal of the Great Commission (see Matt. 28:19-20). However, when many churches side-by-side promote this same objective, it can confuse the potential guest. The reader might feel that every church is the same. As church leaders, we know that this is not the case. Therefore, describe your core competencies in your advertisements so potential attendees will know your strengths and personality.

Employ the Right Advertisement

Marketing students are familiar with the three types of advertisements and the appropriate times to employ them. However, in the religious world, these three types are largely unknown. Here is a brief overview of each, and a graphical representation in figure 11.5 of their appropriate use.

1. **Informative advertisements.** These advertisements provide basic information and announce availability. The ads may give directions to a church or tell about a new worship service or ministry. However, due to their informative nature, they are short-lived. As the new ministry or worship service continues, interested parties will become informed. Thus the informative ad will lose its value.

 Churches overuse informative ads. These ads almost exclusively describe service times, directions, and so on. However, in doing so, they neglect to convey their core competencies. In the marketing world, informative advertising is employed only at the inauguration of a product or service. That should be the same strategy a church uses.

2. **Persuasive advertisements.** These advertisements plainly describe the core competencies of a church and, as a result, what the church offers. They explain the benefits of specific programming in more detail than an informative ad. This is often the missing element in church advertising. Congregational leaders know the rationale and benefits of a new program but sometimes overlook the receivers' corresponding lack of knowledge. Churches must use persuasive advertising to explain how programs and ministries meet the specific needs of the people in their mission field.

3. **Reminder advertisements**. These ads reinforce previous promotional activity. They are usually short, concise, and designed to remind the

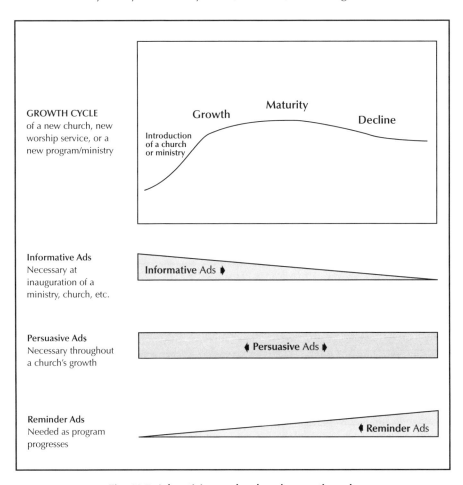

Fig. 11.5 Advertising and a church growth cycle

receiver of the persuasive advertisements they follow.[23] Many churches err by employing reminder ads before they have established their core competencies in persuasive ads.

Figure 11.5 shows how informative, persuasive, and reminder ads are utilized at different stages in the life of a church or program/ministry.[24]

Advertising Media Alternatives

The types and effectiveness of various advertising media are staggering. To help the reader consider the options and their suitability, figure 11.6 compares various forms of media. The "Percent of Total Budget" indicates how much money churches spend in each category.

Media Type	Percent of Total Budget[25]	Advantages for Churches	Disadvantages for Churches
BROADCAST			
Network television	17	Mass coverage, repetition, flexibility, prestige	High cost, temporary message, public distrust; may be reaching a larger geographical segment than the church's mission field
Cable television	8	Same strengths as network TV; less market coverage since every viewer must also be a cable subscriber	Same disadvantages as network TV; however, ads are more targeted to specific viewer segments
Radio	8	Immediacy, low cost, flexibility, targeted audience, mobility	Short lifespan; highly fragmented audience due to differences in musical tastes
PRINT			
Newspapers	19	Tailored to individual communities; ability to refer back to ads	Short lifespan; papers are read quickly

23. *Reminder advertisements* were employed in the 1970s by Campus Crusade for Christ in conjunction with an outreach campaign called "I found it." After laying the groundwork by training thousands of Christians in how to share their faith, Campus Crusade gave these trained workers buttons that said, "I found it." Finally, after the workers had worn the buttons for months, Campus Crusade launched a media campaign showing a young person wearing the "I found it" button. The billboards and TV ads served as "reminder advertisements" to support the young person's one-on-one testimony of faith.

24. Boone and Kurtz, *Contemporary Marketing*, 534.

25. The reader will notice that an estimated 20 percent of total expenditures are not spent on these avenues, but rather on miscellaneous media such as phone directories, transit (bus, subway, train) displays, posters, exhibits, and so on.

Direct mail	19	Selectivity, intense coverage, flexibility, opportunity to convey complete information, personalization	High cost, consumer resistance, dependence on an effective mailing list
Magazines	5	Selectivity, quality image production, long life, prestige	Lack of flexibility
Billboards	2	Quick, visual communication of simple ideas; link to local congregation with directions; repetition	Each exposure is brief; environmental concerns
ELECTRONIC			
Internet	3	Two-way communications, flexibility, fuller information, links to more information	Difficult to measure effectiveness

Fig. 11.6. The church and the media[26]

The Broadcast Media: Network Television, Cable Television, Radio

Traditionally one of the costliest endeavors, the rise of local cable outlets has opened the door for the church on a budget to advertise. Radio stations are also effective, offering relatively low-cost advertising outlets. Here are some guidelines to keep in mind when using the broadcast media.

1. *Oversee quality in your advertisements.* Local cable channels and radio stations are often looking to fill space. Thus they may be less judicious about what they allow to be aired. Radio stations often find it difficult to fill required public service announcement postings or Sunday morning time slots. Because these media outlets often lower their expectations, the church must take it upon itself to ensure a high level of quality that honors God and the church's constituents.

    Today, a number of organizations and denominations offer churches professionally rendered advertisements for print, electronic, and broadcast media. If they can be personalized as well as correlated with a church's core competencies, these prefabricated advertisements can help to increase quality.

2. *Advertise in the right places.* With radio, do not advertise on Sunday mornings because the primary listening audience is Christian (unless this is your mission field). Instead, advertise during drive time, lunch,

---

26. "Advertising Boom in U.S. Ended in '01," *Advertising Age* (May 13, 2002): 24.

and other times when the station's demographics indicate a significant listenership.

Remember that radio listeners are highly segregated by musical style. Investigate various stations and the ages, preferences, and socio-economics of their listeners to decide which station will best help you to reach your mission field.

3. *Broadcast media is especially effective with persuasive and high quality advertisements.* Earlier we saw the need for persuasive advertisements; however, be careful not to appear unreasonable or obsessive. Well-meaning, but overly ardent, Christians have made many listeners wary of Christian advertisements. For that reason, professionally created ads, although expensive, are more effective. On some occasions, the church might want to advertise against its stereotype. For instance, Vineyard Fellowship of Dayton, Ohio, understands that many unchurched people are turned off by churches insinuating they are better than other churches. Thus Vineyard Fellowship advertises its church with the byline, "a pretty good church." Their refusal to compete with their ecclesial neighbors has made them stand out.

The Print Media:
Newspapers, Direct Mail, Magazines, and Billboards

If handled appropriately, the print media continues to be a good place for the church to advertise. Here are some guidelines.

1. *Advertise in the right places.* As noted earlier, churches should avoid running print ads in religious sections of the paper or religious magazines, instead concentrating on areas the unchurched would be more likely to peruse. With direct mail, ensure that you have an effective mailing list and that you are targeting the right mission field (i.e., be sure you are not targeting people too far away to attend, or of the wrong generation).

2. *Write your own stories for newspapers, magazines, and so on.* Smaller community newspapers are often looking for information to fill their pages. When they cannot find enough, they will print space-filling trivia. Whenever a reader sees an abundance of these space fillers, it should be a signal that this newspaper is searching for content. Because journalists at smaller newspapers are not readily available to write stories, a church should pen its own stories. If a local church writes an engaging story and attaches attractive pictures, the local newspaper may gladly print your self-created story. Five to six column inches of a story may translate into several hundred dollars of advertisement. However,

professionalism is important. Look in your church for schoolteachers, journalists, part-time writers, and so on, to entrust with this duty.

3. *Use billboards for impact and to display directions to the church.* Corinth Church's location on an out-of-sight rural lane meant the church had to increase its presence on the nearby bypass. A billboard would be an excellent advertising alternative (and cheaper than relocating the facilities to a more visible site). In addition, the billboard would offer directions to the church.

Electronic Media: The Internet

At one time, the telephone was the greatest communication tool at the consumer's fingertips. The appeal to "let your fingers do the walking" though the phone directory reminded people that it was easier to find out about an organization from their phone directory than it was to visit the organization in person. As a result, churches advertised heavily in phone directories. Today, we might say instead, "Forget your fingers, and let your browser do the surfing." A survey by the Online Publisher's Association discovered that even more than using the Web for communication (e.g., e-mail) or social networking (e.g., Facebook or Twitter), most people use the Internet for gathering information about products, organizations, and news.[27]

The Internet contains more information than any phone directory imaginable. Faster, smaller, and easier-to-use computers, netbooks, and smartphones mean searching for information on the Internet is the norm. Today, churches must offer professional, uncomplicated, but extensive Web sites that are also friendly to mobile devices such as netbooks and smartphones. Here are four keys to Web effectiveness:

1. *Have your Web site professionally designed.* It has been said that building a poor Web site is easier than creating a good one. A brief voyage across cyberspace will confirm this hypothesis. Thus it is wise to employ professional Web designers to create your Web presence.

2. *Make sure the Web site is listed with the major search engines.* It does little good if people cannot find your Web address. Use services or software that keep your Web site listed with the popular search engines.

3. *Update your Web site on a regular basis.* Just as you would not think of distributing the same church bulletin with the same outdated information week after week, you must continually update your Web site. To-

---

27. "Consumers Are Spending the Lion's Share of Their Time Online with Content," Online Publishers Association, September 17, 2009, http://www.online-publishers.org/press-release/consumers-are-spending-the-lionshare-of-their-time-online-with-content.

day most communication and data gathering takes place via the Web. Generation X and Generation Y are especially adept at using the Web to gather information. If a young person wants to know about your church, chances are that person will begin by looking up your Web site. The last thing you want to do is to present them with outdated information, which can give them the impression that you are slow to respond or at worst archaic.

4. *Use online questionnaires to maintain research related to your mission field.* Businesses are discovering the advantages of online questionnaires, which allow community residents to anonymously share their ideas, requests, and even complaints. Online questionnaires can easily provide a great deal of information on your targeted mission field.

Miscellaneous Media: Posters, Flyers

Probably the least effective advertising avenue for the church is the use of flyers, handouts, and posters. Because of a growing appreciation for keeping the environment unspoiled and clean, distributing flyers or posting posters has steadily lost effectiveness. These can be appropriate avenues at private events, such as church gatherings, where distribution and posting is controlled. But for public spaces and events, the other advertising avenues mentioned above are preferred.

IT CULMINATES WITH THE RIGHT PERSPECTIVE

While many readers will grasp the importance of marketing, others will find it challenging to introduce these principles to congregations that historically eschew such practices. Therefore, to promote such understandings, the church will need to see itself as growing out of a learning organization into a teaching organization.

Becoming a Learning Organization

In the business realm, effective organizations are often praised for becoming "learning organizations." Noel Tichy, professor of Organizational Behavior and Human Resource Management at the University of Michigan Business School, and researcher Eli Cohen describe learning organizations as those who "in order to succeed in a highly competitive global marketplace . . . need to be able to change quickly; [thus] their people must be able to acquire and assimilate new knowledge and skills rapidly."[28]

---

28. Noel M. Tichy and Eli Cohen, "The Teaching Organization," *Training and Development* 52, no. 7 (July 1998): 27.

Moving Toward a Teaching Organization

In their investigation of successful companies, Tichy and Cohen found that being a learning organization was not enough. In order for a company to thrive, it also had to become a "teaching organization."

In the church context, where teaching biblical truths is a central task, the idea of the church as a "teaching organization" can be confusing. Therefore, let's differentiate what is meant in the business world by a "learning organization" and a "teaching organization." Figure 11.7 offers a comparison.

The Learning Organization	The Teaching Organization
	Adopts all of the learning organization's characteristics but adds these:
1. Insists that leaders become learners; encourages leaders to see learning as a responsibility	8. Insists that leaders become teachers; encourages leaders to see teaching as a responsibility
2. Studies the marketplace	9. Studies training principles
3. Changes quickly to reach a changing market	10. Adapts new teaching skills, tools, and procedures to reach a changing workforce
4. Encourages people to acquire and assimilate new knowledge	11. Encourages people to pass knowledge on to others
5. Encourages people to acquire and assimilate new skills	12. Encourages people to pass skills on to others
6. Helps leaders and workers understand the ideas and concepts that drive the company	13. Helps leaders and workers master the ideas and concepts that drive the company
7. Focuses on developing strategies	14. Focuses on developing leaders

Fig. 11.7. Comparing learning and teaching organizations

Thus the "teaching organization" goes beyond learning, embracing as a core competency the ability to pass skills and knowledge on to others. Tichy and Cohen put it well:

In teaching organizations, leaders see it as their responsibility to teach. They do that because they understand that it's the best, if not the only, way to develop throughout a company people who can come up with and carry out smart ideas about the business. . . . A teaching organization's insistence that its leaders teach creates better leaders, because teaching requires people to develop mastery of ideas and concepts.[29]

A teaching organization is often characterized by the following:

1. *Leaders are committed teachers.* Larry Bossidy, who transformed AlliedSignal in the 1990s, is an example of a committed teacher. Bossidy didn't slash and downsize AlliedSignal on its way to success. Rather, Bossidy spent hundreds of hours teaching senior leaders about strategy and goals and inculcating an atmosphere of "teaching." The remarkable turnaround of AlliedSignal in only five years is a tribute to Bossidy's success as a committed teacher.

2. *Leaders are models.* The late Robert Goizueta, CEO of Coca-Cola, was a quiet engineer with a thick accent. His success at Coca-Cola and its battles with rival PepsiCo are legendary. Goizueta frequently recounted to his employees his personal experiences with his family's business in Cuba, drew on the wisdom of Spanish poets, and often quoted his grandfather. He served as a model of teaching in a humble self-effacing manner.

3. *Leaders are coaches.* AlliedSignal's Larry Bossidy wrote personal letters to each manager after meetings, encouraging and guiding them in their performance. He took it as his personal responsibility to let managers know that he was there to laud good performance and diplomatically redirect poor performance.

4. *Leaders identify workers' goals and help them develop a "leadership pipeline" toward their dream career.* GE develops a career map for each employee called a "leadership pipeline." Regularly consulted by managers, this visual graph details the jobs an employee has held and the positions that employee wants to hold in the future. The leadership pipeline helps managers to identify the goals and aspirations of workers and assist them in fulfilling their dreams.

5. *Leaders ensure that teaching becomes a core competency of the organization.* GE, under Jack Welch's legendary leadership, inculcated its teaching orientation with the Six Sigma approach.[30] By developing six memorable traits, Welch ensured that employees would be embraced and that a far-flung GE organization could see itself as one large but unified organization.

---

29. Ibid., 28.
30. General Electric, "What is Six Sigma?" http://www.ge.com/en/company/companyinfo/quality/whatis.htm.

When a congregation becomes a teaching organization, and not just merely a learning organization, its leaders will more readily embrace the important principles of outreach and marketing. As a result, marketing and outreach will inherit their rightful meanings as the methods through which the church presents Jesus' good news.

12

LEADERSHIP PRINCIPLES
THE FOUR CS OF LEADING A CHURCH

Stephen W. Dillman
PhD, District Superintendent, Pittsburgh District,
Church of the Nazarene

———————————◆———————————

The educational outline for preparing ministers in one denomination calls for instruction in four categories: character, content, competency, and context.[1] This outline is applicable to the broader subject of Christian leadership and, specifically, the church leader—both clergy and laity. It is true, as Winston notes, that "leadership is leadership—regardless of the type of company or organization."[2] However, Winston moderates this statement by pointing out that leadership should begin with an internal value system that is scripturally based and rooted in *agapaō* love.[3]

CHARACTER

Proverbs 23:7 says, "For as he thinketh in his heart, so is he" (KJV). Trevecca Nazarene University, in Nashville, has an interesting motto: *Esse quam vederi* (To be rather than to seem). The motto is a reminder that genuine Christian character precedes and accentuates academic excellence.[4] This is just one example of a Christian institution acknowledging the primacy of character.

Forgiven. Being precedes doing. Leadership emanates out of one's character. Church leaders must be Christian leaders. For that to be true, these leaders must acknowledge that by faith in Jesus Christ, their sins are forgiven, they are reconciled to God, and they are committed to exemplifying Christ in their life. For Christian organizations, David McKenna rightly calls this "incarnational

---

1. *Manual: Church of the Nazarene 2005-2009* (Kansas City: Nazarene Publishing House, 2005), 193-94.
2. Bruce Winston, *Be a Leader for God's Sake: From Values to Behavior* (Virginia Beach, VA: School of Global Leadership & Entrepreneurship, 2002), iii.
3. Ibid., 1. Note: The verb form of *agapē* is intentionally used to emphasize the active character of this love.
4. Mildred Wynkoop, *The Trevecca Story: Seventy-Five Years of Christian Service* (Nashville: Trevecca Press, 1976), 227.

leadership." With the help of the Holy Spirit, he says, persons are transformed so that the living Word is once again embodied in the human flesh of the Christian leader.[5]

Holy. The incarnational life goes on, by scriptural mandate, to call us to holiness. It is the will of God that you should be holy because God is holy (see 1 Thess. 4:3 and 1 Pet. 1:16). Holiness is not an option. It is part of the saving, sanctifying work of God that cleanses the leader from self-sovereignty and enables the leader to serve in the same selfless way as Christ (see Phil. 2:5-8). A Christian leader who has been sanctified can be trusted to lead without self-serving ambition and self-promoting agendas.

Humble. Filled with the Spirit of Christ, the Christian leader models the self-emptying of Jesus through humility. Humility acknowledges one's strengths and faces one's limitations.[6] Warren Bennis splits this continuum into magnanimity and humility, saying that humble people take compliments with a grain of salt and take intelligent criticism without rancor, learning from their mistakes and not harping on the mistakes of others.[7] Building on these definitions, Christian leaders live in total dependence upon God's love and mercy. Self-sufficiency and self-centered pride are stripped away until these leaders naturally (or supernaturally) want to serve others above themselves.[8]

Committed to service. The humble Christian leader lives to serve. Service is more than just the behavior of helping. It is connected to the character of a Christian leader, because the motive to serve emanates from a moral caring for others above self and thus acts to benefit another person at the risk of diminishing one's own power and authority.[9] An example is the pastor who jumps in to help stack chairs after a fellowship dinner so that the volunteer staff will not have to stay late.

Live with integrity. Like adding rows of block to a wall, the Christian leader builds integrity with every act of selfless service. The popular culture understands integrity as walking the talk and practicing what one preaches. David

---

5. David McKenna, *Power to Follow, Grace to Lead: Strategy for the Future of Christian Leadership* (Dallas: Word Publishing, 1989), 22.

6. S. J. Sandage and T. W. Wiens, "Contextualizing Models of Humility and Forgiveness: A Reply to Gassin," *Journal of Psychology and Theology*, 29 (2001): 201.

7. Warren Bennis, *Managing People Is Like Herding Cats* (Provo, UT: Executive Excellence Publishing, 1997), 58.

8. C. Gene Wilkes, *Jesus on Leadership: Discovering the Secrets of Servant Leadership* (Wheaton, IL: Tyndale House Publishing, Inc., 1998), 48.

9. Stephen W. Dillman, "The Person-centered Lifestyle of Servant-Leadership" (Unpublished, 2007), 5.

McKenna observes that we are held accountable for our integrity "every day, and especially in those moments when our leadership is put on the line by personal temptation and pivotal decisions."[10] John Bowling says that integrity must be demonstrated consistently by always taking responsibility for one's words and actions and justly balancing the needs of people with those of the organization one leads.[11] Robert Greenleaf says that "the ability to lead with integrity depends on the leader's skills for withdrawal and action, listening and persuasion, practical goal setting and intuitive prescience."[12]

Trustworthy. As integrity is practiced, the Christian leader becomes trustworthy. According to Max De Pree, trust grows when followers see "that leaders can be depended on to do the right thing."[13] The authority and power to lead is a gift granted to the leader by those who follow. The more trustworthy the leader is, the greater the gift of authority and power followers will grant to the leader. Thus it is fair to say that trust is earned.[14] Trust builds credibility, which James Kouzes and Barry Posner have shown to be the cornerstone of effective leadership.[15]

Sacrificially loving. The progression of the leader's character reaches its pinnacle in the words of Jesus: "Trust in God; trust also in me. . . . If it were not so, I would have told you. I am going there to prepare a place for you" (John 14:1-2). Trust becomes exemplified in sacrificial love—*agapē*. *Agapē* love is love that will do anything to accomplish its desire. In its highest moral sense, this love is expressed as a consuming, total, holistic giving of oneself to God and to others (see Matt. 22:37-38). In the context of leadership, sacrificial love seeks to enrich and empower the lives of others in the same measure as Jesus, who said that he "did not come to be served, but to serve, and to give his life as a ransom for many" (Matt. 20:28). The Christian leader loves God so completely that loving God's people becomes a "passion"—a word rooted in the crucifixion of Jesus. The well-being of the follower is more important than the well-being of the leader.

---

10. McKenna, *Power to Follow,* 145.

11. John C. Bowling, *Grace-Full Leadership: Understanding the Heart of a Christian Leader* (Kansas City: Beacon Hill Press of Kansas City, 2000), 77-83.

12. Greenleaf, *The Servant As Leader,* 7.

13. Max De Pree, *Leading Without Power: Finding Hope in Serving Community* (San Francisco: Jossey-Bass, 1997), 129.

14. Marcus Buckingham and Curt Coffman, *First, Break All the Rules: What the World's Greatest Managers Do Differently* (New York: Simon & Schuster, 1999), 116.

15. James M. Kouzes and Barry Z. Posner, *Credibility: How Leaders Gain and Lose It, Why People Demand It* (San Francisco: Jossey-Bass, 1993).

CONTENT

This section builds on the character of the Christian leader by discussing the issue of personal development—not our internal qualities—but our external capabilities. Winseman, Clifton, and Liesveld, writing about the development of Christian leaders, use five terms that outline this discussion: "call," "skill," "talent," "gift," and "strength."[16]

Call. A call is God's invitation to live up to the expectations for which he created you with the assurance that he will see you through. The *Lutheran Book of Worship* contains an appropriate prayer for Christian leaders: "Lord God, you have called your servants to ventures of which we cannot see the ending, by paths as yet untrodden, through perils unknown."[17] In writing to the Thessalonians, Paul says, "The one who calls you is faithful and he will do it" (1 Thess. 5:24). "To what are we called?" is linked to the question, "For what were we created?" At creation, God breathed his Spirit into what had just been dirt, making humankind in his own image. Humankind became the living embodiment of God—an incarnate witness to the relationship that God desires with all human beings. Those who acknowledge this relationship are called the people of God.

Corporately, God calls his people to be witnesses to the nations, inviting others to join his kingdom. From the beginning, the people of God were to be leaders in the mission to go and make disciples.

Christian leaders develop a sensitivity to this call, respond affirmatively, and draw on its divine assurance when things are not going as well as expected. Leading a ministry is not a job; it is a calling. A ministry vocation is not selected simply on the basis of one's personal interest or on the encouragement of family and friends. God calls Christians to ministry and equips the called to accomplish his mission.

Skill. Skill is the ability to perform the steps of an activity with competence and expertise. It is a capability that can be transferred or taught to one person by another.[18] The Christian leader does not have to have every skill imaginable—only those skills necessary for his or her calling. Those called may not even have the obvious skills for ministry at first. However, they will develop the skills God deems necessary. As the calling matures, the leader's skill set will expand through learning and experience.

---

16. Albert L. Winseman et al., *Living Your Strengths: Discover Your God-given Talents and Inspire Your Community* (New York: Gallup Press, 2004), 3-5, 189, 216.
17. *Lutheran Book of Worship* (Minneapolis: Augsburg Fortress Publishing, 1978), 137.
18. Craig E. Johnson, *Meeting the Ethical Challenges of Leadership: Casting Light or Shadow* (Thousand Oaks, CA: Sage Publications, 2001), 63.

How does a person identify the skills he or she might need? Johnson suggests that leaders take inventory of the skills they already have by examining their major activities and evaluating those areas at which they excel. On the flipside, he suggests that leaders take stock of their significant failures to understand their limitations and identify areas where skill development is necessary.[19] Great leaders, who understand their own skill mix, will also surround themselves with people who have complementary skills.

Talent. Talent is a naturally recurring pattern of thought, feeling, or behavior that can be productively applied instinctively and with great satisfaction. Talents themselves are not special. Everyone has them. However, when people find themselves in a position that is suited for their talent, they become special—they are "talented."[20]

Consider charismatic leadership as an example. Of the many types of leaders (e.g., autocratic, participative, servant, transactional, and transformational), charismatic leaders are defined, in part, by their personal talent.[21] If Buckingham and Coffman are correct, charismatic leaders are not just talented. They apply their talent naturally and instinctively in a way that so fits the mission and their role in the organization that others recognize and want to follow them.

The Christian leader who is called will not only identify his or her innate talents but also be able to discern how those talents can be used by God to accomplish his purposes. Amazingly, some Christians deny their talents in the belief that if they enjoy something or are naturally good at it, God will probably ask them to do something else as a test of commitment. There is no scripture to substantiate this belief, and observable evidence demonstrates the opposite. It is even possible that ministry burnout can be avoided when the leader is serving in his or her area of talent and interest.

Gift. A gift is a God-given ministry area, often broad in scope, that equips God's people to advance the cause of Christ. Paul writes in his letter to the Corinthians that God has given everyone a spiritual gift (see 1 Cor. 12:11). As these people become part of the Body of Christ, God mixes their gifts together to accomplish his purpose (see v. 18).

Identifying his or her spiritual gift is the first step in helping the Christian leader know what God wants to see accomplished through his or her life.[22] The discovery of a person's spiritual gift is not just a matter of personal growth or

19. Buckingham and Coffman, *First, Break All the Rules*, 83.
20. Ibid., 91.
21. Jay A. Conger, *The Charismatic Leader: Behind the Mystique of Exceptional Leadership* (San Francisco: Jossey-Bass, 1989), 96-98.
22. Winseman et al., *Living Your Strengths*, 189.

discipleship. Spiritual gifts exist within community to accomplish God's missional purpose to reconcile the world to himself. While talents are natural abilities, such as the ability to do complex math or paint or fix machines, gifts equip the Christian leader in an area of God's concern. For instance, if God needs his people to be more compassionate, he equips some of his people with the gift of mercy. In the process, he may take advantage of someone's natural cooking ability or organizational ability so that his gift will be maximized in the life of that person.

Strength. A strength is the ability to provide consistently high performance in a given activity both naturally and through the acquisition of knowledge and the development of skills. The Gallup Organization's 2002 national study of congregation members revealed that 53 percent of them do not believe they have the opportunity to do what they do best.[23] While spiritual gifts surveys and inventories have been around for quite a while, the Gallup study shows that there is still an overwhelming loss of ministry potential.

Understanding strengths helps the leader to flourish rather than simply function. It does so by helping the Christian leader build on these strengths in order to apply his or her gifts and talents more effectively. For instance, someone might have the gift of evangelism and feel frustrated when asked to do evangelism according to a methodology being taught at their church. In reality, this individual and the person whose evangelistic method is being taught have the same gift of evangelism but have a different mix of strengths. The one who is strong in aggressive achievement might prefer going to someone's home to share the "Four Spiritual Laws." The one who is strong in building personal relationships will probably prefer joining a gym to meet non-Christians where casual conversations can lead to the sharing of one's faith.

The study of strengths falls into a fairly recent category of science called Positive Psychology. The Gallup Organization supports this science with their massive databases and their ability to pull researchers together. The current edition of their book *StrengthsFinder 2.0* (found on Gallup's StrengthsFinder Web site at http://strengths.gallup.com/110440/About-StrengthsFinder-20.aspx) is the doorway to a rich study and practical application of strengths for personal development and positive outcomes.

COMPETENCY

If character and content have to do with *being,* competency has to do with *doing.* According to Barna, churchgoers expect their pastor to juggle an average

---

23. Ibid., ix.

of sixteen major tasks—a recipe for failure since "nobody can handle the wide range of responsibilities that people expect pastors to master."[24] This section will not attempt to detail the duties of a Christian leader and, possibly, discourage Christian leadership. Instead, this section will focus on seven competencies, or macro-skills, that empower the Christian leader to deal successfully with the multiple tasks of ministry.

Forgiving. The competent Christian leader will be forgiving toward followers. The corporate world's best practices include forgiveness. There it is called learning from mistakes, turning weaknesses into strengths, and understanding limitations. Craig Johnson takes an interesting look at forgiveness in the corporate setting, seeing it as a way to combat the "shadow" side of leadership. He says that "forgiveness is one of a leader's most powerful weapons in the fight against evil."[25] Forgiveness appears to absorb or defuse evil. Those forgiven are released from resentments, enjoy a higher sense of well-being, have better health, and develop more positive relationships between themselves and others. Forgiveness is an investment in the future of one's followers. De Pree calls this *restoration* and sees it as recognizing the potential that lies in a person's future.[26] Winston agrees but calls it *mercy* "that allows us to forget that which is not necessary for the future."[27] As Robert Greenleaf points out, anyone can reach a goal through the efforts of perfect people, but no one is perfect. The forgiving leader recognizes that imperfect people are "capable of great dedication and heroism."[28]

Listening. Another competency that must be developed by the leader is the ability to listen. Banks and Ledbetter highlight its importance when they say that sometimes leaders need to be silent where silence is "not an empty space but a holding space where what is important and necessary can be heard."[29] Bennis defines listening as "having the empathetic reach to understand another" and says that the best way to build trust is by deep listening—relating to the context in which the other person is reasoning to understand where that person

24. George Barna, "A Profile of Protestant Pastors in Anticipation of 'Pastor Appreciation Month'," *Barna Update* (September 25, 2001), http://www.barna.org/barna-update/article/5-barna-update/59-a-profile-of-protestant-pastors-in-anticipation-of-qpastor-appreciation-monthq.

25. Johnson, *Meeting the Ethical Challenges of Leadership*, 84.

26. De Pree, *Leading Without Power*, 75.

27. Winston, *Be a Leader for God's Sake*, 65.

28. Don M. Frick and Larry C. Spears, eds., *On Becoming a Servant Leader: The Private Writings of Robert K. Greenleaf* (San Francisco: Jossey-Bass, 1996), 308.

29. Robert Banks and Bernice M. Ledbetter, *Reviewing Leadership: A Christian Evaluation of Current Approaches* (Grand Rapids: Baker Academic, 2004), 54.

is "coming from."[30] Goldhaber cites the work of the Sperry Corporation and lists ten keys to effective listening. They are (1) find areas of interest; (2) judge content, not delivery; (3) resist judging until comprehension is complete; (4) listen for central themes; (5) take fewer notes; (6) demonstrate listening by body language; (7) avoid being distracted, concentrate on what the speaker is saying; (8) strive to understand complex issues and not just deal with the easy stuff; (9) be sensitive to the emotion of the speaker; and (10) use the "spaces" between the speaker's words to think, weigh the argument, and plan a response.[31]

Empowering. The competent leader will be an empowering leader. Empowerment is the process by which leaders give significance to followers by giving them responsibility and authority for the mission of the organization. Empowered followers see themselves at the center of things and not on the periphery.[32] Among Christians, McKenna calls this "incarnational transfer."[33] Think of it in biblical terms. When in Acts 1:8, Jesus said, "You will receive power when the Holy Spirit comes on you; and you will be my witnesses in Jerusalem, and in all Judea and Samaria, and to the ends of the earth," he was saying that the power he had been given to fulfill the mission of his Father was going to be transferred to the disciples who would be empowered for the same mission. As Christian leaders follow the example of Jesus, they will transfer authority and power to their followers.

Visioning. Somewhere along the line, vision became a verb. Visioning is the act of casting a preferred future and helping others to see that future with the same clarity as the leader. It answers the questions, "Where are we going?" and "Why?" It cannot be a personal vision, however. It must become a shared vision. Those who have a shared vision want to accomplish something as much for the other person as for themselves. Peter Senge says that shared visioning requires the leader to develop skills of *enrollment* (where people feel that the vision is their own), *commitment* (where followers have a sense of responsibility for making the vision happen), and *compliance* (where people support the vision because they see its benefits).[34] Visioning does not focus primarily on organizational goals. Visioning sees the potential in people to fulfill their God-designed destiny and sees how those same people fit into the vision of the organization.

30. Bennis, *Managing People Is Like Herding Cats*, 75, 134.

31. Gerald M. Goldhaber, *Organizational Communication,* 6th ed. (Madison, WI: Brown & Benchmark Publishers, 1993), 229.

32. Bennis, *Managing People Is Like Herding Cats*, 178.

33. McKenna, *Power to Follow,* 165-66.

34. Peter Senge, *The Fifth Discipline: The Art & Practice of the Learning Organization* (New York: Currency Doubleday, 1990), 218-19.

Risking. Great leaders are competent risk takers. They are not reckless. Risk takers are usually very good at being visionaries—seeing the future, looking over the horizon. Doug Murren points out that the great leaders of the Bible were risk takers who "have the ability to see a new thing, to perceive a bright future, to tap into the power of God."[35] Christian leaders who are risk takers trust that God is so much in control that they can relinquish their self-sovereignty over the situation. Earthly things such as ego, security, and popularity are set aside for the eternal benefits that may be realized by following the plan of God.

Lifelong learning. This competency has two sides. First, the leader must be committed to being a learner for life. Ongoing education is not necessarily lifelong learning. As abstract as it sounds, the essence of lifelong learning is discerning what shapes our thinking and acting. To do so, leaders must subject their thinking to the judgment of others whom they trust.[36] It may be a continuing education class for ministerial leaders or an informal coffee shop conversation with a parishioner or ministerial colleague. Regardless, the Christian leader is adding knowledge to what he or she already knows, comparing it with prior experience, and considering future applications. Second, the leader must inspire followers to become lifelong learners. Senge calls this *team learning*, which is the process of aligning and developing the capacity of a team to create the results its members truly desire.[37] However, this does not happen naturally. It goes through discernable phases: fragmented learning, pooled learning, synergy, and continuous learning.[38] Individuals gain insights that they later share with others. This leads to a collective way of thinking that people apply to everything, and so much so that it becomes part of the DNA of the organization.

Skill development. Where learning is more about the process, skill development is more about the outcome. A desired outcome may require an ability that a ministry leader does not possess personally or have within the skill sets of others. When that happens, the leader must learn a new skill or recruit someone who already has it. For instance, a church may need to add its first ministerial staff member. If the pastor has never had staff, he or she must learn skills such as developing a job description, interviewing candidates, holding staff meetings for delegation and accountability, and more. Another example is the building committee that adds experts or brings in consultants to successfully complete each step of the project. The wise leader avoids becoming the "jack of all trades and master of

35. Doug Murren, *Leadershift* (Ventura, CA: Regal, 1994), 128.

36. Thomas R. Hawkins, *The Learning Congregation: A New Vision of Leadership* (Louisville, KY: Westminster John Knox Press, 1997), 99.

37. Senge, *The Fifth Discipline*, 236.

38. Hawkins, *The Learning Congregation*, 119.

none." While a leader may need to develop a new personal skill, involving others with the skills necessary to positively affect an outcome is preferred.

CONTEXT

This section deals with the context or environment of Christian leadership. Leaders, in general, function within three frameworks. Who is leading the leader? Who is the leader leading? And, what are the systems or networks in which the leader is leading?

Leader of leaders. "It's lonely at the top" is a common concern of leaders. It begs the question, "Who is leading the leader?" Two words are associated with leading leaders—"coaching" and "mentoring." Coaching refers to training and specific guidance, while mentoring refers to advising and education.[39]

Coaches are known for their experience, knowledge, and expertise. As leaders develop or take on new responsibilities, new skills may be needed. A wise leader will seek out a coach to help gain those skills in less time than it would take to learn them by trial and error. Peter Block notes that coaching should be seen as temporary and useful during a transitional stage.[40] Taking Block's advice, Christian leaders might consider finding a coach during the early years of their development as a leader or at the start of a new assignment.

Mentors, on the other hand, are helpful over a longer period of time. According to Bass, mentors should be older, more experienced, generally of the same gender as the leader, viewed as competent in their field, skilled at listening, relational, even-tempered, respected, able to communicate complex ideas concretely, and able to think rationally.[41] Christian leaders are not generally focused on career advancement. However, a good mentor can provide encouragement, assurance, blessing, and advice and may even be influential when a leader's ideas or initiatives need to be advanced beyond the leader's current situation.

Being mentored, especially within a Christian organization, provides an accountability partner for the Christian leader. The mentor helps the leader maintain integrity and identify and avoid temptations, observes deviations from the norm, and has permission to challenge anything that might diminish the character of Christ in the leader being mentored.

---

39. Bernard M. Bass, *Bass & Stogdill's Handbook of Leadership: Theory, Research, and Managerial Applications*, 3rd ed. (New York: Free Press, 1990), 833.

40. Peter Block, *Stewardship: Choosing Service over Self-Interest* (San Francisco: Berrett-Koehler Publishers, 1996), 105.

41. Bass, *Bass & Stogdill's Handbook of Leadership*, 835-36.

In the height of the Industrial Age, mentoring had a machine or parental quality with phrases such as "greasing the skids" and "pulling strings." In the Christian organization, mentoring is changing from helping someone learn how to "do" to helping someone learn how to "be." Greenleaf offered this "test" of servant leaders: "Do those served grow as persons; do they, while being served, become healthier, wiser, freer, more autonomous, *more likely themselves to become servants?*" (italics added).[42] Robert Bly calls mentoring a vertical process by which young members of society learn how to "be" in that society because, if they fail in this, the organization will become a sibling society—one in which its members live out a perpetual adolescence.[43]

Leading followers. Kouzes and Posner, respected authorities on leadership development, make a profound statement: "Liberate the leader in everyone, and extraordinary things happen."[44] Studying the leadership of John Wesley, Lovett Weems Jr. suggests that Wesley understood the principle of *multiple leadership*—the idea that everyone has the potential to lead for a specific time or specific task.[45] The classic Christian doctrine of the *priesthood of all believers* sees all believers as ministers, having a ministry for which God has uniquely equipped and called them. Successful Christian leaders recognize this and find multiple ways to liberate the leader in everyone.

Wilkes offers five steps for equipping others to be leaders in ministry.[46] First, the leader must encourage followers to serve. The call must be to a cause worthy of the time and effort being asked of the follower. The leader must also come alongside the follower to urge him or her forward when discouragement sets in. Second, the leader must qualify followers to serve. Training is needed if the follower is to succeed. Expectations need to be clear, and the mission must always be the focus. Third, and extremely important, the leader must understand the needs of the followers. The Christian leader observes and listens. Observing a strength, the leader affirms the follower. Observing a weakness, the leader can offer remedial training or constructive criticism. Through listening, the leader can respond helpfully—sometimes with the obvious answer and sometimes with counsel that comes from "reading between the lines." Fourth, the leader must instruct followers in the art of leadership. Not to be confused

42. Greenleaf, *The Servant As Leader*, 7.

43. Robert W. Bly, *The Sibling Society* (Reading, MA: Addison-Wesley, 1996).

44. James Kouzes and Barry Posner, *The Leadership Challenge: How to Get Extraordinary Things Done in Organizations*, 2nd ed. (San Francisco: Jossey-Bass, 1995).

45. Lovett H. Weems, Jr., *Leadership in the Wesleyan Spirit* (Nashville: Abingdon Press, 1999), 59-70.

46. Wilkes, *Jesus on Leadership*, 189-205.

with micromanagement, the instruction by the Christian leader deals with the issues of the kingdom, the mission of Christ, the power of the Spirit, and the purpose of the church. Fifth, the Christian leader enables others to become leaders by praying for them. Through prayer, God gives the leader insight into his purposes for a follower's life. Through prayer, the leader intercedes for others so that God's power is released in and through their lives. The Christian leader recognizes that the power to accomplish God's mission does not come from a person's developed skills or natural abilities. This kind of power comes from God, and the leader prays that his or her follower-leaders will recognize it as well. Through prayer, the Christian leader is able to support the ministry of others even when not directly involved in the ministry.

An important aspect of leading followers to become leaders themselves is the development of teams. It is common in Christian organizations today to see structure built around ministry teams. This is laudable. However, teams are not committees or groups that have been assigned a task, even if that task is a ministry. A team is an intentional effort to help people accomplish more together than they could working individually.[47]

Sims and Manz have done extensive study of teams, concluding that contemporary teams are characterized by empowering multiple leaders with a variety of skills to make decisions, initiate action, and take risks on behalf of the entire organization.[48] For the Christian organization, a team may emerge as a ministry need becomes apparent or a ministry team may be created to address a need that arises and fits the missional purpose of the organization. The Christian leader can help teams be more effective by evaluating the skills of the team and the team's group dynamics, suggesting additional team members whose skill sets might strengthen the team's ability to accomplish its ministry, and monitoring group dynamics so that relationships and influences detrimental to accomplishing the mission are confronted and resolved.

Leading within systems. The two previous leadership contexts emphasize people—those who can lead the leader and those whom the leader leads. People are at the heart of our leadership. However, leaders usually lead within the context of some kind of system or structure. Even if the leader is determined to avoid institutional constraints, it will not be long before organization naturally occurs. Sometimes, Christian leaders like to talk about creating movements and

---

47. Myron Rush, *Management: A Biblical Approach* (Wheaton, IL: Victor Books, 1983), 42.

48. Henry P. Sims, Jr. and Charles C. Manz, *Company of Heroes: Unleashing the Power of Self-Leadership* (New York: John Wiley & Sons, Inc., 1996), 161.

dismiss the institution as a hindrance to the work of God. The talk is noble, but the reality is that institutions grow around mission. If the mission is the flesh, then the institution is its bones, and the body needs both. This biblical metaphor emphasizes the organic and dynamic nature of ministry institutions. It also avoids the mechanistic and, sometimes, impersonal perspective that can value the institution more than the people being served.

Inagrace Dietterich observes that it is not enough to develop an ecclesiology around the secular disciplines of social and management sciences. The mission organization, whether it be a church or parachurch ministry, must be systemically and holistically ecclesial.[49] Staying with our metaphor, the body's "skin" identifies the organization as being missional—it is what we see. The body's "bones" give the mission structure but do not define the essential nature of the body. For that, we have to go to the level of the DNA where our true ecclesiology lies.

Dietterich goes on to say that bureaucratic frameworks afford the necessary context for supporting and enabling the formation of individuals into missional communities. However, an uncritical view of the institution will result in a distortion where mission is associated with a place that is morally and religiously neutral rather than a dynamic community of people called, redeemed, and empowered for mission.[50] This both-and approach brings the secular and the sacred together—reuniting theology and polity in an imaginative and dynamic relationship in order that God's people may become both more faithful and more effective in their ministry and mission."[51]

The concept of a missional community goes beyond a local organization. A local congregation, for example, may be part of a larger geographical area that includes other local churches that may be within their faith tradition or be quite different. This same congregation may be part of a denomination with a global mission. And this congregation may come to realize that they are one part of the church, historical and universal, sharing in its traditions, affected by its problems, and holding in common its core value of loving God with all one's heart and its core mission of making disciples in all the world.

On a cautionary note, the leaders of a local community of faith must never allow the people to become selfishly centered on their own organization.

---

49. Inagrace T. Dietterich, "A Particular People: Toward a Faithful and Effective Ecclesiology," in *The Church Between Gospel and Culture: The Emerging Mission in North America*, ed. George R. Hunsberger and Craig Van Gelder (Grand Rapids: William B. Eerdmans Publishing Company, 1996), 347.
50. Ibid., 355.
51. Ibid., 369.

As the scope of the community shrinks, the local organization is diminished (though not necessarily in size), reflected by less effectiveness and a lower missional impact on the world. The local organization develops tunnel vision, a myopic affliction that sees no need but its own. This self-focus may infect the individual members of the organization to the point that the local organization itself becomes a victim of the very disease it fostered. The cure is a vision and involvement that includes a mission to the world as part of the broader community of faith. As vision becomes more farsighted and involvement becomes more outward-focused, the sense of community grows, responsibility for others increases, and the local organization becomes healthier and often larger to meet the ever-growing sense of mission.

SUMMARY

Winston, one of the resources for this chapter, emphatically shouts his admonition: "Be a leader for God's sake!" Godly leadership begins with the character of the leader. Christian leadership studies have always emphasized this point. However, more recent discussions about leadership styles and their relative effectiveness may have dimmed the lights on the fundamental truth that a leader is only as good as his or her character. Organizational leadership studies that cover a broad range of organizations such as businesses, educational institutions, health care institutions, and more are bringing the spotlight back to character issues. Recent corporate debacles and the mismanagement of financial institutions have convinced many researchers and writers that character is paramount with respect to leadership. This should be obvious for the Christian leader, but it isn't always. It is well to be reminded that the character of a Christian leader defines the quality of that individual's leadership.

Moving from internal to external qualities, the content of a leader's life focuses on the leader's call, skills, talents, gifts, and strengths. This might be called the leader's personal resources for leadership. For the Christian leader, there is the understanding that God calls and equips individuals for his purposes. Even the desire to pursue education and training is a motivational gift from God. As the created, we honor the Creator by acknowledging who we are and what we were created to be through the development of our natural abilities and the pursuit of excellence.

Competent leadership is more than the ability to accurately read a spreadsheet or speak with eloquence. This chapter has focused on leadership competencies that enhance the leader's standing among followers. Competency attracts followers, increases the effectiveness of the leader in accomplishing desired outcomes, and encourages the development of leadership qualities in others. The competencies of forgiving, listening, visioning, empowering, risking, lifelong learning, and skill development are a core set of competencies. Once a leader masters the core, he or she is prepared to add other, task-specific competencies.

Leadership without a context is like owning a fully rigged sailboat with no place to sail. For the Christian leader, the context is both inwardly and outwardly focused. As the leader ministers to the church, the congregants are prepared to join the leader in reaching out to the world that God loves. The bodies of water upon which a real sailboat sails can be unpredictable, variable, and even threatening. But well-equipped boats and well-trained crews navigate these waters often and with a high percentage of success. Like a skipper of such a boat, successful Christian leaders will know themselves, become skilled "captains," and train their followers in order to fulfill the mission of Jesus Christ.

13
SERVANT LEADERSHIP
VALUING PEOPLE AND BUILDING COMMUNITY

Bruce L. Petersen

DMin, Professor of Pastoral Ministry, Mount Vernon Nazarene University

Any pastor will acknowledge the truth that leading a church is a unique, challenging, and sometimes frustrating responsibility. Finding leadership material to read is not the problem. Bookstores and libraries have shelves of books on the subject. So why write a chapter on a topic that has already been so thoroughly researched? Isn't leading a church an obvious thing that comes naturally to all that lead? The focus of this chapter will be on an approach to leadership, servant leadership, that is particularly useful in churches and Christian organizations.

One of the best definitions of leadership comes from former pastor and leadership consultant John Maxwell: "Leadership is influence. That's it. Nothing more; nothing less. My favorite leadership proverb is: He who thinketh he leadeth and hath no one following him is only taking a walk."[1] Influence can come in many forms—good or bad, positive or negative, effective or less than effective. What means of influencing people will be most effective for the church that develops at the beginning of this new millennium? Servant leadership is an approach to guiding the church that is well suited for the twenty-first century. It is not a technique as much as an attitude or spiritual commitment, based on biblical principles, to humbly serve those who are being led.

In reaction to the dictatorial leadership style of the 1970s, Robert Greenleaf, a leadership expert with Quaker roots, wrote a landmark book directed to the secular business field, *Servant Leadership: A Journey into the Nature of Legitimate Power and Greatness*. Robert Greenleaf borrowed from his scriptural heritage, recognizing that the leadership principles of Jesus applied to all who would be leaders. "For Greenleaf true servant leaders are those who are prepared to take the initiative. But before embarking on a course of action, they

---

1. John C. Maxwell, *Developing the Leader Within You* (Nashville: Thomas Nelson Publishers, 1993), 1.

listen to God and to the voices around them in order to determine what God requires of them. They are committed for the long haul, maintaining faith and hope, patience and fortitude."[2] If Christian principles can work within a business setting, they are even more appropriate within the context of the church.

What does servant leadership look like in a church setting? Alan Nelson says, "Servant leadership is about a group of people mutually submitting to each other for the purpose of achieving something they could not achieve alone."[3] This is what Paul was telling the Roman church: "Do not think of yourself more highly than you ought, but rather think of yourself with sober judgment. . . . Just as each of us has one body with many members, and these members do not all have the same function, so in Christ we who are many form one body, and each member belongs to all the others" (Rom. 12:3b-5).

Servant leadership does not imply a passive, vacillating, wishy-washy, or uninvolved approach. "Christian leaders are servants with credibility and capabilities, who are able to influence people in a particular context to pursue their God-given direction."[4] There is no question, servant leaders should be leaders. But servanthood and leadership are not automatic. "You can be a servant and not a leader. You can be a leader and not a servant," Nelson observes. "But to be a servant leader, you must first become a servant. A servant leader is one who both serves by leading and leads in such a way as to exemplify a servant's attitude."[5] To be a Christian leader means to follow the pattern Jesus demonstrated while on earth.

THE SERVANT LEADER'S MODEL

The idea of being a servant or slave was not a popular one for the people of Israel in Jesus' day. Memories of their ancestors serving 430 years of slavery in Egypt were enough to make their tempers boil in anger. Add to that the humiliation of their captivity in Babylon. If God delivered them from their forced times of bondage in the past, why would they ever want to go back to being servants again? Thus Jesus' talk of being a servant did not strike a positive cord, even among his fellow Jewish followers.

Being a servant didn't resonate with the citizens of the Roman Empire either. Slavery was a common situation for some unfortunate people throughout

---

2. Eddie Gibbs, *LeadershipNext: Changing Leaders in a Changing Culture* (Downers Grove, IL: InterVarsity Press, 2005), 29.

3. Alan E. Nelson, *Leading Your Ministry* (Nashville: Abingdon Press, 1996), 77.

4. Aubrey Malphurs, *Being Leaders: The Nature of Authentic Christian Leadership* (Grand Rapids: Baker Books, 2003), 33.

5. Nelson, *Leading Your Ministry*, 78.

the Roman world. If one became indebted to someone and could not pay back the debt, the only recourse was to become a slave until the debt could be paid back. The problem for slaves was that they didn't earn any money, and so it was impossible for them to ever buy back their freedom. "According to the Greeks, some were born to nobility and others to subjugation. Slavery was for others—the vanquished, the weak, the prisoner."[6]

You can see why no one, Jew or Gentile, came to Jesus and begged that he tell more about how to become a servant. No one listed "being a servant" in the disciple application blank after the question, "Goals in life?" The only way Jesus could get the point across to his followers was to demonstrate it with his own life.

The earliest recorded hymn of the early church, probably written before any of the Gospel accounts of Jesus' life, is found in Philippians 2:5-11. It begins with these challenging words:

> Your attitude should be the same as that of Christ Jesus:
> Who, being in very nature God,
> did not consider equality with God something to be grasped,
> but made himself nothing,
> taking the very nature of a *servant,*
> being made in human likeness.
> And being found in appearance as a man,
> he humbled himself
> and became obedient to death—
> *even death on a cross!*
> (vv. 5-8, italics added)

Those early Christians sang about identifying with the servant nature of their Lord and Master. This was shocking, revolutionary music that harked back to the sayings of Jesus passed from church to church in oral and written form. We can read some of Jesus' summary teaching on the subject today in Matthew 11:28-30; 20:25-28; 23:11-12; 25:14-30; Mark 10:42-45; and John 13:1-17; 15:11-17. If there were only one or two verses in the Gospels on being a servant, it could be argued that Jesus was just making an offhand comment. But Jesus' many statements in various settings indicate that servanthood was a major theme.

One intriguing episode in Jesus' ministry involved James and John requesting a promotion up the corporate pyramid to become the top two disciples among the Twelve. Matthew said it was their mother who made the request.

---

6. Robert D. Dale, *Leadership for a Changing Church: Charting the Shape of the River* (Nashville: Abingdon Press, 1998), 53.

Mark reports that it was James and John themselves. But whatever the origin of the request, the response of Jesus was astonishment. If he were speaking today, he would say, "You guys just don't get it! The kingdom is not about position. It's all about service." Greg Ogden observes,

> Jesus instructed his followers to walk away from the prevailing Gentile and Jewish models of prideful leadership where dominance ("lording it over"), coercion, titles, and public recognition were the goals. . . . Jesus spoke of leaders who serve. Servant leaders still do things leaders do—direct, organize, envision. But with *servant* qualifying *leadership*, the kingdom of God—not one's personal fiefdom—becomes our motivation and shapes our style of leadership.[7]

As Jesus' ministry phase drew to a close, he began to demonstrate the principles of servanthood with his life. "When Jesus washed the feet of the disciples, he was transitioning his focus from the visionary/direction part of leadership to the implementation role."[8] Jesus waited until the night before he died to introduce the official uniform of the servant leader—the towel. He took the basin and water and moved around the room washing the dirty feet of every man in the room. So the teaching moment would not be missed on the twelve men in the upper room, Jesus clarified what had just happened. "Now that I, your Lord and Teacher, have washed your feet, you also should wash one another's feet. I have set you an example that you should do as I have done for you. I tell you the truth, no servant is greater than his master, nor is a messenger greater than the one who sent him" (John 13:14-16). It was a powerful life statement none of them would ever forget. "In essence he was saying that if you want to get people to come willingly, if you want to influence people from the neck up, then you must serve. Legitimate leadership, influence, is built upon serving, sacrificing, and seeking the greatest good of those being led."[9]

The ultimate demonstration of Jesus' servant spirit was his death on the cross. Jesus concluded his servanthood discourse in Mark 10 with this prophetic statement: "For even the Son of Man did not come to be served, but to serve, and to give his life as a ransom for many" (Mark 10:45). When the actual moment was about to unfold on the eve of Jesus' death, John opens the scene in the upper room: "Jesus knew that the time had come for him to leave this

---

7. Greg Ogden, "Servant Leadership" in *Leadership Handbook of Management and Administration*, ed. James D. Berkley (Grand Rapids: Baker Books, 1994), 150.

8. Ken Blanchard and Phil Hodges, *Servant Leader: Transforming Your Heart, Head, Hands & Habits* (Nashville: Thomas Nelson, 2003), 53.

9. James C. Hunter, *The World's Most Powerful Leadership Principle: How to Become a Servant Leader* (Colorado Springs: WaterBrook Press, 2004), 73.

world and go to the Father. Having loved his own who were in the world, he now showed them the full extent of his love" (John 13:1). The full extent of love was not found in washing between the disciples' toes. It was laying down his life. Chuck Colson, founder of Prison Fellowship, once said, "All the kings and queens I have known in history sent their people out to die for them. I only know one King who decided to die for his people."[10] Jesus never demanded that his followers physically give up their lives, although many have died across the centuries of the church's history. He does call all servant leaders to die to their right to be first.

THE SERVANT LEADER'S CONTEXT

Many will remember people around the world counting as the last seconds of the twentieth century disappeared forever. The giant globe descended on Times Square in New York City and the new millennium began. Most of the Y2K (Year 2000) fears that computers would not work on January 1, 2000, were baseless. But the beginning of the twenty-first century has not been simply a repeat of the past. Forces beginning in the 1980s and 1990s have spawned a new culture that is only beginning to be understood. Some are saying that this cultural shift is as significant as the changes brought about by the invention of Guttenberg's moveable-type printing press in the late fourteenth century. Consider briefly a few of the shifts that directly impact the church beginning today and stretching into the future.

The Postmodern Paradigm Shift

To better understand the impact of the move from a *modern* to *postmodern* mind-set, Robert Dale gives three characteristics of this new world: (1) The postmodern world has moved to a cultural understanding that has *no rules*. Processes and routines are not as well defined as in the past. Dale says, "To survive and thrive in a world without rules, leaders need principles based on character and integrity."[11] (2) The world in which we live has *no speed limit*. Change is coming so rapidly that some people live in perpetual panic. "The speed of change is so great that paradigms have shrunk from millennia to centuries to mere decades. . . . Values and character have a huge advantage for leaders in chaotic circumstances; they are portable and sustain us on the run."[12] (3) For many people living in this world, there are *no boundaries*. The informa-

---

10. Quoted in Blanchard and Hodges, *Servant Leader*, 57.
11. Dale, *Leadership for a Changing Church*, 20.
12. Ibid., 21.

tion age has made almost any fact about any person or idea available to anyone who has a computer and access to the Internet. Indiscretions or misstatements of public figures are revealed immediately for everyone to see and read, not by news organizations, but by anyone with a video camera or cell phone. "In our boundary-transcending information society, leaders are persons who can sort through the glut of data and make some sense of our world."[13]

From Pyramids to Level Ground

The use of hierarchical business charts to define corporate or church authority structures is being replaced by an image of leaders standing on level ground with those being led. Leadership roles are functional as everyone finds a place of responsibility and service within the church. Nelson explains, "In leadership, the leader fills the key role because without this person or persons the quality of the relationship would be severely reduced. At the same time, the leader is considered a peer, just another part doing her unique job. . . . A linear peer relationship conveys servanthood because it equalizes everyone when the tendency is to elevate leaders, even servant leaders."[14] Even in business, leaders are now realizing that implementing the vision of the organization means a change in approach. Blanchard and Hodges report, "Effective implementation requires turning the hierarchy upside down so the customer contact people are at the top of the organization and are able to respond to customers, while the leaders serve the needs of employees, helping them accomplish the vision and direction of the organization. That's what Jesus had in mind when he washed the feet of the disciples."[15] Jesus said, "The Son of Man did not come to be served, but to serve" (Matt. 20:28). Jesus served the plan laid out by the Father, thus serving in advance the people who would benefit from God's divine plan. It is this same kingdom plan that servant leaders are called to today.

Leadership Built on Trust

In a climate of moral failure where political, corporate, sports, and even religious leaders have capitulated to greed, lust, and an unbridled misuse of power, people are suspicious of anyone in a leadership position. The most important question on people's minds as they view potential leaders, whether those seeking political office or a new church pastor is simply this: "Can this person be trusted?" Malphurs states, "Trust is so important to leadership because people won't follow leaders they don't trust. And trust is at the core of the leader's cred-

---

13. Ibid.
14. Nelson, *Leading Your Ministry*, 79-80.
15. Blanchard and Hodges, *Servant Leader*, 54.

ibility and essential to effective leadership in today's ministries."[16] Earning the trust of the led is essential for church leaders. "A servant leader in the image of Christ must be by nature a truth-teller and a realist. Honesty in communicating the price to be paid for serving and living out the values of servant leadership is a crucial test of the integrity of the leader."[17]

Community Openness and Disclosure

When information is so readily available from many sources, people in the community of faith expect to know what is going on in the church as well. "The leader must identify with all other members of the congregation. . . . There should be a climate of trust, in which people learn to trust their own abilities and those of others, unthreatened by constant changes in policy and program."[18] There are certainly conversations spoken by people in confidence to a pastor that should not ever be shared with anyone. However, when it comes to financial issues such as monthly and annual reports, such information should be available to anyone in the church. People do not give with generosity and confidence if they don't know how their money is going to be used. Paul describes the unity of the church in Romans 12:5: "So in Christ we who are many form one body, and each member belongs to all the others." Openness and disclosure promote unity.

THE SERVANT LEADER'S ROLES

Leaders in the twenty-first century are constantly looking backward to the Scripture as they move into the future. Both the Old and New Testaments are rich in leadership imagery. Robert Cooley mentions four biblical images that will be further expanded.[19]

Shepherd

This term refers to the pastoral care and concern that is a part of all in servant leadership within a church or religious organization. In the Bible, leading sheep usually meant direct contact because sheep were considered to be unreliable in their choices. Shepherds tended their flocks. "This tending includes

---

16. Malphurs, *Being Leaders*, 50.

17. Blanchard and Hodges, *Servant Leader*, 59.

18. Kenneth O. Gangel, "The Meaning of Leadership," in *Leadership Handbook of Management and Administration*, ed. James D. Berkley (Grand Rapids: Baker Books, 1994), 155.

19. Robert E. Cooley, "Learning from Biblical Images of Leadership," in *Lessons in Leadership*, ed. Randal Roberts (Grand Rapids: Kregel Publications, 1999), 90-92. His use of the terms "shepherd," "servant," "steward," and "leader" form the structure for this section.

a variety of functions which follow the analogy of shepherding such as feeding (teaching), nurturing (exhorting, reproving, correcting, comforting), leading or guiding, calling to follow, knowing by name, modeling and leading in hope."[20]

Shepherds in biblical times really got to know their sheep because they spent a lot of time alone with them. Jesus, in John 10:14, described himself in shepherding terms: "I am the good shepherd; I know my sheep and my sheep know me." There is understanding and concern implied in Jesus' words. A shepherd/pastor loves the congregation and sees ministry as the way to promote the well-being of everyone in the group. Nelson writes, "Servant leadership involves a much kinder, gentler approach to leading. It can be equally forceful and dynamic, but does not reduce the self-esteem of followers. Effective leading rarely leaves bodies strewn along its path due to blowing people over who will not bend to the new goals and vision."[21] Shepherds really care about the people inside and even outside the flock.

Servant

Some people watch a television program depicting children starving or groups of people suffering under the oppression of a corrupt political regime, and soon tears of concern flow down their cheeks. But concern itself accomplishes little without some kind of action. James confronts the issue directly, "Show me your faith without deeds, and I will show you my faith by what I do" (James 2:18). A servant cannot sit idly by when someone is in need. In serving others we become God's physical representatives here on earth. "The spiritual leader is one who voluntarily or willingly submits to the sovereign authority (Lordship) of Jesus Christ to obey him as directed for his benefit."[22]

Being a servant is not always casually done in a clean, antiseptic atmosphere. You can usually identify a servant leader by dirt under the fingernails and scrapes on the knees. Servants are not always treated with honor or viewed as heroes. They are often ignored, misunderstood, and even despised by onlookers. Sometimes it takes courage to be a servant. Ken Gangel tells the story of Loren Sanny, former leader of the Navigators, who was once asked, "How do you know when you have a servant attitude?" Sanny answered, "By how you react when you are treated like one."[23] Many Christians choose to identify with Christ by wearing a small cross. It is interesting that Jesus never commanded his

---

20. Edgar J. Elliston, *Home Grown Leaders* (Pasadena, CA: William Carey Library, 1992), 24.

21. Nelson, *Leading Your Ministry*, 80.

22. Elliston, *Home Grown Leaders*, 23.

23. Kenneth O. Gangel, *Feeding and Leading* (Wheaton, IL: Victor Books, 1989), 56.

followers to wear crosses around our necks. He did command us to tie a towel around our waists and serve (see John 13:14-17).

Steward

A steward assumes responsibility for the care and management of the monetary and physical resources of an individual, community group, or an organization. Jesus' familiar parable about talents in Matthew 25:14-30 illustrates the importance of stewardship. Three servants were entrusted with portions of the property of a man who was going to be away for a period of time. These servants were not given specific instructions. They only knew that they would someday answer for how they managed their master's property. When the owner returned, two of the servants reported that they invested the resources wisely and gained a profit for their master. The third servant did not spend or waste what was entrusted. This person simply buried it in the ground. It was not lost, but neither was it used. The first two were honored for being good stewards. The third was punished for being lazy and neglecting his responsibilities. In Scripture a steward acted as a representative of the master, making decisions for the benefit of the owner's estate.

The pertinent question for any steward, then or now, is this: "What would the master want me to do with the resources he has entrusted to me?" I have yet to meet a pastor who has said that his or her church has more money, facilities, or workers than they can possibly use. Most churches would like to do more if they just had more resources. As servant leaders, the stewardship question centers on how to use the limited resources to best build the kingdom of God. The money does not belong to the pastor or ministry leader. It doesn't even belong to the church. All of these resources—physical, financial, and human—belong to God. And all of us as leaders will someday answer for our stewardship of his kingdom assets.

Seer

The seer role of leadership refers to the visionary quality of seeing the present and future with faith. Old Testament seers were the prophets who saw hope and restoration in the future when all around them was corruption, idolatry, or even captivity. The apostle Paul, in a nighttime vision from God, shifted the focus of his missionary journey away from Bithynia to cross over to the European continent (Acts 16). It was a big step in fulfilling his call to be the apostle to the Gentiles outside the Middle East. Even John in the Book of Revelation spoke to a persecuted church about a vision of hope for better days ahead.

How important is vision? Dale Galloway says, "Vision—the place where tomorrow is shaped—motivates ministry and determines achievement. Vision unleashes creativity and helps a body of believers visualize a magnificent future." He continues, "Vision provides an energizing force for a congregation even as it produces a picture of a faith-inspiring future that can be brought into being by individual and group actions, commitments, and priorities."[24] Vision is imagining God's preferable future that he has uniquely planned for the church. What is this preferable future? Preferable means it is something that is better than today. It becomes a direction or roadmap for the church to follow as it moves to the future. It is a snapshot, sometimes clear and other times fuzzy, of what God wants the church to become and do. Servant leaders stimulate faith in that vision—what God wants to do among the local body of believers. "Servant leadership begins with a clear and compelling vision of the future that excites passion in the leader and commitment in those who follow."[25] Vision comes first to the leader and is then fleshed out by the church. Effective servant leaders who are seers are able to visualize God's dream of hope and then communicate that image to the community of faith.

THE SERVANT LEADER'S PERSONAL QUALITIES

Drawing an exact picture of a servant leader would be impossible. They may be female or male, tall or short, young or old, skinny or stout. Some may influence large groups of people while others may know only a few. While it may be impossible to identify the physical makeup or the ministry context of a typical individual, there are some qualities that are common in most servant leaders. And while no one exhibits all of the characteristics, these qualities help to build a profile of the inner makeup of those who serve and lead in the name of Jesus.

Character

Character is the consolidation of moral and ethical qualities at the inner core of an individual that motivate behavior. It is who we are at the heart or center of our being. The nineteenth-century lay evangelist Dwight Moody defined it this way: "Character is what a man is in the dark."[26] Why is good character important? Greg Ogden says, "Servant leaders base their authority on character, not the position they occupy. Moral authority arises from a person's integrity

---

24. Dale Galloway, "The Incredible Power of Vision: Discovering God's Extraordinary Plan for Your Future" in *Leading with Vision*, ed. Dale Galloway (Kansas City: Beacon Hill Press of Kansas City, 1999), 11.

25. Blanchard and Hodges, *Servant Leader*, 45.

26. Quoted in James C. Hunter, *The World's Most Powerful Leadership Principle: How to Become a Servant Leader* (Colorado Springs: WaterBrook Press, 2004), 141.

and consistency before Christ."[27] The more people learn of the good character of a servant leader, the more willing they are to follow. Trust, based on character, promotes confidence among those who are led.

For this reason leaders need to live consistently, motivated by those core character values. Former major league baseball pitcher Tim Burke tells how he learned this lesson. Tim and his wife, Christine, became Christians while he was playing minor league ball in Buffalo, New York. God immediately delivered him from a serious alcohol addiction in his life that had threatened their marriage. After Burke made it to the major leagues, playing for the Montreal Expos, he had even begun sharing his testimony of deliverance with teammates and at churches. One night Christine called after the game and recognized right away that he had been drinking. For Christine, it brought back all the memories of Tim's alcoholism in the past. Tim asked for Christine's forgiveness, but it took her some time to get over the hurt and disappointment she felt.[28] Trust is easily lost and difficult to regain. Aubrey Malphurs writes, "Credibility and trustworthiness rest on the foundation of your character. To compromise your character is to compromise your leadership and erode the trust of followers."[29]

Humility

Humility is an honest appraisal of our strengths and a recognition of our weaknesses. In his book *Humble Leadership*, Graham Standish writes, "Humility, in the end, is a state of being in which we willingly try to seek and serve God's will in everything. We do our best to discern God's will and follow it, and in the process, we willingly set aside, to the extent possible, everything that gets in the way."[30] Leading with humility can be challenging, especially when people brag on your leadership skills. There is a tendency in the current church culture to emphasize strengths and accomplishments. When television pastors vie for the title of who has the largest church, servants like Mother Teresa are ignored as models of ministry. The issue is not only that you serve but also how you serve. John Maxwell writes, "The higher your status or standing in a kingdom assignment, organization, or local congregation, the harder it is to remember that you are always a servant to the people of God and that Jesus is Lord and Master. Titles, authority, being boss, controlling budgets, and perks must always

---

27. Ogden, "Servant Leadership," 151.
28. Tim Burke and Christine Burke, *Major League Dad* (Colorado Springs: Focus on the Family Publishing, 1994), 111-17.
29. Malphurs, *Being Leaders*, 56.
30. N. Graham Standish, *Humble Leadership: Being Radically Open to God's Guidance and Grace* (Herndon, VA: Alban Institute, 2007), 16.

be used under the ultimate Lordship of Jesus."[31] There is no room in a servant leader's makeup for a big ego.

Love

Love is an indispensable quality of those who would be servants. The problem with the term "love" is that it is used to describe everything from a preference in food ("I just love steak!") to the emotional feeling of two fourteen-year-olds who discover romance, to a sign-off on the phone ("Love ya!"). Most students of the New Testament are familiar with the Greek word *agapē*, which describes a self-giving love that demands nothing in return. James Hunter explains this concept of love to secular business leaders: "The act(s) of extending yourself for others by identifying and meeting their legitimate needs and seeking their greatest good."[32]

When Jesus, the Master Servant Leader, wrapped the towel around his waist to wash the disciples' dirty feet, the disciples were outraged. It was true that there were probably no house servants there that evening. But a teacher would never wash the feet of his students. Jesus knew that custom, but his attitude was different. His kind of love required action. He wanted these men to understand servant love, so John wrote that Jesus "now showed them the full extent of his love" (John 13:1). This gets to the driving force for leaders serving. Nothing is as powerful a motive as *agapē* love. "How would you know a servant leader if you saw one? Jesus was a servant leader incarnate. And he's taught us by his example that servant leadership is *humble service to others based on our love for them.*"[33]

Courage

How would you like to be the leader to follow Moses, the greatest leader of the Hebrew people in the Old Testament? Joshua, the heir apparent to the leadership role, had served under Moses' leadership for many years. Joshua apparently didn't feel he was capable of stepping into Moses' sandals. After assuring Joshua that he would be with him, God challenged Joshua four times to "be strong and courageous" in Joshua 1. In fact, in verse 7 he added a word for emphasis, "be strong and *very* courageous" (italics added). Joshua could not be the leader God needed him to be if he didn't have the strength and courage to act when it would be easier to move cautiously or sit and do nothing. Courage

---

31. John Maxwell, "How to Be a Christlike Servant Leader," in *Leading with Vision*, ed. Dale Galloway (Kansas City: Beacon Hill Press of Kansas City, 1999), 54.

32. Hunter, *World's Most Powerful Leadership Principle*, 86.

33. Malphurs, *Being Leaders*, 43.

is required in ministry because the job is so challenging. Leith Anderson tells of hearing the late business writer Peter Drucker say to a group of large church pastors, "Other than president of the United States, the three most difficult jobs in America today are president of a large university, administrator of a large hospital, and pastor of a large church."[34]

Having courage doesn't mean always needing to be right or being unwilling to consider other's opinions. "This kind of courage displays itself in leaders' willingness to stand up for their beliefs in difficult situations, challenge others, admit mistakes (be vulnerable), change their views when wrong, and not quit. The payoff is exceptional credibility, because followers like what they see in courageous leaders."[35] Such courage arises out of the conviction that the God who calls will guide the leader in the right direction toward his vision for the church.

Empowering

Servant leaders can only be successful as they help people to, in the words of the old U.S. Army slogan, "be all that you can be." In this organizational climate change from hierarchical to team leadership, a servant leader needs to have the best equipped, qualified, Spirit-led people available to be a part of the leadership team. Stephen Dillman defines the role of the empowering leader as "motivating others, providing guidance, resourcing those being led, and developing environmental supports to facilitate their tasks. Implied in this definition is the responsibility of the leader to help followers succeed and to remove obstacles that might hinder them from succeeding."[36]

The concept of empowerment suggests that the leader's confidence and trust are in those assuming responsibilities. No one wants to feel as if he or she is being used to do tasks that are merely busy work. That is why people need to be valued, first of all, for who they are, and not simply for what they can do. "What makes a leader a servant leader is first and foremost the type of motivation in the leader. When the motivation of the leader is to unleash the potential of the followers and primarily benefit the needs of the organization, that person is a servant leader."[37]

Community Building

Servant leaders strive to eliminate any sense of "us versus them," or "clergy versus laity," pitting leaders against followers. Being a clergy or lay leader does

---

34. Leith Anderson, *Leadership That Works* (Minneapolis: Bethany House, 1999), 25.

35. Malphurs, *Being Leaders*, 63.

36. Dillman, "The Person-Centered Lifestyle" (quotation used by permission).

37. Nelson, *Leading Your Ministry*, 78.

not automatically place a person into a category that elevates him or her above others. Everyone in the church fills a unique role, but all are part of the unified Body of Christ. Dale says, "As community builders, leaders help link persons and ideas into meaningful connective patterns. . . . We help people who don't know each other become acquainted. . . . Leaders link the old and new in order to lend continuity and to make sense of our worlds."[38] Paul emphasized the importance of community in 1 Corinthians 12:12-13: "The body is a unit, though it is made up of many parts; and though all its parts are many, they form one body. So it is with Christ. For we were all baptized by one Spirit into one body—whether Jews or Greeks, slave or free—and we were all given the one Spirit to drink." Servant leaders play a key role in creating an atmosphere where community can develop and flourish. Maxwell offers this challenge to all who would be servant leaders: "(1) Whatever I do, I want to *honor God.* (2) Whatever I do, I want to do it with *all my heart.* (3) Whatever I do, I want to do it with *others.* (4) Whatever I do, I want to *honor and add value* to others."[39]

CONCLUSION

Just in case you still think that servant leaders are part of a special, exclusive group of people, such as Jesus, Paul, Francis of Assisi, and Mother Teresa, consider these words from another person who might be put in this category. Martin Luther King Jr. once said, "Everybody can be great because anybody can serve. You don't have to have a college degree to serve. You don't have to make your subject and verb agree to serve. You only need a heart full of grace. A soul generated by love."[40] With the Holy Spirit's empowering presence, you, too, can be a servant leader.

FOR FURTHER READING

Dale, Robert D. *Leadership for a Changing Church: Charting the Shape of the River.* Nashville: Abingdon Press, 1998.

Gibbs, Eddie. *LeadershipNext: Changing Leaders in a Changing Culture.* Downers Grove, IL: InterVarsity Press, 2005.

Nelson, Alan E. *Leading Your Ministry.* Ed. Herb Miller. Nashville: Abingdon Press, 1996.

---

38. Dale, *Leadership for a Changing Church,* 36.
39. Maxwell, "How to Be a Christlike Servant Leader," 53.
40. Quoted in ibid., 44.

14

CHANGE MANAGEMENT
LEADING THE CHURCH THROUGH CULTURAL AND ORGANIZATIONAL CHANGES

Edward A. Thomas
PhD, Associate Professor of Management,
Mount Vernon Nazarene University

The time has come to make a change. Change will happen just as the sun rises, and everyone can be certain of that. Good change does not just happen. It happens only with the understanding that people must change their behaviors. Most leaders—whether in the church or in a business—do not understand the complexity of how the change process affects people. Change is simply not something that is announced and then it happens.

How many times have you heard, "We have done it that way for thirty years and we will continue to do so" or something to that effect? People basically don't like change. But if a church has been operating a program or process the same way for thirty years, then it may be time to look at what is happening. This is not so much a matter of the church's theology as it is the church's traditional methods of ministry, outlook, or way of thinking. Times have changed. The Bill Gaither Trio, the gospel group, was big thirty years ago, and though many still enjoy them because they are very good, the style of song ministry has changed. The contemporary style of Generation Y (born after 1980) features lyrics that are more personal than theological and favors drums and guitars over the piano and organ. In some circles even the use of hymns has almost disappeared. But this is the music many today will listen to, and church leaders have to pay attention to it. At the same time, they cannot ignore the preferences of older generations in trying to fashion a healthy blend of worship music. Change happens. Look at the many different versions of the Bible. The Bible has been translated into the modern vernacular so the gospel can be widely communicated and understood. This author has actually heard this bold statement: "If the King James Version was good enough for St. Paul, it is good enough for me!" Think about it.

For most leaders change is something that is not taught. In business most change comes by way of a formal one-time announcement accompanied by an organizational restructuring. A boss might announce that on a certain date there will be a new way of doing things along with a change in the company's hierarchy. Sometimes an illusion of progress is created just by moving the organizational structure around. Often this activity results in the change of a few things and much confusion for the people over what happened. So instead of doing what was intended, people go back to doing what they have always done. Why? Because the behavior of people must change before the organizational structure is changed. Just as this process happens in business, so does it happen in the church.[1] The church is no different when it comes to the change process.

PURPOSE

Most people want to believe things will always remain the same and change will not happen. Ben Franklin said that the sure things in life are death and taxes. He should have added change. People, circumstances, and things will never stay at the status quo. The world is revolving at breakneck speed. Things change at our workplaces, and circumstances change at our church.

Black and Gregersen tell us it is human nature to seek the status quo, while nature tells us things are changing.[2] The church is one of the bastions of stability and most resistant to change. The key to overall strategic change is to change the behavior of the people before changing the culture or organizational framework. This is the way to give birth to real, lasting change. Most organizations try to change the structure before the behaviors, but simply changing titles and moving offices to formulate a new organizational chart does very little. Change is not easy, but it does not have to be painful. It is less painful when trust is built first.

J. D. Duck gives two prerequisites for change leadership:
1. Predictability—proven consistency
2. Capabilities—competencies for leadership and training others.[3]

These two factors mirror the traditional requirements for trust: fairness, honesty, and integrity. The pastor needs to get to know the people first before a major change in ministry takes place. Pastor, build trust between yourself and your congregation.

---

1. J. Stewart Black and Hal B. Gregersen, *Leading Strategic Change: Breaking Through the Brain Barrier* (Upper Saddle River, NJ: Prentice Hall, 2002), 8.
2. Ibid, 21.
3. J. D. Duck, "Managing Change: The Art of Balancing," *Harvard Business Review,* November/December 1993, 108-18.

Even in business school and leadership conferences, the topic of change is not taught often, because it is a soft issue. Business schools like to teach the hard issues, or quantitative problems, because getting one's hands around hard numbers is easier. And clearly it appears fancier to work with long equations and spreadsheets. But when it comes to change, leaders of organizations are expected to be experienced. Yet how can they be if they were never taught this change paradigm? The ones that learn the process are light-years ahead in their professional leadership development. For readers of this book, this is now an opportunity to learn the process that others have found so valuable.

To begin, we must understand, as mentioned earlier, that individual behaviors must change first. Then together the people can change as a movement to fulfill their gospel mission and stand before God on that last day to hear, "Well done, good and faithful servant" (Matt. 25:21).

STRATEGY

Kotter recommends an eight-stage process to accomplish the highly improbable task of moving the congregation or any group of people in a new direction. The steps of the process are (1) create urgency; (2) build a guiding coalition; (3) develop a vision and strategy; (4) communicate the vision and strategy; (5) empower the people; (6) realize short-term wins; (7) consolidate gains; and (8) anchor the gains.

The first step is to create an atmosphere of urgency.[4] Keep stressing from the pulpit and in church communications the importance of the mission objectives and how they will be achieved. This will set the tone for the members to be ready for the next move. Use visual images to remind the people that there are mission objectives still to be accomplished. If possible, keep the church's physical surroundings simple. When the physical environment of the church building itself is shouting success, then the congregation may feel they have arrived and become complacent.

Next build a guiding team. Look for these characteristics: *(a)* early volunteers, *(b)* positive critics, *(c)* informal power, *(d)* versatility, and *(e)* emotional intelligence.[5]

It will be all right as well to include those with formal power (power by virtue of a position or office), but be sure they can be positive contributors. The bottom line is that most churches have an organizational board, but their pur-

---

4. Kotter, *Leading Change,* 36.
5. Quy Nguyen Huy, "In Praise of Middle Managers," *Harvard Business Review,* September 2001, 72-79.

pose is set to maintain the status quo. Use functional groups to move the change process forward. It will be their purpose to make a change happen.

Third, develop a vision and strategy. Show the path the congregation will travel (the strategy part), and assure them that they will arrive safely at the targeted destination. People need to see where they are going. Just as plane passengers must know their itinerary and be convinced before takeoff that they will land safely once the flight is over, so must church members be confident of the route they are taking and that they will reach its end in one piece.

Church members do not want to be led in the wilderness. Following their exodus from Egypt, the Israelites arrived at the outskirts of the Promised Land and sent out twelve spies into it (see Deut. 1). The spies reported back that it was a land of milk and honey, but ten spies said that there were giants in the land and that they would be unconquerable. Joshua and Caleb were the only ones to report that the Hebrew nation could win the battle for the land. Most of the people believed the ten. Therefore, except for the two spies who had faith to believe that God would help them, God did not allow any of that generation to enter the Promised Land. A new and trusting generation had to be raised. People need to believe that they can reach their destination safely and competently.

The next step is to communicate the vision and strategy. People need to be clearly and repeatedly told where they are going and that there is a safe arrival. Black suggests that the message must be communicated at least five to six times, not just in a one-time announcement.[6] People need to rehear the message to establish its importance and renew it in their minds. Some marketing experts tell us that we need to recall an advertisement 10 to 12 seconds after we have experienced it to remember it.[7] Don't just repeat the message of the vision once. Repeat it again and again. Don't fall into the "I get it" mistake of only stating the message one time because you "get it" but nobody else does.[8]

Also, when communicating the details of the strategy, give only 20 percent of the plan at the outset. Give only the details that are most important for the people to know at the moment.[9] There is a concept that organizational behaviorists call selective perception. People tend to choose what is familiar and leave out the rest. So if the messenger gives out too much information too soon, people will garner only what is familiar or what they want to hear and will thus

6. Black and Gregersen, *Leading Strategic Change*, 50.

7. J. W. Mullins, O. C. Walker Jr., and H. W. Boyd Jr., *Marketing Management: A Strategic Decision-Making Approach* (Boston: McGraw-Hill/Irwin, 2008), 111.

8. Black and Gregersen, *Leading Strategic Change*, 50.

9. Ibid, 146.

defeat the change process. They will latch on to the old process themes and discount the new ones.

One more thing, Black tells us that people want a safe arrival. This was mentioned earlier, but now the emphasis is on communicating it clearly. So show them how they are going to start from point A and arrive at point Z safely. Give them the resources they need to be competently ready to meet the new program. Make sure they receive whatever training, equipment, and personnel they need to make the change. Ask volunteers and personnel what skills, competencies, and training they think they need.[10] See if their viewpoint matches that of the leader. If not, get them the necessary resources.

Reward people, not with money, but with intrinsic motivators (outlined below using the acronym ARCTIC) that bestow the feelings of self-actualization and self-worth when the task is completed:[11]

1. **A**chievement
   a. Accomplishment—meeting goals
   b. Competition—comparing performance of individuals and groups
2. **R**elations
   a. Approval—being appreciated
   b. Belonging—being part of a group. Make this need a little harder to come by, for sacrifice locks in commitment
3. **C**onceptual/**T**hinking
   a. Problem solving—finding solutions
   b. Coordination—integrating and managing the pieces of the process
4. **I**mprovement
   a. Growth
   b. Exploration—seeking out the new
5. **C**ontrol
   a. Competence—becoming capable; trained
   b. Influence—becoming a knowledgeable expert

Church members will be motivated by one or more of the factors listed above. Use them to motivate a few before motivating the many. Jesus did this with the twelve disciples.

Next, empower the people to take the reins of the carriage of change and drive it. When the winds of change are in movement, people may begin to feel worthless and unneeded and their commitment to the church may wane. Make

---

10. Ibid, 157.
11. Ibid, 11.

them feel useful.[12] Give responsibilities so that they may feel a sense of owner-ship. Nothing that comes easy is worthwhile. Let them achieve their place using one of the motivational factors mentioned earlier. Hard work, even some sacri-fice, allows for increased commitment, gives them their sense of purpose, and becomes a natural turn on.[13] When they have a vested interest in what is going on, they will turn their energy toward the new project. Give them something they love to do. They will give their heart to the ministry and see that it proves successful. They will commit themselves to the new project. When the pastor takes control, the church member is robbed of a rewarding ministry. Most pas-tors will allow parishioners to perform their ministries. But there are some who need to micromanage and do everything themselves. This deprives parishioners of their joy and their fulfillment in God's work.

Sixth,[14] realize short-term wins. A machine tool company from Wisconsin had an incentive plan called the Scanlon Plan. When the company showed improvement in its efficiency, a cash reward was given out. Part of this reward went into a yearly pool of money. If the firm failed to show improvement, the money went to the company, but if improvement in efficiency was quantifiable, the money went to the employees. What made this strategy work was the hand-ing out of monthly bonuses for improvements. By realizing short-term wins, the workers could say, "We've done it." This factor builds confidence. It energizes people to continue their efforts. Think of a pro baseball team. They need to win in the regular season to make it into the fall playoffs. Without short-term wins they would neither qualify nor feel confident that they could meet the challenge of the playoffs. So when the church shows that it can accomplish a difficult task, the members will try other challenges.

One thing churches do well is plateau. After a church works hard and reach-es a target or objective, it exerts no more effort. Some members may have a sense of "arrival" or mission accomplished. For example, many churches in the evangeli-cal movement still hold revivals with special speakers once or twice a year. One of their major hopes is that their people will get enthused or "fired up" in their spiritual commitment. Everything done in those meetings comes with a sense of urgency. This continues only until the speakers and musicians have left for other meetings. The pastor then feels that the church has arrived. Emotional encourage-ment may last a short time, but soon the people are doing the same thing they did

---

12. Price Pritchett, *Firing Up Commitment During Organizational Change,* 2nd ed. (Dallas: Pritchett & Associates, 1996), 12.
    13. Ibid, 14.
    14. Kotter, *Leading Change,* 117.

before the revival services, being complacent or plateauing (coasting): "We are here, why try harder!" Most of the time, but not always, this scene will play itself out. Then the church will start yearning for the revival process all over again. And pastors often come to depend on this. Jesus' disciples had this problem.

On the Mount of Transfiguration, Jesus was revealed as the Son of God. The three disciples wanted to build altars because of this event and stay on the mountaintop. But they could not remain there, and Jesus led them back down the mountain to the real work in the valleys where people lived and worked (see Matt. 17:1-9). It is great to be on a mountaintop spiritual high, but one must see the needs in the valley. The three disciples wanted to rest on the mountaintop or plateau. Likewise, the church that continually yearns to rest on the mountaintop experiences of revivals but plateaus out between every revival service must begin ministering to people working and living in the valleys of everyday life. This is the way to escape from the revival-plateau cycle and move on to real ministry and purpose. A church must find a way to make its new accomplishments—revived lives or otherwise—permanent.

Consolidating gains that are achieved and bringing permanence to change is thus the seventh step suggested by Kotter.[15] This stage has the following features:

1. More change not less: each short-term win from the previous stage is used as a stepping-stone to tackle new projects.
2. More help: new people are brought in, trained, and given responsibilities.
3. Leadership from top management: this group steers the way and keeps everyone accountable and on track.
4. Project management and leadership from below: the lower hierarchy carries through and implements the projects plus reports the completion.
5. Reduction of unnecessary interdependencies: remove obstacles to change and unneeded processes.[16]

If completed projects are not recognized and used as steps to move on to the next plateau, then some folks may try to halt the momentum and assert that the progress made is enough. The key to this section is No. 5 listed above, the reduction of key interdependencies. This may include certain organizational structures, levels of management, and specific departments, programs, and processes. The more clutter in the way, the less chance for success. Dead weight drags momentum backward. If there are factors that get in the way of change in the church, remove them. If it is people, find something they can do. Prayer

---

15. Ibid, 131.
16. Ibid, 143.

would be a good place to start; then move into the auditing of programs and budgets. And who knows, a church may be able to unleash some budgetary money by the elimination of processes and programs. A handy method is zero-based budgeting. This method works by taking all the current budgetary lines, removing any current figures, and setting each line to zero, then going through each line and asking whether the item is really needed and, if so, how much. This will give a true picture of a budget. The lines that are needed or new ones added will be kept, and the excess or unneeded lines will be discarded. The zero-based method can also be used for a start-up process.

Keep the process of running the church organization lean. Keep the process and methodology effective and efficient as you minister in love and holiness. Time and money are precious resources that should never be taken for granted. You are the chief steward of the church's resources. Use them well. People will donate more time and money if they see that good stewardship practices abound.

The eighth and final step in the process that Kotter recommends is to anchor the wins and the gains made in the culture.[17] Make the gains part of the new values of the church. Rewrite the vision and mission statement. Celebrate the new goals and values so that the members experience the new culture. Remember you must facilitate changing individual behaviors before the culture can change. This may take months or even years, but do it. Black and Gregersen give a bit of advice: there are people and groups that fail to finish because they grow tired or get lost. This happens when change takes the long-term route.[18]

Robbins states that there are five reasons for individual resistance: habits, security, economic factors, fear of the unknown, and selective information processing. They will be discussed in the order given.[19]

1. Habits—people revert back to the ways that have proven successful.
   a. People drive the same way to work every day. They have the same habits and follow the same processes that have worked well for them at work.
   b. In church, they sit in the same seats and worship the same way they have done for years.
   c. Reason: these habits have worked well for them and have been successful in the past. Why change even though they are less fruitful today?

---

17. Ibid.
18. Black and Gregersen, *Leading Strategic Change,* 91.
19. Stephen P. Robbins and Timothy A. Judge, *Essentials of Organizational Behavior,* 9th ed. (Upper Saddle River, NJ: Prentice Hall, 2008), 269.

2. Security/stability—this goes hand in hand with the first point.
   a. The status quo is more satisfying and less risky.
3. Economic factors—fear of a loss in income and monetary status.
   a. A high monetary status equals stability.
4. Fear of the unknown—trying something new.
   a. Fear of poor performance or looking incompetent.
5. Selective information processing—hear only what one wants to hear.
   a. The individual listens for what is familiar; ignores the rest of the message.
   b. Churches become petrified in ministry when time and culture have passed them by. They do not hear the call of change.

Robbins states that these old individual reasons listed above also bring about resistance to organizational change through structural and group inertia, a limited focus on changes, and threats to relationships and resource allocations:[20]

1. Inertia—Every process moves the same as it has in days gone by.
   a. Nothing new is done.
2. Limited focus on changes.
   a. Original culture or viewpoint remains constant and moderate in response to any large change that upsets the status quo.
3. Threats to relationships and resource allocations.
   a. Individual fears loss of belonging to a group.
   b. Individual fears loss of control.
   c. Individual fears loss of identity.

There are three obstacles, or "brain barriers," to overcome in the challenge of changing behaviors:[21] a failure to see, a failure to move, and a failure to finish.

First, there is the failure to see. Again, people are creatures of habit. They will follow the same procedure day after day. Because they are comfortable with the way things are done or going, they will need to be awakened from their sleep. The parable of the ten virgins in the Bible (see Matt. 25) reinforces this principle. They all fell asleep waiting for the coming of the bridegroom. They awoke, and five went looking for more oil for the lamps to light the way for the bridegroom. While they were gone, they missed his coming. In that same vein, church members fall asleep to the calling of the church's mission. It will take a large shock to awaken them.

To overcome the failure to see, try using the tools of contrast and confron-

---

20. Ibid.
21. Black and Gregersen, *Leading Strategic Change.*

tation.[22] In contrast, give the listener a before and after picture of the desired change or new behavior. Also use these methods:[23]

1. Give only 20 percent of the details initially in presenting the future.
    a. This avoids selective perception from people hearing too much detail at once.
    b. Avoids people latching on to what they know and understand, forgetting the rest of the details they don't understand.
2. Show the differences in the before and after descriptions.
    a. Use word pictures.
    b. Use stories and applications of the new concepts that must be understood.
    c. Use a bit of humor.

Getting people to see their faith's purpose can also be accomplished by creating a confrontational experience using these methods:[24]

1. Repetition (five or six times)
    a. The message must be repeated to demonstrate the importance of the message and details.
    b. Also this repetition is needed for recall. Marketers know that a person needs to be able to recall a commercial with its message at least five to ten seconds after he or she has seen it in order to remember the message much later.
    c. The people must remember and recall the importance of the message and purpose of the new directive.
2. Create high-impact, inescapable experiences. Provide an exposure to other groups. Visit the people to whom you are targeting your energies and resources. Read and study alternatives to the way you have been doing something for the last thirty years. Remove something from your church facility or a piece of your worship service to show the congregation what might be missed if things do not change. In others words, show a high contrast from where the people are now and where they should be. This is the inescapable experience. (See b-(4) below.)

    a. People cannot easily ignore the experience.
        (1) If they cannot get around the new experience, they will be forced to deal with it and not ignore what they hear and see.
        (2) This eliminates most selective perception.

22. Ibid, 46-47.
23. Ibid, 146.
24. Ibid, 55.

(3) This places them with a choice to try a new way or lose out in experiencing a new and joyous adventure.

b. People must be engaged in the activity (sensory).
   (1) Allow them to use their senses: touch, taste, sight, hearing, and smell.
   (2) Put them in a situation to experience the change dynamics and processes.
   (3) Do not give them the opportunity to turn to the left or right or any moment to retreat. Only forward momentum.
   (4) Let them try it firsthand. Samsung executives couldn't understand why their products did not sell in the United States. A visit to the States showed them that their Korean products were relegated to the discount section in electronic stores. This perception had to change. After they saw what was happening, only then did they go back and develop a marketing plan to change that perception.

c. Stay focused.
   (1) Focus on your core values and any new values that you want to instill in your church members.
   (2) Remember, this is how they will discover the importance of the change decision.

The second obstacle in successful motivation is the failure to move.[25] Black and Gregersen present the argument that even though the people see what must be done, they must overcome the fear of trying something new. This paralysis comes from the fear of not understanding how the new change is to be done and whether or not they will have the knowledge and skills to do so. Other fears stem from ignorance about the process or from peer pressure and fear of what others will think. Now is when true leadership must take over. The old habits will not work. The same mental and emotional responses will not be effective. Leadership again will need to colorfully present a roadmap from point A, the beginning, to point Z, the finish, showing all the points along the way that include training-and-encouragement stopping points, resting stops, and milestones for celebration of achieved objectives. Here are the three steps by Black and Gregersen.

1. Show the destination.
2. Give the skills and resources needed.
3. Deliver rewards.[26]

---

25. Ibid, 65.
26. Ibid, 76.

In the first step, people need to know where they are going and how they will get there. How does a pastor know this? He needs to ask the people. Allow them to express what they are concerned about. Does this data match the map that the new change calls for? Is their map of the new path the same as the pastor's?

Second, what are the resources needed to make it from point A to point Z? Again, ask the members what they may need to make the journey. Human nature tells us that if the members are not provided resources, then they will try to find a way to get around the new pathway of ministry or avoid it altogether. Some examples of this behavior may include:

1. Becoming busy in other ways.
2. Refusal to participate.
3. Initially joining in but gradually fading out of the picture.
4. Complaining.

Remember, the level of the members' confidence is imperative. If the members feel they will get training, support, leadership by example, and monetary resources in the budget, only then will they develop confidence in the journey to their point of arrival. A sales company once urged its sales force to push the new product lines developed by its research and development division because sales were low. But the salespeople had no knowledge or expertise in the new product lines, so they were afraid to push the sales because they would look incompetent. Finally, management ordered training for the sales staff. Pastors, the "sink or swim" method very seldom works in any vocation or aspect of life. "Just do it" won't build a winning team. Give your people the resources they need to be successful.

The third strategy to overcome the failure to move is to present rewards. Find and discover ways to motivate. Motivate through the use of ARCTIC[27]— an acronym for achievement, relations, conceptual/thinking, improvement, and control. This concept was presented earlier in this chapter. This method helps get people off dead center and moving toward the goal of becoming a mission-minded church. The members need to experience a personal appeal to their hearts that moves them. Pastor, don't announce a new plan and expect it to happen. Get them motivated from the inside out.

The last motivational obstacle to get people to change is the failure to finish. Black and Gregersen state that two things happen: (1) people get tired and (2) people get lost.[28]

---

27. Ibid, 83.
28. Ibid, 91.

The pastor happens to be the most changeable piece in the church. He or she may come and go for different reasons. The church members have become experts at riding the crest of change as one pastor exits and another arrives through the front doors. As it is with any organization, there is a wait-and-see attitude. If they wait long enough, circumstances will stay the same and not change. The members have grown tired of change. The answer to this (from earlier in this chapter) is trust. Become predictable in your leadership and managerial abilities. The people in your church need to feel that you have integrity and fairness in all your dealings and preaching. Second, demonstrate that you have the tools to lead in change. Church members will want someone to train them—someone who will be around when success calls and will not leave the parish too quickly. A pastor's failure to stay when change comes can kill momentum and spirit.

Next, people tend to lose their way. Men no longer need to worry about damaging their egos from asking a stranger for directions when they get lost. The GPS device has come to their rescue. When change comes, it does not actualize overnight but may take months if not years. Then people lose sight of their destination. Black and Gregersen give us two answers to prevent a failure to finish: *(a)* chart the progress and *(b)* provide champions.[29]

First, measure how far you have come.[30] Determine what you want to measure—what you are changing. Then set a baseline measurement. What is the old value, standard, or number that you are working to change? Next, what is your goal? Set an objective to measure.

An objective should be an infinitive phrase, starting with "to" and an action verb such as "achieve" or "build." Next, be specific and measurable in the objective: "to achieve 5 percent growth in membership . . ." Then include a time sequence: ". . . in one year." Objectives should outline specific results that are measurable and timely.[31] This step will aid in identifying concise objectives.

Once the objective is defined, set a time line to measure the actions or behaviors that are to take place and when. Do not bunch measurements into one short period. Space out the interval between measurements.[32] Measure to chart the progress. This tool is an aid to visualize when changes in attitudes and behaviors should occur.

---

29. Ibid, 106.
30. Ibid, 170.
31. Robert N. Lussier, *Management Fundamentals: Concepts, Applications, Skill Development* (Mason, OH: Thompson Higher Education-Southwestern, 2006), 158.
32. Black and Gregersen, *Leading Strategic Change,* 171.

Second, provide the champions or cheerleaders who will propel the change movement forward.[33] These are people on the frontlines. They are early volunteers who are open to a new vision or challenge. Most importantly they are teachable. Once they learn the new way, then they can teach others. That is the best way to master a subject. To get them ready for launching the change, analyze what change behaviors are needed to sustain momentum. Write the names of the cheerleaders next to each behavior described for the change process. Put checkmarks next to their names if they have the knowledge or behavioral traits already, or place question marks next to their names if they do not exhibit such skills. Then write next to the question marks what training, if any, is needed to achieve the skills required. The idea is that when the new program is launched, the cheerleaders will be there to champion the cause if others begin to fall short of the new attitude or behavior. They will be able to encourage, instruct, and aid the others to keep going forward, and they can report the progress or problems encountered to those in charge of the change project. They will know what to do as the change is happening. Thus the church has its cheerleaders.

These steps, as laid out by Black and Gregersen and Kotter, along with others mentioned in this chapter, provide unique tools to build leadership and give change a chance. A gardener does not weed a garden of flowers with a book. That is the wrong tool. A leader must manage the art of change and understand that individual behavior must change before a church's organization or culture changes. These are the tools to put in the tool belt along with the Bible, good preaching, and, wrapped around it all, holy prayer. Make a difference. Lead and manage the church for lasting success.

---

33. Ibid, 166-67.

15
CONFLICT
THE MANAGEMENT OF CONFLICT IN THE CHURCH

Houston Thompson
EdD, Department Chair, Social Work and Criminal Justice,
Olivet Nazarene University

CONFLICT CONCEPTUALIZED

The word "conflict" generally incites negative thoughts and emotions. In part, this is due to the very definition of the word. *Webster's New World Dictionary* describes conflict as "a fight; struggle; sharp disagreement; opposition; an inability to reconcile."[1] Based on this definition, the idea of conflict sounds like something of which the church wants no part. Conflict feels incongruent with the church's mission and message.

One reason conflict generally promotes negative thoughts and emotions is that it is most often heard or used when one is describing a situation or dynamic that is perceived to be negative and possibly destructive. Any variance is frequently blamed for strained relationships and the lack of progress, especially in institutions like the church. Conflict is often seen as a parasitic evil potentially destroying the church. Consequently, the definition and imagery of conflict just does not resonate with the vocabulary and picture of a healthy church.

The truth is that conflict will happen in the church. In spite of definitions and nuances, conflict does not have to be viewed as a force adversely affecting the church. It is true that it can be; however, generally speaking, disagreement is not always a negative from which negative outcomes are to be expected. Conflict, properly understood, accurately assessed, and appropriately intervened, can be a building block upon which the church furthers its mission and strengthens relationships.

---

1. *Webster's New World Dictionary of the American Language*, 2nd college ed., s.v. "Conflict."

Within conflict is opportunity. Conflict brings situations, circumstances, issues, and relationships to the forefront and often mandates they be addressed. An inappropriate response will most likely result in negative outcomes; however, an appropriate response lays the foundation for using the conflict to achieve positive outcomes. Conflict provides those in leadership the opportunity to create dialogue, to be proactive, to act rather than react, and to model Christlike behaviors and responses.

INFLUENCERS AND STRESSORS

There are many factors that may influence conflict in the church. These are dynamics that exist and are generally beyond the control of anyone. Local church history, familial ties, status of members, church and community culture, and doctrine are some of the major influencers. Every church, regardless of its age, has a history. It was started with passion and purpose. It is probable that underlying today's existence is a memory of yesteryear casting a forward shadow. Familial ties lead to strong homogeneous bonds that may form natural groups within the church. These groups may have tendencies to think, act, and respond in similar manner. Seniority, prestige, position, or wealth among members or leadership may provide the credential for those individuals to be internal leaders with significant influence.

Understanding the church's and the community's culture is critical. Most likely, these cultures are woven together by the values, norms, and expectations that have naturally established themselves. While the church will be, and should be, different, the influence of the community as a whole will influence attitudes, perspectives, and coping skills of the people within the church. For many churches, affiliation with a denomination or group provides already defined statements of beliefs and rules. In a postmodern society where some do not choose a church for its dogma, the church becomes a body with a variety of beliefs from which conflict can arise and therefore stress occurs.

Stressors are those things that individually contribute to conflict. In some cases they may be ongoing and in other cases they may be isolated incidents. They are acts, events, decisions, circumstances, and relationships that become stress points within the church. Generally, they may not appear to be tied to the influencers; however, the influencers often create the context in which the stressors can be seen. For example, the youth Sunday School class schedules a fun activity night that includes a disc jockey and dancing. Most of the youth do not see a problem with this; however, some of the church members express concern. While this is an isolated event, there are dynamic forces at play, including history, the culture of the church, and the perspectives of some members.

Seeing conflict in context helps the leader understand it. One of the smartest things a leader can do is try to visualize all sides of an issue through the lenses in which others are viewing it.

There are numerous circumstances, situations, and events that can be stress points for the church. Paradoxically, they are common among churches, and yet each incident is unique to the individual church. Some of the common stressors include the level of spiritual maturity of leadership; resources and finances; leadership style of the pastor; resistance to change; worship style preferences; lack of communication; and rumor and gossip. Other stress points often overlooked are ambiguity of doctrine, vision, mission, or values; situations where people feel threatened for any reason; feelings of entitlement; crisis, disaster, fear, loss, or separation; economic, social, and moral shifts in the community; generational differences; a change in pastoral or lay leadership; role confusion; norms and unwritten rules; ethical positions; convictions; commitment to outreach; competition between churches; and issues new attendees bring into the church. Any one of these can create a conflictual situation for the church.

PERSPECTIVES ON CONFLICT

There are some factors that must be considered when thinking about managing or resolving conflict. These are issues that are larger than the conflict itself and directly affect the way the church or its leadership addresses the conflict. To begin, one must consider the ecclesiastical structure. If the church or denomination has a manual or similar document, it may prescribe or dictate how certain kinds of conflict should be handled. This may be especially true in regard to the discipline of a clergy or church member for an illegal or immoral act. Likewise, in some cases the manual may detail a grievance procedure for those who are accused. Leaders dealing with serious conflict involving pastoral staff or church members should consult and follow the protocol outlined in the governance policies of the church or denomination.

The style of decision-making leadership in the church may dictate who is responsible for managing the conflict and how it should be handled. If a church has an authoritarian style of leadership, it may be the leader who is ultimately responsible for managing a dispute or leading any initiative toward resolution. On the other hand, if the church is congregational, it may be that this kind of responsibility becomes the work of a committee or board, and the pastor is less involved, if at all. For churches that have a blended or democratic style of leadership, the process may include the leader and a committee or board depending on the issue and the need. Understanding the leadership expectations of the church will be critical in knowing how to best deal with conflict.

A major issue in understanding conflict is the ideological foundation.[2] If one's ideology purports that conflict is wrong or sinful, one of two responses is probable: ignore the conflict and pretend it does not exist; or identify the person or persons seemingly responsible for the conflict and conclude that the person or persons are spiritually immature. Either way, this ideological approach may be detrimental to the leader or the church as it does not recognize conflict as a legitimate process in the church. Norman Shawchuck states, "When the church ignores or suppresses conflict, it may be hindering the work of Christ within the congregation. When pastors teach that conflict in the congregation is sinful, they may be hindering the work of the Spirit."[3] This is not to suggest that some conflict may be fraught with evil intent and needs to be addressed as such. It is to say that conflict cannot be ignored or people written off because one's ideology views conflict as sinful.

The opposite ideology may be just as detrimental. If one's ideology believes that conflict is an inevitable component of relationships and consequently should be freely expounded and acted upon, then the leader and the church may be in constant turmoil. It may be possible that individuals within the church can survive the tumultuous environment; however, it does not provide a positive witness to those on the fringes. Peripheral people presume that the church, and consequently her people, live in unity and love for one another. Finding congruence between open conflict and unity may be difficult as their perspective of the church does not match the present reality. Overt conflict, embraced as the norm, may destroy the testimony of the church.

In the middle of these two extremes is an appropriate ideology of conflict. Conflict is an inevitable component of relationships and processes even in the church.[4] Conflict often arises from the core values and beliefs individuals hold. Generally speaking, when people are vocal, it is because they believe something to be true or right. Consequently, conflict should be seen as a dynamic where individuals express themselves and begin a process of finding a positive outcome. Conflict does not need to be irrationally charged with emotion, argumentative, or dogmatic. It is the hearing and sorting out of beliefs, values, feelings, and emotions that will lead to positive change for the church.

---

2. Norman Shawchuck, *How to Manage Conflict in the Church*, vol. 1, *Understanding and Managing Conflict* (Leith, ND: Spiritual Growth Resources, 1983). In this volume, Norman Shawchuck provides an excellent presentation on the theology of conflict.

3. Ibid., vol. 2, *Conflict Interventions and Resources.* This volume has models of addressing conflict with small groups as well as sermon ideas and readings for the church.

4. For examples, see the degradation of the temple, Matthew 21:12-13; dispute and debate, Acts 15; disagreement between Paul and Barnabas, Acts 15:36-41; and divisions in the church, 1 Corinthians 1:10-13 and 3:1-23.

CAPACITY BUILDING

One of the first things a leader can do to manage conflict is to build capacity. Generally, this may be done on three fronts. The first front is congregationally. It behooves the leader to spend some time teaching scriptural principles on the value of relationships, the meaning of conflict, forgiveness, injustice, and righteous anger. It is important that the congregants understand that conflict does not have to be a negative but may be the springboard to opportunity. Learning to disagree agreeably is fundamental for the healthy church. The Bible has numerous examples that may be used to demonstrate biblical principles and Christian conduct.[5]

A second front is institutionally. As previously noted, some churches and denominations have standard operating procedures for dealing with conflict in the church. These are a great resource; however, they are often limited as they usually address major infractions. In addition to these procedures, it may benefit the church to prepare its own protocol for dealing with conflict. This is not to say that the church should plan for every contingency and have a huge manual. It is to acknowledge that certain principles, procedures, and processes can serve as a foundation for dealing with future issues.

The third front is personally. Every leader should spend some time studying the dynamics and mechanics of dealing with conflict in the church. Being able to assess situations, knowing if one should intervene, who should intervene, how to intervene, and when to intervene, is critical. People look to their leaders for guidance. Leaders should know how to begin a process of conflict management.

Another dimension of capacity building has to do with the intentionality of the church's vision and mission. The leadership of the church must be intentional in keeping the vision and mission of the local church in the forefront of everything. Without a vision, people focus on all kinds of things including the selfish, petty, and inconsequential. The more focused people become on themselves, instead of the kingdom work at hand, the more likely conflict will arise. A great tool in managing conflict is simply keeping the focus on the vision and mission of the local church.

Capacity building also has to do with building relationships within the church. A respected church leader, educator, and author said, "The quality of fellowship, separate from tasks in the church, is so important. It is harder for

---

5. For examples, see forgiveness, Matthew 6:14-15 and 18:21-35; judging and personal accountability, Matthew 7:1-5; a Christian who sins against another, Matthew 18:15-17; and a woman caught in adultery, John 8:1-11.

destructive conflict to arise if people like each other."[6] Being intentional about developing fellowship is a key component of minimizing negative conflict. The utilization of small groups, fellowship dinners, and recreational activities goes a long way toward creating an atmosphere of genuine concern, love, and well-being for each other.

ASSESSING CONFLICT

Before any management or resolution work can be done, the leader must know, to the degree possible, exactly what he or she is facing. To do this, the leader should thoroughly assess the gathering of information and ascertain the facts. The leader must be as objective as possible. Even if intuition or fact suggests something, the leader needs to be able to demonstrate objectivity and the ability to move forward without bias. The leader also must show empathy without judgment. Empathic listening is critical to understanding the person's or group's point of view and collecting accurate information.

A variety of methods and tools may be used to gather information. A leader can make this process as simple or complex as necessary. True conflict management can only happen when all the facts are gathered and the root cause, not just the symptoms, of the conflict is the issue at hand. Some damage control may need to be done in helping people work through the emotional and relational baggage of the conflict, but the focus must be on the conflict. Assigning blame is of no value and only hurts relationships and the problem-solving process.

One really good method of information gathering is using the ecological perspective.[7] This involves not only collecting general information but also looking at the history, environment, and culture surrounding the issue. Historically speaking, one must ask if there are events, relationships, or issues in the past that have a bearing on the present conflict. Knowing where something has been sheds light on knowing where it is, and will be helpful in knowing where it should go. A leader must think environmentally and ask what is going on in and around the situation. What influencers or stressors are affecting the situation?

The leader must also understand the culture in which the conflict is occurring. This includes knowing the community, the church, and the people in the church. It includes looking at traditions, customs, the general philosophy of life and living, values, norms, and problem-solving strategies.

---

6. Mark Quanstrom, personal communication, April 4, 2008.
7. The ecological perspective is used in helping professions, including social work, to thoroughly assess and understand people and situations in context.

Assessing and managing conflict includes thinking systemically. Parsons and Leas state, "Systemic thinking assumes multiple causes—not a simple cause; it assumes that there are many contributing factors to any given set of circumstances."[8] Rarely does conflict begin and end with a simple, single stimulus. Generally, there are several factors in play, including the influencers and stressors addressed previously. Consequently, the conflict most likely affects a greater part of the church, if not the whole church. When the leader assesses the conflict, the systemic impact should be assessed. The leader must think about the whole rather than isolating individuals or incidents. The caveat is not to make it larger than it needs to be. The more public conflict becomes, the harder it is to address.

Another systemic perspective of the church is to think about the church as a family. Family Systems Theory suggests that a congregation behaves like a family.[9] The family has learned to accept and love each other, interact and respond with each other, and recognize the idiosyncrasies of each other. They learn behavior and communication patterns, coping skills, and acceptable norms. Families utilize conflict management skills to deal with issues in the family. This norm of managing and adapting is homeostasis, the predisposition to maintain a sense of stability.

It should be noted that this process involves a lot of time and energy. It is a process that demands confidentiality on the part of the leader. One will learn, hear, and observe things that should be considered private. Confidentiality is critical to presenting an objective agenda in managing the conflict. As a rule of thumb, maintaining confidential notes is helpful to the leader. A conflict may be ongoing or last for an extended period of time. Being able to review the information gathered is helpful. Relying on memory can be risky.

MANAGING CONFLICT

Once the leader ascertains the nature of the conflict, a decision must be made about how it will be addressed. Each issue will be different and require a unique response. Sometimes, a leader will choose to respond one way only to discover more information or observe that the intervention isn't working. It may be the conflict has shifted. Norma Cook Everist suggests conflict has fluidity,

---

8. George Parsons and Speed B. Leas, *Understanding Your Congregation As a System* (Bethesda, MD: Alban Institute, 1993), 19. This volume includes many strategies for addressing conflict.

9. Shawchuck, *How to Manage Conflict in the Church*, vol. 3, *Dysfunctional Congregations*. This resource discusses Family Systems Theory and how to manage conflict in dysfunctional congregations.

ranging from the destructive to the productive and potentially including escalating, widening, contagious, or habitual behaviors.[10] Shawchuck and Heuser state, "Church conflicts are often habitual and escalate into ever tightening cycles of destructive behavior."[11] Knowing how and when to respond is therefore critical.

Shawchuck suggests there are two major issues that must be considered when choosing how to manage conflict. These are the personal relationships of those involved and the goals and interests of those involved.[12] Every conflict will involve people where the quality of the relationships between them is at stake. Even for God-fearing, sincere Christians, conflict has a way of straining relationships. Since much of the church's work is relational, great value and consideration needs to be given as to how the conflict, and the management of it, will affect the relationships of those involved.

Knowing the goals and interests of those involved in the conflict is likewise extremely important as one place to start. Leaders are at risk of assuming that everyone who challenges something, brings up an alternative, or resists change is just not in tune with the vision, mission, and program of the church or is not following the leadership. It is easy to categorically group these individuals as having spiritual problems or, at the least, not being progressive. Many times, if not most of the time, people are not trying to be vicious or vindictive on purpose; they are just stating their values, beliefs, and opinions. David Lieberman states, "We argue over the right to be heard, the right to have our beliefs validated, and the right to be who we are."[13] A wise pastor recognizes the strengths inherent in people expressing themselves and responds with respect, dignity, and objectivity.

Generally speaking, people's stated positions arise out of their own traditions, life experiences, sense of purpose, and their understanding of what it means to be a Christian and a part of the church. Granted, these may be misguided at times, but a leader needs to be gracious and open-minded by looking beyond the surface statements to the heart. Conflict is generally not as much about the person as it is the issue.

---

10. Norma Cook Everist, *Church Conflict: From Contention to Collaboration* (Nashville: Abingdon Press, 2004), 26-34.

11. Norman Shawchuck and Roger Heuser, *Managing the Congregation: Building Effective Systems to Serve People* (Nashville: Abingdon Press, 1996), 249.

12. Shawchuck, *How to Manage Conflict in the Church*, vol. 1, *Understanding and Managing Conflict*, 30.

13. David J. Lieberman, *Make Peace with Anyone* (New York: MJF Books, 2002), 64.

There are several models of conflict management styles.[14] These models basically outline the different frameworks for understanding how to manage the conflict at hand. Even in the church, there are options. In some cases, church policy and operating procedure or denominational polity may dictate how the leader should respond. In many cases, those guidelines are not applicable and the leader must address the conflict with his or her gained knowledge and skill set.

One paradigm of conflict management styles is the Six Cs Model. This model consists of approaches, or styles, ranging from stepping directly into the conflict to working on a win-win outcome. The styles are ordered so that the probability of successfully managing or resolving the conflict is greater and more value is placed on relationships with the approaches lower on the list. Likewise, the lower the listing of the style, the less the associated risk to the leader. The six Cs are confrontation, complacency, coordination, communication, cooperation, and collaboration. The following outlines these styles:

- *Confrontation.* Confrontation is the act of confronting the conflict head-on. The leader, based on his or her assumptions or knowledge about the conflict, dives into the issue and confronts it and, if necessary, those who are involved. Confrontation may generally be seen as the use of authority to deal with conflict. The leader may find this style to be risky, challenging, and at times threatening. This style places the leader directly in the conflict and often aligned with one side of the issue limiting his or her influence with the other. With confrontation, the leader becomes the aggressor.
- *Complacency.* Complacency is where the leader basically chooses not to do anything. This generally means ignoring the conflict, pretending it does not exist, or hoping that it will resolve itself without intervention. In some cases, the leader may acknowledge the conflict but assume someone else, some other process, or just time itself will take care of the issue. The severity of the issue may be a determining factor in choosing this style. If it is inconsequential or not relevant to the church, compla-

---

14. Shawchuck, *How to Manage Conflict in the Church*, vol. 1, *Understanding and Managing Conflict*. Shawchuck proposes five styles of conflict management: avoiding, accommodating, competing, compromising, and collaborating. He presents a matrix where the concern for relationships and the concern for goals and interests of those involved are considered with each style.

Speed B. Leas, *Discover Your Conflict Management Style* (Bethesda, MD: Alban Institute, 1993). Leas offers six strategies or conflict management styles: persuasion, compel or force, avoid or accommodate, collaboration, bargain or negotiation, and support. Leas also provides information on knowing when and how to use the conflict management styles as well as the probable outcomes.

cency may be a good option. Complacency should never be a cop-out. It is an intentional response that protects the leader from getting involved where he or she should not be involved. With complacency, the leader becomes a bystander.

- *Coordination.* Coordination is the work of arranging or organizing the conflict and outcome. This may involve the intangible, such as relationships, or the tangible, such as policy and programs. Essentially, coordination is an attempt to convince people or to control circumstances, to the degree it is possible, to achieve the desired outcome. Coordination may feel like manipulation because one is managing the conflict as a conductor leads an orchestra. This style may have varying degrees of success and risk depending on the issue. Typically, like confrontation, the leader's views are generally made known. In coordination, the leader becomes the director.

- *Communication.* Communication involves active and empathic listening and using the information gathered to help individuals address the conflict themselves. When individuals have the opportunity to express themselves without being judged, it is empowering. This may instill the participants with the confidence to address the conflict. Several things can happen. First, it is easier for everyone to be more open and objective. Second, it helps those involved to own their part of the conflict and take responsibility, thus leading to less blaming of others. Third, it helps people think about using their own problem-solving skills to effect change or may make them open to learning new skills. With communication, the leader is working toward getting all parties to honestly and openly work through the conflict and find resolution. Communication is a great style for helping others resolve the conflict without becoming personally vested in it. With communication the leader becomes the mediator.

- *Cooperation.* Cooperation is about bringing all parties together for the purpose of managing or resolving the conflict. Inherent in cooperation is the basic assumption that it will be a process of exchange theory. This means all parties will give up something to get something. To varying degrees, all parties will win and all parties will lose. In some ways, cooperation includes consensus building. Everyone comes to a place where he or she can live with the outcome even though it may not have been the preferred choice. The leader may expend substantial energy in helping all parties present their case and come to a cooperative resolution. In cooperation, the leader becomes the negotiator.

- *Collaboration.* Collaboration is the art of getting all parties to work together for the benefit of all and the common good. Rather than approach the conflict as a give-and-take proposition, collaboration thinks win-win. Collaboration is a process of looking for ways to manage or resolve conflict where everyone agrees with the final outcome or product and feels good about it. Collaboration is a much harder conflict management style to implement; however, it pays the greatest dividends. Generally, people feel they have had a voice and have been a contributor to the outcome. In collaboration, the leader becomes a facilitator.

Perhaps one of the most difficult decisions a leader makes in conflict is the decision to intervene. While there are no easy answers to the dilemma of choosing to do so, there are some guidelines. If the conflict is affecting the church corporately, intervention is necessary. Examples include a compromise related to the vision, mission, or values of the church; a contradiction to the statement of faith; and an ongoing conflict where relationships are in jeopardy and many in the church will suffer. If the conflict has moved beyond the walls of the church, intervention may be necessary to preserve the witness and work of the church in the community. Generally speaking, the more global or universal the conflict, the more likely the need will be for intervention.

If the conflict is minor and does not affect the church at large, the leader may choose complacency or communication over other conflict management styles. To the degree possible, the path of least resistance should be utilized. Conflict management should be focused on the real issue and involve only those who are a part. In committees and board meetings, conflict needs to remain in the boundaries of the group. Confidentiality among members of the group is an important component.

Occasionally, there will be situations where management does not work and resolution does not appear to be an option. These kinds of situations are extremely difficult for the leader and the church. It may be that all parties involved will need to agree to disagree. In the best case scenario, the work of the church will move forward. If the tension is so great that it hinders the ministry of the church, then the involved parties need to seek permanent resolution. This may include utilizing the cooperative management style to negotiate a course of action that may have extreme outcomes. The assistance of a mediator may be necessary.

One way of thinking about intervention is with a pyramid. At the top of the pyramid are those things that are really nonnegotiable. There may be many or a few; however, those are the things that just cannot be compromised. They may be scriptural truths, convictions, vision, or values. The closer you move toward the bottom of the pyramid the more negotiable things become. The bottom of the pyramid may be preferences and idealism. In between may be programs, polices, and goals where expectations have been developed but can be negotiated. When choosing a conflict management style, knowing where the issue fits in this pyramid may help determine what kind of style to use. The question of changing the church's commitment to children is much more significant than which wattage of lightbulbs to put in the foyer. When talking about children's ministry, the leader will want to think about collaboration or, at least, cooperation. When thinking about lightbulbs, complacency may just be a good option.

The truth about conflict management is that the higher one climbs on the pyramid the more narrow it becomes. Realistically, there are fewer items that are nonnegotiable than there are that are negotiable. Many of the issues over which church conflict occurs are really areas where consideration is an option. A wise leader will recognize this and choose the conflict management style that best fits the situation.

One helpful perspective in managing conflict is looking for the strengths in the conflict. Every person, situation, or issue has positive attributes, qualities, and advantages. Often, particularly in conflict, there is a tendency to identify the weaknesses, negative aspects, and those things that are threatening. While these cannot be overlooked, identifying strengths and those positive qualities that do exist is a good way to begin building a foundation for managing or resolving the conflict. It is much easier to build on the strengths of a person or situation than it is to try to repair the negatives. For example, a faithful parishioner is upset over the change in the focus from evangelism to discipleship in the Sunday evening service. There may be a lot of reasons why this decision was made. Trying to convince this person why the church is moving in a different direction is extremely difficult when the person feels so strongly about it. On the other hand, recognizing the individual's passion for evangelism, affirming that passion, and exploring ways in which the church can be more evangelistic is easier and may just open up more opportunities. Focusing on strengths is a great way to frame conflict management and be more objective.

A Leader's Example

The manner in which the leader handles and addresses conflict is vitally important. People will remember how something was handled more than they will remember what the issue was or how it turned out. There are three criteria for thinking about a leader's response in conflict management: it must be biblically sound; the leader must be a person of integrity; and the leader must demonstrate a Christian spirit. A leader who compromises any one criterion will compromise his or her ability to lead and manage conflict.

For the leader, preserving relationships is a fundamental core value. It is critically important that the leader's relationships with others be as positive and rewarding as possible. A leader should acknowledge and accept three truths. First, most disagreements are generally not personal attacks on the leader and therefore the leader should not take everything personally. Second, as a district church leader once advised a young pastor, "Develop rhinoceros skin." A leader cannot let everything get to him or her. Third, a leader must choose those things carefully for which he or she is willing to engage in intervention. These truths help keep the conflict in perspective and allow the leader to keep the right focus on conflict management and the maintenance of positive relationships.

A leader should deal with intrapersonal conflict before attempting to address conflict in the church. If the leader is personally conflicted, struggling with spiritual or leadership issues, this internal turmoil should be resolved before attempting to manage other conflict. The leader will find solace through prayer and Scripture. As needed and appropriate, the leader may seek the counsel of a confidant or pursue professional counseling or coaching. The bottom line is for the leader to have competence in conflict management; personal issues that could potentially create barriers and stumbling blocks must be resolved. The witness of Christ and relationships with people are at stake.

The leader needs to be able to make the right decisions, at the right time, for the right reasons. Lieberman observes that a person makes a decision with one or more of the following motivations: what feels good, what makes a person look good, and what is good or right.[15] A leader who makes a decision based on feeling or appearance usurps the real purpose of conflict management. In such cases, the conflict will most likely escalate. Making decisions based on what is good or right speaks to the integrity of the leader and the principles of Scripture.

UNITY IN CONFLICT

For the church, the perception is that unity comes with the absence of conflict. Since unity is an attribute the church values, the church strives not to have conflict. This thinking is a misperception. As previously noted, not all conflict is negative and all conflict does not have to end with negative outcomes. Within the church, there will be different opinions, beliefs, and values. Unity does not mean uniformity. The church can have unity centered in Christ, fo-

---

15. Lieberman, *Make Peace with Anyone*, 5.

cused on the vision, mission, and values of the church, and still have respect for, and the diversity of, individual opinions, beliefs, and values.[16]

When the issues, relationships, or outcomes of conflict are negative, the ultimate goal is reconciliation. The focus has to be not only on resolution but also on the restoration of relationships. For this to occur, the church needs to be spiritually sensitive. Speed Leas states reconciliation is not totally in the hands of people. Our theology tells us that God provides reconciliation. Our goal is to help create environments where reconciliation can occur.[17] The restoration of relationships helps resolve conflict and maintain unity.

Conflict management is the art of understanding the dynamics of conflict, being able to thoroughly assess conflict, and knowing how and when to appropriately intervene. David Kale states, "Our goal is conflict transformation where God is allowed to work through the conflict to bring new life into the church, providing it with power and resources it did not previously have for achieving his commission."[18] Conflict management is about recognizing the opportunity and strengths in conflict and using those not only to manage or resolve the conflict but also to propel the church into a brighter future for the cause of the kingdom.

---

16. First Corinthians 12:12-31 is a great passage for illustrating unity in the diverse body of believers.

17. Speed B. Leas, *Moving Your Church Through Conflict* (Washington, D.C.: Alban Institute, 1985), 9-12.

18. David W. Kale, *Managing Conflict in the Church* (Kansas City: Beacon Hill Press of Kansas City, 2003), 20.

16

ACCOUNTABILITY

BEING TRANSPARENT AND RESPONSIBLE TO GOD, TO THE CHURCH, AND TO THE LAW

Jim Dalton

EdD, Professor of Accounting, Bachelor of Business Administration Chair, Mount Vernon Nazarene University

◆

"Accountability" and "responsibility" are two words that are often considered synonymous. These words do link with each other but have very different meanings. The word "responsibility" refers to a person being legally, morally, or ethically liable for the care and welfare of himself or herself and of others. This care and welfare not only encompasses physical needs but also mental needs, emotional needs, and the actions of self and others. In addition to himself or herself, a pastor is responsible for his or her family and church.

Being accountable can be defined as being answerable. Any person is accountable for those things over which he or she has responsibility. Since pastors have responsibilities for self, family, and church, they are held accountable for these areas of responsibility. To whom is a pastor accountable? Pastors are accountable to spouses, to children, to family, to church boards, to congregations, to denominations, to legal authorities, but most of all to God.

THE PASTOR'S RESPONSIBILITIES AND ACCOUNTABILITY FOR SELF

God has given every person a mind, a body, and a spirit. People are responsible for how they use and develop their minds, their bodies, and their spirits. As with any person, a pastor is responsible for *(a)* his or her education/development (the mind), *(b)* the care/maintenance/development of his or her physical body (the body), and *(c)* the nurture and growth of his or her relationship with God (the spirit).

Daily time must be allocated to these three personal areas of responsibility (mind, body, and spirit). The pastor who neglects to read, study, and continually learn will become stagnant, stale, and antiquated. Society and the world are ever changing. People today are different from people just a few years ago.

Technology is always changing, and technology in the church is here to stay. The pastor who is not keeping up with change will be left on the "side of the road" as the contemporary church of today speeds on by. Who is the pastor accountable to for developing the mind? The answer to that is fairly easy: the pastor is answerable to everyone! Pastors are answerable to themselves, to family, to church, to denominations, to society, and to God. God wants and expects everyone to learn, grow, and develop his or her mind.

God has given us bodies to use while we are on the earth. Some have even used the word "temple" to describe these physical bodies. Development and care of the body is necessary for life to continue. What is put into the body, what is done with the body, and what is done to the body are the responsibilities of each person. There is a saying that all have likely heard: "Garbage in, garbage out." If the body is fed with garbage and is treated like garbage, then the outcome will be a body made of garbage. If the body is treated like a "temple," then the outcome will likely be a body that is holy and acceptable to God. All are ultimately held accountable for how they have treated their bodies.

As the "shepherd of a flock," the pastor has an important responsibility for the spiritual development of the people in the church. Even though this responsibility is great, a far greater responsibility is the spiritual development of himself or herself. If the pastor does not have a growing, vibrant, dynamic relationship with God, then how can he or she successfully lead others in their spiritual development? If the pastor's spiritual development is weak, everyone will suffer the consequences. The pastor will suffer, the family will suffer, and the church will suffer when the pastor neglects the responsibility of personal spiritual development.

The Pastor's Responsibilities and Accountability for the Family

When God created the first man and woman, he created the family. Families are typically made up of fathers, mothers, and children. Some pastors are fathers and some are mothers. In either case, pastors and their spouses are leaders in their family units. All fathers and mothers are responsible for personal education/development (the mind) of the family, for the care, maintenance, and development of the physical bodies of family members (the body), and for the nurture and growth of the family's relationship with God (the spirit). Since mothers and fathers have significant family responsibilities, they are in turn held accountable for these same responsibilities.

Providing learning and mental development opportunities for family members is the responsibility of all parents. Learning opportunities can include reading to children, frequenting a library, visiting museums, becoming involved in schools and school activities, traveling and taking vacations to historical places, and much more. Actually, almost every experience in life can lead to learning. Never neglect an opportunity to have a "teaching and learning" moment with the family. Preparation for family members' college education is a parental responsibility that can never begin too soon. College education is expensive, while a pastor's salary is typically not generous. The pastor must begin early to plan and save for a college education for his or her children.

Since most pastors are the main breadwinners for the family, it is important that the pastor ensure that the physical needs of the family are met. Obvious physical needs include food, shelter, and clothes. A not-so-obvious need is the physical development of family members. Development takes on many forms. For some, physical development is through sports. For others, this development is through vacations, "family nights," or through school and church activities. The one common thread through all these activities is time together. Spending time with each other as a family playing, working, or traveling is a major part of a family's physical development.

A pastor is the spiritual leader of a church and its congregation. That is his or her vocation. A pastor is the spiritual leader of his or her family. That is his or her responsibility as a spouse and parent. It is not unusual for a pastor to be successful in church-related spiritual responsibilities and unsuccessful in family-related ones. Every one of us can list immediate family members of pastors who are "away from the Lord." How sad it is that those closest to the pastor can be the most challenging to reach for the Lord. All pastors must keep in mind that serving in a church is temporary, but the family is forever!

Pastors must never forget that the family is a top priority; it must not be neglected. Family members must never sense that they are second-class citizens when compared to people of the church and to the pastor's church responsibilities. The pastor who is not successful with family responsibilities will likely be unsuccessful with church responsibilities too!

THE PASTOR'S RESPONSIBILITIES AND ACCOUNTABILITY FOR THE CHURCH

"We want to avoid any criticism of the way we administer this liberal gift. For we are taking pains to do what is right, not only in the eyes of the Lord but also in the eyes of men" (2 Cor. 8:20-21).

Good stewardship and accountability involves both the pastor and the people of the church. The pastor and the people must develop a respect for each other; must treat the other as an equal; must be open, honest, and truthful in communicating with the other; must help the other to grow by using talents and abilities; and must share in responsibilities. God has gifted different individuals with different talents and abilities. To use this God-given giftedness, the pastor must be aware of the expertise of members and encourage them to use their gifts in areas of pastoral responsibility such as finances. There must be openness and transparency about how funds are spent. A pastor who believes things should be hidden has a wrong mind-set and demonstrates a lack of love and respect for the people he or she serves.

The pastor is not ordained to administer the finances of a church, but it is an *ex officio* responsibility. Very few pastors are trained in finances and management, yet they are held responsible for church finances. Very few pastors have knowledge of the many civil laws that affect both finances and employment, yet they are bound to follow these laws. The pastor need not rely on personal knowledge and skills because practically every church has people whom God has gifted with the knowledge and expertise in the "business" areas of the church.

God's people want to help. Most are willing to help if asked. It is their church, but they must be asked and given the freedom and necessary information to help the pastor fulfill leadership responsibilities. Pastors and church people must be given the freedom to make mistakes once in a while and then to learn from these mistakes.

Every church, even the smallest of congregations, generally has a trained person with the expertise to assist in the daily financial responsibilities and to advise a pastor on his or her many administrative tasks. A pastor attempting to do these things alone will have greater burdens and anxieties and may not have the time and energy needed to perform his or her many functions as the congregation's leader. Working alone leads to frustration and to burnout. An important part of church leadership is the pastoral ability to discern and use the talents of the people and to call them to roles of service in ministry. Ministry definitely includes service in the administrative needs of the church.

Many of the administrative responsibilities of the pastor can be assumed by others. Delegation is an "art" that must be learned and put into practice. This is not only true for paid personnel but also for volunteers who have appropriate skills. Pastors are not usually trained in human resource management and its requirements when there are staff members employed in a church. Outside assistance from experts in this area could help in the proper evaluation of staff. These experts could better address the following questions: Are the staff members fulfilling their job descriptions? Do they have proper job descriptions? Do they have the skill to fulfill their job descriptions? Is a more qualified person needed on the church staff?

Churches should not hire someone to help them out; churches should hire someone to fulfill specific duties. If staff members who are "good people" do not have the abilities that are needed for the job, problems will definitely arise that the pastors will be forced to address. People with appropriate expertise, both paid and volunteer, give the pastor the freedom to delegate and thus more time to minister to people.

Pastors should not hand over decision-making power to just anyone. Pastors should consult others and seek to come to a consensus on most decisions but have the responsibility for making the final decision on serious matters. The pastor cannot abdicate authority and responsibility. Working in collaboration with people in the church and sharing in responsibilities does not mean abdicating the pastor's authority.

As a shepherd, the pastor is responsible and is held accountable for the training and development of church members (the mind); the care, maintenance, and development of the physical needs of the church (the body); and the congregations' relationship with God (the spirit). Although the earlier discussion in this chapter about a pastor's responsibilities and accountability for self and for family is highly important, the balance of the chapter will address a pastor's many "business" responsibilities and his or her accountability for those responsibilities in a church.

Most students preparing for ministry learn in their college and university classes about their responsibilities to the "mind" and "spirit" of church members. What is generally not emphasized in course work for ministry preparation are the pastor's responsibilities for the care of the church's "body," that is, the "running of the business."

A church is a business and should be run like a business. Some might take offense to this statement, but legally and in actuality, it is a true statement. A church is considered a not-for-profit business whose mission is to meet the spiritual needs of the people it serves. In business terms, the pastor is the chief executive officer (CEO) of the organization. The pastor is a legal corporate officer. As a corporation, a church normally has three officers approved to operate as its legal representatives: the pastor, as the CEO of the corporation; the treasurer, as the chief financial officer (CFO); and the board secretary. In most cases, these three individuals have the legal authority to sign documents for the church. As corporate officers, those filling these three positions are liable for the actions of the corporation (the church). A part of this liability includes being potentially *personally* liable for the actions of the corporation. That is, the pastor, the treasurer, and the board secretary can be personally held liable for the decisions and actions of a church. This can be a scary thought and is a huge responsibility. As the CEO of a church, the pastor can legally be held account-able for what the church does!

Society as a whole has high expectations of churches. The different needs of people in the world are vast. If the church is to truly meet its mission, it must address these needs. Church members usually want to respond and do what they can do to assist the church in meeting societal needs. People can contrib-ute two things to meet these needs: their time and their money.

Donors want to feel confident that money they sacrificially give is used ap-propriately and that the church is actively involved in ministry that meets needs and is pleasing to God. Financial responsibilities and accountability for them should be extremely important to a pastor.

Financial Accountability

Financial accountability is founded on the concept of stewardship. Most people understand that the foundation of a house is the most important part of the structure. If the house's foundation is bad, the whole house will crumble. Stewardship is similarly important to the basic components of financial account-ability. Any person who is responsible for the finances of an organization is placed in a position of stewardship, a position that requires that person to exer-cise responsible management and care for monetary and nonmonetary assets that belong to others. Good stewardship includes a reporting system where the steward must report to others. The pastor of a church is such a steward. He or she is subject to a system of accountability consisting of the church board, the people in the congregation, donors, and those having legal and spiritual author-ity over the church and pastor. The government's Internal Revenue Service (IRS) is one such legal authority. It allows special tax treatment of churches; churches are potentially violating full-disclosure obligations if they do not fully and ap-propriately disclose all their financial matters.

Financial Reports

The church treasurer should prepare and present financial reports that are meaningful and easily understood by the reader. What good is it to have financial information that makes no sense whatsoever to the reader? Revenue and expense categories should be detailed enough to be understood. The "lumping" together of categories should be avoided, and the number of line items listed under "mis-cellaneous" should be minimal. If there is an entry in miscellaneous, it should be detailed and explained in supplemental notes to the financial statements.

The Statement of Revenues and Expenses

Because churches are considered not-for-profit organizations, they should not prepare income statements. Churches are not in the "business" to make income! Churches should prepare a Statement of Revenues and Expenses. This statement should show meaningful revenue and expense accounts for the church. The bottom line should not be designated "Net Income" or "Net Loss"; rather it should be designated "Excess Revenues over Expenses" or "Excess Expenses over Revenues."

Comparative Financial Information

It is best to present comparative financial information. Usually, presenting comparative financial data would mean showing current year information compared to the previous year(s) information. A reader can make decisions much easier if this sort of trend information is available.

The Balance Sheet

Churches routinely prepare some type of revenue and expense statement. However, very few churches prepare a Balance Sheet. A Balance Sheet lists all of the resources of the church and then lists the claims against those resources. Resources of the church are called assets. Bank and creditor claims against these resources are considered liabilities. The difference between the assets and the liabilities of the church is considered the church's share of ownership in its assets. Some call this ownership share equity; some call it net worth; while others call it net assets. Church Balance Sheets are very different from typical business Balance Sheets. Churches usually follow cash-basis accounting, while businesses are required to follow accrual-basis accounting. Even though church Balance Sheets are not as meaningful and standard as business Balance Sheets, they can still be a valuable tool in financial accountability.

An Annual Financial Report

Most not-for-profit organizations are required to file an annual report with the IRS. This report is filed on Form 990. The good news for pastors and churches is that churches are specifically listed as exempt from this filing requirement. Even though the church is exempt from filing an annual report with the IRS, churches still have a responsibility to fully report financial information to the congregation.

Audits: External Versus Internal Audits

Most churches do not have audits conducted by external independent auditors. The primary reason for this is the cost. Only large megachurches believe an external audit is cost beneficial. If an official external audit is not possible, at the very least an internal review of the financial records should be conducted. This review can be conducted by a committee of the board, by a member of the congregation, or by someone independent of the church treasurer. The review results should be presented directly to the church board, not to the pastor or treasurer. What is the result of not conducting some type of audit? Church employees, volunteers, and those who handle church finances are left at risk, and the door is "wide open" to potential harmful accusations.

Cash and Offerings

Churches must be very careful with how they handle cash and offerings. Following these guidelines will help avoid or reduce potential issues with offerings: (1) offerings should never be left in the church uncounted, (2) they should never be taken home by a member to count later, and (3) they should not be handled by only one person. As soon as offerings are collected, they should be immediately counted by a group of people (two or more). Once counted, these counters should make the bank deposit. At no time should the pastor or the treasurer handle cash and offerings. Good financial responsibility, good financial accountability, and good internal control occur when accounting functions are invested in different individuals. In a "perfect world," the person responsible for the receipt of cash (offerings) is different from the person who disburses cash (the treasurer), who again is different from the person who records donations and issues year-end "Giving Statements." If two or more of these three functions is vested in the same individual, financial impropriety is possible and accountability is destroyed.

Pastoral Staff Payroll

Churches are not legally required to disclose salary information about the pastor, associate pastors, or other paid church staff. Just because the law does not require this disclosure does not mean that it is a secret. The church board should have full disclosure and approval of all salary and benefit information on all church employees. If requested, the church should provide church members with this information. Annual reports to the congregation do not need employee-by-employee detailed information; however, employment category and salary range information should be available.

Discretionary Funds

Many churches make available funds for distribution to homeless, indigent, and other needy people. Most of the time there is little, if any, accountability for these monies. If the church chooses to allow the pastor to handle this discretionary type of fund, there must be an adequate accounting by the pastor of all distributions. Who received the funds, the amount given, and the purpose of the gift are typically provided as documentation of the disbursement. Nothing can ruin a pastor's reputation faster than an accusation of financial impropriety. If at all possible, churches should not give the pastor discretionary funds for this purpose; rather they should have discretionary funds distributed through a properly accountable fund under the direction of the church treasurer, or other designated individual. While discretionary funds can be valid, churches must demand adequate documentation and reporting.

Benevolence Funds

The church must establish policies for gifts donated for benevolence purposes. Donors often have some intent when it comes to the benevolence gift they are making. If the donor's intent is to make the gift for the benefit of a specific individual, then the gift is not considered a gift to the church but a gift to the individual. Generally, this type of gift is not tax deductible and should not be accepted by the church. The best solution for this situation is to establish an official benevolence fund that is operated by specific church-adopted policies that follow IRS guidelines. Church policies should indicate who is approved to make distributions and how distributions are handled. Policies should prohibit the acceptance of donations designated for any specific individual. Donors may make donations and "suggest" how the funds are used; however, the donor cannot mandate a specific individual recipient. Another issue related to benevolence funds is the rule that no pastor or church employee should be the recipient of funds from a benevolence fund. The IRS's opinion on this is that if a pastor or an employee needs financial assistance, the church should pay that person through payroll. For pastors and employees, benevolence funds received are considered taxable compensation; however, for nonemployees, benevolence funds received are nontaxable.

Donor-Restricted Gifts

There are three general categories of gifts that donors give to the church: unrestricted gifts, temporarily restricted gifts, and permanently restricted gifts. The donor's intent must be honored by the church and cannot be reclassified without the donor's approval. Tithes and offerings are considered unrestricted gifts that may be used at the discretion of the church's leaders.

Temporarily restricted gifts are restricted with time and/or purpose restrictions. For example, a donor might give a gift for a future children's wing to be built by the church. This donation is restricted for this purpose and this purpose only. When the children's wing is built, the donation may be used. The donation cannot be used for any other purpose. If the donor gives a gift and instructs the church to hold the funds for ten years and then use it for any need, this is an example of a temporarily restricted donation for time. The funds must be held for ten years before their use by the church.

A permanently restricted donation must be held forever: the principal part of the donation may never be spent. Income earned by this donation can usually be spent by the church at the direction of the donor. This permanently restricted donation is what not-for-profits call endowments.

There is often no differentiation among gifts that are donor-restricted for building projects, for missions' projects, for debt reduction, or for benevolence; the church must separately account for each of these funds. All too often churches combine unrestricted and restricted funds. This combining leads to confusion and violates good accountability for donations.

Personal Use of Church Funds

Church funds must *never* be borrowed to pay for the pastor's personal expenses. Church funds have been given by donors for the purpose of meeting the ministry needs of the church, not for the personal use of the pastor (even if only used temporarily). Any pastor will be held accountable and liable, even possibly civilly and criminally, for such actions.

Board Accountability

Church boards are very important to the organization. Active board participation and involvement tends to ensure integrity. This integrity can be in the pastor, in finances, and in ensuring that board guidelines and policies are being followed. On the other hand, a church board's neglect of financial accountability can often lead to suspicion and mistrust of the leadership and finances of the church.

A church board should meet regularly. Meetings typically involve listening to the pastor's and associate pastor's reports. Having a board that truly "listens" is of much more importance than having one that just "rubber-stamps" pastoral recommendations and/or decisions. Boards must listen and provide input into the decision-making processes of the church.

Board size and membership are generally recommended by denominational leadership. In any case, board size should be no less than five individuals, with no member being on the staff of the church. Family members of the church's staff should also not be members of the board. The exception to this guideline is that the senior pastor is often considered an ex officio member of the board and all committees.

Board Action Records

As with any formal organization, written records (minutes) of meetings and actions of the church board should be maintained. These minutes are typically taken, dated, signed, and distributed by the secretary of the church board. Minutes are to be approved at a subsequent meeting of the board.

Church boards are responsible for the following: (1) church administrative and/or legislative policy, (2) financial accountability for all church funds, (3) church budgets, (4) church acquisitions (property, equipment, and assets), (5) pastoral compensation packages, and (6) outside audit or review of the financial records of the church.

Financial Stewardship of the Pastor

1. The pastor has the duty and responsibility for good financial stewardship over all funds entrusted to the church. The funds of the church belong to the people of God, not to the pastor.
2. The pastor has the responsibility to administer the finances and material goods of the church.
3. The pastor is to be a good steward safeguarding church funds and using them only in accordance with the needs of the church and the intention of donors.
4. The pastor should obtain the advice of people with proper expertise and give them the information needed to monitor the use of church funds.
5. The pastor must see that proper controls are in place for the collection of monies, the counting of monies, and the spending of the funds, with the oversight of the church board.
6. Financial stewardship includes good management principles in running the church. The pastor should obtain the assistance of people with proper expertise.

Good stewardship and financial accountability are essential to being a good pastor and administrator. With the above principles and norms in place, and with openness and honesty in reporting to the people, there will not be any cause for gossip and accusations, either against the pastor or against people in the church responsible for handling the finances of the church. By establishing and submitting to a system of financial accountability, pastors, staff members, and churches can eliminate unnecessary suspicion of financial mismanagement and mistrust.

Financial accountability for churches is much more than preparing and distributing charitable contribution receipts. Honest and open disclosure to the congregation is of utmost importance in good financial accountability. This disclosure can provide the congregation members with trust in knowing that donations are used properly and accounted for by the church. Not providing open and honest disclosures can easily lead to a lack of credibility with church members.

Ethics and Pastoral Accountability

Every person alive faces temptation, and pastors are not exempt! The key to success as a pastor in the face of temptation is to anticipate that it will happen and then know how to respond. Response should be thought out and well planned in advance, not just something considered for the first time once temptation arrives. Pastors must not try to decide on a proper response each time temptation occurs; that unplanned response will likely lead to a potential obstacle if not failure in ministry. Well-established guidelines must be developed and implemented to ensure that the pastor is ethical in all he or she does while leading the church and working daily with the people of the congregation.

A pastor's behavior will greatly affect the ministry and the church. There are important guiding concepts that must be considered as a pastor develops a plan to handle situations once temptation occurs.

Accountability

Pastors, as well as all of us, must be accountable to another person. If accountability to others is ignored, attitudes of arrogance and isolation develop. Going it alone can be an unwise decision. Accountability requires that the pastor meet with others to share honest thoughts and feelings, weaknesses, and potential personal and spiritual "road-blocks." This action forces the pastor to see his or her personal vulnerability and understand that everyone faces temptation. Satan would love to "take down" a pastor. When the pastor falls, Satan will likely take down many in the church, if not the whole church.

Responsibility

The highest standards of professional and ethical behavior must be maintained by the pastor. The truly successful pastor can balance desires for professional excellence while addressing personal and professional relationships. Pastors have a huge responsibility! They must be able to balance the demands of the church, family, and personal life: all of this for 24 hours a day, 7 days a week, and 365 days a year. If a balance among these three demands cannot be achieved, the pastor is guaranteed to face significant struggles.

Integrity

Authority and power are naturally vested in a pastor because of his or her leadership position in the church. How does the pastor use this authority and power? Is it vested in one person or is the power shared with others? Is power used with compassion? Is power used to elevate ego? The effective use of power occurs when it is used with honesty and integrity. Integrity in church finances is obvious, but true integrity requires the appropriate application of power and authority. With an appropriate balance of power, authority, and integrity, trust can be produced.

Conclusion

Everything discussed in this chapter needs to be put into action in the daily life of a pastor. How does this happen? It happens as the pastor accepts personal responsibility and daily evaluates accountability and ethics in all he or she does. Daily the pastor should consider how to answer these questions and then implement the change necessary for improvement.

Questions That Relate to the Pastor's Responsibilities and Accountability for Self

1. Have thoughts and actions been appropriate toward members of the opposite sex?
2. Have feelings toward others been Christlike?
3. Have personal emotional and spiritual needs been met?
4. Are motives pure?

Questions That Relate to the Pastor's Responsibilities and Accountability for the Family

1. Has sufficient time been spent with family members?
2. Have the family's spiritual needs been met today?
3. Is the family second only to God, not second to the vocation?

Questions That Relate to the Pastor's Responsibilities and Accountability for the Church

1. Have dealings with people today been totally honest?
2. Have financial dealings been above reproach?
3. Have obligations and responsibilities to the church been met today?
4. Is God pleased with what he sees in the pastor's life, in the pastor's family, and in the pastor's church?

For Further Reading

Brooks, Leonard J. *Business and Professional Ethics for Directors, Executives, and Accountants.* 4th ed. Mason, OH: Thompson South-Western, 2007.

Busby, Dan. *Zondervan Minister's Tax and Financial Guide.* Grand Rapids: Zondervan, 2009.

Ricchiute, David. *Auditing.* 8th ed. Mason, OH: Thompson South-Western, 2006.

17

FINANCIAL MANAGEMENT
PRACTICING GOOD STEWARDSHIP OF THE FINANCIAL RESOURCES OF THE CHURCH

Dan Schafer
DBA, World Mission Finance, International Church of the Nazarene

◆

In Christian circles, we often use the word "stewardship" to describe how we handle church finances. We can trace the use of this concept back to the New Testament Scriptures where the idea of stewardship is captured by the Greek word *oikonomos,* which primarily denotes "the manager of a household or estate."[1] This same Greek word is translated as "treasurer" (of the city) in Romans 16:23 (NKJV), is used to challenge us to be "stewards of the mysteries of God" in 1 Corinthians 4:1 (NKJV), and is used to employ us to serve "as good stewards of the manifold grace of God" in 1 Peter 4:10 (NKJV). In each of these cases, an individual is the recipient of something valuable and is given the responsibility of using that valuable possession for the benefit of others.

According to the *Oxford English Dictionary,* our English word "steward" has a similar connotation and has its origins in the eleventh-century word *stigweard,* which conveys the thought of a keeper (*weard*) of the house (*stig*). Among the current definitions offered by the *Oxford English Dictionary* for "steward" we can find these:

- One who manages the affairs of an estate on behalf of his employer
- One who transacts the financial and legal business of a manor on behalf of the lord
- A layman appointed to manage the financial affairs of a congregation or of a circuit (used in the early Methodist Church)

---

1. W. E. Vine, Merrill F. Unger, and William White, *An Expository Dictionary of Biblical Words* (Nashville: Thomas Nelson, 1984), 1087.

The *Oxford English Dictionary* also includes the following definitions for the word "stewardship":

- Conduct of the office of steward: administration, management, control
- (Ecclesiastical) The responsible use of resources, especially money, time, and talents, in the service of God.[2]

Like its Greek counterpart, the English word "steward" carries the idea of an individual who is entrusted with the valuable resources of another and has the responsibility to wisely manage those resources for their true owner. Thus, the use of the word "stewardship" in our Christian circles acknowledges something unique about the funds that we direct—they do not belong to us. As financial stewards of the church, individual Christians have entrusted us with their gifts to God to be used for the ministry of God.

Gifts to God for the Ministry of God

When individuals accept positions that either manage the church's finances or have influence over how the finances are managed, they have entered into a trust relationship with the church donors. They have implicitly agreed to manage these donors' gifts to God in a manner that is in keeping with the donors' intentions. That is, they have taken on the role of stewards.

In their roles as stewards, they "must be in tune with the spiritual nature and intent of the congregation," and make "certain that resources are used to produce desired results."[3] Exploring this concept a bit further, we see that although donors technically give up control of the funds they donate to the church, there is an expectation that those funds will be used in a specific manner, that is, in a manner in keeping with what the donors believe to be appropriate ministries of the church.

Whenever the stewards make decisions that appear to be contrary to these expectations, the donors may interpret such decisions as a violation of the trust they placed in the stewards. Given the spiritual nature of the stewards' assignments, such perceived violations may also be interpreted as failures on the part of the stewards to fulfill their spiritual responsibilities. Thus, individuals who assume the roles of financial stewards must take the responsibilities related to those roles very seriously. They must endeavor to maintain the trust of the donors by affirming the expectations of those donors and by becoming wise managers of the resources in their care.

---

2. *The Oxford English Dictionary*, 2nd ed., s.vv. "Steward," "Stewardship."
3. Douglas W. Johnson, *Let's Be Realistic About Your Church Budget* (Valley Forge, PA: Judson Press, 1984), 112.

EIGHT STEPS TO MANAGING THE FINANCES OF THE CHURCH WISELY

Often, church leaders are overwhelmed with the how-to of managing financial resources wisely and in a manner that fulfills the expectations of donors. However, this fundamental principle of stewardship does not need to be viewed as such a besetting impediment to a successful ministry. In reality, church leaders can handle this challenge in a professional and confident manner by focusing on eight simple steps to managing the church's finances:

1. Develop a scriptural view of money (a biblical theology of money).
2. Align expenses with the ministry vision of the church.
3. Develop a system to protect designated funds.
4. Avoid inappropriate personal gain.
5. Avoid the "church treasurer syndrome."
6. Provide management reports.
7. Develop a reserve cash fund (a contingency fund).
8. Avoid giving charitable receipts for personal gifts (understand what is charitable and what is not).

Step One—Develop a Scriptural View of Money

Undoubtedly, somewhere along the way you have heard the saying "You can tell a lot about a person by looking at his or her checkbook." This familiar adage acknowledges that a peek into an individual's checkbook gives you insight into that person's soul. For as we understand how individuals spend their money, we come to understand what they value most in their lives. It is hard to say who first made this observation, but down through the years, caring pastors have repeatedly conveyed the truth of this proverb to their congregations. Why do these loving pastors present this axiom to their people? They know just how important it is for people to consider what their lifestyle is demonstrating about themselves. Pastors use this saying to challenge people to allow the Scriptures to influence not only their lifestyles but also their entire view and usage of money; that is, they challenge people to develop a scriptural view of money.

In his book *Finance in Your Church* Douglas Johnson suggests that the "relationship between money and lifestyle is a theological issue." This author declares that pastors have a responsibility to help people develop a scriptural view of money, which he refers to as a "biblical theology of money." He declares that unfortunately most pastors are not prepared to help their congregations deal with finances from such a theological perspective.[4]

---

4. Douglas W. Johnson, *Finance in Your Church* (Nashville: Abingdon Press, 1986), 14.

Johnson maintains that there are two common positions that stand between pastors and their ability to provide the church members with a scriptural perspective on money. First, many pastors have been infected by the belief that money is "an evil force" or at best a "necessary evil." In contrast, many other pastors have adopted secular concepts about money that "de-emphasize ethical considerations about the ways one acquires and uses money." The result is "these types of pastors tend to ignore their need to think about money in theological terms."[5]

However, "church members rely on their pastor to help them think about money theologically. They need theological guidance from the pastor as they acquire and use money." It is only when the pastor takes seriously his or her responsibility to proclaim a scriptural view of money that the laity will be "challenged" with their "need to use money for God's purposes."[6]

Step Two: Align Expenses with the Ministry Vision of the Church

Aligning the church's expenses with the ministry vision of the church is the second step to wisely managing church finances and fulfilling the expectations of its donors. This step assumes that the church has a common ministry vision and/or plan. If such a ministry vision does not exist, the pastor needs to work with the congregation to develop and adopt such a vision. Once a common ministry vision is adopted, the vision should be routinely announced and published in a highly public manner.

A well-publicized ministry vision will help guide the expectations of those individuals who are donating funds to the church by constantly holding up before these donors what the church plans to accomplish with its resources. The result is that donors are purposefully giving to the church so that it can accomplish the vision it has outlined and championed. Then, as long as the organizational expenditures are aligned to this common ministry vision, those expenditures will most likely be aligned with the expectations of the donors.

A common ministry vision is not only essential to fulfilling donor expectations, but, as Kennon Callahan suggests in his analysis of healthy financial habits within the church, it is also essential to establishing effective financial practices within the church. He states, "The more you advance your mission, the more

---

5. Ibid., 14-15.
6. Ibid., 15.

likely you are to develop effective church finances. . . . Advance your mission; then develop your budget. Advance your mission; then raise your giving."[7]

When the ministry vision of the church is advanced, an alignment between organizational expenses and ministry vision is much more likely to occur. The natural result of such an alignment is a more effective use of the money donated to the church. This concept becomes self-evident when you remember that by definition the word "effective" denotes success in producing a desired or intended result.[8] The greatest potential for producing the desired result will exist when there is an alignment among organizational expenses, donor expectations, and ministry vision.

Step Three: Develop a System to Protect Designated Funds

Up until this point, our focus on stewardship has been related to the general finances of the church. However, one of the greater challenges that individuals will face as financial stewards is in relationship to what are often called designated gifts or funds. Designated funds are unique to churches and other nonprofit organizations. These funds are gifts that are donated to the organization for a specific project or purpose, and, thus, are restricted for the specific use identified by the donor.[9] For example, the church might receive funds from a donor with instructions to use his or her gift to buy a new piano, to repair an air conditioner, or to send students to youth camp. Absent such specific instructions, a gift is considered to be undesignated or unrestricted.

Once the church "accepts a restricted gift, it has an obligation to follow the donor's instructions" concerning the use of that gift.[10] If the church fails on this obligation, the church's members will lose trust in their leaders. Unfortunately, failure on this particular issue is far too common. Thus pastors and other church financial stewards need to implement three safeguards in their financial systems to ensure that this type of failure does not happen within their organization.

First, if church leaders are to ensure that all designated funds are used in accordance to the instructions of the donor, they must implement an accounting system that is capable of tracking those designated gifts separately from the general church funds. The normal practice for designated funds is to "segre-

---

7. Kennon L. Callahan, *Effective Church Finances: Fund-raising and Budgeting for Church Leaders* (San Francisco: HarperSanFranc disco, 1992), 153.

8. *The Oxford American College Dictionary*, s.v. "Effective."

9. Joel G. Siegel and Jae K. Shim, *Accounting Handbook*, 3rd ed. (New York: Barron's, 2000), 662.

10. Malvern J. Gross, *Financial and Accounting Guide for Nonprofit Organizations* (New York: Wiley, 1983), 27.

gate those assets and report separately on their receipt and disposition."[11] These separate funds help "to ensure accountability and expenditure [of the funds] for [their] designated purposes."[12]

In this sense, church accounting is different than general accounting. This type of accounting is often referred to as fund accounting and is actually a very sophisticated and complex form of accounting. Even many trained accountants who daily practice their profession have limited experience with fund accounting. The challenge for many churches is that this type of accounting, with its greater than normal complexity, is sometimes being done by volunteers with limited or no accounting experience. Without some additional training for these volunteers, this can be a recipe for disaster.

The second safeguard to ensure the proper usage of all designated funds is the adoption of a written statement from the church governing body to the congregation pledging that no designated funds will be used for any reason other than those identified by the donors. This precaution is purposefully listed after introducing the reader to the fund accounting system described above because it will be nearly impossible to maintain such a pledge until a fund accounting system is implemented in your church.

However, once the fund accounting system is in place, there must be commitment on the part of the church leadership not to divert designated funds from the donor's intended purpose. This is important because leaders will face significant pressures to use these funds for purposes other than their official designation. Often, these requests will simply be to redirect funds temporarily to avert some impending financial crisis. Sometimes the pressure comes from well-meaning advisors that simply do not share the vision of the original donor and believe the funds would be better spent elsewhere.

When organizations misdirect designated funds away from the specific ministries that were intended by their donors, regardless of whether the cause is poor accounting systems or the purposeful choices made by leaders, the ministry wreckage can be devastating. Through the years, the author has been aware of different Christian ministries that have suffered the consequences of this type of misdirection of funds. They were left having to clean up the chaos created by such decisions, including the loss of their donors' trust, months or even years of reduced operational funding while putting money back into the designated accounts from which it was "borrowed," and defending themselves against possible accusations of misconduct and dishonesty. Thus to protect your organiza-

11. Ibid., 12.
12. Siegel and Shim, *Accounting Handbook,* 483.

tion against such difficulties, the author strongly recommends that you practice these two safeguards.

The third and final safeguard to ensure the proper usage of all designated funds is the implementation of a monthly designated-fund report. This report is very simple and is created after the church books are closed at the end of each month. This report is divided into two parts. The top part of the report lists all cash and cash-equivalent assets, such as CDs or money market accounts, and gives a total of these cash assets. This report does not list noncash assets, such as property and accounts receivables. The bottom half of the report lists each designated fund (or account) by its designation (or name) and any amount related to each account. At the bottom of the report, the sum of all the designated accounts plus any accounts payable balance on the church's books is subtracted from the totals of all cash assets. If this difference is positive, then the church has sufficient cash assets to cover all designated funds. If this difference is negative, then the church does not have enough cash to cover all of its designated accounts. A negative balance would indicate that the church has dipped into the cash that was set aside for these designated accounts to fund some of its regular operations. A church in this latter category would be on a fast collision course with the expectations of its donors. If a church will faithfully produce this report on a monthly basis, the information it provides can be used by the church leadership to guard against ever using designated funds for regular operations.

An additional benefit of this report is that the bottom-line balance that it shows is, by logical deduction, the total of all the cash held by the church that is not designated for any particular project or already committed for the payment of any outstanding bill. If this report is done monthly, then these bottom-line balances can be trended from month to month.

By using this trended information, it is possible to get a good understanding of how a church's income matches up to its expenses. If the trending of this report shows that the balance of church funds that are not designated is decreasing month by month, then the church is spending more money on operations than it is receiving for operations. In such cases, the church leadership can use this report to address their impending financial challenge before it becomes a real problem.

The opposite is true if the bottom-line balances on these reports are growing each month. An increasing number indicates that the church operating income is routinely greater than its operating expenses. In such cases, the church leadership may want to search out ways to invest these accumulating funds into other ministries that are in keeping with the stated ministry of the church. Finally, if this bottom-line number is remaining at a level that is approximately the same from month to month, then income and expenses are well matched.

Step Four: Avoid Inappropriate Personal Gain

As financial stewards, we sometimes have the ability to access money in a manner that others might consider inappropriate, or even unethical. Unfortunately, due to the conflict of an individual's own personal interest, it is easy to become blind to such inappropriate personal gain. Thus to protect ourselves *from* ourselves, we should adopt a few principles we can use to test the reasonableness of all expenditures of the church's money that we may authorize. Individuals should use these two simple tests of reasonableness to evaluate each potential ministry expense before authorizing such expenditures.

First, if the average layperson in the church were reviewing this expenditure would he or she conclude that, given all the circumstances, the purpose of the expenditure represents a legitimate ministry expense and that the amount of the expenditure is within reason? If the answer is no, then it is very unlikely that the expense that is being considered is an acceptable ministry expense.

However, there may be cases where the answer is no, but the individual still believes that there is possible ministry justification for an expenditure. In such cases, the individual should seek the opinion of his or her supervisor or, in the case of the pastor, the opinion of the church board before spending ministry funds. Seeking this second opinion should help to ensure that a proper decision is made.

A second test recognizes that not all expenses that might be deemed legitimate in purpose and size are still appropriate. A second test of reasonableness is whether expenditures help the ministry and support the church's mission or whether they are potentially counterproductive and could hurt the church's mission if those inside or outside the church were aware of these expenditures. If a potential expenditure falls into the latter category, it should not be made.

By applying these principles, financial stewards will be able to more objectively analyze potential expenditures that they are considering. If these principles will be applied faithfully and followed honestly, they will protect financial stewards from making expenditure decisions that would result in bringing inappropriate personal gain to themselves.

Step Five: Avoid the "Church Treasurer Syndrome"

The position of church treasurer is a specialized role for a financial steward. It has been my experience that those who serve in this special position are faced with unique challenges that other financial stewards are not. In most churches, the treasurers have the most intimate knowledge of the church's finances. Through their experience, they develop a good sense of what is needed to balance the church's income with its expenditures. Since church finances are often tight, it is very easy for them to internalize the pressures of meeting all the weekly financial obligations. In addition, they are constantly exposed to the differing money value judgments that are expressed by the many church members. They must also continually deal with the opposing money priorities that are being promoted by the leaders of the different ministry areas within the church. As a result, these fine servants of the church are susceptible to developing a condition that could be termed as the "church treasurer syndrome."

This condition is by no stretch of the imagination universal among church treasurers. However, once a treasurer exhibits the symptoms of this syndrome, his or her effectiveness as a financial steward of the church is compromised. The church treasurer syndrome is characterized by treasurers who become defensive about how the money is spent. Frequently, they will express their displeasure with and to anyone who suggests that the church's funds be spent in a manner that is not in agreement with the treasurer's own value judgments. The church treasurer syndrome is really the result of treasurers forgetting that the essence of their job is to fill the role of a steward of the funds entrusted to them. Instead of acting as stewards, these individuals start acting more like owners of the church's resources. It is important to identify individuals who are exhibiting the characteristics of this syndrome and to help them develop healthier views of their role.

Step Six: Provide Management Reports

Another important element that is essential to managing the church's resources wisely is providing the pastor with financial management reports. Most pastors are not trained accountants. Thus many of them will need some assistance when it comes to interpreting the financial data as it is listed on the standard accounting reports. The financial stewards who prepared these accounting reports must resist the temptation to force the pastor to learn enough accounting to properly interpret these reports. This temptation is strong, especially if those preparing the reports are trained accountants, because to these preparers these accounting reports seem so logical and the information that the pastor needs from these reports seems so straightforward and easy to access.

However, what seems so simple to the accountant is many times overwhelming to the pastor. Thus, in addition to the standard accounting reports, a manager's report needs to be developed for the pastor and other church leaders who make decisions based on the financial information within the report. There is no standard format for a manager's report because each one is unique. In order to develop an effective manager's report, whoever is preparing the standard accounting reports should sit down with the pastor, determine what information the pastor needs to lead the church, design a report around that information, and then format that information in a manner that makes sense to the pastor. A pastor's management report might include a comparison of weekly income and expenses, updates on special projects, and the percentage of church families that are contributing to the church. Yes, this does represent an extra step in the monthly report preparation process, but the benefit is well worth the extra investment.

Step Seven: Develop a Reserve Cash Fund (A Contingency Fund)

Financial stewards must also become proficient in managing the cash positions of the church. Like any other organization, churches have irregular flows of cash into and out of their bank accounts. Cash donations to churches typically ebb and flow during the year. Many churches experience specific times during the year when donations are significantly higher. One typical time period for higher than normal donations is during the Christmas season. Another time of the year when churches might see an increase in their giving is around Easter. Unfortunately, there are also certain time periods when donations are lower than normal, such as during the summer months.

In the same manner that church income fluctuates, so also do expenses. Some expenses, such as utility bills, are seasonal and rise and fall in relationship to the weather. Other expenses occur rarely but, when they do occur, carry big price tags. An example would be the unexpected costs associated with the replacement of an air-conditioning unit that breaks down just before the hottest Sunday of the year. A scheduled replacement of the roof on the church would also be an example of this latter category.

"The primary consideration in managing the cash flow cycle is to ensure that inflows and outflows of cash are properly synchronized."[13] This constant and significant fluctuation of both income and expenses results in the high risk of churches experiencing cash flow problems. That is, churches have a very high probability of experiencing times when they do not have sufficient cash in the bank to meet their obligations. Thus the financial stewards of churches must become skilled in managing the cash within their organizations so as to

---

13. Stanley B. Block and Geoffrey A. Hirt, *Foundations of Financial Management*, 12th ed. (New York: McGraw-Hill/Irwin, 2008), 186.

avoid embarrassing situations that both damage the church's reputation within their community and the trust that the other parishioners have placed in these financial stewards.

In order to avoid running out of cash, the financial stewards of the church must maintain adequate cash reserves. The level of cash that needs to be held in reserve may vary significantly from church to church.

One of the major factors dictating what represents an adequate level of cash reserves for a particular church is the predictability of the cash flow for that church. The more predictable the cash flow patterns of an organization, the less cash that needs to be maintained.[14] Many churches will be able to avoid cash flow problems by keeping enough cash in reserve to cover the average expenses of the church for a period of two to four months. Churches with more predictable cash flows may be able to operate quite effectively on the lower end of this scale. However, churches with high volatility in relationship to their cash flow may want to keep four or more months of cash on reserve.

Occasionally, you will encounter someone who believes that establishing a cash reserve is paramount to a lack of faith. Unquestionably, we should constantly pray for and depend on God's abundant supply for the church's ministries. However, we should not be presumptuous about God's provisions. Jesus wasn't. When Satan tempted Jesus to throw himself down from the pinnacle of the temple, Jesus reminded Satan (and us) that the Scriptures state, "Do not put the Lord your God to the test" (Matt. 4:7). James also teaches us that "faith without deeds is useless" (James 2:20).

Jesus took for granted the value that one should "estimate the cost" in order to ensure that "enough money" is available (Luke 14:28). It is not a lack of faith to prepare for what is needed to navigate the inevitable ebb and flow of church income and expenses. Thus, establishing an adequate cash reserve fund will extend the effectiveness of the church's ministry and will help maintain the trust of the congregation in its leaders.

The hazard of running out of cash due to the cyclical nature of cash flows could also be addressed through a line of credit at a local bank. However, the author does not recommend that approach for a couple of reason. First, the church runs the risk of falling into a pattern where it is regularly operating on debt. Second, a line of credit will likely be distasteful to the fiscally conservative members of the congregation.

---

14. Ibid., 174.

Step Eight: Avoid Giving Charitable Receipts for Personal Gifts (Understand What Is Charitable and What Is Not)

The United States Congress has passed a series of tax laws that are referred to as the Internal Revenue Code. This code governs all matters related to the assessment and collection of federal taxes in the United States. Embedded within this huge array of tax laws are legal guidelines that establish whether a donation to any organization can be considered a charitable contribution. This charitable contribution designation is important because it reduces the taxable income of the donor by the amount of his or her charitable gift and thus exempts the amount of the gift from any U.S. federal income tax obligation. Congress has assigned the enforcement of this federal tax code with its charitable giving guidelines to the United States Internal Revenue Service (IRS).

The IRS interpretations of the tax codes that relate to charitable giving are presented in IRS Publication 526, which is appropriately titled *Charitable Contributions*. This twenty-three-page publication outlines what types of donations are considered tax deductible and what types are not. It identifies limits on deductions, describes the record keeping required to substantiate the charitable nature of donations, and outlines how and when to report deductions.

These IRS interpretations about charitable contributions are important to the financial stewards of the church for a variety of reasons, not the least of which is that, in many cases, the IRS charges the financial stewards of the church with the responsibility of officially acknowledging donations to the church that meet the IRS charitable-giving requirements. In recognition of meeting these IRS requirements, the church is given the responsibility of issuing a charitable-giving receipt that the donor, if required, can officially present to the IRS to substantiate the tax deductibility of the donor's gifts to the church.

There are two main principles that the financial stewards of the church must keep in mind when using the IRS guidelines to determine the tax deductibility of a gift to the church.

Principle No. 1

Gifts must be given to a qualified organization to be considered charitable. "Generally, you can deduct your contributions of money or property that you make to, or for the use of, a qualified organization."[15] In order to meet this requirement, churches must be officially registered with and recognized by the IRS as charitable organizations. Often churches are registered under the aus-

---

15. IRS, "Charitable Contributions," http://www.irs.gov/pub/irs-pdf/p526.pdf (accessed August 21, 2008), 3.

pices of their denomination, but many times they are registered directly with the IRS. This registration is under section 501(c)3 of the Internal Revenue Code, and so churches as well as other charitable (often called nonprofit) organizations are frequently referred to as 501(c)3 organizations.

Principle No. 2

Contributions must be "a donation or gift to, or for the use of, a qualified organization."[16] This principle goes a step beyond the first principle to recognize that a gift is not charitable just because a church receives it. It must also be for the use of the church. Publication 526 further elaborates on this principle as follows: "A gift or contribution is 'for the use of' a qualified organization when it is held in a legally enforceable trust for the qualified organization or in a similar legal arrangement."[17] That is, the financial stewards of the church assume the responsibility through the church's legal structure to ensure that the funds are used for a recognized ministry purpose of the church.

Compliance to this second principle is many times a challenge to the financial stewards because they may receive requests from their parishioners to provide them with a charitable receipt for a gift given to the church that is "earmarked" for a particular person or persons. For example, the church may learn that a particular family within their congregation is experiencing extremely difficult financial challenges. However, "when the beneficiary is designated by name, the gift" is considered personal and, by virtue of that classification, is not considered to "have the characteristics of a charitable gift" and is thus not tax deductible.[18] Publication 526 very clearly states that in order for gifts to be tax deductible, contributions must "not [be] set aside for use by a specific person."[19] In such cases, the financial stewards must resist the pressure from donors to issue tax-deductible receipts.

The scenario described above can be quite unpleasant for the financial stewards of the church as they attempt to stand their ground to comply with the IRS regulations. However, there is a practical way by which churches can avoid such situations. Rather than accepting donations for specific individuals in a time of personal financial crisis, churches can set up benevolence funds that can be tapped during such times. Helping people who find themselves in dire financial circumstances is well within the charitable-ministry scope of a church.

---

16. Ibid.

17. Ibid.

18. Dan Busby, *Donor-Restricted Gifts Simplified* (Winchester, VA: Evangelical Council for Financial Accountability, 2007), 39.

19. IRS, "Charitable Contributions," 3.

Thus churches can set up non-person-specific benevolence funds to which their congregants can make donations, and since these donations would be to a qualified organization and for a recognized purpose of that organization, such donations would be considered tax-deductible contributions. Then, individuals who are in financial need can be given assistance from these benevolence funds. This avoids the situation where individuals are donating gifts for a "specific person."

A similar approach can be taken with gifts for scholarships, assistance for children to attend youth camps, and so on. Again, the key is that the funds are given to the church and distributed by the church in a manner that is not person-specific, and that the reason for which the funds are given is in keeping with the recognized ministry purposes of the church.

Sometimes churches attempt to funnel donations to a specific person by "creatively" using non-person-specific accounts so as to justify the issuance of a charitable receipt for what would otherwise not be a tax-deductible gift. Not only are such actions unethical but they are also illegal.

These "creative" tactics will not withstand IRS scrutiny because the IRS uses a practice called "substance over form" to look behind the veil of non-person-specific accounts to ascertain the true nature of the economic transaction that occurred. To the IRS, it is not the form in which a gift was processed that matters but the actual substance of the transaction that dictates whether a gift is tax deductible. Organizations and donors that deliberately practice such tactics will face significant penalties and sanctions from the IRS.

SUMMARY

Financial stewards serve an absolutely essential function in every church. No church can hope to successfully fulfill its ministry goals without the faithful service of these individuals. They are called upon to wisely manage the church's financial resources while fulfilling the various expectations of the congregation. This role can be overwhelming. However, by following the eight steps outlined above, serving in this role can be both fulfilling and rewarding. My prayer is that you will be strengthened for this work through these materials.

FOR FURTHER READING

Busby, Dan. *Zondervan 2010 Church and Nonprofit Tax and Financial Guide: For 2009 Returns*. Grand Rapids: Zondervan, 2010.

Carter, Doug. *Raising More Than Money: Redefining Generosity—Reflecting God's Heart*. Nashville: Thomas Nelson, 2007.

18

MANAGERIAL ETHICS
BECOMING A LEADER AFTER GOD'S OWN HEART

Robert S. Barnard Jr.
PhD, Military Chaplain, Free Methodist Church

Becoming a leader after God's own heart means learning to lead the way God leads in order to accomplish what is important to God. The desired result is a world redeemed and in full relationship with God. Most ministries are non-profit organizations. The bottom line for all nonprofit organizations is a changed human life.[1]

In the Christian church and other Christian ministries, this is ultimately about making disciples (see Matt. 28:19)—seeking lost people, presenting the gospel, and nurturing responders into mature images of Jesus. The marks of a disciple are found in several scriptures, including Galatians 5:22-23 (the fruit of the Spirit) and Matthew 5:1-12 (the Beatitudes).

Most readers can recount local and personal experiences that highlight ethical dilemmas and challenges. Congregations and religious ministries encounter challenges similar to those found in corporate life because all organizations are made up of human beings. Recent research indicates that, on the average, Christian Evangelical Ministry/Mission Organizations (CEMOs) have a 75 percent probability of encountering a significant event of staff-related Dysfunctional Behavior (DB) requiring senior-leadership or board-level intervention in a twelve-month period.[2]

---

1. Peter F. Drucker, *Managing the Non-Profit Organization* (New York: Harper Collins Publishing, 1990).

2. Robert S. Barnard, "An Examination of Dysfunctional Behavior In Christian, Evangelical, Mission Organizations and Strategies for Managing the Consequences of Dysfunctional Behavior" (thesis, Oxford Centre for Mission Studies, 2004).

The purpose of this chapter is to give the reader practical tools to manage the consequences of dysfunctional or unethical behavior in order to become a leader after God's own heart.

STRATEGIC THINKING

Interviews[3] of members of various levels of CEMOs revealed three broad approaches to strategic thinking and strategic planning in the organizations. The researched CEMOs were divided into groups of different sizes according to the three perceived approaches. The group with the largest number of CEMOs approached the concept of strategic thinking and planning as if it were an event, engaged in annually or less frequently, to be referred to upon occasion for authoritative purposes. In this first grouping, most interviewees had given little thought about the nature of strategic thinking.

The group with the smallest number of CEMOs practiced strategic thinking and planning as a total mind-set or lifestyle, in which strategy was an ongoing learning process. Also, they applied the *New International Version*'s wording of Proverbs 29:18, "Where there is no revelation, the people cast off restraint," as opposed to the King James Version's, "Where there is no vision, the people perish."

In the middle group, strategic thinking was simply a business or military activity that threatened to undermine principles of faith and contaminate the work of the Holy Spirit. At least one Christian writer speaking of management principles and servant leadership encourages this perspective.[4] Here strategic thinking and planning were largely absent because organizations of this grouping relied only on a holy calling.

SCOPE OF ETHICS IN MINISTRY

Practical Approach—Philosophical Approach

Carter McNamara claims that much of ethics literature is written from either a simplified "what would/should you do?" view or an academic and philosophical view.[5] There is a lack of concrete training in practical complex scenarios. The content of this chapter seeks to lay the foundation for a concrete approach to managerial ethics.

---

3. Ibid.
4. David McKenna, *Wesleyan Leadership in Troubled Times* (Kansas City: Beacon Hill Press of Kansas City, 2002), 9.
5. Carter McNamara, A response to David Gebler's blog "Ethics at a cross roads," http://managementhelp.org/blogs/business-ethics/2010/04/01/ethics-at-a-cross-roads/ (accessed July 26, 2010).

Social Responsibility and Spiritual Responsibility

According to McNamara, the social responsibility movement is but one aspect of the overall discipline of business ethics.[6] Social responsibility is focused on businesses promoting the public welfare.

Spiritual responsibility, for the CEMO, adds the dimension of accountability to God and the mandates of Scripture. Regardless of the theological position of a ministry, a clearly defined operative mandate establishes the nature and direction of its ethics and operations.

The Bottom Line: Three Types of Organizations with Differing Motivations

The bottom line is a clear indicator of the motivational force in an organization. When properly understood, the bottom line is used to assess the success of an organization regardless of whether it is a for-profit, nonprofit, or government organization. Clearly, the bottom-line concern for profit-generating organizations is the amount of profit generated. The bottom-line concern for nonprofit organizations is changed lives.[7] Thus, success is measured in the quantity and quality of positively changed lives. The standard of success for a government organization may be an oxymoron to some. However, the best bottom line for government organizations is effective services.

Effective Christian ministries[8] measure themselves according to a standard of changed lives. Stewardship issues are essential and require clear standards of fiscal accounting. Christian ministries thus establish codes of ethics according to spiritual mandates, people issues, and fiscal responsibility.

CLARIFYING CONCEPTS

Working definitions of various terms used throughout this chapter are presented here for clarity.

1. Strategic Integrity

Strategic integrity is the condition in which all aspects of an organization (i.e., identity, structure, policy, operation, culture, and climate) reflect the organization's mission, purpose, values, and vision. Attaining strategic integrity results

---

6. Carter McNamara, "Business Ethics: Managing Ethics in the Workplace and Social Responsibility," Free Management Library, http://www.managementhelp.org/ethics/ethics .htm#anchor1932284.

7. Drucker, *Managing the Non-profit Organization*.

8. Christian ministries are usually nonprofits, though not always—i.e., see Stanley Tam, *God Owns My Business* (Camp Hill, PA: Horizon Books Publishers, 1969).

from a process that ensures the congruence of all aspects of the organization's identity and performance through strategic thinking, planning, and implementation.[9]

2. Dysfunctional Behavior (DB)

DB is any behavior that disrupts organizational function. This encompasses unethical behaviors but may also include the "whistle blower" or the self-appointed "prophet."

3. Consequence Management

All DB creates consequences. Ethically managing these consequences is a critical part of the organizational response for CEMOs. The term "consequence management" is borrowed from the federal response to the first attack on the World Trade Center in 1993.

4. Strategic Model Template

The Strategic Model Template (SMT) is a working model/flow chart for systematic consequence management.

FACTORS IN DISCERNING BEHAVIOR AS ETHICAL OR UNETHICAL

Many different factors influence the discernment of behavior as ethical or unethical. Every leader needs to be aware of the factors and is encouraged to develop a working mastery of each, integrating that mastery into a coherent management approach regarding ethics.

1. Culture and subcultures are the working context of the organization's members. Norms, mores, and values are ingrained in individuals and groups by culture.

2. Moral intensity is the nature of a given event to have sufficient moral impact so that the organization and/or society demands some form of corrective intervention. Moral intensity is shaped by and perceived through various factors such as

- Personal versus corporate: Both individuals and organizations reflect differing levels of moral development. Christian organizations are no different.

---

9. Barnard, "An Examination of Dysfunctional Behavior," 185.

- Absolute versus relative: Modern culture promotes the notion that all moral decisions are relative. This opens the door to many interesting interpretations of events. An example is former President Clinton's now infamous statement about "what the meaning of the word 'is' is" during his impeachment trial.[10] On the other hand, CEMOs and their members have a long history of preferring absolute and literal interpretations. The wise leader understands the distinction between absolute and relative and when to apply each.

3. An individual's internal factors have a complex motivational and interpretative influence on managerial ethics for all leaders and stakeholders. These factors become interpretative filters for assessment. These internal factors include an individual's temperament, spiritual gifts, fruit of the Spirit, talents, roles, training, education, life experience, stages of life, trauma, genetics, assumptions, and presumptions.

4. External factors influence ethical responses also. These include media, reference groups, influential leaders, family, social class, and laws.

The Use of Biblical Texts for Ethical Discernment/Judgment

In the New Testament, two words are used that are generally translated "word" in English. They are *rhēma* (ρημασ') and *logos* (λογος). *Logos* is used to point to the absolute expression of God's will and nature, including judgment. Jesus is identified as the Word (see John 1:1). On the other hand, *rhēma* is used to describe the word as the application of divine standards in the context of individual lives as directed by the Holy Spirit. Thus *logos* is more concrete while *rhēma* carries a subjective component to it. This is significant when we are considering the issue of managerial ethics. There appears to be a clear distinction of time and place for both absolute and relative standards. Thus by inference, from a biblical viewpoint, Christian managerial ethics is concerned with both absolute and relative approaches. It is incumbent on the leader/manager to incorporate both approaches. A biblical mandate must be presented in the context of its language and application.

The Unique Nature of CEMOs

CEMOs are unique in several aspects that strongly influence organizational structure and practice.

---

10. Bill Clinton, "Bill Clinton It Depends on What the Meaning of the Word 'Is' Is," YouTube, http://www.youtube.com/watch?v=j4XT-l-_3y0.

1. Members who enter ministry or serve on foreign fields have a unique character. The independent and "maverick" nature of people who intentionally leave their home culture for the sole purpose of presenting a Christian influence in a foreign community may result in an organizationally resistant individual.[11]
2. The sense of an individual divine calling inclines people to assume a divine approval that may preclude submission to various organizational requirements and procedures.
3. There is a self-perceived gap between the management priorities of the sending organization and the field realities and requirements.
4. Organizational systems, structures, practices, and procedures are viewed by many members as restrictive and confining, stifling creativity and, worst of all, quenching the inspiration of the Holy Spirit.
5. The ideological motivation and purpose of CEMOs combined with an implicit assumption of divine guidance may encourage organizations not to analyze various aspects of their operations or invest resources in intentional leadership or organizational development.
6. Resources are believed to be unavailable for organizational development and training due to the resource development practices of CEMOs and the perceptions of backers who insist their contributions go exclusively to field operations.
7. Because of the first six aspects, CEMOs tend to be suspicious of, and resistant to, any influence that is perceived as generated by values, motives, and practices external to a culture based on "divine guidance."[12]

These interrelated reasons are why CEMOs are momentarily unable to manage DB and its consequences.

The Constraining/Enabling Triangle

The Constraining/Enabling Triangle (appendix 18.1) depicts how the effective management of consequences of DB appears to be strongly influenced by the reasons listed above. Those reasons are grouped into three areas of influence based on attributes they hold in common:

---

11. Christopher Sugden, (principal, Oxford Centre for Mission Studies), in discussion with the author, June 2002.
12. Ibid.

1. Personal and Corporate Theology and Identity

Within the community of those organizations that identify themselves as evangelical are many different theological systems that undergird their values and practices. These systems may cause individual CEMOs to view and practice consequence management somewhat differently. Also, individually held theological positions may differ from espoused organizational theology thus creating internal stresses and possible DB with its attendant consequences. Theological assumptions are often untested on the part of individuals and organizations.

2. History, Tradition, Environment, and Context

History, tradition, environment, and context all influence corporate culture, behavior, and capacity.[13]

3. Personal and Corporate Processes and Competencies

Research revealed a wealth of new data and understandings for both DB and its consequences.[14] The establishment of typologies provides part of the foundation for the art and discipline of consequence management.

These three influences may be either positive or negative. The Constraining/Enabling Triangle model depicts the three main areas of influence that have been found to impede or enhance the capacity of CEMOs to effectively manage DB and its consequences.

Personal and corporate theologies significantly influence personal and corporate identity. Given the nature of evangelical theology with its biblical emphasis, change is not easy without a perceived divine mandate. Although DB is depicted throughout the Bible and its consequences are graphically portrayed, the divine mandate appears to be implemented as a way to avoid DB rather than as a preparation for managing it and its consequences. Thus CEMOs become trapped within a theology that calls for perfection rather than a theology that deals with imperfection. The identity and image CEMOs seek to maintain is one of rightness and righteousness, which they perceive as necessary for sustaining support from donors and other benefactors. However, this approach disables the CEMOs as they avoid evidence of "un-rightness."

On the one hand, the very long history of missions is a strong point in their favor. On the other hand, in the context of DB, tradition has become for many CEMOs a barrier to change. In a rapidly changing world (with rapidly changing expectations of donors, members, and host nations), conformity to leadership

---

13. Barnard, "An Examination of Dysfunctional Behavior."
14. Ibid.

and membership patterns of the past is inhibiting the development of practical approaches to present-day problems.

With the emphasis on theology and tradition, the acquisition of new skills and competencies come low, if at all, on the priority list of CEMOs. Without these processes and competencies the CEMOs are trapped in a triangle of constraints.

TRANSPARENCY AND ACCOUNTABILITY

Strategic Integrity

Strategic integrity is the foundational ingredient in transparency and accountability. The concept of strategic integrity emerged and evolved from observing the function of organizations and the responses in the interview process of a PhD research project.[15] However, in 1960 Douglas MacGregor advocated integrating all aspects of organizational strategy and practice, including human resources, as a strategic asset.[16] Authors have continued to emphasize integration and the achievement of congruence, though without the use of the term "strategic integrity."

To shift from integrating organizational strategy, tactics, policy, actions, and plans (an action itself) to possessing strategic integrity (a state of being) means moving from an emphasis on performance to an emphasis on condition; moving from a focus on an implied task of mission to a focus on corporate character. This places "being" as the definitive precursor of strategy and tactics. What you are and what you know determines how you do what you do.[17] This is especially significant for CEMOs and is the central focus of this chapter. How much people accept the ministries a CEMO offers depends on how well the CEMO's behavior coincides with the content of the message it proclaims. Thus the assessment of validity and credibility for a CEMO's work is dependent on strategic integrity.

Restoration and reconciliation of persons and organizations, from an organizational systems perspective, incorporates consequence management, conflict resolution/management, and change management. Two of these domains of managerial practice are dealt with elsewhere in this text. Consequence management is dealt with here.

---

15. Ibid.
16. Douglas McGregor, *The Human Side of Enterprise* (New York: McGraw-Hill, 1960).
17. This is espoused by Peter Drucker, Karl Weick, and Kathleen Sutcliffe, and in U.S. Army field manual on leadership training (formerly FM 22-100, now FM 6-22).

Codes and Standards—Criteria

There are many fine examples of strong codes of ethics on the Internet.[18] Each denomination today has some version available to its members. Every ministry is encouraged to adopt and publish its own code. The test of ethical effectiveness is the extent to which organizational members internalize and live out the standards that are promoted.

STRATEGIC MODEL TEMPLATE

Organizations need to go beyond a code of ethics. They need a strategy of response when ethical dilemmas and DB are encountered. The Strategic Model Template (SMT; appendix 18.2) is suggested as an initial approach for leaders/managers.

The SMT is a framework for consequence management. It may also function as a tangible aid toward establishing strategic integrity.

Combining essential strategic and operational elements into a management matrix for dealing with the consequences of DB takes the form of a taxonomy,[19] or interrelated classification system, in which the failure or weakness of any component will adversely impact overall accomplishment. Thus, based on strategic integrity, the SMT cannot be regarded as a menu of options for use in consequence management. A menu implies a set of choices from which to select or reject for the purpose of consequence management. The SMT is a flow chart of conditions and processes to accomplish effective consequence management. The neglect of any element or elements may, at the least, leave the organization open to reduced effectiveness.

To have strategic integrity, an SMT should consist of the following qualities: it should be comprehensive, have a nonnegotiable core, be flexible to accommodate local contingencies, combine best practices with learning, focus on the consequences of DB, enable consequence management, describe desired end conditions, have a set of resolution criteria, be capable of being used as a diagnostic tool, and provide a process for learning.

The natural flow of events that are the core elements of the SMT are *(a)* sense, *(b)* identify, *(c)* evaluate, *(d)* decide, *(e)* act, and *(f)* learn. Within the six

---

18. See http://ethics.iit.edu/codes/religion.html for examples and a starting place for research.

19. According to the Cambridge Unabridged Dictionary, taxonomy is a means of labeling and organizing information. Taxonomy provides both description and relationship data. It can therefore be depicted graphically in tabular form, wire diagram, chart, etc. Failure of one component within the taxonomy to properly provide its definitive role jeopardizes the integrity and functionality of the whole.

core elements are subordinate elements that provide a comprehensive but not necessarily exhaustive model.

A flowchart depicting the six core elements of the SMT is shown in appendix 18.2.

A. Sense

The sense component of the SMT consists of three elements: awareness of DB and its consequences, an alert system, and the event of DB and its consequences.

1. Awareness of DB and Its Consequences

The initial requirements for consequence management are an understanding of the nature of DB and its consequences and the capacity to recognize their presence as they occur.

Regarding recognition of DB and its consequences, Karl Weick and Kathleen Sutcliffe point out that those unexpected events usually originate in what psychologist James Reason calls "latent failures."

> Latent failures are "loopholes in the system's defenses, barriers and safeguards whose potential existed for some time prior to the onset of the accident sequence, though usually without any obvious bad effects."[20]

They go on to contend that normal operations may provide free lessons on impending incidents, but only if the organization pays attention to operations by frequently assessing the overall performance of the organization.

Focusing on normal operations allows anomalies to be identified early and corrected, preventing an accumulation that leads to trouble. Consequence management, especially in its preventive aspects, seeks to emulate this sensitivity to operations.

2. Alert System

It is impossible to specify the specific components of an alert system for every CEMO due to the diversity of their working environments. Each organization needs to develop the collective wisdom of its members, a typology of sources, and a benchmarking network of likeminded organizations to determine the functional elements of its alert system. Elements to be included in the system are as follows: a means for monitoring available sources of information and an improved focus on communications processes.

---

20. Karl E. Weick and Kathleen M. Sutcliffe, *Managing the Unexpected: Resilient Performance in an Age of Uncertainty* (San Francisco: Jossey-Bass, 2007), 13.

3. Event of DB and Its Consequences

An event is the occurrence of DB or unethical practice. Events are the initiators of consequence management. Simply being able to recognize an event for what it is, as it happens, is the outcome of awareness and alertness and completes the first step of the SMT.

Summary

Sense, the first element of the SMT, provides the capacity to acknowledge the presence of DB and its consequences.

B. Identify

Effective consequence management is concerned with responding to the true nature of the event at hand. As such, the manager will need to determine the facts and the scope of both the DB and the consequences. Four components to this are information sources, typology of dysfunctional behavior, typology of consequences, and stakeholders.

1. Information Sources

The table in appendix 18.3 is presented as a compilation of possible information sources. It is not exhaustive, and organizations are encouraged to develop their own source list.

2. Typology of Dysfunctional Behavior

The table in appendix 18.4 provides a list of behavior categories of DB. The fact that one column is labeled "Ethical" does not preclude the other columns from concern in managerial ethics.

3. Typology of Consequences

It is helpful to have an understanding of the impact or consequences of DB on organizations. The table in appendix 18.5 depicts a broad representation of consequences so that the leader/manager is conceptually positioned to recognize initial indicators. It is certainly possible to expand the table's content, and the reader is encouraged to do so in the context of the reader's ministry.

4. Stakeholders

Stakeholders are target populations on whose important concerns and issues consequence management focuses. They are qualitatively different from shareholders, who are primarily concerned with the monetary return on their investment, though this is changing somewhat.

C. Evaluate

The next element of the SMT is to evaluate what has been identified and to determine the feasibility and timing of consequence management intervention. Subjective methods and inconsistency are the usual features of consequence management within CEMOs. Through the use of the SMT, organizations can engage in a structured analysis of an event. This endeavor does not always need to be deep and time consuming. Nevertheless, use of the SMT would contribute a measure of objectivity to the situation.

An evaluation must determine the severity of the DB, the severity of the consequences, and when a response threshold has been crossed, thus triggering further action by the consequence manager.

1. Severity of DB

The following four levels of severity can be used as an assessment mechanism to help formulate a structured response to a given situation: Level 1: chargeable moral and criminal offenses; Level 2: consenting adults in objectionable or unacceptable behavior; Level 3: appearance issues and emotional bonding that begins to interfere with organizational performance; and Level 4: tolerable idiosyncrasies or irritants. The first three levels trigger the response mechanism and require some form of intervention by leadership.

2. Severity of the Consequences

The severity of the consequences consists of five levels: Level 1: threats to the survival of the mission (organization); Level 2: threats to the survival of one or more projects; Level 3: threats to the continuing employment or function of a group of people; Level 4: threats to the continuing employment of an individual; and Level 5: threats to efficiency and effectiveness.

Each event may be evaluated using a yes or no assessment, ranked in a high-, medium-, or low-risk scale, or assigned values for judgment through some other means.

3. Response Threshold

When DB crosses the threshold of tolerance, CEMOs react. Not all DBs require action, and indeed, some are often tolerated. However, at some point, the consequences may become intolerable, and that is when either knee-jerk reactions occur or well-planned consequence management takes place.

D. Decide

Having identified the issues, evaluated the impact of the DB and its consequences on the organization, and recognized that a response threshold has been reached making consequence management action necessary, key decisions about the response must be made. These decisions concern the rationale for action, desired results, resolution criteria, composition of a response team, and logistics allocated to consequence management. These five decisions may be made by a leader or a committee. Additionally, they may be refined and developed further by the consequence manager/management team as needed.

1. Rationale

The consequence manager will need to clearly expound the rationale for the actions that will be taken. The table in appendix 18.6 depicts several rationales. Other rationales may be added as the organization determines what other appropriate actions it must take. However it is done, the rationales need to be clearly articulated and recorded to protect the CEMO and ensure due process.

Appendix 18.7 illustrates how different rationales might direct strategy within the CEMOs. The elements of a CEMO's Strategic Model Template (SMT) could and should facilitate moving the organization toward the fulfillment of the expressed rationales. The nexus of the different rationales will influence the construction and implementation of the components of the SMT. For each CEMO, the relative strengths of the different rationales can be assigned values, say on a scale of 1 to 10, with 10 being the ideal score for each. The amount of resulting deformity in the star pattern shapes organizational strategy. Strategic integrity requires an informed and balanced approach.

2. Desired Results

The desired results are damage control, repairs and rebuilding, and organizational learning.[21] These should be further clarified from the perspective of the consequences, their severity, and the scope of stakeholder issues that come to light. For example, in a case of a senior CEMO staff member accused of molesting children, some desired results could be as follows: that justice is served for both the host nation and sending nation; that the victims experience physical, emotional, and spiritual healing; that knowledgeable stakeholders are satisfied and express approval of the CEMO's due process and consequence management; that public trust in the CEMO and its remaining on-site personnel is affirmed and strengthened; that the local church observes and learns how to manage difficult situations; and that the perpetrator is removed from all at-risk positions, is submissive to legal authority, is submissive to spiritual authority, and engages in restoration and rehabilitation with a favorable prognosis.

3. Resolution Criteria

Clearly stated resolution criteria for successful actions should be established from the beginning. That is, stated standards for determining when the situation is successfully managed need to be firmly established before action is taken and then pursued assiduously. Such criteria may include backer financial support that remains constant or improves, victims of DB who desire to remain with the CEMO in the same position and location, and a local populace that acknowledges the wisdom of the consequence management.

---

21. Elaine Chao and Margaret McGehy, *Rebuilding Public Confidence*, audiotape, National Conference of Nonprofit Boards, 1993.

4. Response Team

As a practical matter, it is simplest if issues are resolved at the lowest level in the organization. This certainly coincides with CEMO values where members are frequently encouraged to follow the directions of Matthew 5 and 18. These chapters apply to situations where people have grievances, and they encourage a one-to-one resolution of the problem. Essentially, Matthew 5 requires the guilty member to set things right. Matthew 18 requires the observer of DB, possibly as one offended, to go to the offending persons and seek to set things right. In both cases it is implicit that the action lies with the person who spots the problem.

Additionally, Romans 13 describes a magistrate's responsibility to care for the rights of the victimized. When DB requires the intervention of senior CEMO leaders, it should be in line with Romans 13, which directs followers to submit to those in authority, and those in authority to behave as one working for God.

The SMT prescribes the responsible leader(s) who will address the consequences of DB that escalate to this level. In some situations CEMO leaders may designate the intervention person(s) on a case-by-case basis or assign the person(s) to be specifically available for such work throughout the organization.

5. Logistics

The level of resources committed to consequence management needs to be specified if the organization does not have pre-budgeted logistics in place. This may include time, expenses, travel, fees for external support, accommodations, and support services.

Summary

The decide element of the SMT encompasses five crucial decision areas that set in place the final components for the needed actions: rationale, desired results, resolution criteria, response team composition, and logistics support. With these decisions established, the next two elements, to act and learn, are grounded in reality and focused on future effectiveness.

E. Act—The Consequence Management Matrix

The next step is to take action. The Consequence Management Matrix (appendix 18.8) comprises a wide range of options depending on the consequences of the DB and the designated stakeholders.

The Consequence Management Matrix depicts options available to the consequence manager for each focus area of response and each level of impact of the DB. Five levels of impact (personal, relational, project, organizational, and environmental) are listed in the left column and are an expansion and re-organization of the typology of consequences. The foci of response are listed across the top horizontal row (palliative, preventive, emergency, recovery, and reflective). The cells of the matrix give response options at each level available for each response focus.

The options given are presented from a Western perspective and should be interpreted with that in mind. Organizations and responders are enjoined to re-craft the matrix to suit the particular culture and people involved in the event. An explicit statement and understanding of the desired results and identification of pertinent resolution criteria are keys to forming an effective matrix.

F. Learn

At different points in the SMT process the manager seeks to assess lessons learned. Suggested review and analysis venues are listed in the table of appendix 18.9. Furthermore, programmed reviews and analyses add to the effectiveness of consequence management. The results are used by management to prepare for future events and mitigate the extent of consequences.

CONCLUSION

There are ethical concerns throughout the management of CEMOs. This chapter gives a practical application for identifying and dealing with unethical/dysfunctional behavior and its consequences by defining two typologies and explaining the Constraining/Enabling Triangle. Leaders and managers need to go beyond the theoretical and develop a context-specific response strategy for unethical/dysfunctional behavior that begins with a code of conduct or a code of ethics and then incorporates an SMT.

Becoming a leader after God's own heart is challenging and complex. The SMT with the Consequence Management Matrix is a tool to use for generating prevention and intervention strategies within the boundaries of practical managerial ethics.

APPENDIX 18.1

The Constraining/Enabling Triangle

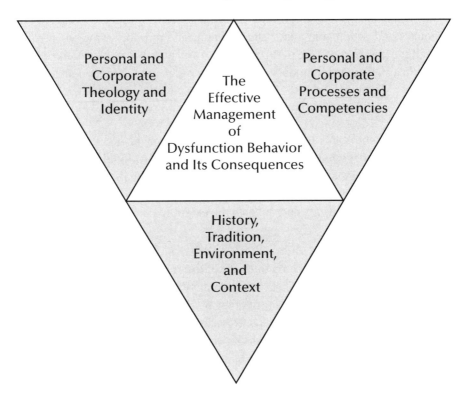

Personal and Corporate Theology and Identity

The Effective Management of Dysfunction Behavior and Its Consequences

Personal and Corporate Processes and Competencies

History, Tradition, Environment, and Context

APPENDIX 18.2
The Strategic Model Template

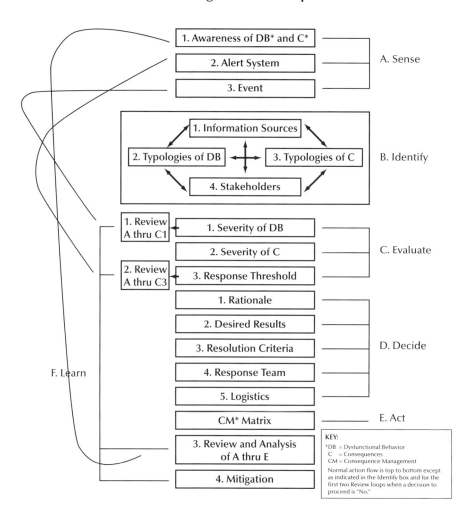

APPENDIX 18.3

Information Sources

Direct Internal Sources	Direct External Sources	Indirect Sources
Supervisor observations	National (host nation)	Health statistics
Colleagues' confidences	Church	Morale
Review & analysis	Government authority	Reduced productivity
processes	Citizens	Attrition statistics
Analyses of reports	Sister agencies	Rumors
Formal evaluations	Media reports	Repeated topic of concern
Climate surveys	Initiated legal actions	in community meetings
On-site inspections	Criminal charges	Turf battles
Performance evaluations	Civil suits	Defensiveness
Post-tour debriefs	Regulatory violations	Critical spirits
	Concerns by backers	Back stabbing
	Injuries to reputation	Disharmony

APPENDIX 18.4

Types of Dysfunctional Behavior

Competence/ Capacity	Moral/Legal/ Ethical	Organizational Dysfunction	Medical/ Physical
Intrapersonal	Substance abuse	Turning the blind eye	Depression
Interpersonal/ personal/family	Funds and resources (e.g., gambling, indebtedness, waste, fraud, and misuse)	Corporate incapacity and structure inadequacies	Seasonal adjustment disorder
Inadequate work/ professional competence and skills	Other illegal acts	Systems failures	Posttraumatic stress disorder
Philosophy/doctrine/ theology	Liability, personal injury and loss (safety)	Inconsistency, favoritism, and nepotism	Stages of grief
Cultural/cross-cultural	Inappropriate sexual behavior	Collusion	Physical illness
Cross-generational	Lifestyle issues Antagonistic behavior	Non-learning	Injury

APPENDIX 18.5

Types of Consequences

Personal Consequences	Corporate Consequences	Stakeholder Consequences
Stress	Damage to team cohesion	Defamation of God's
Health problems	Declining morale	reputation
Demoralization—	Disharmony	Erosion of donor base
sense of betrayal or	Damage control becomes	Loss of relations with host
disillusionment	a priority	nation
Negative emotional	Reduced efficiency	Adverse impact to
states—rage, grief,	Personnel attrition	relations with
exhaustion, disbelief,	Loss of "brand" confidence	sending nation (home
etc.	and public trust	churches, collegial
Survival mind-set	Declining recruitment	agencies, state
	Diversion of resources	department, etc.)
	Termination of a program	Impact to sister agencies

APPENDIX 18.6

Rationales for Consequence Management
Relational values
Task completion
Protection of reputation
Quality assurance
Stewardship of resources

APPENDIX 18.7
Motivation Direction of Rationale for Consequence Management

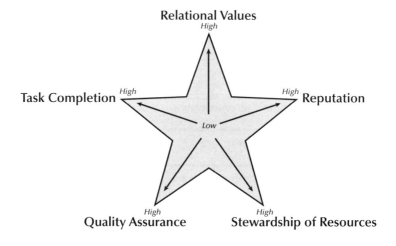

APPENDIX 18.8

Consequence Management Matrix

Focus of Response Impact of Dysfunctional Behavior	1 Palliative Response Management	2 Preventive Response Management	3 Emergency Response Management	4 Recovery Response Management	5 Reflective Response and Learning Management
1 Personal	Suppress Reassign Retrain Support	Choose Inform self Foster multi-cultural diversity Train Personally master Appraise	Confront Counsel Remove Dismiss	Confront Counsel Coach Mentor	Review Evaluate
2 Relational	Suppress Reassign Retrain Support	Give structure Disclose Appraise team Set tone Improve team-work	Confront Mediate Remove Dismiss	Confront Counsel Coach Mentor	Generate ideas Plan
3 Project	Suppress Wind down Limit authority Increase account-ability	Develop systems Resolve resources Set goals and priorities	Confront Control Suspend Close	Confront Refocus Standardize Set procedures and pro-cesses	Implement Communicate
4 Organizational	Suppress Isolate Contain Limit resources	Instill a philosophy Develop values Envision Set policy and principles	Control Suspend Transfer Close	Change leader-ship Communicate Change culture Set procedures and pro-cesses	Train Test
5 Environmental	Limit damage Distance Scapegoat Salvage	Scan Monitor Provide feed-back	Control Communicate Manage media Manage stake-holders	Change iden-tity Change com-munica-tion Change image Rebuild rela-tionships	Reevaluate Continually improve

APPENDIX 18.9

Review and Analysis Types

Review Type	Review Definition	Agenda Concerns
In-process review	Convened for the purpose of assessing the progress toward a given goal	Standards Deadlines Information flow Coordination of activities
After-action review	Formal review convened to determine the effectiveness of a program or event upon its completion	Goals and objectives Lessons learned Recommendations for future endeavors Conclusions
Annual and quarterly reviews and analysis	Assessment of overall operations, programs, etc.	Targets Budgets Calendars Standards
Crisis postmortem	Special assessment convened in the aftermath of a crisis, such as a member's attempted suicide or a failure of critical components.	What happened Lessons learned Conclusions Recommendations

19
CHURCH ADMINISTRATION AND THE LAW

William J. Russell
JD, Professor of Business Law, Northwest Nazarene University

This chapter will discuss a number of key legal issues that are pertinent to the administration of a church or a church-related institution, from the perspective of both the institution and the clergyperson working within that institution. The discussion is not exhaustive and is intended only to highlight a number of key legal issues that can impact such persons and organizations.

Law varies significantly from place to place (state to state, country to country, and governmental level to governmental level). This chapter will focus generally on legal principles extant in the United States, but other legal systems (and the laws therein) may or may not be similar. The legal systems of the former British Commonwealth (Canada, Australia, New Zealand, South Africa, India, etc.) have some similarity and are close to that of the United States. That said, the issues identified in this chapter all require local analysis.

OBTAINING LEGAL COUNSEL

At the outset, legal problems are difficult to understand on the basis of a cursory discussion in a textbook. After reading about legal issues in this chapter, the most important "take away" you need to recognize is that obtaining professional counsel is often a necessity. Nobody likes having to hire a lawyer, but a failure to do so can be disastrous. When a legal problem arises, it will usually be costly. (A discussion of insurance later in this chapter will describe one partial solution to legal costs.) Legal costs are inevitably a "cost of doing business" in the operation of any church or religious organization. It is unrealistic to assume that your church will never need to hire a lawyer, and churches that make such an assumption are often unpleasantly surprised. The first step is to include legal fees as a budget item in the operation of the church. If there is no need to spend that money, those funds can be viewed as a wonderful windfall. But the need to budget for legal costs is manifest, and a failure to plan ahead for something that has a high likelihood of occurring represents a failure of stewardship.

When the time comes to hire an attorney, the most natural thing for a church to do is to hire somebody from the congregation. This is not the proper criterion for choosing professional help. Consider: If your spouse or child required brain surgery, you would not blink at demanding the best brain surgeon in the city, even if there are other doctors in your congregation. The same holds true for attorneys. Go with the best, and the best may not be a member of your church. Additionally, there are many specialized areas of legal practice, and the congregant may or may not be specialized in your area of need. Even if your church has the best bankruptcy attorney in the state, you cannot expect that person to provide topflight legal counsel on a matter of defamation. Find the best and look outside of your own church as a matter of first resort. Don't hesitate to ask around and seek references. The online attorney locator martindale.com includes a rating system for some lawyers. If it turns out that the best attorney in your area is sitting in your pew, count it as an unexpected blessing.

THE LEGAL SYSTEM

The structure of the legal system is not straightforward, but it has a great impact on the ways laws can affect citizens. When you understand the structure, you will better understand how laws work.

Basic Structure of the Legal System

In most places, government is comprised of layered levels of structure arranged in such a way that the residents of any given locale may be governed at several levels, often called "jurisdictions." In the United States, there is a federal government and fifty state governments. Both levels have the power and authority to create laws: federal laws apply to all citizens of the country, and state laws apply to citizens of each respective state. In all fifty states, the state government has created additional levels (sometimes multilayered levels) such as cities, counties, special districts, boroughs, townships, and parishes. These levels also have the power to make laws, and they apply equally to their residents. Thus, three, four, or more layers of government may all have laws that apply to you or your church.

Moreover, at each level of government there may be distinct parts of the government that can make laws. At the state and federal levels of the United States government, laws are properly made by the legislative, judicial, or executive branch of government. In the executive branch, there are a myriad of administrative agencies that have law-making power. Thus, laws can come from many places. You may have heard that judges are not supposed to make laws. That is erroneous. When our constitution was framed, most laws in existence in the states were comprised of judicial precedents (cases with written decisions) that constitute law.

There are some areas of law (contract, tort, agency) where the entire body of law was created by the decisions of judges. This approach goes back to the Magna Carta in England and was adopted by the colonies and the resulting states.

Application of the Legal System to Churches

For the most part, and unless there is a specific provision to the contrary, the secular legal system treats a church (and a clergyperson) as no different from any other citizen. If there is a law that applies generally to citizens in a jurisdiction, a church should presume that the law covers the church. This is true across a wide range of legal subjects. Thus, laws of contract, tort, employment, agency, property, and other areas apply equally to both secular pursuits and ecumenical activity.

The Constitution and the Church

The so-called establishment clause of the United States Constitution represents an example of a specific definition of a relationship between government and churches.[1] While it is beyond the scope of this chapter to discuss at length the challenges that have resulted from attempts to clarify the meaning of the First Amendment to the U.S. Constitution, it is important to note that in most countries there exists some definition of the relationship between church and state. For example, in the United Kingdom, there has been a historically close identification between the two institutions. (The same can be said for Iran.) Each country defines the relationship, and that relationship will impact the ability of the different levels of government to regulate church activity. Suffice it to say here that the establishment clause of the United States does not broadly exempt churches from compliance with a wide range of general laws. Instances of insulation of churches from general law based on the establishment clause are rare; the First Amendment is directed more specifically at what is perceived to be direct involvement in or control of religious content by government.

The Law of Negligence and Tort Liability

The word "tort" is a legal word that refers to the legal practice of holding people and institutions accountable for the damage that they do to others. Some tort law is about things done intentionally, and some relates to damage done without intent but which results from a failure to be reasonably careful. Tort law does not imply moral or ethical judgment; even where tort law addresses intentional conduct, the conduct need not result from evil or malice. Rather it

---

1. "Congress shall make no law respecting an establishment of religion or prohibiting the free exercise thereof. . . ." U.S. Constitution, amend. 1 (1791).

represents a legal approach to an economic problem. There are several common versions of tort law, but a few occur more frequently in a church setting.

Negligence

When you hear a report of somebody being sued, the lawsuit is most likely based on the law of negligence. Cases involving automobile accidents, slip and falls, defective products, or hot coffee are typically situations where the defendant (the person being sued) is alleged to have acted negligently.

The law of negligence represents a pervasive and far-reaching legal duty that every person owes to every other person. The duty is that we are all required by civil law to act in a manner that is reasonably careful so as not to do injury to another. The duty is ever present and requires churches and clergy (and everybody else) to be aware of risks created by either action or inaction and to take steps to avoid causing damage to others. Again, this is not a law about malevolence or evil; it is nothing more than a decision to allocate the economic cost of careless conduct to the person who has been careless. The law of negligence recognizes that where carelessness occurs, it is fairer to make the person who failed to act in a reasonably careful manner bear the economic results of the negligence than to let that burden fall on an innocent injured party.

In order to create liability in negligence, the person bringing the suit and alleging negligent conduct must prove four things: (1) that the defendant owed a duty of care, which is almost always true; (2) that the defendant did not observe the requirement of care; (3) that the plaintiff was injured; and (4) that the defendant's negligence caused the injury.

It is often true that injury results from the carelessness of both the person being sued and the injured person. Where both persons have contributed to the causation that resulted in the injury, the law will usually allocate the economic responsibility on a percentage basis as determined by evaluating the respective causation of the conduct of the two parties.

Churches and church-related organizations (as well as those who work within such organizations) have no special immunity from the law of negligence. It is imperative that those who work within the church be actively aware of the duty to be careful all of the time. Slippery sidewalks must be treated to prevent falls. Church vehicles must be carefully maintained to avoid accidents. Similarly, a church must never let somebody operate a church vehicle without carefully checking his or her driving ability. Nobody should ever be put in contact with vulnerable populations (especially children, but also the elderly and disabled) without a careful check that the candidate is an appropriate person to place in that position. Premises must be carefully maintained. Personnel must be carefully checked and trained. The list is virtually endless but can be summarized with a simple proposition: the church and its people can never act in a way that deviates from reasonable care to avoid damage to all. The result, should this principle be violated, is that the church or clergyperson (or both) may be sued and made to pay for the damage done by the failure. A suit can result in the taking of church monies or even the church property itself. As will be observed later, one crucial risk management tool in this regard is insurance.

Malpractice

Those who profess to have particular skill in any discipline are required to act with the care expected of others having that same skill or expertise. The word for the application of the law of negligence to a skilled or expert profession is "malpractice." Malpractice is often thought of as relating to doctors or lawyers, but the law actually applies to all professionals. If you represent yourself ("hold yourself out") to be an expert with some professional skill, you will be held legally accountable to conduct your activity in that profession with the same reasonable care that such an expert is expected to display.

Within the church, both clergy and professionally trained social workers or counselors often attempt to help persons with specific needs. Simply put, if a clergyperson attempts to counsel a congregant or member of the community, that clergyperson might be held by a court to act as if trained as a counselor, psychologist, or social worker. What is critical to understand is that any person's attempt to undertake the helping arts that reaches beyond his actual professional training is highly risky. Persons of faith generally want to help others, but they must be careful not to reach beyond actual training. And it is often true that the person being helped is led to believe that there is training beyond that which actually exists. Pastors, who try to help out of good intent, can easily find that the person being helped mistakenly assumes that the pastor has skills that are not present. The safest course of action is to always refer persons in need to those who are actually trained professionally to help in the given area. Overreaching in such matters often leads to a lawsuit. If you choose to do otherwise because you perceive a more compelling need, at least do so knowing that there may be serious legal consequences.[2]

---

2. **Editor's Note:** *Pastors have a calling, as well as the training, to provide counsel to people in the area of spiritual needs. From the earliest days of the church, pastors have been charged with the ministry of caring for souls. Jesus understood the extent of his shepherding role: "I am the good shepherd. The good shepherd lays down his life for the sheep" (John 10:11). People in ministry should never take unnecessary, foolish risks in helping people. But neither is the task of ministry risk free. Pastors are the right professionals to assist people with spiritual concerns. Be clear about your abilities and limitations. Make referrals whenever you*

Defamation

Defamation is a tort that provides a remedy to those who suffer injury to their reputation. On this matter, the law recognizes that injury to reputation is very real and frequently has severe economic consequence. The law of defamation is less concerned with intentional injury to the reputation than injury that occurs by virtue of carelessness, although intentional defamation is equally likely to lead to a lawsuit. Simply put, defamation occurs when there is a communication (written or oral) about a person that is false and that causes injury. True statements about a person will never constitute defamation, but if a statement is untrue, the person making the statement may be sued by the subject to recover compensation for damage done. In some cases the damage may be severe.

Clergy routinely are put in a position to report on members of a congregation or community. Prayer requests and church bulletins often contain information about members. Pastors are often asked to convey needs and frequently talk about congregants out of honest concern. Notwithstanding the good intention, if untrue information is passed along, and if harm results, the pastor may be sued. And it should go without saying that clergy must diligently avoid and discourage gossip, both personally and within the congregation.

Conversion of Funds or Property

Conversion is the tort of wrongfully taking the property of another and the civil equivalent of stealing. If money or other property is taken wrongfully, the person taking the property can be sued for the value of the property. Churches must be careful to properly document and manage all funds that come within their control; misunderstandings about property usage can lead to a suit for conversion. Clergy are well advised to keep careful records and be clear (preferably in writing) about the intended use of the property of others. Notice that this is similar to the crime of embezzlement, although a criminal matter is subject to different rules, processes, and consequences.

INSURANCE

Foundational Risk Management Issues

Any activity encounters risks, some small and some great. Churches and church-related organizations (and those persons operating within such organizations) are no different. To ignore risks, even small risks, and to fail to plan for

---

lack the training to be of help with a specific need. But never lose the shepherd's heart of compassion. BP

such risks is folly. Businesses that fail to include coverage of risks in their business plans face a strong possibility of failure, and churches are no different. The primary mechanism for managing the economic impacts of risk is insurance.

There is an inherent irony in the purchase of insurance. We buy insurance and pay premiums, often significant premiums, so that we will be reimbursed for losses should they occur. If we never make a claim, we are prone to think that our money was wasted. Nothing could be further from the truth; whenever an insurance company pays a claim, something bad has happened. We are actually much better off if we never have to make any claim (an unlikely but possible scenario). Don't ever be fooled into thinking that premium dollars are wasted if no claim is made. The premium dollar represents management of a portion of the world's inevitable risks, and the best outcome available is to pay premiums but never make a claim. The following insurance coverages are essential. The different coverage provisions may be included in a single policy, or you may be required to purchase multiple policies; the important point is to be certain that you have all matters covered and that the amount of coverage suffices.

Property Insurance

Property insurance covers the economic cost of loss to tangible property. Property coverage should be sufficiently broad to cover the sorts of risks that actually exist for church property. Be certain that your agent describes and you understand exactly what is covered (flood, fire, wind, vandalism, theft, etc.) and what is not (mold damage, terrorism, etc.) and purchase additional coverage if needed.

Property insurance can cover the replacement value, the book value, or the market value of the insured property. The best risk management occurs when replacement coverage is purchased, although such coverage will cost more than the other types. Buy enough coverage (expressed in a dollar amount) to replace what you will need in case of a total loss. Deductibles represent that amount you will have to pay before the insurance starts to reimburse the church. The higher the deductible, the lower the premium. Purchase coverage with the highest deductible amount that you can reasonably manage when a claim occurs. Then assume that a claim will eventually occur and budget for the payment of the deductible.

Liability Insurance

Liability coverage protects against lawsuits for tort-based and other general claims. A liability policy will cover both the cost of defending against a lawsuit and the amount of a judgment entered against the church or its people up to the amount of the limit of liability. Absent a liability policy, a person obtaining a judgment against the church could actually take the property of the church. Normally, a church should purchase a primary policy with coverage up to one million dollars. The church should also purchase an excess liability policy (a policy that provides additional coverage for amounts above those insured by the primary policy) for a significantly larger amount. An additional four million dollars is not too much. Consider, for example, the case of a church van that crashes and causes severe injury (or death) to a large group of teenage congregants. If the parents of the injured children sue the church, and if there are serious injuries involved (say, paraplegia), then a total of five million dollars may not be enough. Generally, you will want to save money and will thus want to buy less insurance than the amount called for by the realistic risks that you face; avoid that temptation.

All churches should be certain that the liability policy purchased includes coverage for sexually based claims and discrimination claims. The insurer will probably require that the church adopt practices and policies designed to prevent sexual abuse, and the church should be certain to implement such policies. Often the insurance company will recommend specific steps to take. Failure to take those steps may impair or defeat coverage in the event a claim is made.

Errors and Omissions Insurance

Errors and omissions insurance (referred to as E&O coverage) protects professionals associated with the church against claims based on professional negligence or malpractice. (E&O insurance is sometimes called malpractice insurance.) Clergy and professionals operating within the church should be covered in the event they are sued for failure to exercise reasonable care in the pursuit of their professional activities.

Directors and Officers Insurance

Directors and officers coverage (referred to as D&O insurance) insures the members of the board of directors and other official groups within the church, together with the officers. A lawsuit against a church will often include claims against officers and directors alleging failure to supervise or control the operation of the church. Every church should purchase several million dollars worth of D&O coverage, and congregants may decline (and perhaps wisely so) to become members of the board if there is no such coverage. The pastor needs to understand that directors are being subjected to noteworthy legal risk where there is no such insurance.

CORPORATE STRUCTURE

Churches exist legally as artificial entities created by the provisions of state laws. These laws allow the creation of a legal entity with specific legal rights and protections. In this sense, "corporations" represent artificially created "persons" whose existence is recognized by the law. Such entities from a legal perspective are often governed according to defined schemes.

Incorporation

The most common legal structure (or legal entity) in the United States is the corporation. Corporations are created according to state law, but there are similarities in corporate law from state to state. The primary advantages of a corporate form include specific benefits in the tax structure,[3] protection of owners from the liabilities of the corporation, and knowable structures of governance.

Governance

Author's Note: As mentioned above, laws vary from state to state and each denomination has its own structure that will be interpreted according to the particular law of the state where a church is created. This makes it hard to talk about governance generally. What follows describes the most likely template a court will lay over the denominational structure.

Corporate laws provide for specific structures of power that can apply legally to the church. Power is most frequently vested legally in officers and directors even where there is congregational control according to church procedures; it is possible that the church may practice something that the law does not recognize.

Officers

Officers are hired or appointed by the board of directors (sometimes also referred to as board of trustees or by other similar names). Officers conduct the day-to-day work of the corporation and serve at the pleasure of the directors, subject to employment contracts. The pastor may be recognized for legal purposes as an officer.

Board of Directors

The board of directors constitutes the ultimate controlling body within a corporation, and for legal purposes the church board will usually be held ultimately accountable. The board is responsible for selecting officers but may in some situations look to church members (or shareholders) to elect the officers. Directors are elected by the members or shareholders.

---

3. Section 501(c)3 of the IRS code exempts payment of federal income taxes by certain religious (and other) organizations and provides that contributions made to such organizations may be tax deductible for the donor.

Record Keeping

An array of requirements for keeping legal records faces all organizations. In the United States, a plethora of statutes impose such requirements.[4] The application of such requirements is sometimes unclear. Short of simply keeping everything forever, the best course of action for a church is to obtain the opinion of legal counsel. If the church does not choose to ask for legal counsel, the following guidelines represent a plausible policy: keep employment records until several years after an employee dies, financial records for at least twenty years after completion of transactions, and corporate documents (charters, minutes, policies, etc.) indefinitely.

Two points are clear about record keeping. First, every church should adopt a record-keeping policy and must then follow that policy diligently. Failure to follow an established record-keeping policy is dangerous. Second, once litigation has commenced against the church (or its people) or once a claim is known to exist, nothing must be destroyed.

Similarly, a warning is required about electronic files: although you have purported to "delete" an electronic file (including e-mails), the files are seldom actually erased. They continue to reside in the electronic world and can be recovered by a clever lawyer. If you don't want something to be read aloud in a courtroom, don't write it. And be sparse in what you do write anyway: for example, records (including board minutes) should only record actions, not discussions, content of arguments, or opinions.

PROPERTY OWNERSHIP

Many, perhaps most, churches are owners of a significant investment—the church property. This includes both the land and building (referred to as real property) and all equipment, furnishings, books, and other movable items (referred to as personal property). Real property often represents the largest investment had by the church. There are several types of ownership that might occur.

Terms of Ownership

We often think of ownership in simplistic terms. In fact, real property can be owned completely (ownership) or with limitation, including a right to occupy and use property (lease) or a right to use property for limited times or purposes (easements).

---

4. For example, there are record keeping requirements for OSHA, the Department of Labor, employee files, the IRS, disposal of toxic or hazardous substances (such as paint), and others.

Ownership

Ownership is a name often used to denote what is termed by law to be "fee simple." Fee simple is the highest form of ownership and gives to the owner complete control over real property in the matters of occupancy, use, transfer, and even inheritance. Fee-simple ownership is the best way to have the maximum right in property. When you buy a parcel of property, make sure you are receiving title in fee simple; if not, there will be limits on what you are getting and you must either understand and accept those limitations (which will usually compromise the value of the property) or refuse to proceed with the purchase on such terms.

Lease

A lease (often called a rental agreement) gives the person receiving the lease (the lessee) the exclusive right to occupy and use property for a specified period of time. The lease may be in writing or may be oral. Ownership of the property (usually fee simple) stays with the person granting the lease (the lessor). The lessor may have the right to enter onto the property to protect it from damage or for purposes of public safety, but otherwise the property is surrendered to the lessee for his or her possession during the lease term. The lessee does have an obligation to use reasonable care in the use of the property.

Easement

An easement is a right to use a property for a limited time or purpose without exclusivity and without occupying the property. An easement may allow somebody to cross a property or to use a property for an event or other purpose. Usually any real property conveyed in fee simple is conveyed subject to the existing easements. Utility companies often have easements to place lines or pipes across property. When you buy a property, be sure to find out what easements exist.

Limits on Use

Even where property is owned, limitations may be imposed on the manner in which the property is used. Several limitations on usage of property are common.

Restrictive Covenants

It is not uncommon for a deed conveying ownership, occupancy, or use of real property to contain explicit limitations on the use of the property. By accepting the conveyance (ownership, occupancy, or use) the owner of the real property right is legally considered to have agreed to the usage limitations, and a court will enforce those limitations as a matter of contract agreement. Only those who were privy to the contract (usually the prior owner or members of a common subdivision) can complain or enforce the restrictive covenant. When accepting ownership of property, it is important to read the deed or transfer document carefully; you should also study carefully all materials given to you by a title insurance or escrow company at closing. Those documents collectively should tell you if there is a restrictive covenant. This is another time that good legal counsel can really help you to understand what you are getting into.

Zoning

Zoning laws are legal limitations on usage that are created and enforced by the jurisdiction within which a property rests. Zoning is usually created by a city or county and occurs as a part of a planning effort designed to control and manage growth within that area. Zoning laws are enforceable, and you will not be allowed to use property in a manner that is inconsistent with zoning.

Eminent Domain

Eminent domain laws reflect a preemptive right of a government to take privately-owned property for use in public purposes. Where eminent domain is a right vested in government (as is true in the United States), the government may take away your property. In most jurisdictions, including the United States, the government must pay you the fair market value of the property. Governments exercising eminent domain will usually offer what they believe to be fair value, but you can dispute that value and have the right to litigate or arbitrate the value.

SPECIAL ISSUES

Privacy

Despite the notoriety of a so-called right to privacy applied in Roe v. Wade,[5] actual rights to privacy in most legal systems are rare. One example of a right to privacy that has received much attention is the statute referred to as HIPAA.[6] HIPAA is really about the rights of privacy associated with medical records, coupled with the right of an employee to move from job to job without adverse health insurance implications. HIPAA actually rarely applies to a

---

5. Roe v. Wade, 410 U.S. 113 (1973).
6. Health Insurance Portability and Accountability Act of 1996 (HIPAA). For an explanation of rights under HIPAA, see the government explanation at http://www.hhs.gov/ocr/privacy/hipaa/understanding/summary/index.html.

church, but the increasing popularity of the mythical right to privacy means that many congregants expect that information concerning them will be treated with privacy. The wisest course of action for any church is to protect the privacy of its members. A lawsuit by an outraged congregant based on a right to privacy might stand a very high chance of dismissal, but prudence calls for the avoidance of such claims. The church should disclose private information only with documented permission from the person affected.

One common situation involves prayer requests. As a general practice requests for prayer should avoid disclosure of the actual ailment or specific need. Remember that God knows what you are praying for; there is no actual need in prayer to recite the details of the needs. Sometimes interested persons want to know the juicy details, more out of curiosity than from a legitimate need to know. The best practice is to ask for prayer for a specific person, and leave the details to God.

Confidentiality

Whenever you talk to somebody about any problem or sensitive matter, that person will probably expect that you will keep his or her matters secret. As a practice, you should strive to keep personal information confidential to the extent possible. You need to be aware, however, that a court may not recognize your right (or the right of your confidant) to keep your discussions secret. While the rules on the right to keep secrets vary from state to state, generally there is little legal basis for claiming a right to confidentiality once a court wants to know what was said. This means that if a court (or an attorney operating within a court by way of a lawsuit) wants access to information, you will almost always be compelled to disclose that information. Courts tolerate virtually no secrecy, so don't fool yourself into thinking that something will never be known because you agreed somehow to keep it "confidential." Still, confidentiality is the wisest legal course of action to pursue to the extent that you are not ordered by a court to reveal some secret.[7]

---

7. **Editor's note:** *This presents a dilemma for clergy. Various denominations have statements on clergy confidentiality. One example is the statement of the Church of the Nazarene: "It shall be the duty of every minister of the Church of the Nazarene to hold in trust and confidence any communication of a confidential nature given him or her by a counselee of the congregation while he or she is acting in his or her professional character as a licensed or ordained minister of the Church of the Nazarene. The public dissemination of such communication without the express written consent of the declarant is expressly condemned. Any Nazarene minister who violates the above regulation subjects himself or herself to the disciplinary sanctions set forth in Part VI, Subsection V of this* Manual." (Church of the Nazarene Manual, *2005-2009 ed. [Kansas City: Nazarene Publishing House, 2005], 211.)* BP

Clergy-Penitent Privilege

On a state-by-state basis, information obtained by clergy pursuant to a confessional (or similar) activity may be protected from disclosure to law enforcement officials. Usually, the protection applies only to information concerning crimes or activities done in the past; a confessional disclosure of any intent to commit a future crime is not protected from disclosure in most states, and the clergy may be required to disclose an upcoming crime to officials. This privilege does not usually attach to information that comes to the clergyperson outside of the confession. If you learn that a congregant or other person has committed or is about to commit a crime, it is important to contact legal counsel immediately. If you have a reasonable belief that serious harm is about to occur, you can reasonably choose to bypass legal counsel and call law enforcement, but there will be some residual risk; if you are somehow wrong, you could be challenged as to the reasonableness of your belief.

Subpoenas, Search Warrants, and Summonses

The law can come calling anywhere; churches are not immune. Official legal actions usually come to a church or a pastor in one of three forms: a subpoena, a search warrant, or a summons. The items are each specific legal documents that might be either received in the mail (sometimes certified, sometimes ordinary mail), served by a process server, or delivered by a law enforcement officer. There is no ambiguity about the proper course of action in each case—contact legal counsel immediately. There are no exceptions. In the case of a search warrant, the process will proceed without giving you time to talk to your attorney, but you should still contact counsel as soon as possible.

Read the document carefully. It will be confusing, but in each case the word "search warrant," "subpoena," or "summons" will appear somewhere on the document. If the document is a subpoena, it will require you to go somewhere at some time (specified on the document) to give testimony or provide documents in your possession. You may be required to go to a court or to an attorney's office or to some other place such as a hotel conference room. If the document is a search warrant, it will come to you with police or law enforcement officers and they will want to immediately enter the premises specified in the document to conduct a search. They do have the right to do so, and you must not resist. You are entitled to receive a copy of the search warrant. It is generally wisest to not allow a police officer to search unless there is a search warrant; this principle may be compromised where there is some clear emergency that you understand to exist. Otherwise, allow the police to guard your premise while they get a search warrant. The last document, a summons, means that you have been sued. You will usually have a period of time (twenty to thirty days) to respond officially in court. You must contact counsel immediately—do not delay. Failure to respond to a summons in a timely manner can result in the entry of a judgment against you for large amounts of money.

Reporting Child Abuse

One of the most challenging issues facing any clergy is the question of how to respond to the knowledge of child abuse. This issue is particularly difficult because the information usually comes to the pastor through one of two equally difficult communication lines: gossip and confession. In either case there is a natural reluctance to move forward, given the incredibly adverse impact that a false report can have on any person accused of such misconduct. That said, there is frequently a strong legal need to report suspected child abuse to appropriate authorities. Clerical counseling does not suffice in such situations, and the clergyperson should be prepared to take necessary steps to report information to governmental agencies or risk adverse legal consequences.

In some jurisdictions the answer to reporting decisions is found in laws specific to the state or jurisdiction where the clergyperson resides or serves. For example, many states in the United States have strict requirements concerning the reporting of situations where there is reason to believe that abuse has occurred. It is essential that every clergyperson determine what law applies in his or her jurisdiction and comply strictly.

Any course taken by a pastor will involve risks, both legal and relational. The safest (but not risk-free) course is normally to err in favor of protecting the child. What is clear is that ignoring information that child abuse has occurred is dangerous, not only for the child's welfare but also in the matter of legal liability.

CONCLUSION

Law presents a noteworthy challenge for clergy. It is often true that the course of action strongly suggested by legal risk management will conflict with the training and instincts of the clerical mission. The best way to reduce legal interference in the church mission is to be aware of legal requirements. If you choose to take a riskier course for Kingdom reasons, do so with eyes wide open.

FOR FURTHER READING

Hammar, Richard R. *Pastor, Church & Law.* Matthews, NC: Christian Ministry Resources, 1991.

APPENDIX 19.1
Summary of Federal Employment Laws

The following summary identifies various laws pertaining to the employment and treatment of employees. These laws apply generally throughout the United States pursuant to either state or federal statutes. In the United States, some states may also impose similar requirements that are more stringent than federal law. Some other countries also enforce similar laws relating to employment. Descriptions below are very brief; however, complex and extensive details often accompany the laws.

Generally speaking, the statutes identified may provide exemptions or special treatment for churches (or in some cases, other religious organizations). In all cases, the application of the exemptions or special treatment to churches is at best complex and detailed, thereby giving rise to substantial ambiguity; exemptions may apply only (if at all) to pastoral staff or persons who are ordained or licensed. Moreover, the laws frequently specify a minimum number of employees of the organization before the statute applies; churches may employ fewer people than required to invoke the statute. For all of the following legal provisions, it is important to understand that the requirements might apply and that exemptions or special treatment should not be assumed to apply without advice of legal counsel.

FAIR LABOR STANDARDS ACT

Wage and Hour Law

Minimum wages must be paid to certain workers. Pay differential based solely on gender may be prohibited. For hourly or some other workers, overtime pay may be required for work in excess of certain hours.

Child Labor Law

Children under age 18 may be limited with regard to hours worked or the type of work assignment allowed.

Unemployment Compensation

Federally mandated state systems provide pay for a limited amount of time to workers who become unemployed. These systems do not usually provide benefits for employees terminated for just cause or voluntarily. Unemployment compensation is paid with taxes collected from employers.

Workers' Compensation

State legal systems pay for costs and damages in cases where a worker is injured on the job and pursuant to job duties. These systems typically provide immunity from tort liability for employers in return for coverage. Employers are typically required to purchase insurance to cover payments.

Family and Medical Leave Act of 1993

Workers facing an unexpected medical catastrophe or the birth or adoption of a child must be allowed a certain amount of time off from work without risk to their jobs. This applies to employers of fifty or more employees. Leave is typically twelve weeks; it may be unpaid, but health and medical insurance benefits must be continued and the employee must be fully restored to his or her prior position (or equivalent) upon return.

OSHA (Occupational Safety and Health Act of 1970)

Federally mandated requirements, determined on an industry-by-industry basis, set standards intended to protect the health and safety of workers in the workplace. Regulators have broad and intrusive rights to inspect for safety violations, impose penalties, and require remediation of noncompliant conditions.

Employee Privacy Rights

A number of complex and interrelated laws govern employees' right to privacy in the workplace. Where an employee has a "reasonable right to privacy," the employer may be limited with regard to electronic monitoring or the intentional interception of the electronic signals of employees, unless the practice occurs as part of the ordinary course of business. Drug testing as a condition of employment may be permissible as long there is no discrimination or violation of the Americans with Disabilities Act.

Title VII (Civil Rights Act of 1963)

Discrimination with regard to any decision affecting an employee may not be based on certain "protected classes": race, color, religion, sex, or national origin. The prohibition against discrimination on the basis of sex reaches to gender-based harassment of any sort. Title VII does not, according to the U.S. Supreme Court, prevent decisions based on sexual preference, only actual gender. Discrimination may be permitted where a bona fide qualification for employment is evident; this has been deemed to allow a religious organization to set employment standards based on a requirement of similar religious belief. Illegal discrimination can occur by virtue of either a direct decision based on protected class status or general requirements that adversely impact a particular protected class. An extensive system of public and private enforcement mechanisms supports the law; enforcement may involve either civil or criminal penalties (monetary compensation in the case of civil enforcement or criminal penalties, including incarceration, in the case of criminal enforcement).

Equal Pay Act of 1963

Based on factors of skill, effort, responsibility, and working condition, employers must pay both men and women equally where respective jobs are substantially equal. Bona fide systems of seniority, merit, quality review, or factors other than sex may justify differences without violation of the act.

Age Discrimination in Employment Act of 1967

Employers may not refuse to hire, terminate, or otherwise discriminate in compensation, benefits, or work conditions on the basis of an employee's age. This law applies to employers with twenty or more employees in certain industries where there is an impact on interstate commerce. (Churches operating directly under ecclesiastical authority would not normally be covered under this law, but related religious activities such as schools or other social programs would usually be covered.)

Americans with Disabilities Act of 1991

Employers must make reasonable efforts to accommodate workers with disabilities. Where accommodation presents an undue hardship on the employer, the accommodation may not be required. Employment decisions may not be based upon disability status. A disability qualifying for protection may be a physical, an intellectual, or a mental disability. This act applies to employers with fifteen or more employees. Employers are not required to hire otherwise unqualified disabled employees.

ERISA (Employee Retirement Income Security Act)

ERISA sets minimum standards and requirements for welfare benefit plans offered to employees. Generally not applicable to plans offered by churches, but legal counsel should be consulted with regard to any welfare benefit plans providing insurance, health care, unemployment, disability, retirement, pension, or similar benefits. Requirements, if applicable, are complex and carry significant penalties for violation; legal counsel should always be involved in decisions about employee welfare benefit plans.

COBRA (Consolidated Omnibus Budget Reconciliation Act of 1985)

Workers who lose their job or eligibility for health and medical insurance may continue to receive insurance coverage for a limited time. Workers must pay for the coverage, often at a higher rate than the group policy under which they were formerly covered.

20

PERSONAL MANAGEMENT
MANAGING THE LIVES OF CLERGY AND THEIR FAMILIES

Timothy B. Pusey
DMin, Pastor, Meridian Valley Shepherd Nazarene, Meridian, Idaho

In all professions the overall integrity of a leader's personal life is important, but for pastors it is especially essential for effectiveness throughout the course of a career. Such personal consistency also offers a needed model for laypersons within the congregation.

Wise pastors are motivated to cultivate and maintain integrity in the worthy pursuit of "finishing well." They do this as a matter of faithfulness to the Lord, embracing the long-haul perspective of a life intentionally given in service to the Lord through his church. They also do this in pursuit of the approval of God, desiring at the end of life to hear his words, "Well done, good and faithful servant" (Matt. 25:21, 23).

The shepherd of a flock is additionally motivated by the earnest desire to be a worthy example for others to follow. The apostle Paul said to those under his charge, "Follow my example, as I follow the example of Christ" (1 Cor. 11:1). The pastor lives with a keen awareness that others are watching his or her life. It's truly as God designed. The desire to live an exemplary life stirs the pastor to bring godly counsel and wisdom to the management of his or her personal life.

One way to explore personal-life management is under the umbrella of biblical stewardship. We are called to be wise stewards of what God entrusts to us. Stewardship acknowledges that all we have not only has been given to us by our creator God but also, ultimately, still belongs to him. As the manager of a business is accountable to the owner of a business, so are we accountable to our heavenly Father for every resource he makes available to us. The pastor must acknowledge that as a person he or she must be a wise steward in handling his or her time, energy, relationships, and finances. The pastor must also give careful attention to the stewardship of his or her physical, spiritual, and emotional well-being.

THE STEWARDSHIP OF TIME

To each of us God entrusts twenty-four hours a day, seven days a week. No more; no less. He was the one who created days and nights and who marked off our lives in seasons. Time is not intended to be our enemy but our friend. Jesus set the marvelous example of one who was neither worried nor hurried by time. And what we are called to accomplish in each of our lives will by God's design take place within the framework of time.

Managing our time is up to us. The stewardship of time encompasses the challenge to maximize the ministry hours in each day and week, as well as to build in God-ordained times for family, rest, and renewal. The unique challenge of the pastor is to balance the passionate pursuit of fulfilling our ministerial calling alongside an intentional and disciplined plan for family time and for personal rest and renewal. Attention to one is not an excuse for the neglect of the other. Imbalance in either direction has been the demise of many in ministry.

A passion to fulfill our God-given calling should prompt us to be diligent. The work the minister is called to do is the most important "work" in the world. Such a calling demands a built-in motivation and an intentional and honest work ethic, giving the best we have for the cause of Christ. Ministry is not a nine-to-five endeavor. There are many demands requiring much flexibility. Although as pastors we are rarely asked to log our hours, we must be wise and disciplined in our day-by-day work habits. We must adopt time-management principles and practices that work best for us, and however we accomplish it, we must accept the responsibility of managing our time.

Beyond our work habits, we must also acknowledge the need to take a break from our responsibilities. A retired pastor asked me recently if I had scheduled time for vacation. When I affirmed that I had, he said something like, "I made the mistake of not doing that and paid a high price for it. I'm glad you're taking your vacation." Unfortunately, not taking a day off and never missing a Sunday used to be almost a badge of honor for a pastor. How sad that men and women felt so compelled to violate Sabbath principles! Scripture teaches clearly about the importance of a Sabbath rest, and we are not exempt. None of us should feel we are so important that the church cannot do without us for a day, a week, or our given vacation time throughout the year.

Sunday, practically speaking, is not a day of rest for pastors. We need to designate another day of the week and communicate that clearly to the congregation, without apology. In a multiple-staff ministry, encouraging different days off allows for responsibilities in the church to be met with less of a chance for unexpected ministry demands to interrupt any one person's day off.

The biblical model of Sabbath rest goes beyond one day a week. Jesus modeled the pattern by retreating from others for times of personal renewal. Admittedly, sometimes his plan to retreat was thwarted by the needs of the people, and he took the time necessary to respond. But such interruptions did not deter him from later pursuing his desire to retreat. If Jesus needed such time, most likely all of us do too. Pastors today find different ways to retreat for extended prayer, for reading, for contemplation, or merely for physical and emotional rest. Intentionally scheduling such times away from regular church demands can be an essential element in maintaining a healthy balance in life and ministry.

God has created us in such a way that work is good for us. For pastors, our ministry is our work, and we are to pursue it diligently. But apart from our work we also must have personal time, family time, and time with our heavenly Father. We are at our best only when we intentionally order our days so that we can fulfill all of these needs.

THE STEWARDSHIP OF ENERGY

The "stewardship of energy" principle challenges the pastor to prioritize and diligently carry out what matters most in ministry without giving in to nonproductive temptations such as worry, senseless battles, and compulsive people pleasing. When we fail to be faithful stewards of our energy, we become frustrated and prime targets for ministerial burnout.

Every now and then I say that I need to paint a wall so that I can stand back at the end of the day and see what I've accomplished. Why would I say that? Because ministry seldom offers such a view. And hanging on to such expectations only fuels discouragement. The investment of our lives in the lives of others offers few quick fixes and few glimpses of work completed. However, as I look back over nearly thirty years in ministry, the satisfaction and fulfillment of recalling lives forever impacted by the investment of my life and energy is extremely rewarding.

Few would argue about the amount of stress placed on pastors. The challenge of being CEO, shepherd, preacher, counselor, and manager can become more than overwhelming. It reminds me of my panicked effort to swim upstream in rushing rapids after being thrown out of the raft on a whitewater rafting trip. While the effort may be futile, in the panic of the moment it sometimes seems to be the only thing to do. And when we become panicked in the rapids of the many demands of ministry, we easily waste our energy on matters that are not productive. The "stewardship of energy" principle begs us not to waste our energy in such a way.

The conscientious pastor can easily suffocate under the barrage of expectations. Lay leaders in the church likely have differing expectations of what the pastor should be doing. The people in the pews may have a whole other set of agendas for the pastor. For those serving in a denomination, there are the expectations placed on the pastor by the church hierarchy. There are the expectations that pastors sense from their families. And on top of it all are the expectations pastors place upon themselves. Accentuating the challenge is the reality that many of these expectations are in direct conflict with each other, and many of the expectations by themselves are absolutely unrealistic. It's enough to drive even the best men and women to the brink!

And what we haven't yet mentioned are the expectations of our heavenly Father. My personal conclusion is that if I become consumed with trying to live up to everyone's expectations, I will become totally distracted from what matters most and miss living up to the expectations of the One who created me and who has called me into his ministry. Being a wise steward of my energy helps free me from the tyranny of trying to keep everyone happy and releases me so that I can please the One I am most committed to pleasing, even when others neither understand nor appreciate what I do.

Other chapters of this book offer much help and guidance for carrying out the administrative functions of ministry. These matters are essential to being an effective pastor. Such wise counsel points us to the faithful stewardship of our energy. However, we can also become slaves in our attempt to do it all, consuming every ounce of our energy to lead the church. When that happens, we neglect the heart of ministry and miss out on the personal sense of fulfillment and joy that God wants us to experience as we live our lives in partnership with him. When we become slaves to the tasks of ministry, our energy is sapped and our joy depleted. Our heavenly Father has a better plan for each of us. We find that plan as we learn again the simple matter of having childlike faith in him. When we trust the Lord as he invites us to trust him, he guides us to become dependent upon his wisdom and strength. Such a trust steers us away from frantically wasting our energy on worry and fear.

Matthew 6:19-34 contains the guidance of Jesus for worry and stress. We are admonished to store up for ourselves "treasures in heaven" rather than on earth. We are taught to be single-minded in serving one Master. We are not to worry about having our personal needs met, but we are to trust the One who feeds the birds and clothes the flowers of the field in such beauty. We are to be people of faith.

So do not worry, saying, "What shall we eat?" or "What shall we drink?" or "What shall we wear?" For the pagans run after all these things, and your heavenly Father knows that you need them. But seek first his kingdom and his righteousness, and all these things will be given to you as well. Therefore do not worry about tomorrow, for tomorrow will worry about itself. Each day has enough trouble of its own." (Matt. 6:31-34)

THE STEWARDSHIP OF RELATIONSHIPS

To cultivate and maintain personal balance in life, every pastor must give attention to the stewardship of relationships. These relationships include our relationship with our heavenly Father, our relationship with our family, and our relationships with trusted friends.

Let's begin, appropriately so, with our relationship with our heavenly Father. Indeed, that's where the call to ministry begins. Somewhere at a teen camp, at a church altar, in a quiet time of deep personal searching for God's will, or perhaps in a blend of such settings, we "hear" the voice of God calling us into his service. Others affirm that call and encourage us in its pursuit, but it is the call of God that launches us into ministry. Our relationship with the Lord is what sets us on this journey.

It's frightening how easily we can lose sight of the primacy of that relationship. In the busyness of doing all the things we believe we must do to be effective pastors, the one relationship that sets this all into motion is easily put on the back burner so that we can *do* all the things we believe God is calling us to *do*.

Across the ages, volumes have been written as guides to day-by-day holy living. There are not enough pages within this chapter to begin to explore the significance of nurturing and maintaining such a daily walk with the Lord. The significance of the daily disciplines of prayer, Scripture reading, and inspirational reading cannot be understated. In the busyness of life and ministry, pastors cannot afford to neglect these. No amount of training or education and no résumé of impressive years of service can satisfy what can take place in the life of a pastor as he or she daily places trust in the Father and commits anew a life of service to him. Of all relationships, this is first and foremost. We must both guard and nurture our relationship with our heavenly Father.

In God's providence, he brings into our lives those we lovingly call family. Our families are a great treasure to us, certainly one of the greatest blessings God has entrusted to us, for which he asks us to be faithful stewards. Marriage is used as a symbol in Scripture to describe the mystical union between Christ and his church. Scripture commends it as an honorable relationship. Scripture also uses the model of parenting as a means by which we understand the deep love that our heavenly Father has for us and our families.

The marriage relationship is a sacred covenant of love. My wife and I made that commitment to one another before she knew she was marrying a pastor, and yet we have shared our commitment to follow his will, at all costs. We have experienced together the many joys of pastoring and shared the many hurdles that go with it. My call to ministry has become a significant part of our journey together. And yet, while the God-given call can be a rallying point to enhance a marriage and bring a united sense of calling and purpose to a couple, it has also proven to bring much stress into the marital relationship. Many ministry mates find themselves in competition with the church for the attention of the pastor. This threat becomes more complicated because God is the Lord of the church and he has placed the call upon the pastor. Suddenly, the ministry mate seems to be in competition with God himself.

Nothing could be further from God's desire. God's plan is for marriage to be a lifelong commitment between two people. Our desires for companionship and for sharing mutual love and support are by God's design. God is not expecting the pastor to neglect his or her marriage for the sake of the church. Time and energy are to be reserved for the marriage. It is not God's design for church to ever become a threat to the pastor's marriage. But to safeguard what in our humanness might otherwise take place, we must assume the responsibility of being wise stewards of this significant relationship in life. The challenge is to look for ways in which the marriage can be strengthened and enhanced by the opportunity to serve in ministry.

The stewardship of family often includes the privilege of parenting. The relentless expectations upon pastors can easily distract even the best-intentioned pastor-parent. Yet the sacred trust of parenting demands a conscientious balancing of time and energy so that children receive the guidance and encouragement they so much need. While ministry places more demands on the parsonage family than might be the case in most other professions, there is also a flexibility in scheduling that isn't present in all careers. The wise pastor-parent can make that work to the advantage of family life by being involved in daytime activities in which other parents may not be able to participate.

A worthwhile goal of the pastor-parent is that the preacher's kids would come to love the Lord and to love his church too. Children of pastors, like spouses of pastors, may too easily find themselves competing with the church for the attention of the pastor and resenting it. There are certainly occasions when the pastor must fulfill ministry responsibilities that may override family plans. The stewardship of the relationships within the home demand that, ultimately, the family comes before the church in the pastor's priorities. Although the pastor's relationship to the Lord must come first, the Lord does not want a pastor to neglect his family for the sake of the church.

I had a conversation with a layman about a pastor who seemed to have lost all of his children to the church while being a workaholic pastor. I then commented, "I don't believe God is calling me to do that." And the wise layman heartily agreed.

In the stewardship of relationships, this is a good place to affirm the role that friends must play in the life of the pastor. Gone are the days when the church concluded that the pastor must not have close friends within the church, but prudent is the pastor who chooses such friends wisely and exercises discernment in what is shared. Pastors, whether single or married, are not exempt from needing close, intimate friendships in life. The absence of such leaves the pastor and the pastor's family isolated and alone, an unnecessarily vulnerable position for anyone. The pastor is no different from the rest of humanity in his or her need for support, encouragement, and nurturing relationships. We need a support system in place when life becomes difficult. It's not an option for pastors; it's essential.

I met with a young pastor for lunch one day, shortly after he had begun his first pastorate. I asked if he was connected with other pastors or if he was feeling pretty much "alone" in ministry. His honest response revealed his loneliness, and I kindly challenged him, "You can't make it that way!" We began a mentoring relationship that blossomed into a mutually beneficial friendship that lasted the duration of my ministry in that place and beyond. I have come to see that my stewardship of relationships includes the tremendous opportunity I have to build supportive relationships with others. It is both a responsibility and a joy.

How grateful I am for the individuals the Lord has placed in my life as friends! They include laypersons and fellow professional ministers, people who have become "closer than a brother." Carving out time for the nurturing of these relationships has provided a lifeline in the many challenges of life. These individuals have helped me to be at my best, "as iron sharpens iron."

How blessed we are for the relationships the Lord has provided in our lives. To have the privilege of walking with the Lord in close fellowship day after day is a privilege like no other. For those who are married and for those who have children, there are no relationships that compare with the potential for joy and companionship that our families bring throughout our lives. The longer I live, the more I cherish as rare treasure the friends the Lord has brought into my life. All of these relationships are blessings from the Lord, blessings that require our careful stewardship. In all of the demands and busyness of professional ministry, may we not lose our grip on the stewardship of these vital relationships.

THE STEWARDSHIP OF FINANCES

When we think of stewardship, our minds first turn to the stewardship of money, and appropriately so. Jesus taught the principle of stewardship from the vantage point of material resources (see Luke 12 and 16). The effective pastor/leader must model the stewardship of personal finances by responsible money management, giving faithfully and generously—even beyond the tithe—and carefully avoiding unreasonable debt and the continual cultural cry for more.

Some pastors would quickly say that the stewardship of money is no problem to them. "What money? We don't have any!" The reality of ministry is that many pastors are underpaid. Unlike other professions, there is no natural ladder climbing, with increased income and increased retirement benefits as years go by. Education does not automatically raise the income level, nor does inflation always have much of an impact on the pastor's salary. Many in ministry must depend on an outside job for income, the income of the spouse, or both.

But when it comes down to it, the pastor is no different from other believers in needing to be a wise steward of all financial resources. We must live within our means. We must give back to the Lord from out of all we earn. We do it, as noted earlier, in response to the Lord and as part of our worship. But our wise management and generosity are also used by the Lord as a model to others, an example to the flock.

The tithe is the biblical standard for giving. It dates back to Abraham (see Gen. 14:20) and was affirmed by Christ himself (see Matt. 23:23; Luke 11:42). It is the minimum standard, giving back to the Lord 10 percent of all that he has entrusted to us. Offerings beyond the tithe are to be brought before the Lord as well. Throughout Scripture, the Bible teaches the principle of practicing generosity with the Lord and with others. It is to be a key descriptor of our lives.

Such generosity is not possible if we are burdened with unnecessary debts. The ease of attaining consumer debt is mind-boggling, and many, including parsonage families, are suffocating under a heavy load of debt. Too often there is little to show for the debt. It is merely a reflection of a culture that preaches that we must have more and more to be better and better. However, one of the realities of ministry today is the growing debt ministerial students accumulate in the process of receiving their education. Because of large loans, they can graduate and be unable to afford to go to the churches where they are needed. Godly wisdom and discretion are needed at every point in our lives in controlling debt and living within our means.

Failing to manage our money nurtures a spirit of discontent in life and in ministry. Marriages suffer when personal finances are not managed wisely. Growing debt fosters a defeatist attitude of never being able to earn enough, with a tendency to fault the church for not providing adequately. And while it may be true that a pastor is underpaid, the biblical challenge for the pastor and spouse is to learn to live within their means and thus be wise stewards of all God provides.

THE STEWARDSHIP OF LIFE

God is only going to give me one body. It is up to me to take care of it. Considering that reality, it is essential that the pastor learn to give careful attention to the stewardship of his or her own physical, spiritual, and emotional well-being.

We have dealt already with the significance of a pastor's personal soul care. If we believe what we preach, we quickly acknowledge that it is the most important dimension of being a faithful steward of our lives. Christians throughout many years have been motivated by this simple phrase written by missionary Charles T. Studd: "Only one life, 'twill soon be past; only what's done for Christ will last." For me, it is not merely "what's done for Christ" that is the issue; it is, even more significantly, how my own life is lived *in* Christ. My life lived in Christ is shaped by the attention I give to my own soul care: learning more about Christ himself, applying the truths of Scripture to my own life, dealing with my own temptations, allowing him to mold and shape my life, listening for the Holy Spirit's voice, and learning to wholeheartedly trust and obey him. On the day of judgment, I must give an account to the Lord for my own life, whether or not I have lived a Christlike life. I must be a diligent steward of my own soul care.

I'm also keenly aware that as I live this life, I must be a good steward of the physical body God has given me. Unfortunately, pastors do not have a good track record for modeling the care of their bodies. Too many are overweight and out of shape. We may be quick to speak of the evils of tobacco and alcohol, but our propensity to overeat screams of inconsistency.

Any lack of discipline in this realm is further intensified by the amount of stress often put upon the pastor. Add to this the neglect of Sabbath rest and adequate sleep, and the pastor quickly finds himself or herself depleted of all physical reserves. The kind of discerning stewardship required for material resources is the same kind of discerning stewardship needed for our physical well-being. And this will require personal discipline and commitment.

Physical exercise is a known stress reliever and is essential for maintaining our bodies. Establishing a rhythm of consistent exercise throughout the course of every week is foundational to good health. There is no debate on the matter among the medical community. And spending an hour on a treadmill can sometimes be the best way to deal productively with the stresses of ministry.

Excess weight easily takes years off our lives. How can we justify this in light of the biblical concepts of stewardship? For some it is the most difficult challenge of healthy living, but followers of Christ and particularly shepherds of the flock must find ways to deal with this constructively. It must become a matter of conscience. We need to see the risks of being overweight as a waste of what God has provided for us.

Many pastors are also guilty of trying to "burn the candle at both ends." Our lack of sleep may be due to ministry demands, family demands, or simply a lack of discipline in dealing with the many distractions in our media-centered world. We do not function at our best when we sleep less than our bodies require. I admire those who seem to function incredibly well on four hours of sleep a night, but they are the rare exceptions. Like most others, I find I must have at least seven hours of sleep or I simply cannot be at my best day after day.

We are also coming to terms with the reality of keeping ourselves fit emotionally. Perhaps we have been guilty in the past of assuming that this would take care of itself if we are just faithful in carrying out our ministry. But the experience of many has declared otherwise. Our emotional health is an important facet of our overall health, affecting our physical well-being in significant ways. I prefer to think of our emotional health as a matter of balance in life. And while the habits of spiritual and physical health lend themselves to emotional well-being as well, the reality is that we cannot escape our own humanity. Sometimes the pressures of life seem to become more than we can bear. We must be willing to do the same things we suggest to others in order to maintain our own emotional stability.

Just as we refer parishioners to professional counselors when their problems are beyond our expertise and just as we pursue medical attention when our bodies are sick or diseased, so must we be willing to seek professional assistance when it's needed. There is no shame in doing so; there is only shame in failing to seek help because our pride stands in the way. There are times when pastors, like every other person, must rally every resource they can in order to persevere through the challenges of life. And in God's providence, he has especially equipped some persons to be incredibly effective at helping us understand our emotional needs and to help bring his healing to that important dimension of our lives.

Our personal life management involves many different components, not the least of which is the stewardship of our physical, spiritual, and emotional well-being. There are certainly aspects of this for which we have little control. However, as wise pastors we must do all we can to foster health in these significant dimensions of our lives, thus equipping ourselves to be most effective in all our endeavors, including our professional ministry.

Summary

Whenever the Summer Olympics roll around, we become fascinated once again with the uncanny ability of gymnasts to maintain balance. The feats the female gymnasts perform on the narrow balance beam are astounding. I suppose most of us would be thoroughly challenged to merely walk the length of the beam, let alone do summersaults and twirls. But these incredible athletes have learned the secret of maintaining their balance.

Amid sometimes unrealistic expectations, occasionally overwhelming demands, and the relentless week-by-week pressures on us, our challenge as pastors is to learn to maintain our personal balance in life. Unfortunately, those closest to us seem to bear the brunt if we fail to do so. Many pastors simply throw in the towel after a few years of service, concluding that it's not worth the stress. Our challenge is to adopt the "long haul" perspective of our calling, determining to be faithful to the end and finishing well.

To do so, we must be willing to acknowledge our own humanity and our personal vulnerability apart from proper care. God provides for us through Sabbath rest, healthy relationships, exercise and healthy eating, and wise money management. Our challenge is to learn what we can about carrying out our responsibilities in the most effective ways. We must learn to let go of the things we cannot change and the people we cannot please. It is our privilege and blessing to encourage one another along the way.

God has always called mere humans into his service. Those he chooses are generally rather ordinary people, through whose lives he determines to work in extraordinary ways. He does so with the understanding that we will be faithful stewards of all he provides for us, trusting him to accomplish with us what we can never accomplish on our own.

For Further Reading

London, H. B., Jr., and Neil B. Wiseman. *Pastors at Risk.* Wheaton, IL: Victor Books, 1993.

Nowery, Kirk. *The Stewardship of Life.* Camarillo, CA: Spire Resources Inc., 2004.

Spaite, Daniel. *Time Bomb in the Church.* Kansas City: Beacon Hill Press of Kansas City, 1999.

21
LIFELONG LEARNING
CULTIVATING GOD'S CALL TO LEARN

Sharon Drury
PhD, Professor, Graduate Studies in Leadership,
Indiana Wesleyan University

◆

"Do your best to present yourself to God as one approved, a workman who does not need to be ashamed and who correctly handles the word of truth" (2 Tim. 2:15).

LINE-ITEM VETO

Larry is an active layman at Paddington Pike Church in Cincinnati. Started in the 1960s, the church has been a stable and solid institution. However, while the church appears to be healthy, the figures show that membership has been slipping by 1 or 2 percent annually for the last sixteen years. Paddington Pike is Larry's childhood church. When he returned from college with an MBA, he chose his home church rather than joining one of the many vigorous suburban churches in the area.

Larry is a senior manager in a large corporation's home office in Cincinnati. At last night's church board meeting, he proposed adding a new item to the church budget: $2,400 for "ministerial continuing education." Immediately, board members Blanche and Edwin "came up for air" and pronounced the line item extravagant. Larry argued that the church's responsibility was to do everything it could to help the pastoral staff stay current professionally. He explained, "My corporation spends more than this per year on some entry-level employees!" Eventually, the board agreed to add the item, but they pared the amount to four hundred dollars. Larry pleaded, "That would barely pay for one seminar a year for just one of our ministers—we have to do better than that!" In the end, Blanche's retort seemed to represent the opinion of the rest of the board: "The church is different from your company. We don't need to be sending our ministers off to get new ideas all the time. In the church we deal with unchanging truths from an unchanging Bible."

Should ministers, like managers and other professionals, be encouraged to continue educating themselves? Should they consider themselves lifelong learners? Or is Blanche right? Does the fact that the church deals with unchanging truths mean that all a minister needs to know can be found in the Bible? Certainly the church deals with unchanging truths, not the least of which is that the foundation of faith is found in the Bible. However, there is much to learn about leading an effective church besides basic Bible knowledge. Even Jesus taught through parables on issues outside the strict interpretation of the Torah, and Paul quoted from the Greek classics. Likewise, ministers need a broad base of knowledge and experience in helping and equipping others to find God's truth for life.

LIFELONG LEARNING: THE NEED

In arguing at church board meetings for new courses of action, pastors can be known to quote a familiar saying: "If we keep on doing what we've always done, we'll keep on getting what we've always got." The idea is that if we don't change, "we'll keep on getting what we've always got." False. The truth is that if we keep on doing what we've always done, we'll not even get what we've always got. Why? Because the environment changes. Ministers are charged with leading their churches to reach and serve people in a new generation by passing on the faith to future generations. While the faith does not change, people do change.

The invention of the printing press meant that people would be able to own their own Bibles—even their own hymnbooks—and the church changed accordingly. "Doing what we always did" would no longer get the church "what they always got." People change. Culture changes. The neighborhood where a church is located changes. Musical styles change, technology changes, and architecture changes. Even the color of carpeting communicates different messages as expectations for interior design change. The minister may deal with unchanging truths, but he or she must do so in a rapidly changing culture.

Lifelong Learner or Lifelong Loser?

Lifelong learning is how ministers "keep up." Since the ministry deals with people, changes in culture are important to ministers. Since ministers deal with communication, shifts in communication styles are significant. Since ministers care about outreach, they constantly must be aware of how the world thinks and receives messages from the church. Since ministers lead people, they must understand new approaches to leading new generations. Thus a minister must either become a lifelong learner or a lifelong loser.

Fortunately, most ministers are wonderful examples of lifelong learning, and so this chapter may be "preaching to the choir." However, people are quick to sense when a minister needs to improve ministry skills, either personally or in the operation of the local church. While the substance of a pastor's message may remain the same, how that message is packaged and delivered should constantly change. After all, a minister is not just trying to make a living or show a profit—a minister is called by God to accomplish his purposes. Learning how to do that more productively and creatively in a changing environment isn't just a minister's idea of "good business"—it is the minister's divine calling.

Most ministers reject the notion that they have learned everything they will ever need to know for a lifetime of ministry. The computer programmer, business leader, or nurse in your church would never imagine functioning efficiently for a lifetime on what they learned in the 1990s. Neither should a minister. While the computer programmer's company may support lifelong learning, and the minister's local church may not, an effective minister will need to find a way to keep up. This chapter is about enhancing and extending that desire for learning.

DEFINING LIFELONG LEARNING: A MODEL

In *The Three Boxes of Life,* author Richard Bolles argues that most Americans live as if there were only three stages in life: (1) learning and formal education; (2) toil and labor, in which learning is no longer important; and (3) retirement and a self-indulgent stage of leisure and recreation.[1] Increasingly, that has become an obsolete idea for most professionals and organizational leaders. Because of the rapid rate at which the world around us is changing, learning is a never-ending necessity. Figure 21.1 illustrates two approaches to learning or, more specifically, two ways of thinking about preparation for a profession.

Static World Approach

Acquire knowledge & skills .... ▶ Practice profession

Changing World Approach

Acquire basic knowledge +
    lifelong learning skills .... ▶ Practice profession and constantly learn

Fig. 21.1. Two approaches to learning

The Static World Approach

The upper continuum of figure 21.1 assumes that you go to school to get "all the knowledge you'll ever need" for a lifetime of professional practice, then

---

1. Richard Nelson Bolles, *The Three Boxes of Life and How to Get Out of Them* (Berkeley, CA: Ten Speed Press, 1978.

you practice your profession based on that initial training. This is a static world approach. For example, a physician with a static world approach would assume that no new medical discoveries or new treatments will occur over the course of that doctor's lifetime. Thus over the next fifty years, the physician would use the same methods and prescribe the same treatments he or she had learned in medical school.

The Changing World Approach

The lower continuum is based on different assumptions. The changing world approach assumes that you go to school to acquire the basic knowledge for a profession *plus* the skills for lifelong learning. This approach considers college or graduate training to be "initial" by nature, ideally teaching students how to continue learning through life. In this model, the professional practices the discipline of lifelong learning throughout life and adjusts and adapts initial learning to reflect the following attributes:

1. Curiosity and desire for more knowledge (which adds excitement to life)
2. Openness to new ideas (especially when the old ways do not work)
3. Awareness that every new situation is an opportunity for learning (rather than fearing the unknown)
4. Capacity for self-monitoring and reflection (thinking about how you are learning; seeking to improve the process)
5. Responsibility for autonomous learning (actively seeking learning opportunities)
6. Ability to develop broad strategies for learning (knowing your best learning style, but adapting for other delivery systems, methods, and subject areas)
7. Confidence and perseverance while pursuing a learning task (tenacity while learning stretches your comfort zone)
8. Ability and willingness to compensate for cognitive and learning deficiencies (seeking others for help; developing the ability to locate, evaluate, and use information from new sources; e.g., the Internet)[2]

The changing world approach with its extraordinary emphasis on lifelong learning is the way of all professions, including ministry, in today's environment. The changing world approach also affects the initial training of ministers. If the world were static, ministerial education as it exists today in many institutions might be able to equip a minister in the content and methodology for a life of

---

2. Adapted from R. Keith Iddings, *Ten Across Workbook* (Marion, IN: Indiana Wesleyan University, 1995), 19-20.

ministerial service. The world is not static, however, so it is impossible to achieve this goal. Thus initial ministerial preparation in a changing world tends to tilt more toward the unchanging basics—theology, church history, and biblical studies—rather than toward practical programming that will change in less than a decade. Ironically, the more the world changes, the more ministerial education should be tilting toward the unchanging basics. For example, the programming courses that seem most relevant today will be the first to become irrelevant.

In a changing world, ministerial education not only must provide ministers with the basics but also equip ministers with skills for lifelong learning, enabling them to keep learning through their ministerial lifetimes. However, if a minister did not develop lifelong learning skills in the past, he or she can develop them now by putting into practice any or all of the eight attributes just listed.

LIFELONG LEARNING: FOCUS ON CONTENT

As is true of most professions today, the ministry is a complex one. A manufacturing company may face changes in markets, new equipment, price structures, or fresh competition—this drives the business person to keep abreast of trends and changes in the business environment. But the ministry may be even more complex because it involves intricate relationships, life change, and the supernatural. What "content areas" are of particular concern to ministers as they seek to stay abreast of changes in their working environments?

New Program Methods

Some criticize ministers for their preoccupation with new methods, but ministers have no choice. There was a day when ten-day revivals, tent meetings, and cottage prayer meetings were the newest and most effective methods to accomplish the church's purpose. But these methods have been replaced by newer methods that accomplish the same goals. If a minister does not stay informed on the best methods applicable to that minister's church, the church will be stuck in the past and find itself ministering only to a dying generation.

Technological Changes

While we readily admit the importance of technology to such professions as medicine or business, we might be tempted to see the church as an ageless institution that is impervious to technology. Not so. The Christian church has often been an early adopter of technology: using the "codices" (hand-copied books of the New Testament) in place of scrolls, as well as capitalizing on the invention of the printing press for Bibles and hymnbooks. When television became dominant, Christians were there. When projection was developed, churches were as quick to install PowerPoint as they were to adopt hymnals centuries before. When the Internet emerged and e-mail became a major means of communicating, ministers were quick to find ways to advertise and communicate through these media. As electronic biblical and theological resources became available, ministers began to use them in sermon preparation. All of this occurred because ministers found it necessary to be lifelong learners. A minister today who is not technologically developing may be as rare as a minister without an automobile. As technology continues to develop, ministers will have to stay informed on technology's continuing application to worship, communication, and personal study.

Shifting Culture

International businesses and missionary organizations have much to teach ministers about ministry as it relates to culture. They approach their work cross-culturally, studying the culture to determine how to approach people based on this knowledge. The competent global worker does not assume "my way" is the right way but allows for methods to develop in the culture's context. Yet what is true in Uganda, Sierra Leone, and the Philippines is also true in Michigan, Arizona, and Ontario. All ministry is intercultural, and all ministers must learn to communicate cross-culturally as they lead the church to reach the unchurched. Thus ministers must be lifelong students of culture. They should consider these questions:

- How do people expect to be spoken to by a public figure?
- What sort of worship music do people most appreciate?
- What terms have a shifting meaning in the culture—and which terms should be abandoned or adopted because they mean something different now?
- What kind of leadership style is most effective with today's people?
- What common experiences do people have (i.e., "real," as in community events, or via television and various media) that can provide illustrations and lessons in preaching?

Admittedly, these concerns are not as important as correct theology and biblical exegesis. However, if a minister is unwilling to become a lifelong student of culture, that minister is likely to wind up delivering an unchanging message to empty pews. Ministers must be able to exegete both the Bible and the culture and bring them together.

The Latest Christian Trends

Ministers must stay abreast of the latest trends in Christendom. These trends are not always wholesome or even accurate, but the minister at minimum must be aware of them. For example, when many Christians were reading *The Prayer of Jabez* or *The Purpose-Driven Life*, a minister could not dismiss these books as irrelevant to the church. Even if the minister sought to refute them, it would be best for the minister to read them first. Christian publishing has "gone mainstream" and now produces best sellers along with the secular press. A minister who is not informed about what Christians everywhere are reading is like a doctor who is totally ignorant of the Atkins diet. Like the secular press, the popular Christian press is capable of producing fad books with glaring errors and omissions. To prevent church members from being led astray, the minister must be able to identify and explain these errors and omissions.

Lifelong learning is more complicated for the minister than for the average businessperson. The latter may be able to survive in a particular field by staying abreast of whatever learning opportunities the businessperson's boss suggests. But the minister often has more than a hundred "bosses" in the church, each suggesting books that the minister "must read." To work through that stack, a minister must be a lifelong reader with wisdom and discernment.

New Developments in the Discipline of Ministry

A minister's lifelong learning is not limited to methodology. Even the foundational educational emphases for ministers—theology, biblical studies, history, practical ministry—are experiencing new developments. Developments in the practical fields are most obvious. These include new methods of counseling, church planting, church development, small-group ministry, and worship. However, even the traditionally static fields of theology, history, and biblical exegesis experience changes in technique, focus, and understanding.

For instance, a minister who last studied the role of women in the church when he was in college in 1975 has missed major subsequent contributions to scholarship on this topic. Likewise, a minister might sit in a Sunday school class today and hear a layperson raise a discussion about open theism. If that minister closed off basic learning in theology in 1980, he or she will be ill equipped to help the layperson. Worse, if the minister does not even know what open theism is, he or she will appear ignorant in his own field—like a dentist who has never heard of a root canal. Ministers must be lifelong students in practical ministry, as well as in the more static disciplines of theology, Bible, and church history.

Breadth of Knowledge

Ministers must be specialists and generalists at the same time. They must be specialists in their field but also acutely aware of areas not directly in their field of study. Why? Because Christianity is about all areas of a person's life. Conversely, a computer programmer may be able to survive, saying, "I never read anything but stuff about computers." A minister could never say that. Ministers must be learners in all fields. Christians do not consider their religion to be a part of their lives. Instead, Christianity is at the center of their lives.

For example, if a minister is totally unaware of genetic engineering, he or she will be unequipped to help people apply their Christian ethics to genetic decisions. Ministers are called to lead people from a myriad of backgrounds and professions. Knowing something about a variety of fields enables that minister to better understanding parishioners. A minister who knows nothing but the Bible and sports likely will preach Bible sermons that are sprinkled generously with illustrations from Monday night football—and completely miss the interests of many in the congregation each week. Ministers must be specialists in the fields of theology, church history, Bible, and practical ministry, but they also must be broadly educated generalists in all areas to which Christianity relates.

LIFELONG LEARNING: ACCESSING THE METHODS

The first part of this chapter has established the breadth and depth of learning a minister must continue to acquire even after completing initial training. So once ministers have finished college or seminary, where do they get additional learning to carry them through the rest of their lives? What are their venues of lifelong learning?

Reading

A minister's primary access to lifelong learning is reading. Effective ministers spend from five to ten hours a week reading current magazines, books, and Internet columns. While a few ministers might claim to have *not* read a whole book since seminary, they are so rare as to be dismissed completely. For ministers even to survive—let alone thrive—in today's world, they must be avid readers. On this point most ministers are examples for their laity—a practice that dates back to Martin and Katharina Luther, who taught many to read in their community. It is not uncommon for a minister to have processed the equivalent of fifty books a year—an average of a book every week. While they may not have *studied* these works, many ministers have mastered them enough to speak intelligently about their content.

Most ministers would be surprised by how much they read beyond their basic book list. Besides books they also read many periodicals regularly, plus the local newspaper every day to stay aware of what is happening in their communities. Every week, most read *Time* or *Newsweek* to stay abreast of the national news. Many read their denominational periodicals once a month or quarterly—but that doesn't take too long—and they usually subscribe to *Christianity Today* and *Leadership Journal*, though they may only read half of the articles. They will also go online and review other pastoral resources such as *Rev! Magazine* and *Preaching Today*. When driving to distant hospitals, they often listen to audio books or podcasts of seminars or sermons. Some pastors may peek through their wives' copies of *Gifted for Leadership* or some other women-in-ministry periodical. Then at the office, the church subscribes to several magazines for the entire staff. So with the leadership team pastors might carefully read *Worship Leader* but only scan *Youthworker Journal* and *Men of Integrity*. Each week there are a series of Internet columns and blogs for pastors to peruse, and sometimes they exchange tips for Internet reading with their ministry friends from college or seminary. If pastors were to write all this down, it would be more reading than they thought at first, and they would consider themselves pretty good readers after all.

Learning Groups

Perhaps the greatest tip for facilitating a minister's lifelong learning is to establish a learning group—a group of ministers who meet regularly to learn together. Most ministers on the cutting edge of learning belong to such a group, although it is seldom actually called a "learning group." Here are some examples:

- Phil meets Charlie and Ted every Monday morning for an accountability group—but it is also a learning group.
- Elizabeth and Kathy drive an hour to eat lunch together once a month— just to stay in touch. They bring a book each time and discuss it—so their monthly lunch is really a learning group.
- Dave, Chad, Rachel, and Gordon all serve as staff ministers with Dennis, the senior pastor. Their weekly staff meetings often last four hours and range everywhere from event planning to brainstorming to assigned book reviews. Every staff person who attends a convention or seminar is required to give a fifteen-minute prepared report on new learning. Therefore, Dennis's staff meetings serve as a learning group.
- Ken is the ordained minister in the family, but his wife, Debbie, is almost as active in the church as he is. They are both avid readers. Several times a week they meet at Subway for lunch and talk about the books and magazines they are reading. While others see them as a busy couple having lunch, Ken and Debbie know this luncheon is the best learning group they've ever been in.

Learning groups are gatherings intentionally designed to help participants learn. Adults learn best when they discuss and process the content in groups.[3]

---

3. Malcolm S. Knowles, *Andragogy in Action: Applying Modern Principles of Adult Learning* (San Francisco: Jossey-Bass, 1984).

Ministers who are effective leaders are involved in a learning group—no matter what they may actually call it.

Seminars and Conventions

Seminars especially designed for ministers are so ubiquitous that a minister theoretically could attend one every single week of the year and never actually do ministry! However, the omnipresence of such seminars is a tribute to the quest for new learning among ministers. While these seminars are often geared to practical (and thus temporary) solutions in the church, this method, along with reading, provides primary input for most ministers' lifelong learning goals. Such seminars are often offered by regional megachurches and educational institutions, or sometimes by for-profit religious companies. They offer practical tips and programming for ministers who understand that they work in a changing world and who are desperate for new approaches to accomplish ageless goals.

Degree Programs and Online Courses

While church history has not changed much since Lois went to school in the 1980s, Lois herself has changed a lot. She is more aware of the diversity of her church and has faced a hundred questions from new members transferring to her church from backgrounds as varied as Presbyterian, Charismatic, Church of Christ, and Lutheran. She vaguely recalls taking a church history course that explored the restoration movement. However, she doesn't remember enough to intelligently discuss the matter with the Spauldings, who came to her congregation from the Church of Christ. She wishes now that she had paid more attention in church history classes—she was so interested in the practical courses then. Actually, it turns out that the evangelism method she was taught then is completely outdated now. Yet the history of how the Church of Christ got started and a summary of its denominational beliefs are intensely relevant to her now. Lois just enrolled in a single online graduate course in church history as a refresher. She is determined to discipline herself "to really study it this time."

Reading, seminars, and learning groups are wonderful venues for the minister who is a lifelong learner. However, they are all strong at the same point where they are weak—since they are usually extremely relevant, they also are temporary. Seminars and the popular press cater to immediate solutions to pressing problems. Most are heavily program driven, as if the minister need only initiate the most recent iteration of a program and all the problems of discipleship and outreach will be solved. The missing elements in many ministers' lifelong learning curriculum are not more practical ideas and programs, as Lois found out, but foundational theology and theory.

Single online courses are being offered everywhere today, but they are only one entry point to lifelong learning. Ministers also are rushing to enroll in both online and on-site degree programs. They do so although few denominations require it, and many local churches do not financially support it. Ministers are so intent on lifelong learning that they will pay tuition out of their own pockets. This trend says something very positive about ministers (and something not so positive about churches and denominations that don't support it). Some ministers have not been able to acquire advanced degrees because of their pastoral schedules. It is difficult for ministers to be away from their churches when they are supposed to be on call locally much of the time. However, online education has remedied that problem. We are now seeing ministers join an even greater stampede to formal degree programs, including the MA, MDiv, and DMin programs, along with other degree programs related to ministry, such as leadership and counseling degrees.

Ministers will always gain immediate problem-solving and idea/program learning from reading and attending seminars. Increasingly, they also want to put a solid foundation under these temporary ideas with courses and degree programs in theology, church history, and biblical exegesis. This is not because these fields have changed substantially (although some have), but because the minister has changed as a person and now sees the relevance of these foundational studies more than before. These ministers now know that a novel approach to a Christmas show that attracts seekers to their church might work for a decade, but a deeper understanding of the incarnation will last a lifetime.

LIFELONG LEARNING: THREE TIPS FOR MINISTERS

We have noted that many ministers provide a wonderful example of a profession bent on lifelong learning. While learning in recent years may have been tilted more toward programming that is practical (and often temporary), this is now in a stage of correction as ministers revisit the deeper foundational studies in online and on-site formats. Ministers have hungry minds—even for areas outside their direct discipline. For example, this book offers no quick program to build church attendance. It offers very little that you can work into next week's sermon. But you are reading it anyway. Why? Probably because you already are a lifelong learner—enough of a lifelong learner to read a book relating the MBA curriculum to the ministry. So what ideas might you continue (or initiate) to ensure that you will remain a lifelong learner? Consider these three:

1. **Establish reading goals**. Write down your goals and surprise yourself by how much you already have read. Then expand your reading. Learn to speed-read if you have not yet developed that skill. For further tips and

a resource list on how to read more quickly, visit this Web site: http://www.drurywriting.com/keith/SPEED.htm.

2. **Start a learning group.** You are probably already involved in one, but it may not be intentional. Make it more intentional. Establish a policy of "learning accountability" in your group—each of you *formally* reporting what you learn from conventions, seminars, and books. Even if you do this somewhat with your online friends, make your efforts intentional and learn from one another. God often teaches us the best things through others.

3. **Get your church to financially support lifelong learning.** It isn't selfish to get the church to do the right thing. If you don't have a board member like Larry in your church to suggest the line item, cultivate one or do it yourself. Get your board to support lifelong learning for its ministers—present and future. If a worldly corporation can wholeheartedly support its employees' learning, how much more important is it for a church to encourage and support its ministers' learning? Not to do so is unacceptable—in fact, it is *wrong*. Be more insistent—it is the right thing for the church, you, other staff members, and your successors. Perhaps suggest multiple lines in the church's budget instead of one: a line for periodical subscriptions, another for seminars and conventions, and a third line for credit-bearing courses and degree programs.

MODELING LIFELONG LEARNING

When ministers practice the discipline of lifelong learning, they often do so at great personal expense and with little financial or career rewards. Why? Perhaps because ministers know that if they become lifelong learners and model continuous learning for their members, then the church will be the influential organization it is intended to be in the world. Peter Senge calls this indicative of a learning organization.[4] Leaders of learning organizations model learning by regenerating themselves and providing ways for members at every level of their organizations to grow personally and professionally. According to Senge, "It is no longer sufficient to have one person learning for the organization. Organizations that excel will tap into people's commitment and capacity to learn at *all* levels in an organization."[5]

Ministers also understand that the church is a dynamic organism under the direction of the Holy Spirit. The church may stand for static truth, but it is con-

---

4. Senge, *Fifth Discipline*, 4.
5. Ibid.

stantly under the leadership of the Holy Spirit to learn new ways to accomplish old and enduring purposes. When ministers continue to learn, they model what they want their churches to be—learning organizations that are not static but dynamic, influential organizations. That is important because ministers come and go. They, too, some day will join the ranks of other ministers who have passed from the scene. Ministers who have practiced lifelong learning and influenced their churches to be lifelong learning organizations will not have their life's learning interred with their bones. Those ministers will leave behind lifelong learning churches. And that is a worthy goal, for the church is never ending.